£63.00

50

GW01454247

OXFORD HISTORICAL MONOGRAPHS

EDITORS

R. R. DAVIES   R. J. W. EVANS

J. HARRIS   B. WARD–PERKINS

J. ROBERTSON   R. SERVICE

P. A. SLACK

Governments, Labour, and the Law in Mid-Victorian Britain

The Trade Union Legislation of the 1870s

MARK CURTHOYS

CLARENDON PRESS · OXFORD

OXFORD
UNIVERSITY PRESS

Great Clarendon Street, Oxford OX2 6DP

Oxford University Press is a department of the University of Oxford.
It furthers the University's objective of excellence in research, scholarship,
and education by publishing worldwide in

Oxford New York

Auckland Cape Town Dar es Salaam Hong Kong Karachi
Kuala Lumpur Madrid Melbourne Mexico City Nairobi
New Delhi Shanghai Taipei Toronto

With offices in

Argentina Austria Brazil Chile Czech Republic France
Greece Guatemala Hungary Italy Japan Poland Portugal
Singapore South Korea Switzerland Thailand Turkey
Ukraine Vietnam

Oxford is a registered trade mark of Oxford University Press
In the UK and in certain other countries

Published in the United States
by Oxford University Press Inc., New York

© Mark Curthoys 2004

The moral rights of the author have been asserted
Database right Oxford University Press (maker)

First published 2004

All rights reserved. No part of this publication may be reproduced,
stored in a retrieval system, or transmitted, in any form or by any means,
without the prior permission in writing of Oxford University Press,
or as expressly permitted by law, or under terms agreed with the appropriate
reprographics rights organization. Enquiries concerning reproduction
outside the scope of the above should be sent to the Rights Department,
Oxford University Press, at the address above

You must not circulate this book in any other binding or cover
and you must impose this same condition on any acquirer

British Library Cataloguing in Publication Data
Data available

Library of Congress Cataloging in Publication Data
Data applied for

ISBN 0-19-926889-4

3 5 7 9 10 8 6 4 2

Typeset by Regent Typesetting, London
Printed in Great Britain
on acid-free paper by
Digital Books Logistics Ltd

In memory of

MY PARENTS

ACKNOWLEDGEMENTS

My thanks are due to the archivists, librarians, and other holders of records who have enabled me to consult materials in their care. Over many years I have received great assistance from the staff of the Bodleian Library, the Modern History Faculty Library, Oxford, John Wing and his colleagues at the library of Christ Church, Oxford, David Webb of the Bishopsgate Institute, and Richard Storey and the staff of the Modern Records Centre, University of Warwick. I am grateful to Mr B. A. Shillito of the Office of the Parliamentary Counsel for granting me access to that department's papers, to David Holland for enabling me to consult the papers of S. H. Walpole, and to the many individuals who helped to locate manuscript materials. Gordon Phillips, archivist of *The Times*, kindly identified the authors of leading articles in that newspaper.

This book is based on research undertaken while I was the holder of a postgraduate studentship funded by the Department of Education and Science. I also wish to acknowledge financial assistance from the governing body of Christ Church, Oxford.

I owe a longstanding debt of gratitude to David Steele, who introduced me to the problems of the mid-Victorian period through his special subject at the University of Leeds. His advice, suggestions, and personal support have been vital throughout the preparation of this work. To those who patiently heard the preliminary results of my researches, in papers delivered to the Oxford seminars run by Ross McKibbin and Philip Waller, and to others who read the widely circulated typescripts of those papers, I owe an apology for the long delay in bringing into print a revised version incorporating the comments which they took the trouble to make. I am also grateful to the participants of seminars at All Souls College, Oxford, the University of Liverpool, the Institute of Historical Research, London, and Trinity and All Saints College, Leeds, for their suggestions. At the outset I learnt much from John Davis (who kindly passed on transcripts of the Wemyss MSS), Nicholas Fishwick, Michael Hart, and Paul Johnson; latterly, my colleagues at the *Oxford Dictionary of National Biography*—especially in the 'vic' room—have provided a congenial and stimulating atmosphere in which to complete the work. Mark Pottle's encouragement has also been invaluable. I was fortunate to be employed on the History of the University of Oxford project under Michael Brock, and to have benefited from his guidance over many years; I am also grateful for his practical help in enabling me to obtain unpaid leave to complete the thesis in which this book has its origin. The examiners of that thesis, Lord Briggs and Professor Paul Smith, pointed out corrections and made many helpful suggestions for improvements. I wish to thank the Oxford Historical Monographs Committee for the opportunity to return to this subject, and Jose Harris, who read the typescript on behalf of the committee, for her penetrating comments. Brian Harrison kindly read two sections at a very late stage and his suggestions led to some important adjustments. Lawrence Goldman generously shouldered the burden of reading the entire typescript; I owe much to his candid criticisms and advice. I am also indebted to Nancy-Jane Rucker for the great care with which she edited the final text, and to Kay Rogers for guiding it through the press. Responsibility for remaining errors and shortcomings remains mine alone.

My debt to the late Colin Matthew exceeds what can be expressed here. First as thesis supervisor, then as Editor of the *Oxford DNB*, he was a source of inspiration, encouragement, criticism, and innumerable personal kindnesses. The subject was his idea and he continued to support my work on it even when the demands of other employments led to seemingly interminable delays in its completion. It is a matter of immense sadness not to be able to present him with this attempt, however inadequate, to respond to his original suggestion.

A further cause of regret is that my parents did not live to see the book finished. I am grateful to Judith for sharing some of the trials which accompanied the later stages of this project.

CONTENTS

ABBREVIATIONS

ASCJ   Amalgamated Society of Carpenters and Joiners
ASE   Amalgamated Society of Engineers
ASRS   Amalgamated Society of Railway Servants
CAT   Conference of Amalgamated Trades
CLAA   Criminal Law Amendment Act, 1871
CPPA   Conspiracy and Protection of Property Act, 1875
DLB   *Dictionary of Labour Biography* ed. J. M. Bellamy and J. Saville (10 vols., 1972–2000)
DNB   *Dictionary of National Biography*
FSIF   Friendly Society of Ironfounders
GBA   General Builders' Association
GLCC   Gas Light and Coke Company
GUCJ   General Union of Carpenters and Joiners
H   Hansard *Parliamentary Debates* (prefixed by series number)
Matthew, *GD*   H. C. G. Matthew (ed.), *The Gladstone Diaries*, vols. 5–6, 1855–68 (1978); vols. 6–7, 1868–74 (1982)
NAPSS   National Association for the Promotion of Social Science (or Social Science Association)
NAUT   National Association of United Trades
NFAEL   National Federation of Associated Employers of Labour
NFBTE   National Federation of Building Trades Employers
OBS   Operative Bricklayers' Society
OPC   Office of the Parliamentary Counsel
OSM FR   Fortnightly Returns of the Friendly Society of Operative Stonemasons
PP   *British Parliamentary Papers*
RCLL   Royal Commission on the Labour Laws, 1874–5 (chairman: Sir Alexander Cockburn)
RCTU   Royal Commission on Trade Unions, 1867–9 (chairman: Sir William Erle)
SCCL (1825)   Select Committee on the Combination Laws, 1825 (chairman: Thomas Wallace)
SSA   Social Science Association (or National Association for the Promotion of Social Science)
TRHS   *Transactions of the Royal Historical Society*
TUC   Trades Union Congress
TUCPC   Trades Union Congress Parliamentary Committee

Introduction

'We legislate for individuals, while we are, in fact, surrounded by corporations', a newspaper writer commented in November 1853, as the lengthy strike in the Preston cotton trade showed no sign of collapse.[1] That celebrated dispute exposed the extent of collective activity and organization among both masters and operatives, and challenged many prevailing assumptions about economic and social behaviour. It also posed a practical, and growing problem for legislators: how, in an age which sought to apply 'liberal' principles to issues of government, a viable legal framework could be created for trade unions and strikes.

Many of the difficulties which confronted the mid-Victorians—the need to balance individual and collective freedoms, and to reconcile the anti-competitive tendency of combination with the free working of markets—were not peculiar to their age, and became a feature common to Western industrial societies.[2] In Britain, during the two centuries since the enactment of statutes forbidding combinations (1799 and 1800), each attempted legislative settlement was challenged and either renegotiated (1825), reasserted (1906), or sometimes (as in 1824 or in the period after 1979) overturned. Yet the confidence of those politicians, such as Disraeli, who in the mid-1870s congratulated themselves on having resolved the legal conflict between capital and labour was not entirely misplaced. Admittedly, within a generation of their passage, the statutes of 1871, 1875, and 1876, whose making is the subject of the present work, were undermined in various ways by the courts. But the framework of collective labour law and industrial relations instituted in the 1870s was broadly reaffirmed in the early twentieth century. Upheld by politicians and civil servants, it proved remarkably durable.[3] As late as 1959 it was depicted as a characteristically British, and reasonably successful, approach to the law affecting industrial relations, though by then it was coming under renewed critical scrutiny.[4]

---

[1] *Morning Chronicle* (9 Nov. 1853), 4.

[2] H. Collins, K. D. Ewing, and A. McGolgan, *Labour Law: Text and Materials* (2001), 5.

[3] For Stanley Baldwin's endorsement of the system in the 1920s see P. Williamson, *Stanley Baldwin: Conservative Leadership and National Values* (1999), 193–202; for the civil servants, see R. Davidson, *Whitehall and the Labour Problem in Late-Victorian and Edwardian Britain* (1985), 261–4, and R. Lowe, *Adjusting to Democracy: The Role of the Ministry of Labour in British Politics, 1916–1939* (1986), ch. 4.

[4] O. Kahn-Freund, 'Labour law', in M. Ginsberg (ed.), *Law and Opinion in England in the Twentieth Century* (1959), repr. in O. Kahn-Freund, *Selected Writings* (1978); A. Fox, *History*

Collective labour law has long been recognized as a peculiarly sensitive indicator of wider trends in public policy and of the character of the state itself. Writers in the 1860s and 1870s perceived this clearly enough, and in later life one of them, the jurist A. V. Dicey, yoked the history of changes in the status of unions and strikes to a controversial thesis about the rise of collectivism in Britain.[5] In the mid-Victorian period contemporaries celebrated the tendency of the aristocratic governments to pursue 'progressive' policies.[6] It was by no means self-evident, however, what a 'progressive' policy towards combinations might amount to. For example, if 'monopoly' and 'privilege' were being dismantled elsewhere, how could the state be justified in extending its recognition to associations such as trade unions which appeared to uphold custom and vested interest? Should criminal sanctions cease to be available to deal with the perpetrators of the type of non-violent, but nonetheless coercive, collective action which infringed the individual freedom of other workers or damaged the economic position of employers? A further issue was raised when workers—and particularly strikers—broke their contracts of employment. If the penalties provided by the Master and Servant Acts (1823 and 1867) were removed, might those without property simply walk away from their agreements whenever they thought it convenient to do so, without fear of redress for the loss they caused?[7]

However much practical considerations—electoral ones being not the least of them—influenced official approaches to these problems, politicians and their advisers could hardly avoid engaging with an ideological debate which raised fundamental issues ranging beyond the immediate concerns of unions and employers. One consideration was how far legislation should reflect the dominant orthodoxies of political economy, even supposing that

---

and Heritage: the Social Origins of the British Industrial Relations System (1985), 368–74; for a discussion of the system's persistence see P. Davies and M. Freedland, *Labour Legislation and Public Policy: A Contemporary History* (1993), chs. 1, 11. See the critique, Inns of Court Conservative and Unionist Society, *A Giant's Strength. Some Thoughts on the Constitutional and Legal Position of Trade Unions in England* (1958), 10–12.

    [5] A. V. Dicey, *Lectures on the Relation between Law and Public Opinion in England* (1905; 2nd edn., 1914), xliv–xlviii, 95–102, 153–8, 191–201, 267–73.

    [6] E.g. Erskine May, cited in E. D. Steele, *Palmerston and Liberalism, 1855–1865* (1991), 4, 65.

    [7] Having received comparatively little attention since the pathbreaking article, D. Simon, 'Master and Servant', in J. Saville (ed.), *Democracy and the Labour Movement* (1954), the anomalous persistence of a penal contract law, and therefore of 'unfree' labour, until 1875 has recently been re-examined in R. J. Steinfeld, *Coercion, Contract and Free Labor in the Nineteenth Century* (2001), and D. Hay, 'Master and Servant in England', in W. Steinmetz (ed.), *Private Law and Social Inequality in the Industrial Age* (2000); S. Deakin and G. S. Morris, *Labour Law* (3rd edn., 2001), 24–5.

those fundamental principles in their application to the labour question were agreed upon. A choice had also to be made between contested meanings of 'free labour' when the upholding of such freedom was regarded as a fundamental duty of government. Policy-making at a time when the franchise was being extended needed to concern itself with conceptions of citizenship. This led, for example, to a tension between attempts to frame laws which applied to all citizens without distinction, and those directed towards what were considered 'special' circumstances but which were exposed to the allegation of being 'class' legislation, stigmatizing one group alone.

Responsibility for forming legislative policy in this area lay with the secretaries of state and their officials at the Home Office. The ideas and pressures which formed their 'official mind' are the central focus of this book. Two expert permanent officials, Henry Thring and Godfrey Lushington, successive legal advisers to the Home Office, guided ministers through the legal technicalities involved. Since the Home Office did not retain its papers relating to the preparation of the legislation, Lushington's role, in particular, has had to remain a matter for speculation.[8] His well-known public identification with trade unionism marked him out, potentially, as one of the specialist 'zealots' in the public service during the period before most higher positions in government offices were recruited by open competition. At the same time he exhibited many of the personal characteristics of what became the generalist, administrative class within the civil service, a pattern which his own career subsequently followed.[9] His predecessor, Thring, has received less attention, yet the latter's appointment to head the new Office of the Parliamentary Counsel placed him at the gateway to the legislative process.[10] Owing to the survival of Home Office drafting instructions among the papers of Thring's department the process of policy-making can be more fully established, Thring and Lushington's own roles delineated, and the ideas that they employed to support their recommendations can be examined.

Much inevitably remains unknown given that discussions were often conducted verbally between the home secretary, his legal adviser, the Crown law officers, and the Parliamentary Counsel. The subject rarely

[8] R. Harrison, *Before the Socialists* (1965), 288–9; P. Smith, *Disraelian Conservatism and Social Reform* (1967), 215.

[9] H. Parris, *Constitutional Bureaucracy* (1969), 138–44; G. Sutherland (ed.), *Studies in the Growth of Nineteenth-Century Government* (1972), introduction; C. Kent, *Brains and Numbers: Elitism, Comtism and Democracy in Mid-Victorian England* (1978), 146.

[10] Parris, *Constitutional Bureaucracy*, 176–8; B. McGill, 'A Victorian Office: The Parliamentary Counsel to the Treasury, 1869–1902', *Historical Research*, 63 (1990).

impinged upon the correspondence of successive home secretaries from
1867 to 1875[11]—Spencer Walpole, Gathorne Hardy, H. A. Bruce, Robert
Lowe, and R. A. Cross—for this was not a subject which lay at the root of
party division. Nor did it touch upon the concerns of 'high' politics except
in the negative sense that politicians who had departmental responsibility
for the issue were expected to ensure that it remained beyond politics.[12]
Failures to do so produced the rare occasions when the subject entered
Cabinet deliberations. Then, briefly, it was regarded as a matter of considerable gravity.

Politicians were sensitive towards the labour laws issue because of its
potential to disrupt the unity between classes which underlay mid-
nineteenth-century party politics. Liberals felt this keenly: developments
in labour law could undermine the 'alliance of interests between working
men and employers' upon which organized labour's attachment to the
Liberal party was based.[13] Legislation affecting either combinations or
individuals in their capacity as employers or workers starkly defined the
rights, liabilities, and inequality of the two. In 1825 the debates on the
combination laws impelled one reporter of them, Thomas Hodgskin, to
write what has been described as the first radical text to 'make the conflict
between the labourers and capitalists more important than that between
labourers and landlords'.[14] During the early 1870s, when unionists believed
that iniquitous laws were being perpetuated by the political influence of
capital, their language assumed a very markedly 'class' tone, and was
viewed by some politicians with especial alarm.[15]

From the mid-1820s, governments had tried to keep the economic
conflicts between organized labour and capital out of politics by enforcing
the doctrine which treated industrial relations as matters of private agreement between employers and workers and therefore outside the public
sphere of government.[16] It is open to question, of course, whether such an

---

[11] Cf. the paucity of references to Chartism in ministers' private correspondence a generation earlier, F. C. Mather, 'The Government and the Chartists', in A. Briggs (ed.), *Chartist
Studies* (1959), 372.

[12] J. P. Parry, 'Religion and the Collapse of Gladstone's First Government, 1870–74',
Historical Journal, 25 (1982), 71.

[13] D. A. Hamer, *Liberal Politics in the Age of Gladstone and Rosebery* (1972), 10.

[14] D. Stack, *Nature and Artifice: The Life and Thought of Thomas Hodgskin (1787–1869)*
(1998), 113, 132.

[15] J. Lawrence, *Speaking for the People: Party, Language and Popular Politics in England,
1867–1914* (1998), 90–1.

[16] C. Wrigley, 'The Government and Industrial Relations', in *A History of British Industrial
Relations, 1875–1914* (1982), 135–9; J. Harris, *Private lives, Public spirit: A Social History of
Britain, 1870–1914* (1993), 140; P. Harling, *The Modern British State: An Historical
Introduction* (2001), 72, 108.

attitude can properly be understood as one of neutrality, in view of the pervasive official belief up to about the mid-1860s that workers' combinations were futile and self-defeating, and when market conditions were so generally unfavourable to labour. During strikes the conduct of local authorities, whether magistrates or police, was sometimes flagrantly partial. Yet, so far as the practice of central government was concerned, this area of policy exemplified the theory of the 'minimal' or '*laissez-faire*' state. Governments were nevertheless periodically obliged to legislate in order to adjust the boundaries within which conflict between capital and labour took place, and to do so within the terms of the state's notional 'disinterestedness' as between the two parties.

Such legislative activity might be categorized in several ways. Since it addressed the interests of labour, the legislation was sometimes classified among measures which aimed at raising the condition of the people.[17] Yet, unlike other instalments of social reform, such as elementary education, liquor licensing, and factory and mines regulation, state involvement was minimal and the element of moral improvement, though not absent, was very much a secondary consideration. Legalization of unions, then, was not an exercise in government growth. Another categorization would place it within those types of legislation which sought to develop the democratic principle, by bringing 'previously marginalised social groups' within the political nation.[18] That closely reflected contemporary aspirations: the link between labour legislation and parliamentary reform amounted to more than the obvious, instrumental point that enfranchised artisans were now enabled to make their electoral pressure felt. Like parliamentary reform, the legal status of unions and strikers directly concerned the political standing of labour.[19]

As a problem for government, perhaps the closest analogy lay in the legislative effort by the first Gladstone administration to establish 'right relations' between landlords and tenants in Ireland.[20] Both involved contractual relationships between parties whose interests inevitably conflicted. In both instances, legislative activity during the late 1860s was spurred by violent outrages carried out by groups seeking legal sanction for customary

---

[17] Smith, *Disraelian Conservatism*, 213–18; P. Ghosh, 'Style and Substance in Disraelian Social Reform, *c*.1860–80', in P. J. Waller (ed.), *Political and Social Change in Modern Britain* (1987), 78.

[18] J. P. Parry, 'Gladstone, Liberalism and the Government of 1868–1874', in D. Bebbington and R. Swift (eds), *Gladstone Centenary Essays* (2000), 96.

[19] J. Garrard, *Democratisation in Britain: Elites, Civil Society, and Reform since 1800* (2002), 168–9.

[20] Matthew *GD*, vol. vii, p. lvii; E. D. Steele, *Irish Land and British Politics: Tenant Right and Nationality 1865–1870* (1974).

rights[21]—albeit that the violence perpetrated by trade unions in Sheffield and Manchester was on a smaller and more localized scale than agrarian crime in Ireland. More significant were the similarities between the phases of official policy towards both problems and in the types of intellectual argument which underpinned them. The ideological positions expressed during the debate on legalizing unions approximated very closely to those applied to Irish land tenure. In both cases, the universalist axioms of utilitarian social theory and classical political economy were subjected to an inductivist, historicist critique which, in the case of unions and strikes, cut away the theoretical justification for subjecting them to legal penalties and disabilities.[22]

These critiques were the product of a vigorous public debate about the relations between capital and labour which attracted contributions from economic and legal theorists, occupied two royal commissions, and aroused the energies of pressure groups and publicists. Historical writing has traced the 'struggle for acceptance' conducted by the labour movement in this period and its success in winning over sections of public opinion by evidence of the movement's 'respectability' and the reasonableness of its objectives.[23] In the absence of effective data-gathering by the state itself, the path-breaking empirical inquiry into trades societies and strikes conducted by the newly founded Social Science Association (SSA), whose aim was to introduce the values of 'science, professionalism, and expertise' into policy-making, proved the most influential point of reference for contemporary discussion. The evidence which it gathered illustrated very sharply the shortcomings of economic theory in some of its popular formulations.[24] At the same time, economic thought began to incorporate a rationalization for combinations within a market system.[25] Legal thinkers related the trade union question to their own aspirations for law reform, and brought it

---

[21] S. Pollard (ed.), *The Sheffield Outrages* (1971), intro., ix–xiii.

[22] C. Dewey, 'Celtic Agrarian Legislation and the Celtic Revival: Historicist Implicatons of Gladstone's Irish and Scottish Land Acts 1870–1886', *Past and Present*, 64 (1974), esp. 30–41, 69; G. M. Koot, *English Historical Economics, 1870–1926: The Rise of Economic History and Neomercantilism* (1987), 12, 19, 49; P. Gray, 'The Peculiarities of Irish Land Tenure', in D. Winch and P. K. O'Brien (eds), *The Political Economy of British Historical Experience, 1688–1914* (2002).

[23] A. Briggs, *Victorian People* (1954), ch. 7; W. H. Fraser, *Trade Unions and Society: The Struggle for Acceptance, 1850–1880* (1974); W. H. Fraser, *A History of British Trade Unionism, 1700–1998* (1999), 39–41; H. Phelps Brown, *The Origins of Trade Union Power* (1983), ch. 1.

[24] L. Goldman, *Science, Reform, and Politics in Victorian Britain: The Social Science Association, 1857–1886* (2002), ch. 7.

[25] E. Biagini, 'British Trade Unions and Popular Political Economy, 1860–1880', *Historical Journal*, 30 (1987), 811; W. H. Hutt, *The Theory of Collective Bargaining* (1930) provides a critical appraisal of the economic justifications for strikes developed in the midnineteenth century.

within the range of problems addressed by Victorian intellectuals.[26]

Any account of the formation of the 'official mind' on this subject needs to take into consideration not only the civil servants, and politicians, but also the attitudes and decisions of judges. The area of law affecting workers' combinations was one in which the courts continued to exercise a *quasi-legislative* role, and did so on the basis of their own notions of where the public interest lay.[27] As Dicey and subsequent writers emphasized, the outlook of mid-Victorian judges tended to be coloured by the individualist, utilitarian assumptions associated with one side of the public argument in the 1860s: if the dogmatic individualism sometimes attributed to mid-century liberal thought flourished anywhere, it was in the courts.[28] In a period when unions began to exercise electoral pressure, and increasingly looked to parliament to enshrine their collective freedoms in statutes, the scope for conflict with the courts was inevitable, though allegations of judicial partiality against organized labour remained infrequent and muted.[29] Judicial interventions are therefore central to the chronology of this book which, however, makes no claim to be a legal history. Many such studies exist,[30] and the present author is unqualified to add to them. Instead, in what follows the judges are treated as participants in the intellectual debate on unionism (as some of them clearly understood themselves to be), while their decisions are discussed in the light of the practical problems which they raised for legislators and trade unionists alike.[31]

The legislation enacted in the 1870s conferred upon unions and strikers collective freedoms unparalleled, at the time, elsewhere in Europe, and possibly in the world.[32] Most explanations of how this came about have

---

[26] On the public role of the jurists see S. Collini, *Public Moralists* (1991), ch. 7; C. T. Harvie, *The Lights of Liberalism: University Liberals and the Challenge of Democracy 1860–86* (1976), 167–8.

[27] W. R. Cornish and G. de N. Clark, *Law and Society in England, 1750–1950* (1989), 70; cf. P. S. Atiyah, *The Rise and Fall of Freedom of Contract* (1979), 384–6; on the quasi-legislative role of the common law judges in the early nineteenth century, see D. Hay, 'The State and the Market in 1800: Lord Kenyon and Mr Waddington', *Past and Present*, 162 (Feb. 1999), 158.

[28] K. T. Hoppen, *The Mid-Victorian Generation, 1846–1886* (1998), 116–18.

[29] Harris, *Private Lives*, 10.

[30] The more recent writings include: J. V. Orth, *Combination and Conspiracy: A Legal History of Trade Unionism, 1721–1906* (1991); M. Lobban, 'Strikers and the Law, 1825–51', in P. Birks (ed.), *The Life of the Law* (1993); M. J. Klarman, 'The Judges versus the Unions: The Development of British Labor Law, 1867–1913', *Virginia Law Review*, 75 no. 8 (Nov. 1989).

[31] Following the method adopted in H. A. Clegg, A. Fox, and A. F. Thompson, *A History of British Trade Unions since 1889*, vol. i, *1889–1910* (1964), 305; see A. E. Musson, *Trade Union and Social History* (1974), 3–10, on the lack of data concerning the law's actual effects.

[32] R. I. McKibbin, 'Why was there no Marxism in Great Britain?', *English Historical Review*, 99 (1984), repr. in *The Ideologies of Class* (1991), 28; J. Breuilly, *Labour and Liberalism in Nineteenth-Century Europe* (1992), ch. 5.

been conditioned by a highly influential narrative, established almost from the moment that the legislative process was completed. At the centre of that narrative lay the Trades Union Congress (TUC), which met for the first time in June 1868, and whose formative years were dominated by an agitation to secure the principle of equality before the law, as its constituents interpreted that principle. In 1875, shortly before standing down as secretary to the TUC's Parliamentary Committee, George Howell proclaimed that the legislation recently enacted by Disraeli's Conservative administration 'conceded all, and more than all, the demands made by successive Congresses'.[33] The TUC's achievement found in Howell an early and energetic chronicler. While his preliminary account of the triumphant campaign, 'Labour's wrongs and Labour's victory',[34] was rejected for publication by John Morley, editor of the *Fortnightly Review* (on the ground that it was 'too full of details'), the text provided the substance for Howell's many later writings.[35] Describing how eventual victory was obtained, Howell constructed a classic account of successful pressure-group activity. 'The action for securing this end was constitutional and methodical', Howell wrote: 'the public mind was educated by meetings, lectures, publications, annual congresses, deputations to ministers, and interviews with members of Parliament, and by debates, bills, and petitions'.[36]

Urged on by the Positivist lawyer, Henry Crompton, Howell also explored a second, equally pervasive theme: the relationship between Liberalism and organized labour. Crompton's concern was to highlight why working-class distrust of the Liberal party persisted, a concern which Howell had many reasons for sharing.[37] Like other early labour leaders, Howell had received snubs from whig and Liberal politicians, not least in his attempts to enter parliament. His own position within the TUC had, moreover, been undermined by the uncompromising stance which Gladstone's home secretary, H. A. Bruce, and other members of the government adopted towards the TUC's demands. That friction, which provoked the labour laws agitation, arose from the failure of the Liberals' measure of 1871 to resolve the particular question of the criminal liabilities of strikers. Relations between the TUC and Gladstone's Liberal ministry

---

[33] F. M. Leventhal, *Respectable Radical: George Howell and Victorian Working Class Politics* (1971), 185.

[34] Howell MSS L[etter] B[ook]7, fo. 809.

[35] Howell to Morley, 20 Dec. 1875, Howell MSS LB9, fo. 415; G. Howell, *Labour Legislation, Labour Movements and Labour Leaders* (1902), G. Howell, *The Conflicts of Capital and Labour* (1878; 1890); G. Howell, *Trade Unionism New and Old* (1891).

[36] Howell, *Conflicts*, 126.

[37] Crompton to Howell, 3 Dec. 1875, Howell MSS.

came under strain and Howell's narrative carried an explicit warning to the Liberal leadership that it would be dangerous to neglect labour interests in future.

Such an approach was taken up by Sidney and Beatrice Webb in their *History of Trade Unionism* (1894), written during what has been described as a 'left' phase (1893–4), when disillusionment with Gladstone's last administration led to the Fabians' famous call for the working classes to withdraw support from the Liberal party.[38] Not surprisingly, those sentiments infused the Webbs' narrative of the 1870s, and particularly their account of the Liberals' defeat in the general election of 1874. The Webbs also highlighted the value of a trade union 'cabinet', on the model of that which they took to exist between the late 1860s and early 1870s, with such notably successful results. Their perspective was elaborated in later historical accounts of the work of the 'labour lobby' which promoted law reform in the unions' interests, and was modified only by refinements in the account of the rivalry between the so-called 'Junta' of London union officials and George Potter, founder of the *Bee-Hive* newspaper.[39]

In the mid-twentieth century the overall picture was unsettled when evidence came to light of Howell's susceptibility to the blandishments and financial subsidies of Liberal patrons. What was depicted as the empiricism and practical outlook adopted by Howell and his contemporaries led inexorably, it was now argued, to the sacrifice of class loyalties, and to compromise, collaboration, and in the end corruption.[40] Such a line of argument offered a sidelight upon—and even a crudely material explanation for—what appeared, in hindsight, to have been a puzzling aberration: organized labour's alignment with Gladstonian Liberalism. Furthermore, the 'triumph' of 1875 now seemed to have come about almost in spite of the labour leadership, who had to be spurred on by their legal advisers (the Positivist lawyers) on the one hand, and aggrieved rank and file trade unionists on the other. These external forces succeeded in extracting what over-compliant union secretaries had been reluctant to demand and a Liberal government

---

[38] R. J. Harrison, *The Life and Times of Sidney and Beatrice Webb, 1858–1905* (2000), 253.

[39] H. W. McCready, 'British Labour's Lobby, 1867–75', *Canadian Journal of Economics and Political Science*, 22 (1956); B. C. Roberts, *The Trades Union Congress, 1868–1921* (1958); S. Coltham, 'George Potter, the Junta, and the *Bee-Hive*', *International Review of Social History*, 9 (1964), 10 (1965).

[40] R. Harrison, 'Practical, Capable Men', *New Reasoner*, 6 (autumn 1958), 116; Harrison, *Before the Socialists*; cf. the allegations of venality on the part of the British labour leadership made by Engels in 1874 and Marx in 1878, *Karl Marx and Frederick Engels on Britain* (2nd edn., 1962), 507, 554–5. Simon's study of labour contracts was also concerned to demonstrate the limitations of the 'liberalist' outlook of the leaders of the working-class movement in the 1860s, though without suggesting corruption: 'Master and Servant', 174.

hostile to labour had been unwilling fully to concede. A similar interpretation was applied to the structures of industrial relations which emerged at
the same time as the legal settlement. Some interpreters now depicted
unions and their leaders as being incorporated by employers and the state
into formal institutions at the expense of the members they existed to represent.[41] Responses to this type of explanation contended, in the political
sphere, that the Liberal party affiliation of most trade unionists in this
period could prove a functional one, making possible significant gains,
while interpreting the political activities of the labour leaders within the
radical tradition to which most of them belonged.[42] Whatever view is taken
of the earlier, critical interpretations of Lib–Labism and of the formalization of industrial relations in the mid-Victorian period, the attempt to break
away from an 'unambiguous perception of labour's victories' raised important questions about what lay behind the legislative settlement and
whose interests were served by it.[43]

The Webbs themselves had identified an ambiguity, which they accounted as the 'cost of the victory', in that to achieve their objective, the
TUC had adopted the freedom-of-contract position of their opponents.[44]
Since one of the TUC's demands was that workers and employers should be
placed in a position of formal equality in labour contract disputes, the de-
ployment of such arguments by the labour laws campaign was hard to avoid.
What, however, the Webbs regretted was the later unwillingness of the
labour movement to move beyond the emancipatory phase of Liberal politics: organized labour appeared satisfied to have achieved procedural equality secured through negative freedoms (or 'immunities'). Labour lawyers
developed this perspective in seeking to explain why the nineteenth-
century labour movement did not seek to enshrine in statute a 'positive'
right to combine, as opposed to the simple freedom to do so. The circumstance that powerful unions emerged in Britain, and secured a degree of
industrial recognition, before full political democracy was achieved or a

---

[41] K. Burgess, *The Origins of British Industrial Relations: The Nineteenth-Century
Experience* (1975); V. L. Allen, *The Sociology of Industrial Relations* (1971), ch. 11; these forms
of explanation are discussed in R. Price, ' "What's in a Name?" Workplace History and "Rank
and Filism" ', and J. Zeitlin, ' "Rank and Filism" and Labour History', *International Review of
Social History*, 34 (1989), 62–77, 89–102.

[42] E. Biagini, *Liberty, Retrenchment, and Reform: Popular Liberalism in the Age of Gladstone,
1860–1880* (1992), 5, 8, 86, 148–61; on radicalism see the introduction and essays in E. F.
Biagini and A. J. Reid (eds), *Currents of Radicalism: Popular Radicalism, Organised Labour and
Party Politics in Britain, 1850–1914* (1991), and R. McWilliam, *Popular Politics in Nineteenth-
Century England* (1998), 67–70.

[43] R. Price, *Masters, Unions, and Men: Work Control in Building and the Rise of Labour,
1830–1914* (1980), 2.

[44] Webb, *History*, 276–82.

working-class political party had come into being, has been put forward as the most convincing explanation for the particular, limited type of freedoms to which unionists in the 1870s aspired.[45]

A form of revisionism in precisely the opposite direction to that of the Webbs was offered by Dicey, one of their contemporary opponents. The Edwardian Liberal writer, L. T. Hobhouse, regarded the mid-Victorian legal changes as part of 'a movement to liberty through equality'; Dicey, on the other hand, contended that, as a result of what was done in 1875, combinations had become not equal with other citizens but 'privileged'.[46] Such a contention, much reinforced by the immunity from civil actions granted to unions in 1906, encouraged attempts in the twentieth century to recast the legal framework within which unions operated. It also prompted another form of 'revisionist' interpretation of what was done in the 1870s: legislators were said to have been misled as to the true nature of unionism by the tendentious conclusions of the minority report of the royal commission on trade unions (1869), and conferred 'unreasonable privileges' on unions when the latter were legalized in 1871.[47] No firm conclusion about the credibility of this thesis was possible in the absence of direct evidence on what decision-makers understood or intended. Indeed, despite the weight of historical commentary on the labour laws controversy itself, previous accounts have found the governmental considerations which lay behind it surprisingly obscure.[48]

Although this study is primarily concerned with the functioning of the Victorian state, some indication of the character of the labour institutions with which governments had to deal during the third quarter of the nineteenth century is warranted. During the 1860s the trade union movement remained no more than a shadow of what it later became, and in terms of formal membership (estimated at about 600,000) was far exceeded in scale by the friendly societies. But union membership was in itself an incomplete

[45] O. Kahn-Freund, *Labour and the Law* (2nd edn., 1977), 68–9, 166–7; K. W. Wedderburn, *The Worker and the Law* (3rd edn., 1986), 21–5; G. R. Rubin, 'The Historical Development of Collective Labour Law: The United Kingdom', in M. van der Linden and R. Price (eds), *The Rise and Development of Collective Labour Law* (2000), esp. 291–5.

[46] L. T. Hobhouse, *Liberalism and Other Writings*, ed. J. Meadowcroft (1994), 18; Dicey, *Law and Public Opinion*, 267; cf. W. Holdsworth, *A History of English Law*, vol. xv (1964), 82.

[47] C. G. Hanson, *Trade Unions: A Century of Privilege?* (Institute of Economic Affairs Occasional Paper no. 38, 1973); C. G. Hanson, 'Craft Unions, Welfare Benefits, and the Case for Trade Union Law Reform, 1867–75', *Economic History Review*, 28 (1975); comment by P. Thane and reply by C. G. Hanson, *Economic History Review*, 29 (1976).

[48] For a comment on this obscurity see J. McIlroy, 'Financial Malpractice in British Trade Unions, 1800–1930: The Background to, and Consequences of, *Hornby v Close*', *Historical Studies in Industrial Relations*, 6 (autumn 1998), 44; though see Fox, *History and Heritage*, 153–60; Smith, *Disraelian Conservatism*, 322.

index of collective activity. Many individuals might not, for a variety of reasons, choose to be paid-up members, but would nevertheless act in combination with unionists in the workplace.[49] Unionists therefore exercised an influence disproportionate to their actual number (though hostile observers were more likely to attribute this broad effect to the ability of unionists to intimidate the rest). Furthermore, by any available comparative international measure, the coverage and density of membership achieved by unions in Britain was unrivalled, to the extent that unionism was sometimes seen as a peculiarly British (and even specifically English) phenomenon.[50]

A reflection of unionism's place in the associational culture of mid-Victorian Britain was the compilation in 1861 of the *United Kingdom First Annual Trades' Union Directory*; its appearance caused one reviewer to draw comparisons with the well-established directories of the professions and commerce.[51] Through listings of societies, and their towns and club houses, the directory recorded a movement which, despite the emergence of national bodies with numerous branches, was fragmented into myriad workshop trades, entry to which generally followed a period of apprenticeship. The functions common to many of these artisan societies have been enumerated as: the provision of benefits and relief not only for trade purposes (that is, strikes) but also during unemployment or sickness; placing members with employers seeking skilled labour; organizing the tramping system for members in search of work; regulating the trade through agreed price lists; political lobbying; and conviviality.[52] Their representatives, and especially those of the national organizations with head offices in London, dominated the campaign both to defend unionism against threats to its autonomy in the late 1860s and to achieve changes to the criminal law affecting strikers in the early 1870s. Over that period, there were significant changes to the composition of the movement which they led. Delegates to the congress held at Sheffield in 1874 claimed to represent nearly 1.2 million unionists, the numbers being swollen by coal-miners, factory workers from the cotton industry, agricultural labourers, and even general labourers. All these groups had extended their organization during the upsurge of unionism which accompanied exceptionally buoyant economic conditions, and therefore low unemployment, during 1871–3.

Much has been written about the differing characteristics of unions

---

[49] Price, *Masters, Unions, and Men*, 62–5.

[50] M. Chase, *Early Trade Unionism: Fraternity, Skill, and the Politics of Labour* (2000), 226–42.

[51] *Builder* (24 Aug. 1861), 583–4.

[52] I. Prothero, *Radical Artisans in England and France, 1830–1870* (1997), 49–62.

in this period—the variations in their forms of government, industrial strategies, and the typicality and novelty or otherwise of the amalgamated societies.[53] Such distinctions were very incompletely understood by politicians, and impinge only marginally upon the following narrative. Certain general features are, however, important to note. Perhaps the most significant was the capacity of organized labour to be integrated within the political and industrial system. That tendency was not always obvious to contemporaries who, especially during the debates on the franchise, displayed varying degrees of confidence in its force. Palmerston, for example, viewed unions unfavourably as engines of class conflict and as antithetical to the process of individual advancement which he aimed to promote. Yet he also recognized the possibility of attaching the skilled men who composed the bulk of trade society members to the constitution, the defence of property, and the free trade economy. He treated those men as part of the political nation before most of them were actually enfranchised—a lesson which Gladstone, among others, learned and developed in his formal dealings with unionists.[54] Historical accounts have drawn attention to unionists' commitment in this period to a vision of harmony between capital and labour. Ideals of mutual dependence and reciprocity even in unequal market relationships, a recognition of a legitimate role for capital, and even a willingness to embrace elements of political economy when it suited their purpose to do so, were elements of the unionist outlook.[55] As reactions to the Preston cotton strike showed,[56] assent to these fundamental principles helped to legitimize labour's grievances in the eyes of propertied opinion. On this basis, also, unions were enabled to participate in the public argument as to whether their associations were compatible with the policy and practice of the free trade state.[57] Such attitudes should not be confused with passivity, docility, or 'servility': the workmen deemed 'respectable' within the terms of the franchise debate, or during the discussions on legalizing

---

[53] Discussed in Fraser, *Trade Unions and Society*, chs. 1 and 2.

[54] Steele, *Palmerston and Liberalism*, 207–8, 216, 228; Matthew, *GD*, vol. v., p. xliii.

[55] J. A. Jaffe, *Striking a Bargain: Work and Industrial Relations in England, 1815–1865* (2000), 9–11; N. Kirk, *Change, Continuity, and Class: Labour in British Society, 1850–1920* (1998), pt I; P. Joyce, *Visions of the People* (1991), 89–90; P. Joyce (ed.), *The Historical Meanings of Work* (1987), 7–8.

[56] G. Stedman Jones, 'Some Notes on Karl Marx and the English Labour Movement', *History Workshop*, 18 (1984), 126.

[57] On the participatory political–legal culture in which they operated in Britain, as compared to Germany, see Breuilly, *Labour and Liberalism*, 179, 187–91; L. Goldman, 'Civil Society in Nineteenth-Century Britain and Germany: J. M. Ludlow, Lujo Brentano and the Labour Question', in J. Harris (ed.), *Civil Society in British History* (2003), esp. 111.

unions, were often the most tenacious in the defence of their prerogatives at the place of work.[58]

What follows is primarily an exercise in reconstruction. The first two chapters examine the structures which mid-Victorian policy-makers inherited from their liberal-tory predecessors a generation earlier; how those structures functioned; and why they began to fail. Subsequent chapters trace the decisions which brought about a replacement, with the purpose of reinstating the role of government into an established narrative. The emphasis, therefore, is largely upon the view 'from above'. But the politicians and administrators responsible for devising a legal settlement had sooner or later to acknowledge the evidence brought to light by the industrial disputes which punctuated the mid-Victorian period: habits of combination and even of collective bargaining were deep-rooted and could exist independently of the policy of the state. This fact, which fatally undermined policy prescriptions founded upon deductive systems of thought, whether economic or legal, became a commonplace in studies of labour law. It was by no means self-evident to those who participated in the debates of the 1860s and 1870s, and required frequent reiteration. In 1875 the Liberal politician and Christian Socialist Thomas Hughes reminded a royal commission dominated by judges that the repeal of the outright ban on combinations in 1824 had not brought unions into existence—it had merely brought them to light.

[58] B. Harrison, *Peaceable Kingdom* (1982), ch. 4; N. Kirk, *The Growth Of Working-Class Reformism in Mid-Victorian Britain* (1985), 2, 166, 301
[59] See the historical account in RCLL 2nd Rep. Appx. 2–5.

I
After the Combination Acts

After the repeal of the Combination Acts in the mid-1820s, the extent of the freedom to combine, and the wisdom of exercising that freedom, continued to be disputed. Robert Peel, the home secretary responsible for bringing in the measure of 1825, had intended that the scope for legal combination should be kept within very narrow limits. Any combination which strayed beyond those confines should be 'at the risk' of those who took part in it.[1] Peel's whig successor, Lord Melbourne, appeared to take a slightly more relaxed view of what the new statute meant. 'By that law, whether wise or otherwise,' he wrote shortly after the conviction of the Dorchester labourers (or Tolpuddle Martyrs as they were later commemorated), 'unions and combinations for the purpose of raising or of lowering wages—provided they do not resort to violence, fraud, intimidation, illegal oaths, or acts in themselves illegal—are legal'.[2] He took it for granted that they were legal only so long as they broke no contract; and his careful limitation of the lawful purposes of combinations implied that other objectives would not be permitted. Artisan radicals, on the other hand, claimed the liberty to combine on virtually unrestricted terms, provided only that it was peacefully exercised. In 1853 a circular to the trades of Great Britain and Ireland declared that the Act of 6 Geo. IV, c. 129 (the liberal-tory legislation of 1825) was looked upon by 'the working classes' as 'the *Magna Carta* of their industrial rights and privileges' and 'a "Bill of Rights" ceded to them on the same terms as on the masters'.[3]

These differing interpretations led to an uneasy compromise which was consolidated in the face of challenges from within government in the 1830s, but which proved unsustainable in the face of a series of judicial interventions after 1860. This chapter chiefly concerns the criminal liabilities of

---

[1] SCCL (1825), 10.

[2] Melbourne to James Frampton, 26 Mar. 1834, in L. C. Sanders (ed.), *Lord Melbourne's Papers* (1889), 156; also reprinted, with 'forced' for 'fraud' in *The Book of the Tolpuddle Martyrs, 1834–1934* (1934), 178. 'Lowering wages' referred to section 5 of the 1825 Act, which conferred upon combined employers an identical exemption from punishment. C. Griffiths, 'Remembering Tolpuddle', *History Workshop Journal*, 44 (1997), 163.

[3] 'The Law of Combination "a Delusion and a Snare"! Address of the Central Committee of the National Association of United Trades for the Protection of Industry' (18 Jan. 1853), PRO HO45/4963.

strikers after the ban on combinations was lifted; Chapter 2 will consider the status of trade unions as institutions during the same period.

THE LIBERAL-TORY SETTLEMENT

The partial removal of the penal laws against combinations was an element in the 'liberalisation of public policy' during the mid-1820s, when Lord Liverpool's ministry hoped to avert parliamentary reform.[4] Repeal was carried with the acquiescence of the government—and would not have been possible without it—though William Huskisson, the president of the Board of Trade, later admitted that he had not appreciated the sweeping extent of the measure carried by the radical Joseph Hume in 1824. Huskisson's failure to scrutinize its details indicates how repeal was initially seen to be consistent with the broader policy aim of removing statutory interferences from the labour market, and was therefore in itself unobjectionable. The lifting of the ban on combinations accompanied the ending of the state's role in regulating wages, signalled by the abolition of the so-called Spitalfields system: those late eighteenth-century statutes, which allowed magistrates to determine the silk weavers' wages and prevented masters paying less, also forbade combination by the journeymen to obtain more.[5] Contemporaries understood repeal within this context, and applauded or deplored it accordingly. Thomas Chalmers, the Scottish evangelical economist, described it as an instalment of 'the wise and liberal policy of enlightened reformations of [the] economical code'.[6] David Robinson, the propagandist of agrarian protectionism, denounced it as 'part and parcel of what is called the new system of Free Trade'.[7] Like other tory

---

[4] D. Eastwood, 'The Age of Uncertainty: Britain in the Early Nineteenth Century', *TRHS*, 6th ser. 8 (1998), 113. The literature on the repeal of the combination laws includes Orth, *Combination and Conspiracy*, ch. 5, which gives the fullest account of the parliamentary proceedings and their legal implications; Chase, *Early Trade Unionism*, 105–25; B. Gordon, *Economic Doctrine and Tory Liberalism, 1824–1830* (1979), ch. 3; W. D. Grampp, 'The Economists and the Combination Laws', *Quarterly Journal of Economics*, 93 (1979), 501–22; I. J. Prothero, *Artisans and Politics in Early Nineteenth-Century London: John Gast and his Times* (1979), ch. 9; and R. G. Kirby and A. E. Musson, *The Voice of the People: John Doherty, 1798–1854* (1975), 32–8. The governmental perspective has received comparatively little detailed attention, though see J. Moher, 'From Suppression to Containment: Roots of Trade Union Law to 1825', in J. Rule (ed.), *British Trade Unionism, 1750–1850: The Formative Years* (1988), esp. 90–3; N. Gash, *Mr Secretary Peel* (1961), 344–51; and A. Aspinall, *The Early English Trade Unions* (1949), xxii–xxxi.

[5] Gordon, *Economic Doctrine*, 31–2; 13 Geo II c. 68, s. 3 (Spitalfields Act).

[6] T. Chalmers, *The Christian and Civic Economy of Large Towns*, iii (1826), 220.

[7] D. Robinson, 'The Repeal of the Combination Laws', *Blackwood's Edinburgh Magazine*, 18 (July 1825), 22.

opponents of repeal, Robinson attributed its enactment to the influence of the political economists, meaning the Ricardians. The political economist J. R. McCulloch had provided the most comprehensive statement of the case for allowing workers to combine, though the importance of his arguments probably lay in offering ministers a justification for supporting repeal rather than in influencing their decision to do so.[8]

When they wrested control of the subject from the radicals in 1825, Liverpool's ministers imposed their own, narrower version of a freedom to combine. Instances of actual violence, including murders, attributed to combinations caused Peel to speak of them 'breaking the bonds of civil society'.[9] Furthermore, to a government anxious to secure food supplies and employment for a fast-expanding population, the spread of associations of workers during the speculative economic boom of 1824–5 was viewed with alarm, especially when the effects were seen to be damaging to the vital shipping industry. A select committee, chaired by Thomas Wallace, master of the mint in Ireland, warned of the threat which combinations posed to 'commerce and navigation' and to 'the capitalists and consumers of the country', whose interests it was crucial to protect.[10] Combinations which attempted to control the way in which masters ran their businesses, such as by imposing restrictions on the way work was undertaken, or on who was to undertake it, were to be prohibited. Lawful combination was to be limited to:

meetings and consultations amongst either masters or workmen, the object of which is peaceably to consult upon the rate of wages to be either given or received, and to agree to co-operate with each other in endeavouring to raise or lower it, or to settle the hours of labour.[11]

That description formed the basis of the enabling section in the 1825 Act. A literal reading of the statute suggested that this permission to combine applied only to those persons actually present at such a meeting, and to the conditions which they themselves wished to demand. Huskisson and Peel

---

[8] J. R. McCulloch, 'Combination Laws—Restraints on Emigration', *Edinburgh Review*, 39 (Jan. 1824); D. P. O'Brien, *J. R. McCulloch: A Study in Classical Economics* (1970), 366–70. For conflicting later interpretations of the role of the economists see Grampp, 'Economists', which disputes the view that the classical economists brought about repeal, and Gordon, *Economic Doctrine*, 33, which treats repeal as an achievement of the followers of Bentham and Ricardo. For the ministerial outlook in general see B. Hilton, *Corn, Cash, Commerce* (1977), esp. 304–7.

[9] *2H* xii. 1308 (29 Mar. 1825).

[10] SCCL (1825), 11; Hilton, *Corn, Cash, Commerce*, 179, on Wallace's earlier concerns to develop commerce; examples of job controls imposed by groups of workers were cited by Huskisson and Peel, *2H* xii.1295–7, 1306–8 (29 Mar. 1825).

[11] SCCL (1825), 10.

had denounced the activities of 'delegates' of federal associations, and the wording seems to have been intended to show that such men could not bind others to any decision they made. Nor were majorities to bind minorities.[12]

The freedom to combine which ministers were willing to allow was understood, in terms derived from Adam Smith, as an extension of the right of every man to dispose of his labour to the best advantage.[13] It became an official orthodoxy. Labour being a workman's property, as R. M. Muggeridge, a government-appointed commissioner, declared in 1845, he could dispose of it on his own terms, and 'indeed he might go so far as to combine and concert with his fellow workmen to promote a simultaneous and general strike' if he chose to do so, assuming of course he were not bound by a contract.[14] In 1851 Lord Chief Justice Campbell reaffirmed 'the clear right of English workmen to make the best they could of their own labour, and to refuse to work unless upon terms that they thought were satisfactory; that each might do that, and that the whole might do it'.[15] But men who combined must not interfere with those who did not. This official conception did not recognize the collective interest of 'the trade', as perceived by many artisans, and opened the way for conflicts when combinations attempted to determine the terms of employment of others rather than themselves.[16] Nor, indeed, did it fully carry out the principle, described by McCulloch, of the worker combining with his fellows to sell his labour on whatever terms he chose. Even if not actually in employment, and therefore not bound by any agreement to an employer, workers could still not jointly stipulate other conditions, such as the number of apprentices to be employed, or who else they were willing to work alongside. Wallace's select committee believed that an unrestricted freedom to combine was incompatible with upholding the authority of the masters over their businesses. The liberal–tories therefore sought implicitly to preserve the subordinate position of labour within the employment relationship. That subordination was also enshrined in the Master and Servant Act of 1823, which consolidated and extended the existing law relating to contracts of service. The penal remedies which that statute provided against breaches of contract by workers were, in practice, the most effective legal constraint upon strikes where proper notice had not been given.[17]

---

[12] See Huskisson's comment, 2*H* xii. 1296 (29 Mar. 1825).

[13] *Combinations of Workmen: Substance of the Speech of Francis Jeffrey Esq ... at the Public Dinner given to Joseph Hume Esq MP on Friday 18th of November 1825* (1825), 12.

[14] Report of the commissioner appointed to inquire into the condition of frame-work knitters (*PP* 1845 xv), 123.   [15] *R v Rowlands* (1851) 5 Cox CC 489.

[16] J. Rule, 'The Property of Skill', in P. Joyce (ed.), *The Historical Meanings of Work* (1987), 107.   [17] Chase, *Early Trade Unionism*, 110–11; D. Simon, 'Master and Servant', 171–3.

Liverpool's ministers nevertheless attached great weight to the common law of conspiracy as a means of regulating combinations. Having been surreptitiously extinguished by Hume in 1824, the revival of the common law was the centrepiece of the liberal-tory scheme. Yet no inquiry was undertaken into what that law forbade, or on what grounds it did so. Examples of conspiracy indictments included in contemporary legal manuals seem to have caused ministers to understand that it prohibited all forms of combination likely to prejudice an employer. Legal writers were unsure precisely at what point a combination became a conspiracy, but there was no doubt that there were instances where an act, if not criminal when done by a single person, became indictable 'when effected by several with a joint design'.[18] A late eighteenth-century illustration of the principle, arising from a conspiracy case which did not actually involve a workers' combination, was often cited. By way of analogy, the judge had commented that one journeyman might insist on raising his wages, 'but if several met for the same purpose, it is illegal, and the parties may be indicted for conspiracy'.[19] Legislators in 1825 therefore began with the premise that all combinations to determine the terms on which men sold their labour were liable to indictment as criminal conspiracies, and merely carved out an exemption for peaceful meetings to discuss wages and hours.[20]

To protect the 'free exercise of individual judgement',[21] Peel's Act extended the range of offences, and stiffened the penalties by which magistrates could punish the types of acts which members of combinations were prone to commit against individuals, whether employers or other workers. Not only were acts of violence to person or property, threats, and intimidation subject to special penalties, as had been provided in 1824, but so too were the vaguer offences of 'molestation and obstruction'. Peel described the purpose as being 'to prevent that species of annoyance which numbers can exercise towards individuals, short of personal violence and actual threat, but nearly as effectual for its object'.[22] Underlying this was the principle—admitted by Hume and the supporters of complete repeal—that certain actions became more dangerous if done to further the objectives of a combination. What might ordinarily be minor offences (violent

---

[18] See e.g. J. Chitty, *A Practical Treatise on the Criminal Law* (2nd edn., 4 vols., 1826), iii. 1139, 1141, 1163–9; A. Ryland (ed.), *The Crown Circuit Companion* (10th edn., 1836), 139–56; Orth, *Combination and Conspiracy*, 67.

[19] Sir Nash Grose in *R v Mawbey* (1796) 101 Eng. Rep. 745; W. O. Russell, *A Treatise on Crimes and Misdemeanours*, ed. C. S. Greaves (4th edn., 3 vols., 1865) iii. 116.

[20] SCCL (1825), 10; see Wallace's remarks, *2H* xiii. 1403–4 (27 June 1825).

[21] SCCL (1825), 10.

[22] Peel to Leonard Horner, 29 Nov. 1825, cited in C. S. Parker (ed.), *Sir Robert Peel* (1891), 379.

language, for example) if committed by an individual warranted heavier penalties (up to three months' hard labour) when done to advance collective interests.

By allowing working people collectively and simultaneously to withdraw their labour from the market, albeit within a restrictive framework of criminal law, the liberal–tories intended to create a self-adjusting system. In 1842 Chief Justice Tindal, who had been a member of the parliament which passed the 1825 Act, explained the assumptions which lay behind allowing workmen to strike. In the case of a dispute with their employers,

it was probably thought by the legislature, that if the workmen on the one part refused to work, or the masters on the other refused to employ, as such a state of things could not continue long, it might fairly be expected that the party must ultimately give way whose pretensions were not founded in reason and justice.[23]

The idea of a deregulated system which permitted strikes, and whose excesses would cure themselves by the action of markets, was vividly elaborated by Thomas Chalmers, who envisaged the working-out of a *laissez-faire* system of industrial relations within the framework of Christian political economy fashionable among liberal-tories.[24]

Chalmers strongly defended repeal.[25] Indeed, he thought that ministers had made an error in 1825 by retreating from the principle of a complete freedom to combine, and he hoped that the revived common law would fall into disuse. Like Francis Place,[26] he believed that laws against combination misled men as to the true reasons for their condition: when strikes failed, workers blamed oppressive laws rather than the need to reform their own sensuous natures by prudence and delay in marriages to reduce the excess of population. Men needed to learn in a 'natural way' from their own errors, and could do so only if they were allowed to experience the results of combination. Masters did not need the protection of the law of conspiracy, since they possessed ample power in their own hands to defeat and 'chastise' those who participated in combinations. Strikers could readily be replaced, and in their desperation to find employment elsewhere they would undercut others already in work. It would take only a few such unemployed workmen to reduce the wages of an entire trade, thus 'aggravating the natural

[23] Charge to the grand jury on the Stafford Special Commission, cited in *R v Harris* (1842) 174 Eng. Rep. 679n.

[24] Hilton, *Corn, Cash, Commerce*, 308–13; B. Hilton, *The Age of Atonement* (1991 edn.), 55–70; H. S. Jones, *Victorian Political Thought* (2000), 18–19.

[25] Chalmers, *Christian and Civic Economy*, vol. iii, chs. 20–1.

[26] W. E. S. Thomas, 'Francis Place and Working Class History', *Historical Journal*, 5 (1962), 65.

penalty of these combinations, by making the reaction all the more tremendous'.[27] The experience of 'humiliating prostration' before their masters would teach labourers the folly of combining and would herald a new spirit of 'peace and meekness' between the two parties, of 'kindness' on one side and 'attachment' on the other, as a new relation of mutual dependence was established. Having stood aside from the conflict, government would reveal itself to the labourers in a 'spirit of undoubted benignity and goodwill'.[28] What Chalmers feared was not combination, but that government might give in to 'the sensitive fears or the sordid wishes of traders and manufacturers' and interfere in relations between masters and labourers, with consequences likely to endanger the 'tranquillity of the state'.[29]

GOVERNMENTS AND COMBINATIONS, 1830–1865

Frustrated by the failure of attempts to bring a prosecution against John Doherty's federated union of cotton spinners, whose delegate conference was considered by the government's law officers to be a conspiracy at common law, unprotected by the exemption provided by the 1825 Act, Peel was tempted to ignore Chalmers's warning. In October 1830, shortly before the fall of Wellington's tory administration, he contemplated reimposing a statute against combination.[30] Peel's quest for more effective curbs led to the internal report on combinations drawn up by the economist Nassau Senior assisted by a common lawyer, Thomas Tomlinson, at the request of Melbourne, Peel's successor at the Home Office when the whigs took office in November 1830. The inquiry was Senior's first assignment as an economic adviser to the whigs, and its investigative method and proposals foreshadowed those of the Poor Law commission. From December 1830 he gathered evidence from employers and the authorities in Lancashire, producing a report formally dated 21 August 1832 though it seems actually to have been written, and Melbourne made aware of its content, early in 1831.

Senior and Tomlinson's report assigned a central place to the criminal law in bringing about a free market for labour. Senior's optimism about mechanization and the possibility of combining both high profits and high wages,[31] depended upon removing obstacles to the natural working of the

---

[27] Chalmers, *Christian and Civic Economy*, iii. 211.   [28] Ibid. 234.   [29] Ibid. 221, 243.

[30] Lobban, 'Strikers and the Law, 1825–51', 220–1; Kirby and Musson, *Voice of the People*, 99–100, 106; Peel to J. F. Foster, 30 Oct. 1830, Foster MS Misc 333/4; S. L. Levy, *Nassau W. Senior, 1790–1964* (1970), 72.

[31] R. Brent, 'God's Providence: Liberal Political Economy as Natural Theology at Oxford, 1825–1862', in M. Bentley (ed.), *Public and Private Doctrine* (1993), 104–6.

economy. His inquiries therefore focussed upon the ways in which combinations prevented the operation of supply and demand in the purchase of labour employed in manufacturing. To explain the apparent inaccuracy of economists' predictions that combinations would prove powerless and might eventually wither away, Senior adduced evidence of 'systematic intimidation', which prevented employers bringing in workers from low-wage areas and therefore stifled the action of the market.[32] His and Tomlinson's recommendations represented a strand of official thinking in the 1830s which sought to deal with combinations by legal repression short of restoring the laws actually forbidding combination. Tomlinson demonstrated that, contrary to popular belief, almost any act committed by members of a trade union would render them liable to indictment for a conspiracy at common law. Senior and Tomlinson wanted this to be made widely known, to encourage employers to bring prosecutions.[33] An array of measures was put forward to limit the spread of unionism by, for example, making it punishable to solicit a person to join a combination or subscribe to its purposes. Picketing—a word which began to be used in official reports during the 1830s—was also to be met with more effective sanctions. Employers would be empowered to arrest, without summons or warrant, anyone picketing a mill or factory and bring them before a magistrate. Convicted prisoners would be deprived of the right of appeal given under the 1825 Act which it was suggested (with some foundation) made punishments more or less nugatory. Unions could usually find sureties to free the men pending the appeal, and in the interval before the quarter sessions the dispute with the employer was likely to be settled on the understanding that the prosecution would be withdrawn.

Many of these proposals were made public in a pamphlet by Edward Carleton Tufnell, a Benthamite commissioner who was, like Senior, brought into public administration by the whigs.[34] Tufnell and Senior's analysis set the tone for other official inquiries during the 1830s, which dwelt on the prevalence of intimidation in industrial areas.[35] Archibald Alison, the sheriff of Lanarkshire, and John Frederic Foster, the stipendiary magistrate of Manchester, impressed upon Daniel O'Connell's select committee on Combinations of Workmen in 1838 that new laws were

---

[32] PRO HO 44/56, p. 26.

[33] PRO HO 44/56, p. 10.

[34] [E. C. Tufnell], *Character, Object, and Effects of Trades' Unions* (1834), 123, 119, 121; S. Webb and B. Webb, *The History of Trade Unionism* (1920), 141n.; R. K. Webb, *The British Working-Class Reader, 1790–1848* (1955), 139.

[35] C. Behagg, *Politics and Production in the Early Nineteenth Century* (1990), 117, 119; J. Rule (ed.), *British Trade Unionism, 1750–1850* (1988), 16.

needed to counter the use of pickets.[36] Edwin Chadwick's first report of the Constabulary Force Commissioners, in 1839, also emphasized the need for a preventive police to suppress picketing and protect 'willing workers'.[37]

Other observers in the 1830s were concerned that, in practice, combinations did not confine themselves to the terms allowed by the 1825 Act. So long as they avoided violence or unlawful oaths, they operated largely with impunity. In 1834 an anonymous writer itemized the law's failures to contain the 'dictation' of the London trades: the statute provision against intimidation had no effect and the common law was hardly ever used.[38] Stonemasons employed on the new Houses of Parliament, who struck for several months in the winter of 1841–2 against an unpopular foreman—the very type of interference in the running of a business intended to be forbidden in 1825—displayed a remarkable confidence that the law would not touch them. The strikers were observed frequently taking shelter from the cold in the vacant seats of the nearby Court of Queen's Bench. Free from any contractual obligations to their former employers, they dozed through the court's proceedings, 'their slumbers undisturbed by any fear of writs or other compulsory process to force them to return to their work'.[39]

Senior's report of the Handloom Weavers commission, signed in February 1841,[40] was the high-water mark of attempts to introduce more restrictive criminal statutes against combinations. His analysis and proposed remedies were, for nearly a generation, a point of departure for commentators influenced by the utilitarian tradition, who sought a more energetic governmental response to the growth of combinations. Senior had earlier developed the idea of 'free labour' as meaning the ability of individual labourers to bargain with employers in an open market. The contrast which he originally had in mind was with the 'servile' labour of the southern counties, dependent on poor relief, but he now described 'unfree' labour as that whose terms were dictated by combinations.[41] Having conceptualized the individual bargain, he wanted to use the criminal law to make 'free bargains' a reality in labour market transactions.[42] The Handloom Weavers commissioners attempted to establish whether 'a

---

[36] Select Committee on Combinations of Workmen (*PP* 1837–8 viii), Qs. 2003, 3325.

[37] First report of the Constabulary Force Commissioners (*PP* 1839 xix), 68–88.

[38] 'Combinations and Combination Laws', *Law Magazine*, 11 (Feb. 1834), 167–8.

[39] J. E. Davis, *The Labour Laws* (1875), 2n. (the particular point which Davis was making concerned the freedom of men out of contract to dispose of their labour as they chose); Price, *Masters, Unions and Men*, 36–9; Steinfeld, *Coercion*, 13.

[40] P. Richards, 'The State and Early Industrial Capitalism: The Case of the Handloom Weavers', *Past and Present*, 83 (May 1979), 113.

[41] On the meanings of free labour, see Steinfeld, *Coercion*, ch. 2.

[42] Jaffe, *Striking a Bargain*, 30, 101.

person who chose to make his own bargain with his employer could do so without fear of injury or annoyance'. That was the crucial test of whether labour was 'free': in the case of Manchester, they concluded—largely on the basis of Foster's testimony—that it was not.[43] Accordingly several of their recommendations were enumerated under the heading 'releasing workpeople from the tyranny of combinations', so as 'to give freedom to the labourer' and to make him 'master of his own conduct'.[44]

Senior's prescriptions for enforcing 'free labour' in 1841 were even more centralizing and repressive than those of a decade earlier. He sought to avoid relying on the common law of conspiracy, which was at once oppressive, yet uncertain and ineffectual.[45] In its place he wanted the legal control of combinations to rest upon new statutory offences, which would be knowable and enforceable. These would punish particular actions which were previously subject to the common law alone: strikes to force the discharge of a particular person (in effect, strikes against men who refused to abide by trade rules), strikes against machinery, and strikes for the general purpose of forcing an employer to alter his mode of managing his business (thus including strikes to restrict the employment of apprentices or against piecework).

In common with other advisers to the whig ministers, Senior was willing to sacrifice civil liberties to an extent that no politician was prepared to carry out. Indeed, the Senior–Tomlinson report had the opposite effect to that which its authors intended. It convinced Melbourne that nothing effective could be achieved by legal changes without serious infringements upon 'the constitutional liberties of the country', to which parliament would never consent.[46] For example, the right of appeal from summary convictions, which Senior wanted to abolish, had been inserted into the 1825 Act in response to an amendment by the whig lawyer (and by 1834, lord chief justice) Thomas Denman. MPs who had regarded the right of appeal as an essential check upon individual magistrates were not likely to tolerate its removal. Practical arguments also weighed against Senior's prescriptions. By the summer of 1831 John Doherty's union was already in decline. Had new measures been used against it, Melbourne commented (in an echo of Chalmers), the failure of the Association would then have been attributed to the law, rather than the futility of its objectives. Moreover, as Melbourne advised the king in April 1834, statutes against combinations had historically been a failure.[47] Lord John Russell's defence of Grey's ministry, that it

[43] Royal Commission on Handloom Weavers (*PP* 1841 x), report, 31, 103–4.
[44] Ibid. 98, 118.
[45] Ibid. 98–9, 113, 115–16.
[46] Melbourne to Sir Herbert Taylor, 26 Sept. 1831, in Sanders, *Melbourne*, 131.
[47] Melbourne to William IV, 2 Apr. 1834, in Sanders, *Melbourne*, 132, 161.

had dealt with the threat of general unionism in 1833 without new coercive legislation of the kind introduced to deal with insurgency in Ireland, was of course disingenuous: the Dorchester labourers had been dealt with by reviving two dormant statutes.[48] But the paradoxical outcome of their famous trial was to reaffirm the official priority, which became a retrospective argument against the combination laws, that it was safer for combinations to be legal, and above ground, than prohibited, and secret.[49] Such an emphasis would not have been self-evident to radicals, watching the subsequent prosecutions of the Glasgow cotton spinners and the appointment in 1838 of a select committee which appeared to herald a new parliamentary attack on combinations. Nevertheless, Senior's proposals of 1841, like their predecessors, were shelved. In the following year the Conservative home secretary, Sir James Graham, reaffirmed that the coercive powers of government in industrial disputes should be confined 'to preserve the peace, to put down plunder and to prevent the forced cessation of labour by intimidation'.[50]

Prolonged strikes and lock-outs during the 1850s merely reinforced the official disinclination to interfere with the 1825 settlement. While disputes might affect a whole industry or the principal employment in a town or region for many months, they threatened neither property, public order, nor the political system. In his monthly reports to the Home Office on the state of the northern manufacturing districts in 1850, General Cathcart treated the outbreak of disputes between employers and their workers as inevitable results of renewed prosperity. Even where disputes were the product of depression, the Home Office received favourable reports on the peaceful conduct of the strikers and their families.[51] Like other contemporaries, the young Conservative peer, the Earl of Carnarvon, was impressed by the absence of crime and violence during the strike and lock-out in the Preston cotton trade from August 1853 to May 1854, despite the privations suffered by the operatives. Yet he was left perplexed that 'such rectitude of purpose' should accompany 'deep error of judgement'.[52]

[48] 3H xxviii. 1251 (25 June 1835); Orth, *Combination and Conspiracy*, 113–14; Lobban, 'Strikers', 223–4.

[49] 3H xxviii. 1259 (25 June 1835).

[50] Graham to Lord Talbot, 25 Aug. 1842, cited in Mather, 'The Government and the Chartists', 402.

[51] Cathcart to Home Office, 4 Jan., 4 March, 11 Aug., 3 Oct. 1850, PRO HO45/3131/1, 3, 10, 13; cf. Cathcart to Home Office, 4 Feb. 1852, PRO HO45/4085H; Hatherton to Home Office, 6 Oct. 1858, PRO HO45/6378. It has been suggested that it was not until after 1867 that strikes played a 'major role in working people's repertoire of contention', J. E. Cronin, 'Strikes and Power in Britain', *International Review of Social History*, 32 (1987), 146–7; their frequency during the 1850s indicates an earlier dating.   [52] 3H cxxx. 8 (31 Jan. 1854).

The Preston dispute drew from J. R. McCulloch a reassertion of the arguments against laws prohibiting combinations. The 'grand principle of the freedom of industry must not be infringed upon', he affirmed, and governments must accept the disadvantages, as well as the advantages, of allowing men to pursue their interests in combination with others.[53] He did, however, insist that free and fair competition—the only test of whether the workmen's demands were reasonable—depended upon combination being voluntary. Individuals must be protected from being forced into joining combinations, or from being prevented from seceding when they saw it in their interests to do so. It was crucial that the law should uphold this. Yet, as the reports of various low-level forms of collective pressure to enforce solidarity during the Preston strike showed, it was not clear how far the law could reach them without resorting to the type of measures put forward by Senior. McCulloch himself proposed no new law, but merely the vigorous administration of that already in force.[54]

While McCulloch continued to expect that 'at no very distant date', working people would learn that no combination could raise wages beyond the 'impassable level' produced by the competition of employers, he was far from ruling out the success of strikes on grounds justified by the state of markets. A more rigid approach was introduced into contemporary understanding of combinations by J. S. Mill in his *Principles of Political Economy* (1848). Mill, of course, strongly agreed with McCulloch in condemning laws against combination. He went on, however, to adopt the methodological step of applying the wage fund theory to the problem of strikes and combinations—a link formerly confined to popularizers such as Harriet Martineau—in order to demonstrate the futility of concerted attempts to raise the rate of wages.[55] Whatever his theorerical intention, Mill's account was seized upon by the insistent voices of the recently triumphant free trade movement. They restated with renewed vigour the contention of earlier utilitarian writers that unions were tyrannical monopolies and strikes self-defeating, a contention which they illustrated by the repetition of lists of recent disputes in which labour had been beaten.[56] No less than formal regulation by the state, trade unions and strikes were seen as 'artificial

---

[53] J. R. McCulloch, 'Combination', *Encyclopaedia Britannica* (8th edn., 1854), vii. 165.

[54] Ibid. 166.

[55] J. Vint, *Capital and Wages: A Lakatosian History of the Wages Fund Doctrine* (1994), 140; cf. D. P. O'Brien, *The Classical Economists* (1975), 284.

[56] H. Ashworth, *The Preston Strike* (1854), 95–8; H. Dunckley, *Strikes Viewed in Relation to the Interests of Capital and Labour* (1853), 28–33; J. Watts, 'On strikes', *Report of the Thirty-First Meeting of the British Association for the Advancement of Science, Manchester, September 1861* (1862), 249–50.

interferences' in the division of the profits of industry.[57] These writers placed the idea of the individual bargain at the centre of their account of the relations between capital and labour and, contrary to actual practice in many areas of industry, denied the possibility of any form of mediation between the two parties collectively.[58] After the strikes of 1842, Graham had encouraged the lord lieutenant of Staffordshire to arbitrate between the masters and the men, and to investigate the miners' grievances; he had also, in his public statements, indicated that strikes might well be warranted and, by inference, could be successful. By contrast, in 1852, Lord Cranworth, shortly to become lord chancellor in Aberdeen's coalition, declined an invitation to arbitrate in the engineers' dispute, and repeated a pervasive belief when he declared that 'in the game (so to say) of combination, the workmen always eventually fail'.[59]

A conference on strikes and lock-outs convened early in 1854 by the Society of Arts, and chaired by the evangelical politician Lord Robert Grosvenor, broke up in disarray after failing to secure any agreement as to a basis for resolving those conflicts.[60] The event had been boycotted by most of the Lancashire masters, who regarded the occasion as an improper intrusion into the private affairs between themselves and their operatives. On those grounds the masters also rejected arbitration. 'The battle must be fought out', John Bright wrote to Richard Cobden, early on in the Preston dispute; 'there remains only to learn who is the stronger'.[61] 'I come to the conclusion that the strikes must be left to settle themselves (agreeing almost for the first time in my life with Cobden)', the earl of Derby confided to Disraeli a week later. Much as he would have liked to 'lay hold of the leaders of strikes', Derby acknowledged that the combination laws were unjust and could not be reinstated.[62]

Permanent officials kept in mind the larger perspective that combinations, and therefore strikes, had been permitted because the state had retreated from the task of regulating wages. When, early in 1854, Palmerston, as home secretary, suggested that a government representative be sent to Lancashire for confidential discussions between the Preston strikers and

---

[57] W. R. Greg, 'The Great Social Problem', *Edinburgh Review*, 100 (July 1854), 175.

[58] C. Morrison, *An Essay on the Relations Between Labour and Capital* (1854), 12; for examples of collective bargaining, see Jaffe, *Striking a Bargain*, ch. 3.

[59] Cranworth to Lord Ashburton, 10 Jan. 1852, repr. in Select Committee on Masters and Operatives (*PP* 1856 xiii), Appx. 4, 285.

[60] *Journal of the Society of Arts*, 2 (3 Feb. 1854), 189–207.

[61] Bright to Cobden, 5 Nov. 1853, BL Add MS 43383, fos. 278–9.

[62] Derby to Disraeli, 14 Nov. 1853, Disraeli MS 109, fo. 122; cf. Stedman Jones, 'Some Notes on Karl Marx and the English Labour Movement', 126.

the employers, James Booth, the secretary to the Board of Trade, asserted what became enshrined as the official view:[63]

the sending of a special messenger by this Board might be open to very serious mis-construction inasmuch as it would appear to indicate an intention of removing the question from the province of Police and making it a matter of trade, or in effect to contemplate the possibility of the interposition of the Government in arranging the rate of wages.

This left the Home Office to carry out its existing practice of backing the police measures taken by local authorities to prevent breaches of the peace and to protect non-strikers from intimidation, or to stir into action those magistrates who neglected to take precautionary steps. Policemen in plain clothes attended the mass meeting of London building workers in Hyde Park at the start of the employers' lock-out in August 1859, to observe whether breach of the peace or disturbance was likely. Their reports en-abled Palmerston, by now prime minister, to report to the queen that the event passed off peacefully. He predicted that the exhaustion of the strike fund would eventually force the men to come to terms.[64]

A challenge to this official detachment came from social-reforming MPs. Acting on the recommendations of select committees of enthusiasts in 1856 and 1860, they sought to establish officially sanctioned courts of concili-ation in wage disputes. The Home Office successfully resisted them.[65] They were opposed as a potential reversion to the principles of 'protective' theories of labour, of the type embodied in the handloom weavers' propos-als for local boards of trade to fix wages which governments had rejected in the 1830s. Occasional requests for central government mediation by local authorities alarmed at the distress and privation occurring in prolonged stoppages, were also firmly rebuffed by the Home Office. 'What right has the Government to interfere in the matter, except to keep the peace?', Horatio Waddington, the department's long-standing permanent secre-tary, commented on an application from the lord lieutenant of Warwick-shire for help to settle the Coventry silk weavers' strike in 1860.[66] In March 1865, when 60,000 men were laid idle during the Staffordshire iron lock-out, mediation was again sought. The home secretary Sir George Grey's response to the local authorities, that his interference could have no useful result, was endorsed by Granville and Charles Wood in a note apparently

    [63] H. I. Dutton and J. E. King, *'Ten Per Cent and No Surrender': The Preston Strike, 1853–1854* (1981), ch. 8; Booth to Waddington, 9 Jan.1854, PRO HO45/5244.
    [64] PRO MEPOL 2/69; B. Connell, *Regina v Palmerston* (1962), 265–6.
    [65] 3*H* clvi. 2014–16 (29 Feb. 1860), clxii. 1758–9 (8 May 1861).
    [66] Lord Leigh to Home Office, 17 July 1860, PRO HO45/6965.

circulated around the cabinet. 'The Government have nothing to do but to watch events', was Palmerston's summary of his colleagues' views.[67]

Non-intervention meant that government would not mediate to prevent the masters sitting back and starving strikers into submission. But during the London building strike it was the employers who attempted to bring the government into the dispute. A deputation of master builders sought to draw from George Cornewall Lewis, the home secretary, a statement of support for their resistance to the men's nine hours' demand. Instead, they received a lecture on supply and demand, and a reminder that if the men were right in their estimate of the state of the market, they would prevail; and if not, they would have to give way. 'The Government must be impartial, and must not appear to favour any class of the community', its function being confined to keeping order and ensuring that men were free to make contracts.[68]

THE WOLVERHAMPTON TRIALS AND THE LAW OF CONSPIRACY

Abstention by the executive left the courts to supervise combinations, as ministers had intended in 1825. During the 1840s judges interpreted the freedom allowed to combinations in a broader sense than the authorities cited by Tomlinson in 1831 suggested, or than Senior would have wished.[69] In the trial of Feargus O'Connor and others at Lancaster in March 1843, Sir Robert Rolfe (later Lord Cranworth), who had been solicitor-general in Melbourne's administration, commended the policy of allowing workpeople to decide jointly not to work on terms less than they thought their labour was worth. He explicitly criticized the old policy of forbidding combinations as out of line with 'modern views of political economy'.[70] In the trial of Henry Selsby, the secretary of the Journeyman Steam-Engine and Machine Makers' Society, and twenty-five other men indicted at Lancaster assizes in April 1847 for conspiring to impoverish the partners in an ironfoundry by organizing pickets to prevent them getting new hands, Rolfe held that peaceful persuasion did not amount to molestation. Since it was lawful for people to agree among themselves not to work except upon certain terms, he reasoned that it must lawful for them to try to persuade the others to adopt the same view.[71]

[67] Docket dated 16 Mar. 1865, PRO HO45/7690.
[68] *The Builder* (13 Aug. 1859), 540; *The Times* (9 Aug. 1859), 10; 3*H* clviii. 1909 (1 June 1860); clxii. 1759 (8 May 1861). [69] Lobban, 'Strikers', 225–8.
[70] *R v O'Connor and Others* (1843), in J. E. P. Wallis, *Reports of State Trials*, n.s. 4 (1892), 1202–3. [71] *R v Selsby* (1847), 5 Cox CC 498.

An apparently narrower view of what the law permitted strikers to do was taken by Sir William Erle, like Rolfe a whig MP before his elevation to the bench. At the Stafford summer assizes in July 1851 he presided over two trials arising out of a long strike in the Wolverhampton tinplate trade in the previous year. The local union and delegates of the National Association of United Trades, a Chartist-inspired federation of trade societies, dissuaded potential recruits from taking employment with the principal manufacturer involved, Edward Perry, and induced those already working for him to leave his employment, paying their fares to other towns and providing them with means of sustenance. Nine men, comprising the secret committee which had organized the inducements to Perry's men, together with the Wolverhampton society's officials and the NAUT's delegates, were indicted on forty counts of conspiring to molest and obstruct Perry and his brother in the conduct of their business. The defendants had been careful to confine themselves to peaceful tactics. But in doing so they injured Perry, and this consideration was crucial. Erle laid down that by jointly inducing Perry's workmen to leave his employment, and even though no threats or intimidation were used, the organizers of the strike had conspired to molest and obstruct him in his business.[72] His ruling was confirmed by the Court of Queen's Bench in November 1851, which sentenced five of the defendants to three months' imprisonment in Stafford gaol, and one to one month, the others being freed.

The Wolverhampton case has been seen as opening the way to a new phase of judicial creativity towards unions and strikes.[73] Its ideological implications were marked. Edward Perry, the force behind the prosecutions, energetically publicized his stand. He was applauded by the free trade press, which held him up as a model English manufacturer, 'resolute and intrepid in the maintenance of great principles'.[74] To his opponents, however, he was the embodiment of a 'dishonourable' employer, who rejected arbitration and whose innovations undercut the 'older established and respectable firms' in the town. One feature of the dispute was the tacit encouragement given by other manufacturers and by the town's authorities to the men's attempts to agree a price list to restrain competition.[75] By his own account uneducated and self-made, Perry was depicted by counsel for the

[72] *R v Rowlands* (1851), 5 Cox CC 462; Orth, *Combination and Conspiracy*, 97–8.
[73] Lobban, 'Strikers', 228–33.
[74] E. Perry, *The Tinmen's 'Strike': A Letter to George Robinson, Esq, Late Mayor of Wolverhampton* (1850), 15; *Stafford Summer Assizes. The Queen Versus George Duffield, Thomas Woodnorth, and John Gaunt* (1851), iii; *Daily News* (8 Aug. 1851), 4; (20 Aug. 1851), 3; (21 Aug. 1851), 4.
[75] *Morning Chronicle* (3 Feb. 1851), 5; *Wolverhampton Herald* (24 Sept. 1851), 5; *Wolverhampton Chronicle* (30 Oct. 1850); Perry, *Tinmen's 'Strike'*, 14.

men as 'a low, cunning, mean-minded man' with a 'vulgar mind', who used 'trickery and deception' to ensnare the unionists into the legal traps he had set for them.[76]

It was the injury done to Perry, though, which weighed most heavily with Erle and the other judges to whom the case was referred. One point revealed in the evidence was that none of the Wolverhampton men organizing the strike was, or had been, in Perry's employment; they worked for firms who kept to the list and who were being undercut by Perry as a competitor. The NAUT delegates from London had no personal interest involved, and were readily depicted as paid agitators. It may be that this circumstance was crucial in the outcome. The law, Erle remarked, allowed men 'to combine for the purpose of obtaining a lawful benefit to themselves' but a combination for the purpose of injuring another was a conspiracy.[77] Reflecting on the case seventeen years later, Erle indicated how strongly he had been impressed by the fact that none of the defendants 'had any monied interest at stake in the strike, so far as I could perceive'.[78] Perry appeared in the light of an individual faced by the combined power not only of a trade society but of a national organization, one of whose delegates, it was heard in evidence, had warned him: 'we have twenty thousand pounds at our command, we will stop the supplies, and you shall not have a single hand to do your work'. With this statement in mind, Sir John Patteson spoke of the NAUT as an association which, if it possessed the very large funds it claimed, must be 'of a very dangerous character, and may be used for very bad and very oppressive purposes'.[79] In fact the NAUT turned out to be penniless and in need of a public subscription to pay its lawyers' costs, which amounted to £2,800.[80] But Patteson's remarks recalled the anxieties about dangerous forms of association which had caused Wallace's select committee to recommend the revival of the common law in 1825.

The involvement of the NAUT, which left such an impression on the judges, made the Wolverhampton case rather peculiar. But like many other unionists, the central committee of the stonemasons regarded the judgment as the outcome of 'a crusade against the rights of labour' by 'wealthy capitalists' who 'proposed riding over the statute law that expressly legalises trade unions'. It was 'a question of liberty', for the imprisoned men had committed no violence and 'done no more than we have done on many

[76] *Wolverhampton Herald* (6 Aug. 1851), 6.

[77] 5 Cox CC 461; cf. the comment in *The Jurist*, 15 (9 Aug. 1851), 273.

[78] 'Memorandum on the Law Relating to Trade Unions', Appx. A, RCTU 11th Rep., vol. i, p. lxxxvii.

[79] 5 Cox CC 492.

[80] *Star of Freedom* (27 Nov. 1852), 252.

occasions when our struck shops have been filled with blacks; and endeav-
oured to persuade such serfs to leave the strike by legitimate means'.[81] The
NAUT went further, alleging that the judgments represented a threat to
the right of combination itself, and campaigned to restore what they took to
have been the intention of parliament in 1825.[82] It received some support
from protectionist Conservatives in its attempt to achieve this. A bill drawn
up by Charles Sturgeon, a Conservative barrister, and introduced in March
1853 by Henry Drummond, the tory MP and patron of the Irvingite
church, and Thomas Duncombe, the aristocratic radical patron of the
NAUT, declaring the lawfulness of peaceably persuading or inducing
others to strike to raise their wages, or reduce their hours of labour.[83]

That the NAUT's bill passed its Commons stages owed much to the
exercise of the constitutional right of petitioning as a means of redressing
the grievances of those excluded from the franchise. Over 77,000 signatures
(some on behalf of meetings or societies numbering many more) were presented to the House of Commons in its support.[84] Their effect was to overcome the initial opposition from Palmerston and the two law officers,
Alexander Cockburn and Richard Bethell, who maintained that the bill was
more than merely restorative and that it would legalize acts of intimidation.
As the volume of petitions built up, however, Palmerston and the law officers unexpectedly agreed to negotiate a form of words with the bill's
sponsors to achieve the NAUT's purpose of declaring peaceful persuasion
to be lawful without permitting any form of intimidation. A letter to the
Home Office from a Liverpool master cabinet-maker, complaining that
pickets watching his workshop deterred men from coming to work for him,
also prompted Palmerston to strengthen the wording 'to render this practice of picketing or watching for the purpose of intimidation illegal'.[85] In its

[81] OSM FR 10–24 Apr. 1851, 24 Apr. – 8 May 1851, MRC MSS 78/OS/4/1/13.

[82] *Report of the Central Committee to the Members of the United Trades' Association on the Law
of Combination* (1852), in PRO HO45/4963. This episode was overlooked by the Webbs, probably for the practical reason that they did not have access to the rare pamphlet which describes
it most fully. It was discussed in Frances Gillespie's pioneering study, *Labor and Politics in
England, 1850–1867* (1927), 48–51, which cites the copy of the *Report of the Central Committee
of the United Trades on the Proceedings Connected with the Combination of Workmen Bill* (1853)
in the Goldsmiths' Library; a copy at Harvard University is cited in Orth, *Combination and
Conspiracy*, 120.

[83] For the parliamentary history of the measure see Orth, *Combination and Conspiracy*,
121–7, which draws a different conclusion about its significance and eventual legislative outcome.

[84] *House of Commons Votes and Proceedings* (1853), 359–699; *Report of the Central Committee*
(1853), 15–16; on petitioning see M. Taylor, *The Decline of British Radicalism, 1847–1860*
(1995), 158–9.

[85] William Turner to Palmerston, 9 June 1853, PRO HO45/4963; docket, 11 June 1853.

heavily amended form, the bill received government support in its final passage through the Commons, and Palmerston asked the earl of Granville to take it through the Lords:

We put in the words forbidding Intimidation and any Endeavours to make Workmen break an Engagement and as the bill now stands it seems unobjectionable. The workmen in the manufacturing Districts are very anxious that the Bill should pass and I think it ought to do.[86]

Its subsequent failure owed much to the strike movement which, in the intervening weeks affected most trades as exceptionally buoyant market conditions created favourable circumstances for combined action not to be equalled again until the early 1870s. The outburst of combination provided some of the momentum for the NAUT's campaign but also, as in 1824–5, provoked a reaction. Influenced by hostile representations from the Staffordshire chamber of commerce, Granville declined to introduce the bill in the Lords, and it was left to other sponsors.[87]

In the House of Lords the unanimous opposition of the judges proved decisive. After the presentation of petitions in its favour by Shaftesbury and another evangelical peer, Kinnaird, Lord Campbell made an impromptu statement, unreported in *Hansard*, before leaving London to go on circuit. Denouncing the proposed bill as 'very inexpedient and mischievous', Campbell described the existing law as 'excellent', giving equal justice to employer and employed.[88] Brougham also made known his outright hostility. Another former lord chancellor, Truro, insisted that the judges' rulings had not differed in substance, a view reinforced by Cranworth, the Lord Chancellor, who denied that the law laid down by Erle differed materially from his own summing up in Selsby's case.[89] Later Cranworth privately explained to Drummond why he had opposed the bill: 'My object was to prevent anything like a sanction of the notion that persons could not be guilty of annoyance or molestation if they did not use actual threats or violence.'[90] This did not mean that he thought the bill would legalize acts short of threats and violence; rather, as he argued in the Lords, it would mislead strikers into believing that it would have that effect, leading them to break the law. Cranworth, as his earlier pronouncements showed, strongly favoured allowing the right to combine. Like other

---

[86] Palmerston to Granville, 30 June 1853, PRO 30/29/23/3.
[87] Petition in PRO 30/29/23/15.
[88] *Morning Chronicle* (13 July 1853), 2.
[89] 3*H* cxxix. 1324 (5 Aug. 1853); Orth, *Combination and Conspiracy*, 125.
[90] Cranworth to H. Drummond, 6 Sept. 1853, Drummond MS C/1/381 (I am grateful to the Estates Office, Alnwick Castle, for supplying a copy of this letter).

judges, however, he believed that strikers, although they might start with 'the fairest and most honest intentions', were almost inevitably led to use improper methods of intimidation during their hopeless struggles against the overwhelming power of the market.[91] For this reason the existing law needed to be strictly upheld. Faced with such determined opposition, the bill was withdrawn.

If the strike wave helped to remove support for the bill in parliament, it also discredited the NAUT's claims of an immediate threat to popular liberties, and heightened the estrangement of the organized artisan trades from the remnants of Chartism. The *Bookbinders' Trade Circular*, edited by T. J. Dunning, pointed out that most of the recent strikes had taken place 'without let or hindrance, much less prosecution' and questioned the NAUT's claim that all trade unionists were imperilled by the imprisonment of the Wolverhampton leaders. He hinted that the NAUT had got up a campaign in order to generate support for a measure whose primary aim was in fact to secure their own, peculiar position as outsiders involving themselves in industrial disputes, which the Wolverhampton trials had called into question.[92] Although Dunning's suspicion of political action may have coloured his views, he was a well-informed writer who had shown vigilance in the face of legal threats to unions in 1838–9.[93]

The NAUT's ideas on industrial mediation reflected a significant body of sentiment among the trades, and its warnings of the potential dangers of the law of conspiracy were irrefutable.[94] By 1853, its own standing was, however, highly dubious. Four or five individuals, apparently self-elected, operating from an office in Tottenham Court Road, constituted its 'Central Committee'. They relied on subscriptions from trade societies, mainly outside London, who were impressed by the committee's apparently authoritative and solemn printed circulars and reports. In January 1854 a London stonemason urged the organizer of the Society of Arts conference not to give credence to interventions from the NAUT's 'presumptuous self styled Executive': not themselves members of trade societies, they were 'princes of jugglers', who 'juggled' the unwitting provincial trades into parting with

---

[91] Cranworth to Lord Ashburton, 10 Jan. 1852, reprinted in Select Committee on Masters and Operatives (*PP* 1856 xiii), Appx. 4, 285.

[92] *Bookbinders' Trade Circular* (Nov. 1853), 153–7; (Jan. 1854), 161–4. By Dunning's interpretation, the crucial words in the eventual statute of 1859 were not those permitting peaceful persuasion, which in itself had never been called into question, but the otherwise puzzling words permitting its exercise not only by workmen but by 'other person or persons ... whether actually in employment or not' (i.e. protecting the NAUT), 22 Vict. c. 34 s. 1. Erle placed a similar construction upon the statute, RCTU 11th Rep. lxxxv.

[93] S. Coltham and J. Saville on Dunning in *DLB*, ii. 127–31.

[94] Chase, *Early Trade Unionism*, 209–15.

subscriptions to support spurious parliamentary campaigns.[95] Branches of the Amalgamated Engineers were warned not to be taken in by the NAUT's appeals for funds.[96] In 1859, when Scottish unions received notices from the NAUT in support of its revived campaign for law reform, Alexander Macdonald of the Scottish Miners' Association advised the Glasgow Trades Council not to become involved. He had discovered that the NAUT was no more than 'a self-constituted body', which employed a Parliamentary agent to get itself noticed—successfully so, judging by the reports of its deputations placed in the court circular columns of the metropolitan press.[97]

It suited the purposes of some politicians of both parties, including the tory and whig lawyers Fitzroy Kelly and Richard Bethell (who was hoping to step into a vacant seat at Wolverhampton), to take the NAUT seriously.[98] In 1859, when Derby's government had returned to power, an amended version of the NAUT's bill was passed as the Molestation of Workmen Act, unopposed and barely discussed in parliament, and largely unnoticed in the press. The statute was sometimes cited as evidence of an enlightened desire to protect peaceful picketing and, over a century later was held up as evidence of the attachment of the Conservative party to the interests of the working man.[99] But Cranworth's comment that the bill would not, in fact, legalize all non-violent acts helps to explain why it could be safely enacted and, equally, why it proved to have no noticeable effect on later court decisions. It did not reverse the effect of the Wolverhampton trials, and the common law drawn upon by Erle remained untouched by it.

For strikers to be affected by the common law depended, of course, on the willingness of aggrieved parties to use its power against them. In his preparedness to incur the costs and inconvenience involved in bringing an indictment, Perry—who twice at his own expense conveyed between thirty and forty witnesses from Wolverhampton to the assizes at Stafford[100]—proved to be an unusually determined litigant. Where a contract was broken, most employers who wished to proceed against strikers chose to stop them in their tracks by the quicker, cheaper, and more certain means of warrants or summonses under the Master and Servant Act. Between 1853

[95] William Johnston to secretary, Society of Arts, 27 Jan. 1854, LMA, Royal Society of Arts MS 10/B/49; cf. OSM FR 22 Feb – 8 Mar 1855, MRC MSS 78/OS/4/1/15.

[96] ASE, monthly report, Jan. 1857, 681–2; *Bookbinders' Trade Circular* (Feb. 1857), 97–8.

[97] *Glasgow Sentinel* (5 Mar. 1859), 3; *The Times* (16 Apr. 1858), 9; (26 Apr. 1858), 8; (16 Mar. 1859), 9.

[98] *The Times* (16 Mar. 1859), 9; (5 May 1859), 7; (31 Oct 1861), 9.

[99] C. Sturgeon, *Letters to the Trades' Unionists and the Working Classes* (1868); C. E. Bellairs, *Conservative Social and Industrial Reform* (1974), 14.

[100] *Wolverhampton Herald* (19 Mar. 1851), 5.

and 1866 only ten conspiracy indictments arising from strikes have been located. Of these only one seems to have alleged a conspiracy at common law of the type which convicted the Wolverhampton men. That arose when a London compositors' chapel refused to work with a former strikebreaker, but it was thrown out by Sir Edward Alderson for want of proof that the defendants had agreed to act together.[101] The rest all resulted from acts of physical intimidation, and therefore referred to the commission of acts prohibited under the 1825 Act. Proceedings by indictment seem to have been brought either to reach the organizers, who might not actually themselves have committed the acts of intimidation, or else to make an example before a higher tribunal of those who had.

When indictments for labour conspiracies came up before assizes in the 1850s and 1860s, judges seem to have been concerned to conduct them more with a view to a moral than a penal effect. In these respects they resembled the pattern of labour cases in the late eighteenth century, and the political trials of the Chartist period, with all the nuances that have been detected in those earlier examples.[102] A blatant attempt by the Preston cotton masters to make partisan use of the law by indicting the strike leaders for conspiracy was thwarted by Sir Cresswell Cresswell, who refused to permit the defendants to be rushed before the Lancashire spring assizes in March 1854. He insisted on deferring the case to the next assizes so as 'to convince the most ignorant that it had been a fair and satisfactory trial' even though this defeated the immediate practical object of the prosecution, which was to stop the interference with strikebreakers.[103] Where convictions in labour conspiracy cases did occur, sentencing was lenient, and in two of the cases judges were content to bind over prisoners found guilty.

Defendants in such trials were marked out from the ordinary run of prisoners, being frequently described as 'respectable', 'intelligent', and 'well-dressed', and judges expressed concern to reason with them. Hence the repeated and extended perorations delivered from the bench explaining the principles which underlay the law. That these were deemed necessary reflected the fundamental tension between popular beliefs as to what the law allowed, and the policy of the law's most senior administrators. These differences, which had briefly surfaced in parliament during the debates on

---

[101] *Political Examiner* (10 Oct. 1853), 104–6; *The Times* (1 Dec. 1853), 9.

[102] Rubin, 'Historical development', 305; J. F. Ariouat, 'Rethinking Partisanship in the Conduct of the Chartist Trials, 1839–1848', *Albion*, 29 (1998), 596–621; for a different appraisal of the judges see J. Saville, *1848: The British State and the Chartist Movement* (1987), 174.

[103] *The Times* (30 Mar. 1854), 9; *Preston Chronicle* (25 Mar. 1854), 6; *Daily News* (23 Mar. 1854); *Economist* (25 Mar. 1854), 308.

the NAUT's bill in 1853, sporadically recurred in the local arenas of the assize courts. On the one hand, the assumption of collective labour was that the right of assembly and protest, to impress their views upon strikebreakers, should not be infringed: anything short of violence, or genuine threats of such violence, or actual breach of the peace, ought to be permissible. Some of the actions which gave rise to the indictments amounted to a form of 'rough music' directed against outsiders who were perceived to be depriving communities of their livelihoods. One conspiracy trial in 1864 involved the leaders of a crowd of 2,000 striking Staffordshire miners who had paraded, to the accompaniment of fifes and drums, around the earl of Dudley's pits where their replacements were working. Their purpose was alleged to have been to terrorize the strikebreakers. In their defence, Edward Kenealy, a radical who later championed the Tichborne Claimant, contended that they were exercising their right of peaceful procession: that they did so at four in the morning merely indicated that they were men 'of early habits'. The threat to English liberty came from the 'Cossack' police who had tried to stop them.[104] In an instance where public order had undeniably been breached by strikers, it was urged on their behalf, at York assizes, that they had been driven to desperate measures by the intransigence of the masters, who refused to deal with the men: it was the masters' conduct, rather than that of the men, which threatened to 'dissolve the social compact'.[105]

The authorities, on the other hand, emphasized the priority attached to allowing every individual to exercise his labour as he chose. Palmerston had reminded the Preston strikers of the 'injustice and cruelty' of using molestation and other improper methods to deter the Irish and other workers who took the strikers' places in order to better their own situation.[106] As Cranworth's comments on the NAUT's bill made clear, judges were determined to refute the popular view that so long as strikers refrained from violence they were committing no offence when they confronted those who took their work during disputes with employers. Strikers were reproached for interfering with the freedom of other men to make their own bargains: they must allow each individual to decide for himself on what terms he was willing to accept employment. In 1853 Sir John Jervis, a whig former attorney-general, addressed the Suffolk labourers on the need to leave markets free. At Leicestershire spring assizes, in 1854, he advised six frame-work knitters, who had pleaded guilty to conspiracy, that strikes

[104] *Staffordshire Advertiser* (17 Dec. 1864), 6.
[105] *Leeds Express* (16 Apr. 1864), 3.
[106] 17 Mar. 1854, PRO HO45/5244B.

were futile and urged them to industrious conduct as the means of improving their lot.[107] Both Jervis and Sir Thomas Platt, who delivered a stern address to the Preston strike leaders when the case against them was dropped at Liverpool summer assizes, propounded the Palmerstonian view that in England there were no barriers to individual advancement; the defendants should follow this path, which offered the prospect of becoming masters themselves.[108]

In 1856 two judges invoked broader imperatives of free trade policy. Sir Charles Crompton, hearing a case of riot involving stonemasons intimidating blacklegs, told the grand jury at Glamorgan summer assizes that interference with the liberty of other workers was 'a very serious offence against the public' since it struck at the freedom of trade and employment which it was 'the great object of all governments to protect'.[109] London shipwrights involved in a disturbance during a strike were told by Sir George Bramwell that their attempts to impose restrictions on individual freedom contravened the policy of removing impediments from industry and abolishing ancient corporate rights. It was a process which involved all classes—'the noblest aristocracy in the world had been obliged to give up the privilege they enjoyed of taxing the people's bread for their own benefit'—and it was the duty of the strikers to follow that example.[110] At the trial of the Staffordshire miners, Sir John Byles, a critic of free trade and *laissez-faire*, offered a less stridently individualistic message. Like other judges, he insisted that all forms of intimidation, 'by word or act', were unlawful. But, stressing his impartiality 'as a perfect stranger to masters and men', he advocated courts of conciliation as preferable to the 'barbarous' system of leaving the two sides of industry to fight out their disputes. In a further attempt to use the trial to restore social harmony, Lord Lichfield, the lord lieutenant, and an advocate of industrial conciliation, made an emotional intervention—which reportedly caused a sensation in the court room—to request clemency for the convicted men, an appeal which Byles heeded.[111]

---

[107] *Ipswich Journal* (30 July 1853); *Leicestershire Mercury* (25 Mar. 1854); *Leicester Journal* (24 Mar. 1854).
[108] *Liverpool Mail* (12 Aug. 1854), 7; Steele, *Palmerston and Liberalism*, 208.
[109] OSM FR 24 July – 7 Aug. 1856, MRC MS 78/OS/4/1/16.
[110] *The Times* (19 Sept. 1856), 9.
[111] *Staffordshire Advertiser* (3 Dec. 1864), 5; (17 Dec. 1864), 6. On Byles see Atiyah, *Freedom of Contract*, 380–3.

THE LAW OF COMBINATION IN THE WORKPLACE

Violent deeds or words formed the bulk of the known convictions by magistrates under the summary provisions of the 1825 Act.[112] Few major disputes in this period passed without a prosecution of either a striker, or a sympathizer—often wives of strikers—for threatening or intimidating blacklegs. Sentencing by Justices of the Peace was frequently more punitive than that of judges at assizes: magistrates did not hold back from imposing the maximum penalty of three months' hard labour. Their observations upon strikers who came before them were also less carefully framed. In 1863 Richard Mitchell of the Yorkshire miners complained that the 'want of mutuality' in the law as administered by the local courts was 'glaringly apparent': magistrates declined to enforce the law regarding the appointment of checkweighmen fairly, yet imposed unduly heavy sentences in instances which they regarded as intimidation.[113] It was sometimes alleged that prosecutions brought for the purpose of redressing injuries suffered by individuals were got up by employers, who sought to use the law as an additional weapon in industrial disputes.[114] When they rejected the appeal of four carpet weavers convicted during a strike at the family business in Rochdale of the radical politician, John Bright, the Salford quarter sessions appeared concerned primarily to ensure that the masters could continue their business unimpeded. The convicted men had gathered in large crowds to jeer at, and follow to and from their homes, 'knobsticks' employed to replace them—whether they were, strictly speaking, engaged in peaceful persuasion was at least open to question.[115] That their appeal was unsuccessful went against the more usual trend. Many convicted defendants who had union backing to raise the sureties necessary to bring an appeal avoided punishment. Of 59 individuals who appealed to quarter sessions against convictions under the 1825 Act between 1859 and 1866, 33 (56 per cent) were successful, a pattern which helped to nullify potential opposition to a harsh

---

[112] It is impossible to establish the precise number of convictions before magistrates as the offence was not separately recorded in the judicial statistics. Over seventy prosecutions (most involving more than one defendant) between 1850 and 1866 have been located in newspapers and trade union records.

[113] *Miner and Workman's Advocate* (19 Sept. 1863), 6. He was replying to a speech by J. A. Roebuck proclaiming the equality of rich and poor before the law.

[114] *Wakefield Express* (31 Oct. 1863), 6; *Barnsley Record* (9 Dec., 16 Dec. 1865); *Nottingham Review* (3 Feb. 1865), 3.

[115] *Rochdale Observer* (23 Nov. 1861), 5; *Manchester Examiner* (10 Jan. 1862), 3; J. Vincent, *The Formation of the British Liberal Party 1857–1868* (1972 edn.), 215; M. Taylor, *Ernest Jones, Chartism and the Romance of Politics, 1819–1869* (2003), 203.

law.[116] Before 1867 unionists continued to rely on the legal remedies available to them to obtain redress, rather than embark on further parliamentary campaigns to alter the 1825 Act.

After 1860 the law took a significant new direction. Those who wanted to ensure that individuals could bargain freely, and that masters were not 'controlled' by the men, had long been frustrated by the criminal law's failure to tackle the 'dictation' and 'tyranny' exercised by organized workers over the productive process.[117] But a series of decisions by the Court of Queen's Bench between 1861 and 1867 placed a much-extended construction upon the 1825 Act. These moved towards the outcome intended by the liberal–tories in 1825, and urged by Senior and others, of making strikes against other workers, such as non-unionists, punishable by summary jurisdiction.

As part of the compromise which ended the strike and lock-out in the London building trade in February 1860, the statute law was brought literally into workplaces. The London master builders, who refused to recognize joint activity by the men and insisted on dealing with them individually, had tried to unsuccessfully to impose an anti-union declaration on the workforce. Lord St Leonards, a former Conservative lord chancellor, proposed that their object would be achieved by hanging a copy of the 1825 Act in every London building site, with a statement explaining the intention of the law to protect the 'security and personal freedom of individual workmen in the disposal of their skill and labour'.[118] After the return to work, a representative of thirty joiners presented a note to their employer declaring that they would strike if he did not discharge two men who had previously signed the employers' declaration and therefore acted against the joint resolution of the majority. In January 1861 the Court of Queen's Bench upheld the decision of a London police magistrate that the ultimatum constituted a threat punishable under the 1825 Act, for which the representative was sentenced to one month's imprisonment with hard labour. The court's reasoning was that the notice constituted a threat to commit an illegal act: while one man could refuse to work with another whom he found objectionable, or any number could each separately decide not to work with an objectionable individual or individuals, if several did so in combination it was a conspiracy at common law. 'It is matter of common learning', Sir

---

[116] Derived from the annual judicial statistics, table 10, 'Number of Appeals from Convictions of Justices', published in *Parliamentary Papers*. For examples of successful appeals see *York Herald* (9 July 1864), 10, (29 Oct. 1864), 10; *Derbyshire Advertiser* (19 Aug. 1864), 8, (6 Jan. 1865), 4; *Nottingham Review* (3 Feb. 1865), 3, (7 Apr. 1865), 3.

[117] Price, *Masters, Unions and Men*, 58, 89, 97.

[118] NAPSS, *Trades' Societies and Strikes* (1860), 69–71.

Charles Crompton observed, 'that what one man may lawfully do alone, he may not do in combination with others, when the act tends to do harm to another.'[119]

That decision (*Walsby v Anley*) was reaffirmed by a further appeal case in 1863 when the Court of Queen's Bench upheld the conviction of John O'Neill, president of the Hull branch of the boilermakers, who had been sentenced by a magistrate to three months' imprisonment. The branch passed a resolution that men belonging to the society should cease to work in a yard where there had been an 'encroachment' on their craft rules (a blacksmith had carried out angle iron bending, work normally reserved for the most skilled of the boilermakers). O'Neill's offence was to warn a society member who persisted in working there that if he continued, he would be 'despised by the club, and have his name sent all over the country, and be put to all sorts of unpleasantness'.[120] One of the stonemasons' shop stewards narrowly escaped imprisonment at York, when the notice of an appeal caused the prosecution to drop the case: the radical attorney W. P. Roberts advised the society's central committee that where a steward faced an unco-operative individual, 'he must confine what he threatens to *himself alone*; he must not say what *others* will do'.[121] What the law objected to was the statement of joint intent. In 1864 there were prosecutions in Leeds of plasterers who sought the discharge of a lapsed member, and in Gloucester of members of the tailors' society, for threatening to withdraw their members from a shop which employed an individual who took work for 'sweating'.[122] Employers in the northern iron trade secured the imprisonment in 1864 of the Leeds district secretary of the National Association of Ironworkers, and a delegate of the jettymen who unloaded ore for the furnaces of C. M. Palmer's Jarrow works. Both had presented ultimata to employers demanding, under threat of strike action, the dismissal of an objectionable individual in one case and reinstatement of dismissed men in the other. It was said in defence of both officials that they were trying to settle matters rather to intimidate the employer.[123]

In a second appeal arising from the Hull boilermaking dispute, the court overturned the conviction of a member of a deputation which met the employer after the strike had begun to explain why they were on strike. In this

---

[119] *Walsby v Anley* (1861) 30 LJMC 123; 121 Eng. Rep. 538 (where another wording is reported); *Spectator* (16 June 1860), 571.

[120] *O'Neill v Longman* (1863) 9 Cox CC 363; *Hull Packet* (24 April 1863), 8.

[121] OSM FR 18 Dec. 1862–1 Jan. 1863, MRC MSS78/OS/4/1/20; for Roberts see R. Challinor, *A Radical Lawyer in Victorian England* (1990).

[122] *Leeds Mercury* (9 July 1864), 11; *Gloucester Chronicle* (25 June 1864), 8.

[123] *Leeds Mercury* (16 Apr. 1864), 12; *Gateshead Observer* (17 Sept. 1864), 5.

instance, the court held, the representative of the men was stating a fact, not making a threat—'the object was not to intimidate, but negotiate'.[124] But the line of distinction was narrow, and in January 1866 the court upheld the conviction of the vice president of a bleachers' union, who had headed a deputation which stated the men's refusal to work alongside a strike-breaker.[125] In November 1866, however, the court decided to press the law no further. A master builder from Stockton-on-Tees, Thomas Bowron, brought a prosecution against two officers of the local branch of the United Order of Bricklayers so that, as he announced to a meeting of building em-ployers, 'they would have it decided once and for ever whether workmen should have the power to dictate to employers as to the number and description of the men they were to employ'.[126] Bowron's bricklayers had suddenly walked out (no period of notice was required). His subsequent enquiries to find out why they had done so elicited a letter from the union branch. This conveyed the resolution of a meeting, at which the defendants had acted as chairman and secretary respectively, declaring that no society bricklayer would work for him until the number of apprentices was reduced and 'expenses' (in effect a fine) paid to the union. The Court of Queen's Bench held that as the resolution was sent to Bowron in answer to his own enquiry, which the court inferred was made in order to achieve a settlement with the union, it could not amount to a 'threat'. Sir Alexander Cockburn, the lord chief justice, reflected generally on the considerations which ought to guide the court: the law should leave labour and capital to make the best for themselves respectively, and should not be strained against the large numbers of men who, lacking wealth, depended upon associations to pro-tect their interests.[127]

A number of constructions might be placed on these cases. The judges were evidently trying to arrive at acceptable limits within which collective pressure could be applied in the workplace. At times they appeared to be wanting to encourage negotiation in place of unilateral regulation. They were undoubtedly carrying out the intention of the liberal–tories, by curb-ing attempts to coerce masters in the running of their businesses. In doing so, they went beyond an interpretation of the 1825 Act to which unionists had been generally willing to consent—although with reservations as to its local administration—that its operation should be confined to violence and breaches of the peace. Contemporary commentators noted that by applying

---

[124] *The Times* (9 Nov. 1863), 9; *O'Neill v Kruger* (1863) 122 Eng. Rep. 505 (which reports a slightly different form of words).
[125] *Shelbourne v Oliver* (1866), 13 LTNS 630.
[126] *Newcastle Daily Chronicle* (24 Apr. 1866), 3.
[127] *Wood v Bowron* (1866) 10 Cox CC 348.

abstract legal reasoning to day-to-day non-violent transactions in work-shops, the courts had merely produced a series of obscure and unworkable distinctions between what was criminal and what was not. Hence the Stockton case (*Wood v Bowron*) was widely applauded as a sign of the court's willingness to encroach no further into the territory which it had perhaps unwisely occupied, though a new statute would be needed to reverse what had already been laid down in *Walsby v Anley*.[128]

In practice, what judges were punishing in the 1860s was a form of collective bargaining on the men's side: a master could not be punished for making an ultimatum to the men, backed by a threat to lock them out, because he was doing so as an individual; a group of workers could be penalized, because the law treated them as acting with a joint design. In labour cases the common law of conspiracy was inherently unequal. As some critics began to allege, it also enshrined the idea, rooted in earlier phases of employment relations, that the withdrawal of labour was an act of coercion against an employer rather than an extension of the labourer's freedom to dispose of his labour as he chose.[129] Such arguments were also raised in Master and Servant cases, where opponents of the existing law sought 'to apply contract doctrine to the employment relationship'.[130] 'The proper view of a strike is not that it is a conspiracy against the masters', Godfrey Lushington—then a young radical barrister—wrote in 1860, 'but a suspension of business until the buyers and sellers of labour can arrange the terms of their bargain'.[131]

The courts disrupted the uneasy compromise which had existed since 1825 at precisely the moment when artisans were being drawn into a revived parliamentary reform movement. In July 1861 the secretary for war, George Cornewall Lewis, who as home secretary had expounded the doctrine of state neutrality, acted swiftly to remove soldiers made available by the War Office to a private contractor constructing new barracks at Chelsea to take the place of striking building workers. Lewis's action failed to avert radical attacks upon the use of the army during an industrial dispute: working people, the protesters claimed, whose taxes paid for the armed services, should be left free from government interference to settle

---

[128] *Solicitor's Journal* (9 Feb. 1861), 253; (17 Nov. 1866), 41–2; *Justice of the Peace* (18 Jan. 1863), 452; *Pall Mall Gazette* (16 Nov. 1866), 1513; *Strikes and Lock-outs: The Law of Combination, by a Barrister* (1867), xviii, 21.

[129] F. D. Longe, *An Inquiry into the Law of 'Strikes'* (1860), 48–9.

[130] For instances of W. P. Roberts doing so from the 1840s onwards, see C. Frank, ' "He Might Almost as Well be Without Trial": Trade Unions and the 1823 Master and Servant Act—the Warrington cases, 1846–47', *Historical Studies in Industrial Relations*, 14 (2002), 40.

[131] NAPSS, *Trades' Societies and Strikes* (1860), 158.

among themselves the terms on which they were willing to sell their labour. That instance of state 'tyranny', which radicals cited in their attempts to persuade trade unions of the need for franchise extension, was soon followed by an agitation to address the inequality of the Master and Servant Act.[132] What Robert Applegarth of the Amalgamated Society of Carpenters and Joiners described as 'the present ambiguous and cruelly·unsatisfactory state' of the law of combinations also began to be cited in appeals for manhood suffrage.[133] The cases which came before the courts, however, brought to light precisely the sorts of workplace 'tyranny' which reinforced anti-reforming politicians in their determination to resist any measure of suffrage extension that was likely to invest unionists with a greater share of political power.[134] Yet it also became apparent that once men lacking wealth were enfranchised, both sides in the bargaining between labour and capital would have to be placed upon an equal standing before the law. This was one of the fundamental issues to be addressed by the legislation of the 1870s.

[132] 3*H* clxiv. 1867–9 (2 Aug. 1861); Gillespie, *Labor and Politics*, 205–6; Lawrence, *Speaking for the People*, 82.

[133] Applegarth to C. Williams, 13 Nov. 1867, Liverpool Trades Council MS 331 TRA 2, fo. 57; G. D. H. Cole and A. W. Filson, *British Working-Class Movements: Select Documents, 1789–1875* (1967), 524, 536, 541; Prothero, *Radical Artisans*, 96–7.

[134] See the example from the Birmingham building trade which left an impression on Lord Stanley, J. Vincent (ed.), *Disraeli, Derby and the Conservative Party* (1978), 235 (5 Sept. 1865); cf. Select Committee on the Elective Franchise (*PP* 1860 xii), Qs. 2126–30.

2

'Under Sufferance': Unions Outside the Law, 1825–1866

Legitimate combinations were conceived of in 1825 as occasional meetings of workmen to decide the level of wages for which they were willing to sell their labour. Such meetings might perhaps occur at the expiry of the term of an agreement, or else when factors such as the demand for labour and the cost of provisions suggested an alteration in the terms they were prepared to accept.[1] Although it failed to take account of the prevalence of journeymen's societies, this conception of combination was not an altogether implausible one during a period when strikes appeared to arise out of temporary, spontaneous forms of organization; many of the groups of workers who sought advances during the strike wave of 1853 were in occupations where there was no tradition of formal unionization.[2] During the 1850s official opinion, based on a theory of an unregulated labour market, more readily acknowledged and accepted—though it regretted—the fact of strikes, than it did trade unionism.

Whether the liberal-tory ministers intended it or not, trade unions after 1825 enjoyed in practice a form of legal toleration. To the high tory David Robinson, it was a particularly deplorable result of the 1825 measure that working people had in practice been permitted to combine 'not for a moment, but *constantly*'.[3] Wallace's select committee earlier in 1825 had been well aware of enduring forms of association, but hoped that the reinstatement of the common law and stiffer penalties against intimidation would reduce their power. Nassau Senior attempted to expose the law's failure to do so, reporting in 1841 that permanent unions were the 'most numerous and most important' type of combinations. In 1862, as he prepared his handloom weavers report for reprinting, he lamented that successive home secretaries had lacked the courage to carry his recommendations into effect. Instead, the growth of unions had continued unchecked: 'combinations are as tyrannical, as unresisted and as

---

[1] 2H xiii. 354 (3 May 1825); [E. C. Tufnell], *Character, Object, and Effects of Trades' Unions* (1834), 116.

[2] Select Committee on Masters and Operatives (*PP* 1856 xiii), Qs. 463, 494; E. W. Evans, *The Miners of South Wales* (1961), 84.

[3] D. Robinson, 'The Combinations', *Blackwood's*, 18 (Oct. 1825), 464.

mischievous as they were in 1831', when he had first alerted Melbourne to the problem.[4]

Observers of the great conflicts of the 1850s were equally impressed by their own re-discovery of the extent and resilience of trade unionism. Many of them shared the perception of the Bradford woollen manufacturer W. E. Forster: pointing to the recovery of the Amalgamated Society of Engineers after the employers' attempt to enforce the 'document' in 1852, he concluded that 'no hostile force will ever be able to destroy Trades' Unions'.[5] Such commentators were led to a different conclusion from that drawn by Senior. As one writer on the Preston dispute commented, combination existed on both sides, the masters acting together as much as the men, 'yet the law does not, and apparently cannot, formally recognise it'.[6] Although the masters' association and the weavers' union were not criminal, neither had a recognized legal standing as an entity in its own right. Both were, as Thomas Winters, the former framework knitter and Chartist secretary of the NAUT remarked in 1855, 'under sufferance'.[7] The question then became, whether the state lost more than it gained by its attempt to keep such associations outside the law; and equally, how far did unions actually wish to be brought within it?

THE LEGAL STATUS OF UNIONS

Although the act of forming a trade union was no longer punishable—provided that its members steered clear of violence or unlawful oaths—trade unions had no legal existence as entities in their own right. Technically they were unincorporated associations; in 1851 the largest and most prosperous union in the mid-Victorian period, the Amalgamated Society of Engineers (ASE), was nothing in law but a giant partnership of some 11,000 members.

Governments kept unions outside the law by denying them the legal rights granted to friendly societies, the voluntary associations which they most nearly resembled. Since 1793 a succession of acts of parliament had granted limited corporate powers to societies for mutual relief in sickness and old age. They were enabled to protect their property and settle internal disputes on condition that their rules were enrolled with justices of the

---

[4] Royal Commission on Handloom Weavers (*PP* 1841 x), report, 31; N. Senior, *Historical and Philosophical Essays* (2 vols., 1865), ii. 116.

[5] W. E. Forster, ' "Strikes" and "Lock-outs" ', *Westminster Review*, n.s. 5 (Jan. 1854), 135–6.

[6] *Morning Chronicle* (9 Nov. 1853), 4.

[7] Select Committee on Stoppage of Wages (Hosiery) (*PP* 1854–5 xiv), Q. 5015.

peace.[8] These legal facilities were offered as a privilege to organizations which the state wished to encourage. There were longstanding anxieties that enrolled benefit societies were often trade combinations in disguise.[9] The official perception that unions might use benefit societies as a 'cloak' for their true purpose was a characteristic contemporary misunderstanding of the nature of working-class institutions: early trade unions frequently grew out of 'box clubs' for mutual support.[10] Official policy nevertheless attempted to draw a distinct line between the two types of institution. In February 1846 the home secretary, Sir James Graham, opposed bringing societies other than purely benefit societies within the Friendly Societies Acts lest trade unions should come within its terms: it was not illegal to combine to raise wages, he acknowledged, but associations for that purpose should not receive the 'advantages' given to friendly societies.[11]

The dangers of forcing popular associations to act outside, and without the protection of, the law were well recognized. In 1848 a House of Lords select committee investigated the position of the affiliated orders of friendly societies (the Oddfellows and Foresters), which for technical reasons were unable legally to register. They nevertheless flourished, with over a quarter of a million members. To the committee it seemed important to give them the protection of the law provided by the Friendly Societies Acts: without 'a sense of protection from the law, or feeling of obligation to the state, such associations may lose their attachment to existing institutions'. But the peers were anxious that any measure to protect the Oddfellows should be drawn up in such a form as 'to prevent Trades Unions and other objectionable Associations from availing themselves' of its benefits.[12]

Since 1829 the process of registration had been centrally supervised by a barrister, Tidd Pratt, who in 1846 became a permanent, salaried official. One of the registrar's tasks was to ensure that 'objectionable' associations did not slip through the net, a task which Pratt performed with assiduity. He insisted that while unions might have objects (such as welfare benefits) permitted by the Friendly Societies Acts, their other unauthorized trade purposes debarred them from registration and its benefits.[13] During the London building dispute of 1859–60 he warned friendly societies against

---

[8] P. H. J. H. Gosden, *Self-Help: Voluntary Associations in the Nineteenth Century* (1973), 30–8, 63–9; B. Supple, 'Legislation and Virtue: An Essay on Working-Class Self-Help and the State in the Early Nineteenth Century', in N. McKendrick (ed.), *Historical Perspectives: Studies in English Thought and Society* (1974), 227–8.

[9] Tufnell, *Character*, 103; Aspinall, *Early Trade Unions*, 383.

[10] Behagg, *Politics and Production*, 111; Chase, *Early Trade Unionism*, 56–8.

[11] *The Times* (26 Feb. 1846), 2; 3*H* lxxxiv. 107 (26 Feb. 1846).

[12] Select Committee on Provident Associations Fraud Prevention Bill (*PP* 1847–8 xvi), Rep., 4–5.   [13] Select Committee on Friendly Societies Bill (PP 1854 vii) Qs. 234–9.

misapplying their funds to support the strikers, and publicized the outcomes of successful legal actions against those that did so. When the strike ended he published examples of the trade union rules sent to him for registration (which he of course rejected).[14] In this he was tacitly lending support to an objective of the Central Association of Master Builders, who also publicized what they called the 'illegal rules' of the trade societies in the building industry.[15]

By 'illegal' it was not meant that such rules were necessarily criminal. Rather, the word was used to indicate that the law would not enforce them, or assist an organization whose purpose was to carry them into effect. The distinction between criminality and illegality was the source of much confusion. Soon after its foundation the ASE sought counsel's opinion as to whether its rules were legal, and received in April 1851 what was taken to be the reassuring advice from the attorney-general (Alexander Cockburn), and another barrister, that 'the members of the society will not incur any penalties in conforming to them'. Their opinion was widely cited as giving full sanction to the union. It was, however, given in answer to a case framed in terms of criminal liabilities, and did not address the other aspect of illegality.[16]

That latter question was discussed in a decision of the Court of Queen's Bench in June 1855 affirmed in the Exchequer Chamber in February 1856. The case of *Hilton v Eckersley* was a further legacy of the Lancashire strikes of 1853 and arose from a bond entered into by each of the eighteen mill owners belonging to the Wigan Master Cotton Spinners Association. For twelve months the signatories to the bond agreed to carry on their works, in matters such as the wages and hours of labour and general discipline, in accordance with the resolutions of a majority of the other signatories. Its purpose was to enforce a lock-out by a penalty of £500 imposed on any individual master tempted to break ranks to exploit some advantage in the market. All had to abide by the decision of the majority. In December 1853 Eckersley, the largest spinner in the town got his mill back to work at full capacity by making a small concession to a key group of workers in defiance of the other masters.[17] When the masters' attorney, Hilton, invoked the law to recover the £500 penalty, the courts refused to enforce its payment.

---

[14] Report of the Registrar of Friendly Societies in England, 1860 (*PP* 1860 xxxix pt I), 9–17.

[15] *The Builder* (22 Oct. 1859), 693.

[16] *Important to Trades' Societies, in the Matter of the Amalgamated Society of Engineers* (1851); Thomas Hughes, who knew the background, later acknowledged that Cockburn's opinion had been misunderstood, 3*H* clxxxvi. 1451 (11 Apr. 1867).

[17] *Wigan Examiner* (16 Dec. 1853, 23 Dec. 1853, 30 Dec. 1853, 13 Jan. 1854). On the case, see Atiyah, *Freedom of Contract*, 410–12.

Two of the three judges who first heard the case held that the bond was in restraint of trade and therefore void. Sir Charles Crompton objected to the bond on the ground that it deprived a party to it of his individual freedom to judge for himself whether or not he wished to open his mill. Each millowner, instead, placed himself 'under the dictation either of a majority or of a committee of delegates'.[18] The parallel with combinations of workmen was obvious, and a significant part of Crompton's judgment concerned the consequences which would flow if such agreements were enforced in the context of combinations among the men. The courts might be called on to force an individual to strike, or oblige him to contribute to a strike, or enforce payment of a fine imposed on him for failing to abide by some collective decision. To Lord Chief Justice Campbell,[19]

A decision in favour of this bond would establish a principle upon which the fantastic and mischievous notion of a 'Labour Parliament' might be realized for regulating the wages and the hours of labour in every branch of trade all over the empire. The most disastrous consequences would follow to masters and to men, and to the whole community.

Both judges wanted to guard against the possibility of combinations legislating for the conditions of employment in entire trades, and therefore establishing a form of legally enforced wage regulation; conversely, counsel for the plaintiffs, on appeal, cited the historic precedent of the judicial enforcement of guild regulations.[20] The judges of the Exchequer Chamber agreed with the decision of the Court of Queen's Bench in regarding the terms of the bond as 'regulations restraining each man's power of carrying on his trade according to his discretion' and therefore not capable of being legally enforced.[21] They, too, feared the consequence of making decisions to strike enforceable at law; if they were, a 'body of delegates' could bring a suit against an individual workman 'who might have been seduced by some designing person to sign an engagement' to take part in a strike so long as a majority wanted to hold out.[22]

One feature of the case was the range of opinion which the judges expressed about the lawfulness of the bond and, by implication, trade unions. Although the majority agreed that it was void, one (Crompton) went so far as to regard it as indictable as a criminal conspiracy, while another (Erle)

---

[18] *Hilton v Eckersley* (1855) 119 Eng. Rep. 785.
[19] Ibid. 789. Campbell's allusion to a Labour parliament referred to the Chartist radical Ernest Jones's initiative in 1854.
[20] Ibid. 790.
[21] Ibid. 792.
[22] Ibid. 793.

took quite the opposite view that, in the light of the 1825 Act, it was perfectly lawful and should be enforceable: assuming men could not be prevented from entering into such agreements (as seemed to be the implication of repeal of the Combination Acts), then it was better that they should be enforced by law than that the parties to them should resort to 'social persecutions, fear and force' to give effect to them.[23] These speculations aside, the ultimate consequence of *Hilton v Eckersley* was that trade union rules were likely to be considered illegal, if ever brought before the courts.

INTERPRETATIONS OF UNIONISM

Association necessary implied the subordination of individuals to the collective will of the majority. On those grounds the whig inspector Hugh Seymour Tremenheere rejected unionism as a solution to the excessively long hours worked by journeymen bakers, on which he reported to the Home Office in 1862. Like the judges in *Hilton v Eckersley* he viewed union restrictions upon individual industry as 'a return to the obsolete principle of the first "Statute of Labourers" by which a certain rate of wages was fixed for all operatives'.[24] The majority judgments in *Hilton v Eckersley* were intended to ensure that participation in combinations was voluntary in the sense that the law could not be used against individuals who chose to break away and follow their own interests. This was an essential condition for reconciling the freedom to combine with the unobstructed working of markets. The judges doubted whether all parties to such associations joined them as an act of free will: the evidence in the Wolverhampton tinplate workers' case of apparently reluctant strikers being plied with drink and sent away to other towns was probably in their minds; so too might the idea, familiar from Chartist trials, that members were 'dupes' led astray by 'agitators'.[25] These perceptions in turn informed contemporary discussion of why combinations persisted and thrived, in spite of the weight of theory pointing to their futility. In 1857 Tidd Pratt reported that in virtually every trade he had found instances of societies regulating the rate of wages; since

---

[23] Ibid. 786.

[24] Report relative to the grievances complained of by the journeymen bakers (*PP* 1862 xlvii), p. lxxxiii; R. K. Webb, 'A Whig Inspector', *Journal of Modern History*, 27 (1955), 358.

[25] *R v Duffield* (1851) 5 Cox CC 422–3; 'Combinations', *Encyclopaedia Britannica* (8th edn., 1854), 163; C. Alderson (ed.), *Selections from the Charges and Other Detached Papers of Baron Alderson* (1858), 184.

they were not enrolled, he had no data on their nature or extent.[26] In 1860 his annual report spoke of 'the unseen power' exerted by collectivities over individuals.[27]

Pratt's choice of expression echoed the conclusion of an article by Harriet Martineau published in October 1859, which aimed to expose the 'secret organization' of the trades and 'the tyranny of a portion of the working classes'.[28] She gathered evidence from employers to demonstrate the extent of the moral pressure by which unions controlled the labour market, and the concealed ways in which they did this. Senior's Handloom Weavers commission report was one of her points of departure, and her argument was essentially an updating of his. Although unions were less prone to violence than a generation earlier, they possessed no less effective means of coercion to infringe the liberty of individuals and impose 'all the fallacies of the protective system'.[29] Unions survived, not because their aims had been proved reasonable by the market, but because members were subjected to a highly effective system of collective control.

Martineau described unions as a challenge to national complacency about the extent of constitutional liberties; trade combinations might avoid violence, and even strikes, but they clandestinely imposed regulations 'more tyrannical' than any government on the continent of Europe would dare to do. The independent working man was prevented from making his own bargains, and subjected to the irresponsible and secret government of union delegates or 'managers' (as she termed their officers). Union rules, such as those of the ASE, the London Society of Compositors, and the flint glass makers, illustrated how individuals submitted to collective dictates: the ASE's elaborate scale of fines enforced discipline not only in workplace matters but also in the sphere of personal conduct, as individual members were supervised and even spied upon by their fellows.[30] Estimating union membership at about 600,000, Martineau reckoned that 2.5 million persons (taking account of dependants) were subjected to their rules, and therefore not able to exercise their labour freely. The remedy lay partly in education and 'the teaching of experience'—union members would ultimately suffer for their economic errors—but also in bringing their proceedings into the open by means of a parliamentary inquiry. This she intended as a prelude

---

[26] Report of the Registrar of Friendly Societies in England, 1857 (*PP* 1857 xxxix), 6.

[27] Ibid. 1860 (*PP* 1860 xxxix pt I), 13.

[28] Martineau to H. Reeve, 9 Mar. 1859, *Harriet Martineau: Selected Letters*, ed. V. Saunders (1990), 174.

[29] H. Martineau, 'Secret Organization of Trades', *Edinburgh Review*, 110 (Oct. 1859), 529.

[30] Ibid. 551–3; on these rules see J. Harris, 'Victorian Values and the Founders of the Welfare State', *Proceedings of the British Academy*, 78 (1992), 174–7.

to the sort of stringent addition to the criminal law and the tightening of its administration which Senior had proposed. Only then would 'true British liberties' be restored to working people.[31]

By the time that Martineau's article was published, an investigation into trades societies and strikes was well advanced, conducted by a voluntary body, the National Association for the Promotion of Social Science (or Social Science Association (SSA) as it was widely known). Pratt and Martineau complained about the dearth of central government data on both phenomena. This deficiency was repaired by the SSA report, whose standing as a pioneering empirical social inquiry has recently been highlighted. Whereas Martineau, like Senior, relied on the unqualified testimony of employers, the reports of the SSA's investigators were, in general, based on a careful balance of testimony.[32] Their principal finding, that unions had grown in membership and become more national in organization, was no more than Martineau had asserted, though they rooted it in firmer evidence. But the SSA committee's comments on the quality of these developments confuted her allegations, directly and scathingly so in the case of her suggestion that union officers were self-elected (much as that would have applied to the NAUT).[33] Indeed, her central thesis was called into question at the outset by the acknowledgement of the openness with which trade societies had dealt with the committee's inquiries.[34] Instead of the 'democratic tyranny' described by Martineau, the SSA report found trade societies offering 'an education in the art of self-government'; instead of the 'shadowy', nameless figures whom she described as forming the organizing committee of the strike in the London building trade, the committee described the leaders of trades societies as 'known and responsible men'.[35] Moreover, their investigations into the actual circumstances of strikes suggested that combination might indeed represent an economically rational strategy for working people. An account of a strike of chain makers in the Midland counties found that the strikers obtained a very considerable rise, earlier resisted by the masters, whose concession could not be attributed to a change in the state of the trade. Had the laws of political economy operated as their proponents said they would, the rise ought to have been

---

[31] 'Secret Organization', 561–3.

[32] Goldman, *Science, Reform, and Politics*, 208–13; Behagg, *Politics and Production*, 153; Fraser, *Trade Unions and Society*, 82–5.

[33] NAPSS, *Trades' Societies and Strikes* (1860), xvi; see also Henry Fawcett's comment on her argument: 'Strikes: Their Tendencies and Remedies', *Westminster Review*, n.s. 18 (July 1860), 2.

[34] *Trades' Societies and Strikes*, vii.

[35] Ibid. xv; Martineau, 'Secret Organization', 528, 555.

conceded long before the strike; the SSA's investigator, Godfrey Lushington, concluded that only by the action of the union had the laws of supply
and demand been set in motion.[36]

These points of difference between Martineau and the SSA established
the terms of a public debate about unionism whose conclusions were
codified in the two reports of the royal commission on trade unions in 1869.
The debate's original context was the political discussion of parliamentary
reform; Henry Reeve had commissioned Martineau's *Edinburgh Review*
article as a contribution to that topic. No one, Bagehot remarked after the
publication of Martineau's piece, could now be unaware that franchise extension in the boroughs would give political power to artisans organized in
unions serving 'a class interest of the worst kind'.[37] Politicians viewed the
practices of unions in that light. Gladstone's defence, in 1864, of his
Government Annuities Bill against the attack of George Potter, whom he
described as 'the far-famed secretary' of the trade unions, included a denunciation of their tyranny over minorities; a deputation from the London
Trades Council who sought to distance themselves from Potter and to refute Gladstone's allegations of their coerciveness caused him to moderate,
but not altogether to withdraw, his allegation.[38] In 1865 he spoke of the un-
soundness of union regulations which interfered with the right of every
man to employ his labour as he chose, and insisted that 'the labouring
classes have the great lesson to learn concerning the rights of minorities'.[39]
John Bright, who had in January 1860 urged unions to use their power for
political ends, tried to get round these objections to wider enfranchisement
by suggesting that political exclusion caused working people to focus their
discontents upon employers; if admitted to citizenship they would be less
likely to resort to strikes and unionism.[40]

To describe combination as a malignant result of an unrepresentative
constitution was hardly more favourable than the utilitarian view of it as the
product of social pressure and popular ignorance. In an attempt to define a
place for unions within the free trade economy and the liberal state, a group
of writers contributed to a different understanding of the persistence of
combination. E. S. Beesly, Henry Fawcett, Frederic Harrison, Thomas
Hughes, J. M. Ludlow, Godfrey Lushington, and Charles Neate claimed,

---

[36] *Trades' Societies and Strikes*, 158.
[37] 'Trade Unions and Reform', *Economist* (22 Oct. 1859), *Bagehot's Political Essays*, ed. N.
St John Stevas, viii (1974), 18.
[38] 3*H* clxxiii. 1577 (7 Mar. 1864); clxxv. 321 (11 May 1864); *Bee-Hive* (19 Mar. 1864), 1.
[39] *The Times* (2 Nov. 1865), 7–8.
[40] Bright to a Blackburn spinner, 3 Nov. 1860, in H. J. Leech (ed.), *The Public Letters of the
Right Hon. John Bright, MP* (1885), 80–1; Steele, *Palmerston and Liberalism*, 132.

as professional men, to be able to review the subject from a vantage point free from class interest. Noting the association of unionism with the extension of education and 'intelligence', they sought rational explanations for its existence.[41] Hence Henry Fawcett's attempt to explain the recurrence of strikes, in the face of the economic assertions of their futility. His conceptualization of strikes as a form of profit-sharing caused Mill, in 1862, to modify his account to acknowledge that markets were not self-clearing, and that strikes played a necessary part in their functioning, as the SSA inquiry had demonstrated.[42] Most of all, they dwelt on the morally beneficial results of unionism, which they identified with independence and heightened public spirit, linking it to the contemporary celebrations of British self-governing institutions and voluntary effort. Theirs was an early attempt to identify unionism with national values.[43]

A vision of moral progress had obvious appeal to observers influenced variously by Arnoldian broad churchmanship, Christian Socialism, and Positivism. Hughes was one of a small group of young politicians and public men in or on the fringes of the Christian Socialist movement, who were drawn into a correspondence with Viscount Goderich in the winter of 1853–4.[44] Goderich (like Marx)[45] had been impressed by the 'bitter class hatred' evident in the published statements of both sides in the Preston dispute, calling it an 'industrial civil war' for which the *laissez-faire* principle seemed to allow no peaceful solution. He and his informants, who also included H. A. Bruce, MP for Merthyr Tydfil, and W. E. Forster, could envisage no legislative solution (for that would involve the protectionist fallacy of wage-fixing), but instead looked to goodwill on both sides, and a moral change on the part of employers. Summarizing some of their conclusions, Forster regretted the unwillingness of the masters to recognize the men as equal bargaining partners, a theme much emphasized by Hughes

[41] Fawcett, 'Strikes', 4, 23; J. M. Ludlow, 'Trade Societies and the Social Science Association', *Macmillan's Magazine*, 3 (March 1861), 362; T. Hughes, 'More about Masters and Workmen', *Macmillan's Magazine*, 4 (1861), 496; E. S. Beesly, 'Trades' Unions', *Westminster Review*, 20 (Oct. 1861), 535; C. Neate, *Two Lectures on Trade Unions Delivered in the University of Oxford in the Year 1861* (1861), 35; F. Harrison, 'The Good and Evil of Trade Unionism', *Fortnightly Review*, o.s. 3 (Nov. 1865), 35–6.

[42] *Collected Works of John Stuart Mill*, vol. iii, ed. J. M. Robson (1965), 932–3; the passage drew upon Fawcett, 'Strikes', 1–23; P. Deane, 'Henry Fawcett: The Plain Man's Political Economist', in L. Goldman (ed.), *The Blind Victorian: Henry Fawcett and British Liberalism* (1989), 100–01; Biagini, 'British Trade Unions and Popular Political Economy', 814–15.

[43] J. P. Parry, 'The Impact of Napoleon III on British Politics, 1851–1880', *TRHS*, 6th ser. 11 (2001), 164–6; Briggs, *Victorian People*, 179; Jones, *Victorian Political Thought*, 45–52.

[44] Goderich to H. A. Bruce, 22 Nov. and 3 Dec. 1853, BL Add MS 43534, fos. 3–4; Goderich to Hughes, 7 Nov., 17 Nov., 29 Nov. 1853, BL Add MS 43547, fos. 104–9.

[45] Stedman Jones, 'Some Notes on Karl Marx and the English Labour Movement', 126.

and Ludlow.[46] The idea had been privately floated in Goderich's correspondence that unions might represent the men in some form of collective bargaining to produce an orderly resolution of the differences between labour and capital. Unions would then become agents of class reconciliation, tending to curb rather than promote strikes. This in turn raised the question of legalization.

Before 1867 two forms of argument were used in favour of state recognition of unions. One was essentially that advanced by the Lords select committee in 1848 in the case of the Oddfellows, which held that it was more dangerous to leave such associations outside the law than to bring them within it. Newspaper correspondents sent to report the Preston strike formed the same conclusion. Since it was clear that combinations, 'however objectionable', could not be repressed, 'the next best thing is to turn them if possible to some account and perhaps gradually to lead them to a wise use of the power which they undoubtedly concentrate', the *Times* special correspondent concluded.[47] James Lowe, a journalist who covered the strike for the radical *Leader* newspaper, thought that in view of the immense losses inflicted on the participants and on the public by the seven-month dispute, the operations of both employers' associations and trade unions should be made more open to account. He had discovered that 'almost every trade in the Kingdom has its union', yet the objects, constitutions and activities of those organizations were shrouded 'in the greatest possible obscurity'. Parliament would have acted with greater foresight in 1825, he suggested, if it had not simply permitted combinations to exist, but had treated them in the same way as joint stock companies, 'defining the limits within which combinations are legal, and providing the machinery for insuring the responsibility of their members'.[48]

A second view, which contained elements of the first, was identified with those of the Christian Socialists whose positive impression of trade unionism dated from their engagement with the ASE during the engineering dispute of 1851–2.[49] Thomas Hughes found, contrary to Martineau, that the ASE enjoyed the confidence of its members, who had good grounds for believing that it represented their best interests. Unions should be legally recognized so as 'to render their influence and action wholly beneficial to the great common interests of the nation'.[50] Those national interests were damaged by the prevailing orthodoxy that capital and labour relations

[46] Forster, ' "Strikes" and "Lock-outs" ', 130, 136.
[47] *The Times* (8 Nov. 1853), 7.
[48] *Leader* (8 Apr. 1854), 326.
[49] Fraser, *Trade Unions and Society*, 77–84.
[50] *Trades' Societies and Strikes*, 187.

could be treated as a purely private matter: that theory overlooked the fact that 'if one is injured, all suffer'. Recognizing unions and giving them a legal corporate existence would both facilitate arbitration, by enabling the men to be bound by agreements, and would help to improve the 'spirit and temper' of the unions themselves.[51]

The Christian Socialist lawyer J. M. Ludlow devised a more elaborate scheme of legalization. Like Hughes, he admired the 'really brotherly spirit' engendered by the ASE (in contrast to Mill's castigation of the 'total absence of any large and generous aims' displayed by the engineers during their conflict with the employers).[52] Ludlow attached enormous significance to the development of working-class associations and became an authority on their legal position.[53] He concluded that friendly society legislation had helped to distort the development of mutual associations by encouraging the severing of friendly societies from trade unions. This arose because what he termed 'the simplest and universal function of trades' societies', the provision of benefit to workers 'casually out of employment', was not one of the objects recognized by the Friendly Societies Acts.[54] Men joined the ASE primarily, he believed, because of the security offered by 'donation' (out of work) benefit which it offered, but in doing so they were obliged to become members of societies which might become involved in strikes. But the Home Office refused to allow societies offering unemployment relief to come within the Friendly Societies Acts; in 1861 the permanent secretary refused permission for a registered society to offer out of work benefit on the ground that to do so 'would be a great encouragement to strikes'.[55]

Ludlow was as opposed to encouraging strikes (though he might support the aims of strikers) as the Home Office, and was prepared to contemplate banning them, which no home secretary was willing to do. At the time of the Wolverhampton conspiracy trials he had denounced the 1825 settlement as no more than 'a solemn duelling code', laying down the terms upon which the 'competitive fight' between capital and labour was to be carried out.[56] Instead, he advocated compulsory arbitration, which was feasible now that

---

[51] T. Hughes, 'More about "Masters and Workmen"', *Macmillan's Magazine*, 4 (Oct. 1861), 497 8.

[52] J. M. Ludlow, *The Master Engineers and Their Workmen: Three Lectures on the Relations of Capital and Labour* (1852), 36; Mill, *Collected Works*, iii. 931.

[53] Ludlow, 'Trade Societies', 314; E. Norman, *The Victorian Christian Socialists* (1987), 62, 78–9.

[54] *Trades' Societies and Strikes*, xx–xxi; Ludlow, 'Trade Societies', 318–19.

[55] Docket by Waddington on Tidd Pratt to H. Waddington, 14 Mar. 1861, PRO HO45/7194.

[56] *Christian Socialist*, 2 (23 Aug. 1851), 113.

data on unemployment and wages rates collected by unions could enable the state of the labour market to be scientifically established and the price of labour to be accurately assessed.[57] Strikes could therefore be forbidden, but unions fully legalized under the Friendly Societies Acts—even compulsorily so, since he saw 'a great social danger' in 'large bodies of men permanently organized' operating outside the pale of the law.[58]

Elaborated for the first time in 1852, at a time when the engineering employers were trying to enforce the 'document', Ludlow's original suggestion that unions should be allowed the same legal rights as friendly societies bore a radical appearance.[59] There was, however, a strong regulatory, even authoritarian, element in his proposals: by recognizing unions his purpose was to use the power of the state to modify them and their policies.[60] His ideas reflected both his admiration for English voluntary associations and the experience of his upbringing in France, where combinations remained prohibited until 1864 but where disputes were settled by officially constituted joint tribunals (*Conseils de Prudhommes*). Another advocate of legalization, Charles Neate, the Liberal MP and Oxford professor of political economy who, like Ludlow, had been educated in Paris, saw any state interference in the free bargaining between capital and labour as incompatible with English 'habits and feelings'. In England the interference of a public official on the subject of wages would be repelled as 'an impertinence'; in France the authority of a prefect would command immediate respect. It was one of the 'set-offs to the many disadvantages of a despotic government' that its representatives assumed a paternal role.[61] Neate, like Goderich's correspondents in the mid-1850s, saw that any legalization of unions would have to be carried out within the existing national practice of *laissez-faire*.

TRADE UNIONS AND LEGALIZATION

The obstacles in the way of obtaining a recognized legal status represented a significant hindrance to the development of certain forms of working-class association. The extra-legal standing of the affiliated orders within the

---

[57] Ludlow, 'Trade Societies', 317.

[58] Ludlow, 'Trade Societies, pt II', *Macmillan's Magazine*, 3 (March 1861), 366–70; Ludlow, *Master Engineers*, 44; *Trades' Societies and Strikes*, 617–18.

[59] Ludlow, *Master Engineers*, 44.

[60] Ibid. 45; Ludlow advised the ASE to register under the Companies Act, see ASE, Abstract Report of Council's Proceedings, April 1862 to December 1863.

[61] Neate, *Two Lectures*, 44–6.

friendly society movement has already been noted; even after 1850, when they were permitted to register, Tidd Pratt did not ease their path.[62] Repeated attempts by the National Charter Association and by the Chartist land plan to achieve a legal form of organization were thwarted by the limited purposes for which registration under the Friendly Society Acts was permitted, and by the prohibitively expensive and ultimately insurmountable obstacles placed in the way of a mass membership association securing incorporation under the existing Joint Stock Companies Acts.[63]

Refused the benefits of friendly society legislation, unincorporated, and illegal in the non-criminal meaning of the term, trade unions were potentially exposed to a number of practical difficulties. Even the most routine transactions, such as renting premises, were conducted on an uncertain basis. In spite of this, unions managed to run their affairs without recourse to the processes of the law. Their difficulties were not those of the Chartists' land plan or of co-operative ventures: unions had no shareholders; they did not trade; and they did not require limited liability. Their anomalous position had not prevented them from accumulating and disbursing funds. Most seem to have used the device of appointing trustees, in whose names money was deposited in banks or property was acquired. After Gladstone's first budget in 1853 the London Society of Compositors bought £400 worth of the new three and a half per cent government stock in the names of three members. The brushmakers deposited funds in a savings' bank through the intermediary of trustees, and in the same way the London Coopers acquired a hall in East London. By the mid-1860s the accumulations could be considerable. In 1866 the ASE, the Friendly Society of Ironfounders, the Amalgamated Society of Carpenters and Joiners, and the Steam-Engine Makers Society had between them funds of nearly £200,000.[64] In 1868 a speaker at the first TUC pointed out that unions already had, for practical purposes, a legal existence: banks did extensive business with them, and the Post Office transmitted annually tens of thousands of pounds on their behalf as funds were moved between union branches and head offices.[65]

[62] J. Belchem, *Industrialization and the Working Class: The English Experience, 1750–1900* (1990), 112–13.

[63] E. Yeo, 'Some Practices and Problems of Chartist Democracy', in J. Epstein and D. Thompson (eds), *The Chartist Experience: Studies in Working-Class Radicalism and Culture, 1830–60* (1982), 372.

[64] MRC MSS 28/CO/1/8/4/1 LSC 22nd Quarterly Report, July 1853; W. Kiddier, *The Old Trade Unions: From Unprinted Records of the Brushmakers* (1931), 84; *Miner and Workman's Advocate* (12 Dec. 1863), 5; *Bee-Hive* (3 July 1869), 4; Howell, *Conflicts*, appendices, 494.

[65] *Bee-Hive* (13 June 1868), 6.

Insofar as mid-Victorian unions sought anything from the state, it was protection for their funds. Financial dishonesty was an enormous temptation to officers and defalcations undermined confidence in the organization, a factor which weighed even more heavily with unionists than the actual amounts lost to fraud.[66] No union suffered a loss on the scale of the £4,000 embezzled from the Manchester Unity of Oddfellows by its secretary in 1848; all but one of the reported cases of dishonesty in unions up to 1870 involved sums under £100. More considerable losses were liable to be incurred through the commercial failure of private banks, as at least two unions who had deposited funds with them found to their cost.[67] After the Overend and Gurney bank collapse in 1866 the Manchester lodge of the stonemasons urged the union's central committee to deposit £7,000 of its funds with the Bank of England 'for safety'.[68] Hence also the famous deputation of the ASE to Gladstone in May 1864 to seek his permission to deposit the union's funds in the Post Office Savings Bank.[69] Their request indicated a weakening of radical fears earlier in the century that the state would not scruple to confiscate the funds of working-class associations. It also mitigated the anti-statist furore generated in March 1864 by Gladstone's plan for the government to provide low-cost annuities, which had been the occasion of his clash with George Potter.

Opposition voiced in the radical press to 'French centralization' and the undermining of self-governing institutions by paternal government were a common currency of political sentiment among all classes during the 1860s. The outcry against Gladstone's bill needs, however, to be treated with some caution, for those popular newspapers which denounced it derived advertising revenue from the collecting societies and industrial assurance companies who were directly threatened by the proposal. Officers of the commercial societies were observed to take a prominent part in the 'monster meeting' chaired by Potter at Exeter Hall, London. An uproarious meeting at Leeds, which was told by Potter—who was now managing the *Bee-Hive*—that the scheme's 'ultimate object was to annihilate trades' unions' and to crush the artisan's 'manly and independent spirit', was reportedly packed with insurance agents.[70] The London Trades Council's

---

[66] J. McIlroy, 'Financial Malpractice', 6–11.

[67] ASE, monthly report, Sept. 1856, 634; *Flint Glass Makers' Magazine* (Dec. 1857), 109.

[68] OSM FR 2 July – 26 July 1866, MRC MSS 78/OS/4/1/29. They were unable to do so because the Bank would not accept deposits in the names of trustees.

[69] Matthew, *GD*, vi. 275 (10 May 1864).

[70] *Glasgow Sentinel* (12 Mar. 1864), 4; *Leeds Express* (19 Mar. 1864), 6. For denunciations see *Bee-Hive* (12 Mar. 1864), 5–6; (19 Mar. 1864), 4 (cited in Biagini, *Liberty*, 85); *Lloyd's Weekly Newspaper* (13 Mar. 1864), 6; *Miner and Workman's Advocate* (19 Mar. 1864), 4. However, *Reynolds's Newspaper* (13 Mar. 1864), 4, supported the measure.

deputation to Gladstone to dissociate themselves from Potter's views showed that the opposition was not unanimous.[71] Nevertheless all would have agreed with the assertion of Richard Harnott, general secretary of the stonemasons, that they were competent to manage their own affairs and administered welfare benefits more efficiently than any government department. Where they differed among themselves was in their pragmatic responses to particular institutional advantages offered to them by the state.

Before 1867, when trade unionists spoke of legalization they usually meant freedom from the criminal law rather than acquiring a recognized legal standing.[72] Indeed, the only piece of enabling legislation affecting them in their institutional capacity arose from characteristically defensive mobilization of trade societies in 1854. A bill to consolidate and amend the law relating to friendly societies, introduced by Thomas Sotheron, a Wiltshire county MP whose preoccupation was to keep the agricultural labourers of the southern counties off the poor rates, aroused such a heated reaction that Thomas Duncombe believed 'no subject had ever made a greater commotion among the working classes' and John Bright warned that its enactment would 'produce something in the nature of a revolt among the population of the north of England'.[73]

An attempted interference with benefit societies had provoked a similar response in 1828,[74] and the reaction was particularly strong in 1854 because of the stigma upon working-class parents implied by the limitations proposed to be placed on the insurance of infant lives.[75] In addition, an indirect effect of the bill was believed to be to prohibit the existence of trade unions as they were then constituted.[76] All societies which received subscriptions for relief in case of sickness, superannuation, or death were to be required to submit to the process of enrolment under the government registrar; but since trade unions embraced objects beyond those permitted by the bill, they were ineligible for registration. Had the bill passed, a trade union

[71] On 16 Mar. 1864; *Bee-Hive* (19 Mar. 1864), 1; Potter had led a deputation to Gladstone on 5 Mar. 1864, Matthew, *GD*, vi. 261.

[72] *Glasgow Sentinel* (6 Apr., 16 Apr. 1859).

[73] 3*H* cxxxiii. 91 (10 May 1854).

[74] Prothero, *Artisans and Politics*, ch.12.

[75] It was alleged that such insurance created a temptation to neglect young children. Pratt to Palmerston, 26 Dec. 1853, PRO HO45/5203; Palmerston to Sotheron, 7 June 1854, Sotheron Estcourt MSS D1571 X98; *Stockport Advertiser* (5 May, 26 May 1854); *Manchester Guardian* (6 Apr 1854); *Times* (12 Dec. 1853), 6; Palmerston, writing to Aberdeen, used its alleged prevalence as an argument against franchise extension, 12 Feb. 1854, BL Add MSS 43069, fo. 212.

[76] *Reynolds's News* (12 Mar. 1854), 16; (19 Mar. 1854), 13; report of the Metropolitan Trades Delegates reprinted in *Friendly Societies Journal* (Mar. 1855), 2, and reviewed in *Bookbinders' Trade Circular*, 2 (Dec. 1855), 44–6.

would have been faced with two alternatives to avoid the substantial penalties prescribed by the Act: either to renounce its trade functions and register, or to cease to offer welfare benefits. The ASE executive saw the proposal as 'the means of breaking up our society, and every Trade Society of a similar character', while branches of the stonemasons reported rumours that the bill was a plot by employers to retaliate for the support given to the Preston strikers.[77] Lobbying against the bill was organized by the committee of London trades delegates, chaired by William Allan of the ASE.

Sotheron's diary indicates that he had drawn the bill some time before the Lancashire strikes began. He did not discover until after the bill was published that unions were likely to be affected by it. Meeting a deputation which included Goderich, William Newton of the Engineers, and other representatives of the trades, he disclaimed any intention to interfere with trade societies.[78] When the bill was referred to a select committee, not only were the offending clauses expunged, but with the assistance of Goderich a clause was inserted permitting societies existing 'for any purpose which is not illegal' to receive the special remedies against fraud enjoyed by friendly societies registered under the Act, by merely depositing their rules with the registrar of friendly societies.[79] Both the committee of metropolitan trades delegates and the ASE executive described it as giving them all the advantages of an enrolled friendly society without having either to alter their rules or to submit to any interference in their activities.[80]

In 1855 the trades were willing to take any advantages which legal recognition might bring so long as their autonomy was not impaired. But they obtained this favourable settlement by what amounted to a 'subterfuge', for Parliament was not made aware of the ulterior object of protecting trade unions.[81] It was based, moreover, upon Cockburn's opinion that the purposes of the ASE, as indicated by its rules, were not 'illegal'. This was vulnerable on two counts: first, the ASE's rules were extremely mild, in that they made only oblique references to strikes, so what held for them might not do so for other unions; and secondly, after 1856, *Hilton v*

---

[77] ASE, monthly report, Apr. 1854, 232; OSM FR 22 Feb. – 8 Mar. 1855, MRC MSS 78/OS/4/1/15.

[78] Sotheron diary, 15 Aug. 1853, 23 Mar., 24 Mar. 1854, Sotheron Estcourt MSS D1571 F403.

[79] McIlroy, 'Financial Malpractice', 22–5; J. M. Ludlow and Lloyd Jones, *The Progress of the Working Class 1832–1867* (1867), 44; Select Committee on Friendly Societies Bill (*PP* 1854 vii), Rep. iv–v; 18 & 19 Vict. c. 63, s. 44.

[80] *Friendly Societies Journal* (Mar. 1855), 3; ASE, monthly report, Aug. 1854, 367; *Bookbinders' Trade Circular* (Dec. 1855), 44–6; cf. ASCJ, monthly report, Sept. 1865.

[81] H. Pelling, *Popular Politics and Society in Late Victorian Britain* (2nd edn., 1979), 71.

Eckersley called into question their legality if anyone chose to raise the issue.[82]

In administering the 1855 Act, Tidd Pratt and his Scottish counterpart effectively prevented any but a small number of unions from taking advantage of it. Both registrars were willing to accept the rules only of those societies which disguised their trade purposes. Requests by the flint glass makers, bookbinders, and stonemasons to deposit their rules were all rejected; Pratt pointed out to the masons, who attempted to deposit their rules following three recent cases of fraud, that they could not benefit from the relevant section as ' "the regulating the price and lessening the hours of labour" is not one of the objects authorised under the Act'.[83]

The vast majority of unions, whose rules were not deposited, were left to rely on whatever remedies against robbery that the ordinary process of the law would allow them. For a small, local society, or a temporary combination formed to carry out a strike, the cost of bringing proceedings made such a remedy of limited value. Some of the well-established societies did successfully proceed against dishonest members and officers. The iron-moulders (forerunners of the ironfounders) prosecuted a branch secretary, who was sentenced at Liverpool assizes to one month's hard labour for a fraud involving £50, and an individual member was sentenced to four months' imprisonment for forging travelling cards which entitled him to relief.[84] Even the masons obtained a sentence of six months' hard labour at Exeter sessions in October 1866 against a lodge secretary who had obtained £19 from central funds to finance a strike which never took place. While counsel for the dishonest official urged the jury 'to discourage such societies as these', the recorder of Exeter insisted that the question of whether the society was 'for good or evil' was irrelevant.[85]

More than the threat of prosecution, unions relied upon the efficiency and probity of their own internal administration to secure their funds. Outsiders were impressed by the meticulous accounting of strike funds— receipts and disbursements were published in the press—and the very rarity of fraud was sometimes cited as evidence of their fitness for recognition by the state. Any desire on the part of the trades for the additional

---

[82] *Flint Glass Makers' Magazine* (Dec. 1859), 552–3.

[83] *Flint Glass Makers' Magazine* (Mar. 1856), 377–9; Tidd Pratt, 26 Feb. 1856, OSM FR 20 Mar. – 3 Apr. 1856, MSS 78/OS/4/1/16; *Bookbinders' Trade Circular* (Jan. 1866), 67.

[84] *Oldham Chronicle* (25 Sept., 18 Dec. 1858); *Staffordshire Sentinel* (31 July 1858). The ironfounders deposited their rules in August 1858 but did not use the summary remedy available to them; see also a successful indictment brought by the boilermakers at Middlesex sessions, *Morning Chronicle* (19 May 1857), 9.

[85] OSM FR 4–18 Oct. 1866, 7–21 Feb. 1867; MRC MSS 78/OS/4/1/29.

security which such recognition might bring was tempered by their unwillingness to be supervised by a government official. In his paper on trade societies, read at the Social Science Association's Congress in 1865 but not published in the association's transactions, the Sheffield compositor William Dronfield described the lack of legal protection to unions as a civil disability and 'an anomaly that ought not longer to exist'. Faced, though, with the sort of legalization advocated by a popular social science tract writer, who demanded that all minutes of union proceedings be published, their accounts submitted to public auditors, and their votes taken by ballot, Dronfield preferred to remain outside the law, and carry the risk of fraud.[86]

Hostile observers suggested a further reason why unions were wary of legalization. As early as 1834 the whig adviser E. C. Tufnell observed that the combination of trade and welfare benefits operated as a powerful disciplinary force against dissidents: a member who was expelled for some transgression of trade rules lost all his rights to benefits and enjoyed no legal redress.[87] To Martineau this represented another means by which individuals were subjected to collective tyranny and prevented from following their own interests.[88] How far the loss of benefits was actually used as a lever to enforce trade rules is uncertain; in 1867 it was alleged that ASE branches were using the threat of forfeiting benefits to enforce the abolition of piecework among their members in Lancashire.[89] Welfare benefits made it more difficult for employers to impose the 'document', since any union member agreeing to sign it would have to give up the entitlement to valuable benefits for which they had contributed over many years.[90] Hence the attempts to set up employer-sponsored schemes, and recurring proposals that unions should be forced to separate their benefit from their trade funds.[91]

In reaffirming that contracts in restraint of trade were unenforceable, the court in *Hilton v Eckersley* wanted to ensure that unions could not take legal proceedings against their members. In doing so the majority of the judges overlooked the greater likelihood that a member might need to proceed against his union. In 1864, when a recalcitrant member of the Brighton branch of the ironfounders who had been expelled for refusing to contribute

---

[86] W. Dronfield, 'A Working-Man's View of Trades' Societies', *Seventh Annual Report of the Executive of the Association of Organised Trades of Sheffield* (1866), 13–14; *Trades-Unions, Strikes, and Locks-Out* (Chambers' Social Science Tracts, 1861), 24.

[87] Tufnell, *Character*, 117; Clegg, Fox, and Thompson, *History of British Trade Unions*, 7.

[88] Martineau, 'Secret Organization', 540.

[89] *Engineering* (15 Mar. 1867).

[90] Select Committee on Masters and Operatives (*PP* 1856 xiii), Q.2886.

[91] FSIF, half-yearly report, Jan.–July 1852, 24; MRC MSS 41/FSIF/4/2/7; *Friendly Societies Journal* (Apr. 1855), 9; *Report of the Executive Committee of the Central Association of Master Builders* (1860), 28–9.

to the auxiliary (trade) fund, sought reinstatement through his local county court, the society's solicitor successfully argued that the society stood outside the pale of the law, and that the matter was beyond the court's jurisdiction.[92] In another case, at St Helens, a member 'who had been excluded for working under wages', attempted with the backing both of his employers and their foreman to sue the ironfounders for sick pay; the union again successfully argued that, being an extra-legal body, the court possessed no power to adjudicate in its affairs.[93] The possible injustice to members was addressed by the majority of the Social Science Association committee, which urged that there should be 'an easy and cheap remedy' to settle disputes about benefits, though this would have required some form of legalization, a step which they were not prepared to recommend.[94]

The anomalous position which trade unions occupied during the mid-1860s was an instance of the phenomenon of 'equipoise': the 'temporary balance of forces', neither planned nor contrived, which has been described as characteristic of the decade before 1867.[95] Unions were allowed to exist, but governments denied them a legal status as permanent associations because their purposes—the regulation of trade and the support of strikes —were contrary to public policy. As Senior complained, ministers shied away from addressing the fact that unionism continued to flourish in the face of official disapproval and discouragement. Charles Neate described the dilemma of government in similar terms: unionism was 'commonly looked upon as a troublesome and dangerous nuisance, which we dare not put an end to by law, and which we hope in vain will die of itself'.[96] For their part, many of the craft unions found a position of 'sufferance' not altogether inconvenient. They could prosper under the minimal state rather as, it has been argued, artisans in the workplace sometimes found the *laissez-faire* framework of industrial relations advantageous.[97] While some form of unregulated legalization might have represented their ideal, they wanted to avoid the sort of recognition which would compromise their independence, and they had good reason to be wary of submitting to the sort of paternalist, arbitrary officialdom represented by Tidd Pratt. Their existing position would have to be shaken by some powerful, external force, before they, or the Home Office, would feel the need to promote change.

[92] FSIF, half-yearly report, June–Dec. 1864, 276; MRC MSS 41/FSIF/4/2/9.
[93] FSIF, half-yearly report, July–Dec. 1865, 294; MRC MSS 41/FSIF/4/2/11; for a case involving the ASE, see *Miner and Workman's Advocate* (12 Dec. 1863).
[94] *Trades' Societies and Strikes*, xix; Ludlow MSS Add 7450/5.
[95] W. L. Burn, *The Age of Equipoise* (1964), 82.
[96] Neate, *Two Lectures*, 49.
[97] Price, *Masters, Unions, and Men*, 93.

3

Union Funds, Free Labour, and the Franchise

When an outrage widely attributed to trade unionists coincided with the parliamentary reform crisis, the Home Office could no longer avoid dealing with their anomalous legal position. The detonation of a canister of gunpowder in October 1866 in the house of a former member of the Saw Grinders' Union in Hereford Street, Sheffield, was not in itself especially remarkable. Acts of similar or greater violence in the town had been brought to the attention of the home secretaries over the previous twenty years, and the Home Office's initial response was routine. A confidential approach by the mayor of Sheffield, seeking assistance in detecting the perpetrators and also strongly implying the involvement of trades unions, was met with the usual departmental procedure of offering a reward for information leading to a conviction, and a pardon to any accomplices who gave evidence.[1]

The Hereford street explosion occurred on the morning of the vast West Riding demonstration on Woodhouse Moor, Leeds, some 200,000-strong, under the auspices of the Manhood Suffrage Association, followed by an indoor rally addressed by John Bright.[2] Anti-reform interests in Sheffield seized on the likely union involvement in the outrage: pressure for further inquiry came from Sheffield Town Council and the Chamber of Commerce, encouraged by W. C. Leng, the evangelical editor of the Conservative *Sheffield Daily Telegraph*, and J. A. Roebuck, whose purpose was to discredit franchise extension in general and Bright's attempt to enlist union support for it in particular.[3] Led by Roebuck, they met the home secretary, Walpole, on 14 November but refused to permit the proceedings to be fully reported;

---

[1] Mayor of Sheffield to Home Office, 12 Oct. 1866, PRO HO45/7921; Belmore to mayor of Sheffield, 15 Oct. 1866, PRO HO43/108, p. 119; S. Butcher (mayor of Sheffield) to Sir J. Graham, 23 Apr. 1846, PRO HO45/1484; *The Times* (16 June 1854), 5; Sheffield Association of Organized Trades to Palmerston, 9 Aug. 1862, PRO HO45/7360.

[2] *The Times* (9 Oct. 1866), 7, 8.

[3] *Sheffield Daily Telegraph* (30 Oct. 1866), 6; (10 Nov. 1866), 3; J. A. Roebuck to Stanley, 17 Oct. 1866, Stanley MSS 920 Der (15), 12/2/2; Sheffield Chamber of Commerce Minutes, 2 Nov. 1866, LD 1986/1 p.71.

three days later a deputation from the Sheffield Association of Organized Trades and London Trades Council requested an open enquiry. Walpole told them that the cabinet was discussing the appointment of a royal commission and had agreed that it should be 'a comprehensive and impartial one'.[4]

These deputations reinforced Walpole in a decision which he had privately come to early in November, that there should be a general inquiry with a view to amending the law on 'unlawful combinations' as well as investigating the whole question of the relations between employers and workers.[5] Unlike the Adullamite MP, Lord Elcho, who urged him to appoint a commission to expose the danger of entrusting the men with electoral power,[6] Walpole attempted to approach the issue in an even-handed spirit, though his idea of impartiality—a commission chaired by a recently retired judge, Sir William Erle, and composed of 'high officials, with four members from the two Houses of Parliament, and the chairman of a great industrial undertaking'—did not include a working man.[7] After representations from George Potter's London Working Men's Association, Walpole added a union nominee to the commission, the Positivist lawyer Frederic Harrison, balanced by an employer (an iron master). Walpole was resolute in defending Harrison's appointment in the face of strong Conservative objections; and he described Harrison's seminal *Fortnightly Review* article of November 1865, 'The good and evil of trades unions', which contained a penetrating critique of economic objections to unionism, as 'temperate and remarkably able'.[8] Walpole envisaged the commission as being 'more or less of a judicial character'.[9] This had the advantage that minutes of the proceedings in London were published at regular intervals, but the proceedings were otherwise closed, and the cross-examinations of witnesses assumed an adversarial form.[10] Unlike other major royal commissions of the 1860s, such as the Children's Employment and Endowed Schools Commissions, no regional or industry-wide surveys were undertaken by assistant commissioners to gather and digest evidence in a system-

---

[4] *Sheffield Daily Telegraph* (14 Nov.; 19 Nov. 1866); *Bee-Hive* (24 Nov. 1866); *Report of the Various Proceedings taken by the London Trades Council and the Conference of Amalgamated Trades in Reference to the Royal Commission on Trades' Unions* (1867), 9–21.

[5] Walpole to Elcho, 5 Nov. 1866, Wemyss MSS. I am indebted to John Davis for this and the subsequent references to the Wemyss MSS.

[6] Elcho to Walpole, 2 Nov. 1866, Wemyss MSS.

[7] Webb, *History*, 265; Fraser, *Trade Unions*, 90–1.

[8] Walpole to Derby, 11 Feb. 1867, 14th earl of Derby MSS 153/4; M. S. Vogeler, *Frederic Harrison* (1984), 64.

[9] Walpole to Lichfield, 17 Jan. 1867, Anson MSS D615/P(P)/4/4/4.

[10] *Bee-Hive* (13 June 1868), 5; Harrison, *Peaceable Kingdom*, 288.

atic way, beyond the two special inquiries into the circumstances of outrages in Sheffield and Manchester.

The Erle commission was appointed during a crisis in relations between employers and organized workmen in the iron industry; of all forms of enterprise, it was alleged, none was 'so distinctively English and National', for both the extraction of raw materials and the manufacturing process were indigenous.[11] A scare about foreign competition exploiting the failings of the British industry was got up in a series of letters to *The Times* published in December 1866 and January 1867 by H. Herries Creed, editor of the *Colliery Guardian*, the organ of the Mining Association of Great Britain, and Walter Williams, a south Staffordshire ironmaster. Following a tour of the iron-producing regions of Belgium, they warned that rival producers were catching up with the British industry, and that whatever competitive advantage the latter still possessed was being eroded by unions and strikes, from which Belgian manufacturers remained unaffected. Creed and Williams's claims were treated with sufficient seriousness for the Foreign Office to address despatches to the British representatives in Belgium, France, and the states of the Zollverein to establish the extent of the threat which developing industries in those regions posed to British trade.[12]

The replies from British missions were inconclusive, and Creed and Williams's statements about the contentedness of continental workmen with a lower standard of living than their English counterparts were seriously undermined by the outbreak of riots in the Belgian coalfields early in February 1867. Their prescriptions nevertheless enjoyed some purchase during the Erle commission's investigations. Creed and Williams elaborated a distinct 'entrepreneurial' programme to create favourable conditions for industry. While trade unions complained of exclusion from the franchise, and the lack of a working man on the royal commission, Creed and Williams described a legislature in which iron manufacturing had few direct representatives. Commissions composed of clergymen and college fellows, who had no understanding of, or sympathy for, the problems of manufacturers, disadvantaged British producers by recommending onerous restrictions on production and by creating an education system with a 'scholastic' bias.[13] Yet in the sphere of industrial relations Creed and

---

[11] H. H. Creed and W. Williams, *Handicraftsmen and Capitalists: Their Organization at Home and Abroad* (1867), 4, which reprints their letters to *The Times* with an introduction.

[12] Correspondence with Her Majesty's missions abroad regarding industrial questions and trade unions, RCTU 11th Rep., appx F, 143–78.

[13] Creed and Williams, *Handicraftsmen and Capitalists*, 4, 17, 21–2.

Williams exhibited diminished faith in *laissez-faire*. Like other contemporary English observers of continental Europe who were occasionally tempted to hanker after statist solutions to their difficulties, they sought close government regulation of workers' combinations and the creation of officially sanctioned arbitration structures which would set prospectively the rate of wages and terms of labour contracts.[14] Their ideas foreshadowed others put before the commission by employers, to end the extra-legal and unsupervised freedom of action which unions enjoyed.

HORNBY V CLOSE AND TRADE UNION FUNDS

The anomalous status of unions was formally exposed when the Court of Queen's Bench delivered its judgment in the famous case of *Hornby v Close* on 16 January 1867, shortly before the royal commission could be announced when parliament reassembled in February 1867. Contrary to what was frequently stated at the time, and repeated since, the court did not decide that union funds could be plundered without redress.

Charles Close, the treasurer of the Bradford branch of the United Society of Boilermakers, avoided punishment for misappropriating nearly £25 of the society's funds, an act of which he was clearly guilty. But the point at issue was whether the boilermakers, who had deposited their rules with Tidd Pratt when Close's and another Yorkshire official's fraud came to light, were entitled to use the summary remedies provided by the 1855 Friendly Societies Act to proceed against him. In January 1866 the boilermakers had successfully used that rapid and inexpensive legal procedure to prosecute a fraudulent branch official; the Leeds borough bench brushed aside the objection that the boilermakers' society organized strikes and was therefore not entitled to use the special procedure allowed to friendly societies, imposing a sentence of two months' imprisonment.[15] A week later, however, two West Riding county justices, both of whom were ironmasters and regarded as far from impartial,[16] dismissed the Bradford case on the grounds rejected by their counterparts in Leeds. On appeal, in the name of John Hornby, the Bradford branch president, funded by a 1s. levy on all the boilermakers' members, the decision of the county magistrates was

---

[14] Ibid. 35–6. Cf. T. J. Hovell-Thurlow, *Trade Unions Abroad and Hints for Home Legislation* (1870), iii–iv, 371; the author, a British diplomat at the Hague, regretted the comparative weakness of the British state in its dealings with unions and strikes.

[15] *Bradford Observer* (11 Jan. 1866), 5; *Leeds Mercury* (5 Jan. 1866), 3.

[16] See their partisan handling of a Master and Servant case involving an ironmoulder, *Bradford Review* (4 Aug. 1866), 5.

unanimously upheld by the higher court.[17] Lord Chief Justice Cockburn declared that the magistrates had been 'perfectly right' in considering that the society did not come within the Friendly Societies Act.[18] Although the boilermakers' society provided welfare benefits, its purposes included those of a trade union and therefore the case was governed by the precedent set in *Hilton v Eckersley*. The boilermakers' rules, like the bond of the Wigan cotton masters discussed in the earlier case, were in restraint of trade and against public policy. Thus the union could not claim the privileges granted by the 1855 Act to societies formed for 'any purpose which is not illegal', though the judges were careful to say that the boilermakers' rules were not unlawful in the sense of being punishable.[19]

Although the *Bee-Hive* jumped to the conclusion that the decision placed unions at the mercy of any of their officers or members who sought to rob them, sources closer to the amalgamated unions initially placed a different construction upon the judgment.[20] The *Commonwealth*, the organ of the London Trades Council, pointed out that while they were deprived of the advantages offered by the Friendly Societies Act to proceed against misappropriation, they still enjoyed the protection of the common law.[21] This was lawyers' understanding of the position: all that *Hornby v Close* had decided was that unions could not enjoy the special facilities granted to friendly societies for the protection of their funds. It did not deny them recourse to the general criminal law.[22] One of the members of the court which decided *Hornby v Close*, Sir Robert Lush, actually said as much when a case came before him at Manchester assizes a year later. A prosecution was successfully brought by Manchester and Salford Trades Council under the ordinary processes of the law against the treasurer of the operative house painters, who was found to have defrauded £800 from his union by forging a bankers' pass book. In sentencing the official to five years' penal servitude, Lush made an emphatic correction to 'an entirely mistaken view which has got into the public mind of what the decision in the case of *Hornby v Close* really amounted to'. It was 'a great mistake' to suppose that the earlier decision 'left the property of those societies unprotected'; the property of trade unions was 'as much protected by the law as [that] of any other persons or

---

[17] J. E. Mortimer, *A History of the Boilermakers' Society, 1834–1906* (1973), i. 72; McIlroy, 'Financial Malpractice', 28–33.

[18] *Hornby v Close* (1867) 10 Cox CC, 398.

[19] 18 & 19 Vict c. 63, s. 44.

[20] *Bee-Hive* (19 Jan. 1867), 4.

[21] *Commonwealth* (2 Feb. 1867); see also a similar interpretation in the Liberal *Daily Telegraph* (18 Jan. 1867), 5; (28 Jan. 1867), 4; (4 Feb. 1867), 4; (11 Feb. 1867), 5.

[22] W. Guthrie, *The Law of Trade Unions in England and Scotland* (1873), 9; Atiyah, *Freedom of Contract*, 533.

societies'.[23] In response to a letter of thanks from the trades council, Lush wrote a public letter, published in the *Bee-Hive*, regretting the 'erroneous views' that had taken hold about *Hornby v Close* and sharing the council's pleasure that these had been dispelled.[24]

There were nonetheless strong reasons why 'erroneous views' of *Hornby v Close* came to be propagated. A construction damaging to the position of unions was enthusiastically placed upon the judgment by the Conservative press. The *Standard* rejoiced that all funds subscribed to unions were now 'lost beyond power of recovery in any court of the kingdom'.[25] To Alfred Mault, secretary of the General Builders' Association, it was an opportunity to promote an employer-sponsored friendly society to draw building workers away from craft union benefit schemes which now no longer looked secure.[26]

Hornby v Close intensified the notorious division within the London trades, between the so-called 'Junta'—principally the amalgamated trades —who dominated London Trades Council, and George Potter's London Working Men's Association.[27] It did so because the judgment had a different immediate effect on the two groups of societies. The court had withheld the privilege of proceeding under the Friendly Societies Act, but only a small number of societies had ever succeeded in getting Tidd Pratt to accept their rules. A little-known parliamentary return, moved for by Russell Gurney, the recorder of London and a Conservative MP who took a special interest in legal subjects as they affected poorer litigants, revealed that only twenty-six out of possibly 2,000 trade societies in England had done so.[28] The essential characteristic of the Conference of Amalgamated Trades (CAT), founded at the instigation of Applegarth's Amalgamated Society of Carpenters and Joiners, was not size, a head office in London, or even character: the Vellum Binders' Society, a mere 266 strong, were members. What united them was the fact of having deposited their rules.[29] Hence the Liverpool-based boilermakers received an invitation to join. It was declined by their secretary on the revealing ground that his union had

---

[23] *R v Dodd* (1868) 18 LTNS, 90–1; *Bee-Hive* (11 Apr. 1868), 5; (18 Apr. 1868), 6.

[24] Sir Robert Lush to W. H. Wood, 21 Mar. 1868, *Bee-Hive* (11 Apr. 1868), 5.

[25] *Standard* (18 Jan. 1867), 4; (12 Apr. 1867), 4–5; *Morning Herald* (9 Feb. 1867), 5.

[26] Minute book of the committee of the General Builders' Association 1865–71, 18 Jan. 1867, p. 73, National Federation of Building Trades Employers MSS; Home Office to secretary of General Builders' Association, 4 Feb. 1867, PRO HO43/109, p. 84.

[27] Ludlow and L. Jones, *Progress*, 210n; Webb, *History*, 254–5.

[28] Return of the number of societies which have deposited their rules *PP* 1867 xl. 521–48 (21 Feb. 1867).

[29] ASCJ, monthly report, Apr. 1867, 74; CAT minute book, p. 18 (28 Jan. 1867), Webb Trade Union Collection, Sect. B (xviii).

suffered far greater losses through the infringements of members of the Amalgamated Society of Engineers 'upon our trade' than those sustained through dishonest officials like Charles Close.[30]

The CAT's aim was limited to protecting the position of societies with deposited rules, but it tried to present the Associations of Workmen bill, introduced in February 1867 by two sympathetic MPs, Charles Neate and Thomas Hughes, as a measure to protect union funds generally. In fact the bill restored the position of only the few privileged societies, and excluded those unions which contemporary rhetoric described as 'strike societies' since they offered no welfare benefits but confined themselves to trade purposes.[31] 'As long as they got within the shelter of the law', the *Bee-Hive* complained of the amalgamated trades, 'what cared they who were left out in the cold?'[32] For practical purposes *Hornby v Close* left the great mass of unions in the same position as before. But once an agitation had begun to reverse the judgment's supposed effects, Potter responded by convening a rival, inclusive, and impressively attended St Martin's Hall Conference in March 1867. A petition complained that unions were 'deprived of all legal recognition' and called for 'the same protection for their funds as are enjoyed by all other classes of Her Majesty's subjects against fraud and dishonesty'.[33]

The actions of the CAT and of Potter's conference—the latter generally regarded as a forerunner of the Trades Union Congress—marked the beginning of the unions' campaign for civil and legal equality. Technically, their initial demands were ambiguous and inconsistent: both organizations sought not simply the protection which other citizens possessed, but the special facilities which a paternalist state had provided for friendly societies. But the funds issue—seen as a failure of the state to protect the property of working men—became a symbol of the exclusion and injustice suffered, as the CAT put it, by the 'artizan class of this country'.[34] At a particularly heated meeting convened by the executive of the Amalgamated Engineers at Exeter Hall in February 1867, William Newton complained that the judges had not only denied the respectability of trade unions, but the fitness of their members to exercise the privilege of citizenship.[35] For the engineers, *Hornby v Close* represented a rejection of their tentative

[30] *Bee-Hive* (16 Feb. 1867), 8.

[31] *Report of the Various Proceedings* (1867), 35.

[32] *Bee-Hive* (16 Mar. 1867), 4.

[33] *Report of the Trades Conference held at St Martin's Hall on March 5, 6, 7, and 8, 1867* (1867), 2, 18, 27.

[34] Fraser, *Trade Unions and Society*, 131.

[35] Amalgamated Society of Engineers, *Full and Authentic Report of the Speeches Delivered at the Great Demonstration of Trade Societies ... 21st February 1867* (1867), 7, 19; *Hull News* (9 Feb. 1867), 4; *Bradford Review* (16 Feb. 1867), 8.

moves, dating back to Cockburn's (misinterpreted) opinion on their legality in 1851, to place themselves in closer relation to the state. Gladstone's opinion of their suitability to be allowed to invest in the Post Office Savings Bank turned out, as they discovered in an interview with Walpole on 1 February, to have no bearing upon their legality. Gladstone himself admitted this when the CAT met him on 7 March 1867.[36] The engineers now complained that the government could, if so disposed, impound and confiscate the funds deposited with it—a remarkable undoing of the popular confidence in the state celebrated by Gladstone in his speech on Edward Baines' Borough Franchise bill in 1864.[37]

For Liberal proponents of legalization, *Hornby v Close* undermined the weight of argument which had been built up following the Social Science Association report. Both Thomas Hughes and Frederic Harrison complained that it put unions entirely outside the law.[38] By applying the doctrine of restraint of trade to the unions, Harrison pointed out, judges had placed them on a level with betting and gambling, public nuisances and immoral considerations, reinforcing the conclusion that 'the working classes are not fully incorporated into the nation as part of society'.[39] The court had thwarted the ultimate object shared by the Positivists and other middle-class patrons of labour, that unions should become recognized social institutions.[40] At the same time, the panic about the security of their funds—which Harrison and the other advocates of legalization did nothing to allay—helped to persuade union leaderships, who had tended with good reason to view the idea with suspicion, to seek a more permanent position under the law.

Another writer who saw beyond the issue of security of funds was Robert Lowe, the Liberal opponent of democracy. He was among the few contemporaries to grasp what *Hornby v Close* really meant. In an anonymous *Times* leader, he pointed out that it was now no longer possible to maintain the official policy of regarding with 'neglect and apathy' the growth and organization of trade unions. Tolerated, but left to grow up outside the law, a union was 'a sort of legal monster'. If unions were allowed to exist then they should be allowed the rights of other recognized bodies, such as friendly societies, and equally the public and their members should be given rights against them. Lowe's argument for legalization nevertheless contained an

[36] *Report of the Various Proceedings* (1867), 27–30, 36–8; Matthew, *GD*, vi. 505 (7 Mar. 1867).
[37] Matthew, *GD*, v xli; 3*H* clxxv. 321–3 (11 May 1864).
[38] *Report of the Various Proceedings* (1867), 27.   [39] *Bee-Hive* (26 Jan. 1867), 4.
[40] G. Lushington, 'Workmen and Trade Unions', in *Questions for a Reformed Parliament* (1867), 55.

unresolved question, for his condition of registration was that all union rules should be conformable to law.[41] So long as the doctrine of restraint of trade was applied to them, there was little prospect that union rule books could ever fulfil Lowe's condition.

Hornby v Close therefore touched on much broader questions than the immediate one of the security of union funds. To writers like Lowe, it illustrated why unions, as then constituted, could not be legally recognized; and, equally, why it was crucial that they should be made to conform to the law. It forced contemporaries to consider the grounds on which unions were held to be 'illegal'. In April 1867 a court upheld the repudiation of an agreement to rent a lecture-room for the purpose of blasphemous lectures on the ground, as Sir Fitzroy Kelly reaffirmed, that 'Christianity is part and parcel of the law of the land' and that therefore the agreement was illegal and unenforceable.[42] By analogy, Lowe went on to insist that 'Political Economy is not exactly the law of the land, but it is the ground of that law': so long as unions stood in opposition to economic science, they would remain in conflict with the law.[43]

A HOME OFFICE VIEW

One of Walpole's objects in setting up a royal commission was, as he admitted, to try to keep the trade union question out of the House of Commons during the debates on parliamentary reform.[44] Ministerial statements were therefore guarded, though Conservative backbenchers were not reticent about expressing their antipathy towards unions. This inevitably encouraged suspicions of governmental intentions. Like many other labour organizations, the Wolverhampton Trades Council believed that the commission had been set up 'for the purpose of some Act being passed to put them out of existence'. In the absence of surviving material in either Home Office or Cabinet papers, this view of official policy has permeated the historiography of trade unionism ever since.[45]

[41] *The Times* (26 Jan. 1867), 8. I am indebted to Gordon Phillips, archivist of the *The Times*, for locating the authorship of this and other leading articles. Lowe had used the expression 'legal monster' during debates on company law, 3*H* cxl. 129 (1 Feb. 1856).

[42] *Cowan v Milbourn* (1867) 2 L R Exch 230; Burn, *Equipoise*, 302–3.

[43] *Quarterly Review*, 123 (Oct. 1867), 365.

[44] *Report of the Various Proceedings*, 33.

[45] *Wolverhampton Chronicle* (5 June 1867), 5; *Bolton Chronicle* (2 Feb. 1867), 3; cf. GUCJ, 40th Annual Rep., MRC MSS 78/GUC&J/4/1/1; Associated Carpenters and Joiners of Scotland, Report of Delegate Meeting, Apr. 1867, 71, MRC MSS 78/C&JS/4/1/1; Fraser, *Trade Unions and Society*, 91.

More substantial evidence of the view from government is provided by a confidential memorandum on the trade union question prepared by the Home Office counsel, Henry Thring. His was the first departmental paper on the subject since Senior and Tomlinson had presented their report on combinations to Melbourne over a generation earlier.[46] Thring had succeeded the Benthamite, Walter Coulson, at the Home Office in 1860, and his recommendations illustrate a generational shift in approaches to the union problem. A highly experienced public servant, Thring had worked closely with executive politicians—Gladstone, Cardwell, who was Thring's brother-in-law, and Lowe—in preparing major legislation. Although a Liberal in politics, he had been entrusted in March 1867 by Derby, who regarded him as 'a very safe man', with the drafting of the government's parliamentary reform bill.[47] It is unclear whether Thring's report was commissioned by Walpole before leaving office as home secretary in mid-May 1867; the paper was in the hands of Walpole's successor, Gathorne Hardy, in June. Its purpose appears to have been to assist ministers pending the report of the royal commission.

The first half of Thring's memorandum was given over to an account of the criminal law relating to workers' combinations, and its central thrust—perhaps surprisingly, in view of what is often said about the attitude of the government in 1867—was that the criminal law should be relaxed. Like other commentators, he disliked the judicial interpretations of the 1825 Act which, since 1860, had extended the terms 'molestation', 'obstruction', and 'threat' so broadly that the element of physical injury to person or property was no longer essential to the offences. Citing Cockburn's remarks in *Wood v Bowron* (1866), Thring argued that the law had already been pressed too far against organized workers, and a recently decided case (*Skinner v Kitch*) reinforced his view. In May 1867 the Court of Queen's Bench upheld the conviction and imprisonment for the maximum period of three months' hard labour of the secretary of the Bridgwater lodge of the General Union of Carpenters and Joiners, who had sent a letter ultimatum to a builder threatening a walk-out unless a non-unionist was discharged. Sir Colin Blackburn remarked that 'a greater piece of tyranny than to insist that a master shall have his work stopped unless he consent to punish the men who are his journeymen for refusing to belong to a union cannot well be', while Lush described the transaction as 'not only a case within the [1825]

---

[46] The only copy which has been located is among the papers of the Office of the Parliamentary Counsel: H. Thring, 'Memorandum on Combinations', OPC Bills and Memoranda (HJ) 1871, 713–745.

[47] Derby to Disraeli, 14 Mar. 1867, Bodl. Disraeli MS 110; the entry on Thring by his successor, Courtenay Ilbert, in *DNB* remains the fullest account of his career.

Act, but *the* case pointed at'.[48] Thring differed from the judges—and implicitly from the liberal-tory policy of 1825—in believing that such circumstances were not appropriately dealt with by the criminal law, which should be confined to punishing actual violence or threats of personal injury.

Thring's reasoning did not spring from any desire positively to encourage unionism, nor from sympathy with many of its methods. He was as hostile to many of the practices identified with unionism as either the 1825 Select Committee or Senior and Tomlinson had been, but in his view those were insufficient grounds for treating them as crimes. Nothing, he asserted, could be more 'wicked' than to ruin a master by withdrawing his workmen to enforce 'some capricious law as to the employment of apprentices or the dismissal of non-unionists'. Many union practices were 'unjust'. But the practical question was 'whether such wrongs are proper subjects of Criminal Law', and he offered strong objections to treating them as such. Prosecutions were occasionally brought, but for practical purposes the criminal law was inoperative in curbing 'the social tyranny' practised by unions. Moreover, penalizing the ordinary activities of unions would drive them into secrecy and, as the experience of the Combination Acts showed, into violence and other illegal acts. Public policy favoured openness, which was the principle behind granting indemnities to those involved in the Sheffield outrages. Like the advanced Liberal writers of the early 1860s, Thring regarded public opinion and improved education as more effective agencies than the criminal law for redressing the wrongs perpetrated by unions.[49]

Thring was a member of the Political Economy Club,[50] and in his review of 'the principles and effects of trades unions', which formed the second half of his memorandum, he assumed the position of an interested and well-read inquirer. Like Walpole, he admired and drew upon Frederic Harrison's insights, and especially the latter's searing critique of the idea that unorganized workers could bargain on equal terms with employers.[51] Thring noted Harrison's observation that, unlike the sellers of other commodities, individual labourers could not as a general rule withold their labour from the market for months on end if the price offered for it was too low. Without the backing of a combination, an 'unaided workman', needing

[48] *Skinner v Kitch* (1867) 10 Cox CC, 495; discussed in *Justice of the Peace* (6 July 1867), 418 and *Solicitor's Journal* (8 June 1867), 735. cf. *Hodgson v Graveling* in *Justice of the Peace* (23 Feb. 1867), 115. For successful prosecutions in similar circumstances in Scotland, see *Nairnshire Telegraph* (3 July 1867; 14 Aug 1867); *Scotsman* (1 July 1867), 6.

[49] Thring, 'Memorandum', 12–13.

[50] *Political Economy Club*, 6 (1921), 362.   [51] *Fortnightly Review*, 3 (Nov. 1865), 47–8.

to subsist, was obliged to sell his labour immediately, and for whatever price was offered. Thring's investigations also revealed how far the debate on trade unionism dating from the Social Science Association report of 1860 had undermined the assumptions upon which policy had previously been grounded. This applied, in particular, to what he identified as the fundamental issue, whether unions could exert any effect on the rate of wages.

Here, the wage fund theory, recently restated by Henry Fawcett, was the starting point.[52] Thring understood the doctrine in its popular formulation as an explanation for the futility of combinations, and took it to be the central theoretical economic objection to union activity. He therefore attached particular significance to a refutation of the theory published in 1866 by F. D. Longe, a barrister employed as an assistant commissioner to the Children's Employment commission, who had already achieved some notice for an original legal-historical critique of the common law doctrines against combinations.

Longe's refutation was traditionally assigned a comparatively minor place in the history of economic thought. He stood outside the inner circle of economists (he was not a member of the Political Economy Club) and his refutation was not considered to offer the most powerful arguments against the wage fund doctrine.[53] More recently, Longe's contribution has received closer attention, and the importance which Thring attached to his pamphlet supports this reappraisal.[54] For while Longe could not claim acquaintance with Mill, he had official connexions and at least one long-standing political friendship, with the whig-Liberal George Goschen, who was later to secure him a position at the Local Government Board. Longe's argument drew upon his practical experience of four years spent investigating the conditions of children in a range of industries where conditions were especially depressed, and which did not come within the protection of the Factory Acts. His final report, dated December 1866 and compiled at the time that he wrote his refutation of Mill and Fawcett, was an account of the exploitation of children and women in the agricultural gangs of East Anglia.

Agricultural labour formed the central example in Longe's account of how competition depressed wages among workers in areas of the labour market, where employers—in this case farmers—were effectively acting in combination. Low wages in turn drew into employment those whom Longe

---

[52] H. Fawcett, *The Economic Position of the British Labourer* (1865), 120; P. Deane, 'Henry Fawcett: The Plain Man's Economist', in Goldman, *The Blind Victorian*, 99.

[53] Fraser, *Trade Unions and Society*, 177, 180.

[54] Vint, *Capital and Wages*, 179 and 179n; see entry on Longe by A. Picchio in J. Eatwell, M. Milgate, and P. Newman (eds), *The New Palgrave: A Dictionary of Economics* (4 vols., 1987), iii. 236.

would have preferred to exclude from the labour market: the elderly 'who ought to be provided for', wives and mothers 'who would better be at home', and children, who should be at school.[55] The argument drew upon a social reforming impulse which sought, as Longe's reports as an assistant commissioner recommended, to extend protective legislation covering women and children. But his principal complaint against the wage fund theory was that it protected from the 'censure' of public opinion employers who paid low wages, by which he meant wages that were insufficient for a healthy male labourer to support a family. He specifically excluded a discussion of the bearing of the wage fund theory upon strikes and combinations, though in passing he urged that well-organized workers should use their power to equalize wages between trades rather than to secure for themselves the benefits of a market advantage. He also hoped that his refutation of the theory would help employers to see the value of combinations among the men.[56]

Although, therefore, Longe was not addressing the wage fund theory in the particular light that concerned Thring, the objections which he raised to the doctrine convinced Thring that it no longer offered a convincing analytical tool for establishing the likely effectiveness of unions. Longe demonstrated that there were no grounds for supposing that a fund of capital designated for the purchase of labour existed except, Thring noted, 'in the imagination'. It was also a fallacy to suppose that such a fund could be distributed by competition among the aggregate body of labourers. A worker in one trade which was depressed could not be assumed to be able to work at another trade that was prospering; and moreover, political economists had confused 'labour' and 'labourers', failing to allow for changes in productivity. Thring thought the assertion of proponents of the wage fund, that if one group of workers gained an increase above the natural rate the fund available for division among the rest would be diminished, of no useful bearing. A mason would not be deterred from striking by the abstract consideration that if he obtained a wage increase it would diminish the proportion of the wage fund available for distribution among tailors. Thring's terse marginal note, 'Theories as to wages of no practical importance', anticipated by nearly two years Mill's observation in his famous recantation of the wage fund, that public policy towards trade unionism could no longer be 'peremptorily decided by unbending necessities of political economy'.[57]

[55] F. D. Longe, *A Refutation of the Wage-Fund Theory of Modern Political Economy as Enunciated by Mr Mill, MP and Mr Fawcett, MP* (1866), 69, 79.

[56] Longe, *Refutation*, 2, 69–70; cf. Fawcett, *Economic Position*, 132.

[57] Thring, 'Memorandum', 17; Mill, *Collected Works*, vol. v, ed. J. M. Robson (1967), 646.

If theories of wages failed to resolve the question, the only concern of workers was whether in practice strikes had a chance of success. Here, a second widespread assumption dissolved under a cursory objective scrutiny. Thring attached great weight to the data assembled by the Social Science Association in 1860 which, in the face of a weight of contemporary propagandizing to the contrary, showed the tendency of strikers to prevail.[58] Another member of the Political Economy Club, Jacob Waley, had recently addressed the same question in a paper read before the London Statistical Society in December 1866 and similarly concluded that the routine condemnation of strikes as failures could not be substantiated.[59] Insofar as trade unions existed to raise wages, Thring concluded, they enabled the market price of labour to be rapidly adjusted 'and to that extent are beneficial rather than the contrary'.[60]

One object of trade unions had therefore survived Thring's test of expediency. His assessment of their other objectives was in places more critical; though, as with wage bargaining, he found aspects worthy of approval. Rules prohibiting overtime and limiting the hours of labour he treated as coinciding with the policy of the Factory Acts to protect the health of the worker, enable him to educate himself, and to reduce the danger of drunkenness, and were therefore to be approved. Nor was he concerned by the danger of foreign competition, of which Creed and Williams's letters had been just one of many warnings; Thring doubted whether disputes between employers and workers could ultimately ruin 'any branch of industry that rests on a solid foundation'.[61] He found the evidence more evenly balanced between those who asserted that unions had improved the 'moral character' of their members, and those who alleged that they had damaged relations between employers and workers; he was unmoved by their claims to be a morally improving agency. Their rules prohibiting piece-work, like craft regulations restricting apprentices, he regarded as 'unjustifiable', while rules against working with non-unionists were seen as part of a system of 'social excommunication', which at its most extreme might be enforced by outrages. The most serious objection to the existing organization of unions was their 'tyrannical' rules, 'restrictive of the development of free labour', an observation which found many contemporary resonances in the press and in the testimony by employers who appeared before the royal commission.

    [58] Thring, 'Memorandum', 18.

    [59] J. Waley, 'On Strikes and Combinations, with Reference to Wages and the Conditions of Labour', *Journal of the Statistical Society of London*, 30 (Mar. 1867), 5–7, 19–20; Price, *Masters, Unions, and Men*, 138.

    [60] Thring, 'Memorandum', 19.   [61] Ibid. 21.

How, then, should the law deal with organizations whose objectives and effects varied so considerably between the beneficial and the unjustifiable? Thring, who recognized that the court in *Hornby v Close* did not deny the boilermakers a remedy against theft but merely deprived them of an advantageous procedure, nevertheless thought the outcome counterproductive. If, by denying unions the benefits enjoyed by legal societies, the courts were likely to cause them to alter their policies, then there might be an argument for leaving them outside the law. But far from responding to 'judicial reproof', it was 'notorious' that unions 'multiply for good or for evil, clinging to their narrow and objectionable regulations'.[62] It was 'hopeless' to expect 'the extinction or repression of trades unions'.[63]

Thring shared Lowe's perception that the unions' extra-legal status tended to reinforce their objectionable characteristics.[64] Members were deprived of a remedy to recover their contributions and minorities found themselves forced to support strikes; the funds of unions—amounting, he believed, to nearly £1 million—were placed in the hands of managers answerable to no authority. His solution was similar to that recently put forward by Bagehot, writing in the *Economist*, who had proposed conferring full corporate rights upon unions in the belief that freedom, with its concomitant exposure to public scrutiny, would prove the most effective solvent of foolish restrictions.[65] Unlike the sort of restrictive legalization proposed by Creed and Williams and other employer interest groups, Thring and Bagehot were proposing complete freedom of association, so long as the purposes were not in themselves criminal. The objection that this would give sanction to 'tyrannical' union practices would be met by leaving the courts to discriminate between those union rules that could be enforced and those that would be treated as void. A member would be enabled to recover any welfare benefits to which he was entitled, but a union could not turn to the courts to force individuals to obey trade rules.

Thring's ideas supplied an official model for legalizing unions and all non-violent forms of joint action. His plan did not depend on a perception that unions were promoters of civic virtue, nor that they were evolving into benefit societies, or might form the basis for a system of collective bargaining. His arguments applied to the most unreconstructed pot-house strike

---

[62] Ibid. 24.

[63] Ibid. 25; cf. H. D. Le Marchant, *Trades' Unions and the Commission Thereon* (1867), 22; Fox, *History and Heritage*, 157.

[64] Lowe elaborated the point in the *Quarterly Review*, 123 (July 1867), 269–71, discussing Godfrey Lushington's contribution on labour law in *Questions for a Reformed Parliament*.

[65] 'The Working of Trades Unions' (27 Apr. 1867), in N. St John Stevas (ed.), *Bagehot's Political Essays*, vol. viii (1974), 20–3.

society as much as to Applegarth and Allan's amalgamated societies; indeed, his proposals made no reference to their evidence of union respectability to the royal commissioners, of which he seems to have been unaware.[66] Paradoxically, his arguments for legalization were reinforced by the revelations of union complicity in the Sheffield outrages, which dramatically emerged during the proceedings of the Sheffield Inquiry Commission within days of Thring's memorandum having been completed.[67] This had long been assumed, and Thring took the culpability of certain unions more or less as read. What the inquiry showed, as William Overend, the presiding barrister, commented in his concluding address in July 1867, was the need to accord unions a satisfactory status.[68]

FREE LABOUR AND THE COURTS

Thring was writing in detachment from political pressures and was largely unconcerned with industrial issues. His account necessarily ignored two developments which helped to shape the terms of the argument: politically, the reaction to the sudden concession of household suffrage in the boroughs; industrially, the emergence of a 'free labour' movement. The two intersected as the forms of language commonly levelled at union or collective work group practices—'tyranny', 'dictation', disregard for the rights of 'minorities'—were seen as auguries for the behaviour of working-class electors. Indeed, the industrial relations conception of the individual bargain, in which each man was to be free to work on the terms he chose, found its political parallel in the argument about whether the new electors would follow their individual consciences or vote as a class. The 'free labourer' might be conceived as the industrial equivalent of the 'independent elector'. His promoters were those who, politically, wished to neutralize the strength of 'the combining class', though their intentions were more likely to be to promote a category of voter independent of pressure from his peers, but very much dependent upon social influence from above.[69]

The most powerful argument for 'free labour' was made in the evidence given to the royal commission by Alfred Mault, secretary of the General Builders' Association, who complained that 'unions hamper and restrict

---

[66] The early evidence was published in late May 1867, *The Times* (22 May 1867), 8.

[67] Thring's paper was simply dated June 1867; the breakthrough at Sheffield came on 19 June and succeeding days.

[68] Pollard, *The Sheffield Outrages*, xvi, 292 (Q.15,370), 450.

[69] *The Diary of Gathorne Hardy, later Lord Cranbrook, 1866–1892*, ed. N. E. Johnson (1981), 43 (28 June 1867).

trade by endeavouring to enforce unreasonable and foolish trade rules'. His allegations about firms being 'dictated to' by craft unions were common to other industries.[70] The Central Defence Association of Master Engineers met in Manchester, in April 1867, 'to establish free trade in labour' and to resist the encroachments of the ASE.[71] These complaints primarily concerned the defence of managerial prerogatives. Other free labour initiatives emphasized the object of upholding the rights of non-unionists. Much publicity was given to Charles Markham's attempt to run the Staveley collieries on non-union lines; the *Daily News* reported on the Walker Alkali works in Newcastle where the unions were kept out. On a visit to Leeds later in the year, the Conservative politician Lord Carnarvon was impressed by an iron works where no unionists were employed.[72] A Free Labour Registration Society aimed 'to secure to its members the free exercise of their rights to dispose of their labour on whatever terms and whatever circumstances, they may individually and independently think fit'.[73] Its founder, colonel F. C. Maude, was a distinguished Indian mutiny veteran. Pledged to the 'total abolishment of Trades' Unions', the agency had an especial appeal to Conservatives, its principal sponsors being noblemen from Lancashire, where the society's strike-breaking activities were particularly energetic. Although Lord Stanley, the foreign secretary in his father's administration, turned down Maude's appeal for '3 or 4000£ of secret service money' to extend its operations, on the grounds that such a payment would be contrary to precedent and of doubtful legality, he assured Maude of his interest in the society, 'which I believe to be doing good'.[74] The claim of Maude's registry to render its clients 'independent' was, however, undermined by a court case arising from its activities. Seven London stonemasons, who were signed up by the agency for twelve months' work in Sheffield, found themselves being required to work for an employer who disregarded craft rules. On refusing to work for him, they were imprisoned for a month under the Master and Servant Act.[75]

The attempt to establish a free market in labour depended—as was recognized in the 1830s and again in the 1890s—on the ability of employers to prevent the use of pickets to obstruct the flow of 'independent' labour. Yet

---

[70] RCTU 1st Rep. Q.3332a; Price, *Masters, Unions, and Men*, 62; *The Times* (23 Apr. 1867; 11, 15 July 1867), 11.

[71] *Engineering* (26 Apr. 1867), 414.

[72] RCTU 6th Rep. Q.11,484; *Daily News* (5 Nov. 1867), 3; Carnarvon diary, 7 Nov. 1867, BL Add MS 60899.

[73] *First Annual Report of the Manchester Free Labour Society* (1870).

[74] Maude to Stanley, 21 Nov. 1867, Derby MSS 920 DER 12/2/3; *Free Labour Journal* (10 Oct. 1868), 18.

[75] *Crane v Powell* (1868) 38 LJMC 43; *The Times* (2 Dec. 1868), 9.

the legality of picketing had not been extensively discussed in parliament or in the higher courts since the debates on the Combination of Workmen bill in 1853, and the subject was not mentioned in Thring's memorandum. It was revived by the system of pickets organized by the tailors' unions in central London during a dispute with their employers, from May to August 1867. The labour question, and the implication of household suffrage, was brought forcibly to the attention of metropolitan opinion, as sometimes disorderly crowds of pickets gathered around the tailoring shops in the fashionable West End. Indictments for conspiracy were brought against the leaders of the two unions involved, the evidence against them being that they had organized the pickets, some of whom had gone on to break the law by abusing and harassing those entering or leaving the shops.[76] Edward Lewis, a London solicitor, had advised the tailors' unions that picketing was lawful so long as intimidation was not used. In bringing a prosecution, the master tailors wanted to demonstrate its unlawfulness and to get the pickets, who had successfully prevented them from breaking the strike, withdrawn.[77]

Sir George Bramwell, the trial judge, placed an extremely wide construction upon what constituted 'molestation'. Summing up the evidence against Druitt, he declared that the law held no right more sacred than that of individual liberty.[78] And this meant not only the liberty of the body, but also the liberty of the mind and will. Therefore a combination to coerce that free will by conduct 'unpleasant and annoying to the mind operated upon' was a crime. If picketing 'could be done in a way which excited no reasonable alarm, or did not coerce or annoy those who were subjects of it' then it was no offence. If, however, it went beyond this narrow limit and 'was calculated to have a deterring effect on the minds of ordinary persons, by exposing them to having their motions watched, and to encounter black looks, that would not be permitted by the law of the land'. If 'black looks' could constitute molestation, picketing could not for practical purposes be done without breaking the law, as Bramwell acknowledged.[79] Sixteen of the defendants were found guilty, but were bound over on the understanding that the picketing would cease. The tailors' strike collapsed.

Bramwell did not confine himself to an exposition of the law, but after the tailors' leaders were found guilty proceeded to address them on the broader questions at stake. In a theatrical peroration, during which 'the learned Baron's ... voice faltered with emotion', Bramwell set about con-

---

[76] *Bee-Hive* (11 May 1867), 5.
[77] *Glasgow Sentinel* (10 Aug. 1867), 6; (17 Aug. 1867), 1.
[78] *R v Druitt* (1867) 10 Cox CC 600–2.   [79] *R v Bailey* (1867) 16 LTNS 859.

vincing them that not only was the law against them, but 'reason and justice are against you also'. It was intolerable to restrict competition:

everybody knows that the total aggregate happiness of mankind is increased by every man being left to the unbiased, unfettered determination of his own free will and judgment as to how he will employ his industry and other means of getting on in the world.

The previous forty years of legislative policy had been directed to this end, with remarkable results: 'There is now no monopoly in this land. There is no class legislation.' As in the case of the London shipwrights a decade earlier, he depicted the policy of the tailors' unions as contrary to modern commercial policy and likened them to the 'corporate guilds' of medieval times.[80] It was in effect an address to the new voters by a member of the bench who shared Lowe's apprehensions that a preponderantly working-class electorate would reverse the policy of free trade; Bramwell had publicly voiced his hostility to franchise extension in 1860, and the passage of household suffrage left him privately in despair.[81]

Bramwell was congratulated on his handling of the tailors' trial by Sir William Erle, chairman of the royal commission.[82] Erle himself was described as having been 'once a Whig', when he sat briefly as an MP some thirty years earlier, 'but like most men who have been raised to high place has become extremely Conservative in his notions'.[83] As the commission went into recess, he began work on his *Memorandum on the Law Relating to Trade Unions*, privately circulated to his fellow commissioners in October 1867, and later published in 1869.[84] An elaborate attempt to explain and justify judicial attitudes towards trade unions, the memorandum also incorporated a vigorous justification of the legislative policy of the parliaments which sat between 1832 and 1867, 'enacted without a suspicion of partiality for any class'.[85] His account of the law was intended to underpin recommendations for imposing a restrictive settlement on unions. Apparently without consulting the other commissioners, he caused one of them, the retired Board of Trade official James Booth, whose views were closest to his own, to draft a final report with proposals for legislation which was circulated early in 1868.[86]

[80] *The Times* (24 Aug. 1867), 11.

[81] C. Fairfield, *Some Account of G. W. Wilshere, Lord Bramwell of Hever* (1898), 111; Bramwell to Sir Frederick Pollock, 21 Mar. 1867, Bodl. MS Eng Hist c. 962, fo. 137.

[82] Erle to Bramwell, 25 Aug. 1867, Fairfield, *Bramwell*, 31.

[83] Chelmsford to Derby, 11 Feb. 1867, Derby MSS 152/11.

[84] Erle to Lichfield, 25 Oct. 1867, Anson MSS D615/P(L)/6/18; Harrison to Beesly, 28 Oct. 1867, Harrison MSS 1/14.   [85] Erle, 'Memorandum', RCTU 11th Rep. lxxx.

[86] Harrison to Erle, 2 Mar. 1868, Bodl. MS Don. c. 71, fo. 151.

Erle's haste to bring the commission's proceedings to a rapid conclusion may have been prompted by a desire for administrative efficiency and to limit the costs to public funds. But the consideration of getting a report out, and legislation enacted, before a general election took place under the enlarged franchise cannot have been far from his mind. Moreover, the state of the public argument—as opposed to the internal views of the Home Office counsel—in August 1867, when the commission went into recess, was potentially favourable to subjecting unions to the types of legal control which Erle and Booth commended. In addition to Mault's evidence of restrictive practices in the building trade, the Sheffield revelations, and the tailors' trial, actuarial reports, drawn up at Mault's instigation and sprung on Applegarth by the commission in July 1867, exposed the likely insolvency of the benefit schemes offered by the amalgamated unions.[87]

Fortified by this evidence, Lowe produced a rancorous review, written in August as the Reform Act received royal assent. In effect a restatement of the arguments of Senior and Martineau, Lowe attempted to show that there was no fundamental difference between the unions who achieved their ends by violent outrage, such as the Sheffield saw grinders and Manchester brickmakers, and those who presented themselves as essentially pacific and respectable. Applegarth's Amalgamated Society of Carpenters and Joiners, 'the most reasonable and moderate' of unions, was based quite as much as the more obviously lawless associations on 'the right of the majority to coerce the minority, on the absolute subjugation of the one to the many'.[88] Of course, the ASCJ did not employ the methods of terrorism associated with the Sheffield saw grinders, but did so no less effectively by the power of confiscating members' benefit subscriptions. Members were lured into unions by 'the promise of benefits impossible to realise' and stood to lose their savings if they wanted to leave. Lowe's solution was to forbid unions to append welfare functions to their trade purposes—the proposal which had been successfully resisted in 1854—and to force all remaining provident societies to come within the law, placing an absolute prohibition on those who failed to do so. The remnants of trade unions 'if [they] existed at all', would be subject to a statute reaffirming the common law, that societies to restrain the free course of trade were criminal conspiracies, making their members liable to summary punishment.[89]

Lowe, like Bramwell and Erle, regarded unions as a 'monstrous excep-

---

[87] RCTU 4th Rep. Q.6539; Webb, *History*, 267–8; C. G. Hanson, 'Craft Unions, Welfare Benefits, and the Case for Trade Union Law Reform', *Economic History Review*, 28 (1975), 251–3.

[88] *Quarterly Review*, 123 (Oct. 1867), 378–9.

[89] Ibid. 382; for another reading of Lowe's ideas see Harrison to Beesly, 28 Oct. 1867, Harrison MSS 1/14.

tion' to the commercial system of free trade. Other classes had surrendered their monopolies, and shouldered the burden of income tax to make up the deficit, yet unions sought a protected status for labour, taxing the rest of the community through restrictions which prevented competition and artificially raised the cost of commodities. Hence they ran up against the doctrine of restraint of trade which, Erle argued, was the ultimate ground for the law's hostility to actions such as picketing. To Bramwell, Erle, and Lowe the common law represented a means to uphold a commercial policy which they feared the reformed parliament could no longer be relied upon to do.

Erle and Bramwell were, in A. V. Dicey's later account, among 'the best and wisest' of mid-nineteenth-century judges.[90] Yet in the aftermath of the tailors' trial Dicey was among the academic Liberal jurists who were highly critical of the way in which the law had been applied. Their views were linked to a broader objection to the law of conspiracy, previously articulated by Bentham:

The word conspiracy serves them [the superior judges] for inflicting punishment without stint on all persons by whom any act is done, which does not accord with the notions they entertain, or profess to entertain, concerning the act in question.[91]

Mid-Victorian commentaries on labour cases developed the point. F. D. Longe had drawn attention to the ways in which judicial interpretations of the law of conspiracy had gradually infringed the right of association. Liability for punishment for unlawful conspiracy did

not depend upon established rules of law, but upon the particular view a court or jury may take of the propriety of the object of [the] combination, according to whatever principles of politics, religion, morality, or political economy they may happen to entertain.[92]

The elasticity of conspiracy was precisely what had commended it to the government's law officers in 1825 as a device for curtailing combinations. In his robustly pragmatic observations to Melbourne, in 1831, Tomlinson, the common law practitioner, had insisted that conspiracy's value lay precisely in its 'ductile' tendency, enabling it to adapt to and 'grapple with' the 'ever varying forms' which the offence of combination might assume.[93] But, as the most forceful and persistent critic, James Fitzjames Stephen, pointed out a generation later, 'in the hands of encroaching judges' the law of

---

[90] Dicey, *Law and Opinion*, 199–200; cf. Orth, *Combination and Conspiracy*, 133.
[91] *The Works of Jeremy Bentham*, ed. J. Bowring, vol. ii (1843), 126.
[92] Longe, *Law of Strikes*, 40, 45; cf. 'The law of Conspiracy', *Jurist* (29 Nov. 1851), 430.
[93] Report on combinations, PRO HO44/56, p. 9.

conspiracy might 'be made at least as dangerous to liberty as the law of libel ever was'.[94] He reiterated the point in articles on labour cases in the *Pall Mall Gazette* and in his professional contributions to the criminal law.[95]

This was also Dicey's objective in demonstrating how Bramwell's train of reasoning represented a significant threat to the freedom of association. In other areas where the law restricted liberty to a greater extent than was generally supposed, such as freedom of discussion and religion, public opinion prevented it from being put into operation. This guarantee of liberty could not always be relied upon. Occasions might arise in which the public—and the implication was a democratic electorate—might encourage rather than check the strict administration of the law, allowing the law of conspiracy to be used to 'impose restraints on the action of any association of which the majority of the public happens not to approve'.[96] No doubt from the best of motives judges were willing to sacrifice the rights of combination to the rights of individuals in trade union cases, but in doing so they strained the law against one class. No one, as other Liberal writers pointed out, imagined applying the law of conspiracy to those instances of social ostracism and collective disapproval common among other classes and analogous to the 'black looks' which Bramwell held to be criminal among the tailors.[97] In doing so, Dicey implied, judges created a dangerous precedent for the future.

Such expressions had yet to make an impact on the wider understanding of the labour question. Both party leaders addressed the subject in speeches towards the end of 1867, and offered traditional prescriptions. Derby, speaking at Manchester Free Trade Hall, acknowledged the lawfulness of strikes, 'objectionable as they are in principle, and injurious as they are to the working classes', but went on to denounce unions' 'tyrannical power' and their protectionist craft restrictions, citing the stonemasons' notorious rule against the use of worked stone.[98] At Oldham, Gladstone affirmed the right to strike but thought that its use did more harm than good, for 'undoubtedly it must limit the whole amount of the fund available for division

[94] J. F. Stephen, *A General View of the Criminal Law of England* (1863), 148; K. J. M. Smith, *James Fitzjames Stephen* (1988), 74.

[95] See the articles on *Wood v Bowron*, where he urged the unions to use their political power to promote codification, and on the tailors' trial; *Pall Mall Gazette* (16 Nov. 1866, 23 Aug. 1867) (Stephen's authorship is indicated by internal evidence); J. F. Stephen, *Roscoe's Digest of the Law of Evidence in Criminal Cases* (7th edn., 1868), 397.

[96] A. V. Dicey, 'The Legal Boundaries of Liberty', *Fortnightly Review*, n.s. 3 (Jan. 1868), 13; Harvie, *Lights of Liberalism*, 167.

[97] Beesly to Crompton, 6 Sept. 1867, Beesly MSS; cf. T. J. Dunning, *Trades' Unions and Strikes* (1860), 12.

[98] *The Times* (18 Oct. 1867), 10.

between the labouring man and the capitalist'. Restrictive rules against piecework, apprentices, or machinery were even less defensible, and they too diminished the wage fund.[99] In February 1868, he repeated many of these strictures to a deputation of trade unionists led by George Potter, famously denouncing the masons' worked-stone rule as 'worthy of savages'. But 'impolitic' rules ought not to stand in the way of protection for union funds against fraud.[100]

When a serious threat to the security of union funds actually did emerge, shortly after Gladstone's meeting with Potter, the Conservative government moved swiftly to protect them. Both Lush and Thring had identified a potential difficulty, which was not confined to unions but was common to all unincorporated partnerships. In embezzlement cases dishonest union members might claim that any money they abstracted from the funds was partly their own property and that their appropriation of it was not an act of theft. In May 1868 the secretary and treasurer of the Shoreditch lodge of the stonemasons, both of whom more or less admitted taking the union's property, were acquitted at the Central Criminal Court having used the argument that they had merely taken their own money.[101] Russell Gurney, the recorder of London, had summed up strongly against the defaulters but was ignored by the middle-class jury; within days of the acquittals he introduced a bill to close the loophole.

Gurney's bill was intended to provide 'a remedy for embezzlement by members of Trade Unions without referring officially to them'. It was similar to an existing statute which dealt with offences of larceny committed by partners in joint stock banks, and to that extent placed unions in a position of equality with other institutions. The Conservative government's reticence about the bill's purpose reflected an unwillingness to be seen to assist unions; nevertheless, with government support, it became law.[102] Yet because ministers declined to advertise what they had done, the protection of funds issue continued to be raised during the general election campaign in 1868. The first successful prosecution under Gurney's Act did not take place until mid-December 1868, a matter of days after polling was over. In the course of that trial the prosecuting counsel commented on the curiosity that during the election 'questions were asked of candidates all over the

[99] Ibid. 19 Dec. 1867, 8; Matthew, *GD*, v. xli; vi. 563 (18 Dec. 1867).
[100] *The Times* (19 Feb. 1868), 10; Matthew, *GD*, v. xli; vi. 576 (18 Feb. 1868); Price, *Masters, Unions, and Men*, 91–2, 303n. The masons' rule prohibited the handling of stone which had previously been worked outside the town or district where the rule was in force.
[101] OSM FR 30 Apr. – 14 May 1868, MRC MSS 78/OS/4/1/34.
[102] Home Office docket, 30 May 1868, PRO HO45/8314; Sturgeon, *Letters to the Trades' Unionists*, 4.

country whether they would support such a bill', a trend which even well-informed Conservative candidates had been slow to anticipate, possibly to their detriment.[103] Once the confusion about protection of funds was finally cleared away, however, public debate could be directed to the really salient issue: on what terms would the state be justified in granting unions full legal recognition?

[103] *R v Blackburn* (1868) 11 Cox CC 158; cf. RCTU 11th Rep. lxviin. Neither Gurney nor the Conservative law officers set the record straight until late in the campaign, *Hampshire Advertiser* (24 Oct. 1868), suppt, 2; (31 Oct. 1868), 6; *Cardiff and Merthyr Guardian* (14 Nov. 1868), 8; *Hereford Journal* (7 Nov. 1868), 5.

4
Reconciling Unions and the Law

Trade unions were denied legal recognition because their aims and practices were regarded as detrimental to the community at large and ultimately also to union members themselves. Thus the Court of Queen's Bench held in 1867 that the provisions in the rule-book of the boilermakers, regulating piecework, supporting strikes, and fining members who found work for non-unionists, were illegal since they restrained the free course of trade, which the court considered to be its duty to uphold. During the debates of 1867–9, advocates of legalization attempted to surmount this difficulty in two ways. Unionists and their supporters claimed that restrictive rules were often justifiable, and that the activities of unions were on balance beneficial. A broader form of argument was put forward (as shown in Chapter 3) by Thring at the Home Office and other observers. This view held that the doctrine of restraint of trade ought not to stand in the way of bringing unions within the law, however foolish or economically erroneous their objectives and practices. Unions' institutional structures and industrial strategies were areas in which it was both futile and impolitic for the state to attempt to interfere. Both these positions concluded that unions should be allowed a more or less unconditional form of legalization.

The contrary view insisted that the law was right to subject unions to disabilities if their objectives conflicted with prevailing notions of public policy, especially those drawn from the maxims of political economy. Legalization should therefore be on restrictive terms, purging union rule-books of those provisions which the courts had held to be illegal, and enforcing changes to the way unions conducted their affairs.

The evidence heard by the royal commission was interpreted as supporting or undermining either of the two policy prescriptions, and the commissioners themselves divided on these lines when they came to draw up their conclusions early in 1869. Before their reports are considered, it is important to note two external developments which materially altered the context within which their recommendations were received. The first, the conciliation 'craze' of the late 1860s, lent weight to the argument that the spread of unionism might serve the public interest; the second, the outcome of the general election of 1868, decisively limited the options available to legislators.

ARBITRATION AND CONCILIATION

Had the royal commission concluded its proceedings upon the completion of the inquiry into outrages and intimidation in Manchester early in 1868, as Erle seems to have intended, the testimony of A. J. Mundella, the most prominent political exponent of industrial conciliation, would not have been heard. The board of arbitration and conciliation in the Nottingham hosiery trade, of which he had been founder and first chairman, had been described at the British Association in September 1867 as a means of resolving the contention between organized labour and capital.[1] Gladstone, chairing the conference on 'Wages and Capital' convened by the Social Science Association in July 1868, cited the idea approvingly as one of those which exhibited the 'practical union of interest between working men and their employers'.[2] Later in July, Mundella's appearance as one of the final witnesses to appear before the royal commission, was a belated opportunity for the commissioners to learn of circumstances in which combination could harmonize the interests of labour and capital;[3] hitherto, the evidence had concentrated on industries, such as coal, where conflict was endemic and influential large employers were opposed to unionism. Those—notably cotton—where examples of joint regulation might have been found, were conspicuously overlooked.[4]

Neither Mundella's board of conciliation nor the boards of arbitration promoted initially in the building industry by Rupert Kettle, a county court judge in the Midlands, were in themselves new. Arbitration, it has been suggested, was a familiar means of resolving disputes early in the nineteenth century and resort to it was routine before the concept of the individual bargain gained ascendancy in the early 1850s.[5] Two aspects of Mundella and Kettle's systems were, however, presented as significant departures.

First, they both aimed to settle the terms of future contracts for labour, as opposed to resolving disputes arising from the interpretation of existing agreements between employers and workers.[6] Legislative proposals in the

[1] E. Renals, 'On Arbitration in the Hosiery Trades of the Midland Counties', *Journal of the Statistical Society*, 30 (Dec. 1867), 548.

[2] NAPSS, *Sessional Proceedings, 1867–8*, 394–5, 410; Goldman, *Science, Reform, and Politics*, 219.

[3] RCTU 10th Rep. Qs.19,341–19,480 (14 July 1868), Qs.19,679–19,715 (22 July 1868); Harrison to Beesly, 25 July 1868, Harrison MSS 1/14.

[4] Le Comte de Paris [Louis Philippe D'Orléans], *The Trades' Unions of England*, ed. T. Hughes, trans. N. J. Senior (1869), 184–2; R. Church, *The History of the British Coal Industry*, vol. iii (1986), 661–4, 685.

[5] Jaffe, *Striking a Bargain*, 223; Fraser, *Trade Unions and Society*, 110.

[6] H. Crompton, 'Arbitration and Conciliation', *Fortnightly Review*, n.s. 5 (May 1869), 622–8.

1850s and 1860s to create equitable councils of conciliation had been confined to settling disputes arising from existing contracts.[7] Kettle insisted that his arbitration boards were merely mechanisms for arriving at agreements to sell labour for a certain price for a fixed period. The umpire—a role which he hoped 'the nobility and gentry' would feel it their public duty to fulfil—was to have the specific function of ensuring that economic laws were obeyed.[8] Kettle's repeated emphasis on this point reflected his anxiety not to be exposed to the critics, such as the economist W. S. Jevons,[9] who perceived courts of arbitration as reviving the principle of statutory wage-fixing or of customary ideas of a 'just' wage. Both Kettle and Mundella saw their schemes as means of adjusting wage rates to changing market conditions without interruptions and conflict, Kettle having observed from his adjudication of small debts cases how extensively the uncertain and fluctuating demand for skilled labour forced artisans to resort to credit.[10]

The other novel feature of the boards devised in the 1860s was their reliance upon trade unions to represent the men. 'Our plan involves the frank acknowledgement of the trades societies. They are no longer with us objects of hatred and dread', Mundella told a meeting at Bradford.[11] Union involvement received heightened emphasis during 1868. The account of Mundella's board presented to the British Association had barely mentioned this feature and Kettle, in his evidence to the commission in July 1867, played down the unions' role. Kettle initially attached less importance than Mundella to the unions' function in ensuring that decisions were carried out, proposing instead that arbitration decisions should be embodied in the employment contracts of individual workers.[12] In practice, though, both schemes relied upon union officers as advocates, and upon the unions themselves as agents of moral pressure to secure their members' adhesion to the outcomes.

A variety of interpretations—both of the costs and benefits to their participants and of the objectives which drew them into the new system—have been placed upon the moves towards the formalization of industrial relations in the 1860s.[13] Evidence from the building and iron industries,

[7] *Trades' Societies and Strikes*, xix.

[8] R. Kettle, *Strikes and Arbitrations* (1866), 6.

[9] W. S. Jevons, 'Industrial Partnerships', in *Lectures on Economic Science* (1870), 3–4; cf. Fawcett's objection, *PP* 1860 xxii, Q.11181.

[10] R. Kettle, *Masters and Men* (1871), 7–8.

[11] A. J. Mundella, *Arbitration as a Means of Preventing Strikes* (1868), 16.

[12] Kettle, *Strikes and Arbitrations*, 20; RCTU 4th Rep. Q.7153.

[13] Webb, *History*, 338–9; V. L. Allen, 'The Origins of Industrial Conciliation and Arbitration', *International Review of Social History*, 9 (1964), 247–9.

showing that conciliation and arbitration were imposed by the employers after lengthy strikes had ended in defeat, raised the question of whether the purpose of incorporating unions into formal structures was to turn them into an instrument to discipline the men.[14] The emasculated role assigned to John Kane's ironworkers' union under the North of England Manufactured Iron Trade Conciliation Board founded early in 1869, had certain similarities to the ideas floated two years earlier in the employers' programme of Creed and Williams.[15] From another perspective, though, the boards could be seen as a partial fulfilment of artisan aspirations towards the regulation of their trades by agreed rules, founded upon ideals of equity and reciprocal obligations. They had the potential—though this was far from the minds of Creed and Williams—to fulfil the popular aspiration for a moralized labour market.[16] Such were the terms in which Ludlow and Lloyd Jones described arbitration in 1867: 'honourable employers' and 'good steady workers' would be brought together in an atmosphere of 'goodwill and mutual respect' to stabilize markets and exclude 'undercutters'—whether unscrupulous employers or workers who violated trade rules and rates. Those ideals were repeated in some of the expressions used by Mundella (an Anglican who, in his youth, had held Chartist sympathies).[17]

Conciliation and arbitration were enthusiastically embraced by politicians—mainly but far from exclusively Liberal—in the summer of 1868, as election campaigning began and the need to reconcile capital and labour became a matter of political urgency. Mundella's ideas accumulated endorsement from the first Trades Union Congress, held at Manchester in June 1868, and from two of the commissioners, Lords Lichfield and Elcho (the support of Harrison and Thomas Hughes being taken as read).[18] Indeed, the political significance of the boards perhaps exceeded their immediate industrial impact. They were a symbol of the formal equality of organized labour; Kettle acknowledged in 1866 that the existing, unequal law of

---

[14] Price, *Masters, Unions, and Men*, 116–24; N. P. Howard, 'The Strikes and Lockouts in the Iron Industry and the Formation of the Ironworkers' Unions, 1862–1869', *International Review of Social History*, 18 (1973), 425–6. For a critique see J. Zeitlin, 'From Labour History to the History of Industrial Relations', *Economic History Review*, 40 (1987), 171–2.

[15] See E. Taylor on John Kane in *DLB*, iii. 120–1; Creed and Williams, *Handicraftsmen and Capitalists*, 35–6.

[16] Prothero, *Radical Artisans*, 56–7; Jaffe, *Striking a Bargain*, passim; P. Joyce, *Visions of the People* (1991), 91–2, 111.

[17] Ludlow and Lloyd Jones, *Progress of the Working Class* (1867), 239–41.

[18] Roberts, *The Trades Union Congress*, 48; Mundella to Leader, 11 July 1868, Mundella MSS 6P/58/5; C. Fisher and J. Smethurst, ' "War on the Law of Supply and Demand" ', in R. Harrison (ed.), *Independent Collier* (1978), 137–8; NAPSS, *Transactions, 1868*, 524.

Master and Servant was incompatible with the principle of his arbitration boards. The new structures also helped to displace the notion of the individual bargain from the central place that it had previously, and very recently, occupied in many politicians' understanding of the labour problem.[19]

INSTITUTIONAL AUTONOMY AND THE GENERAL ELECTION OF 1868

A commitment to settling disputes by conciliation and arbitration was often reiterated in the stream of apologetic which emphasized the unions' respectability and moderation. So, too, was their provision of welfare benefits which, by the Manchester printer W. H. Wood's estimate, accounted for 75 per cent of many unions' expenditure.[20] For the stonemasons, presentations of lump-sum benefits to members or their widows were occasions for public ceremonies when both the financial soundness of the society and the laudability of its aims could be proclaimed.[21] Benefit funds made the unions powerful, and their members 'independent', the flint glass makers insisted.[22] Combined labour, William Macdonald told the inaugural TUC, was 'free labour', and by implication unorganized labour was not.[23]

Such formulations of 'freedom' and 'independence' united the craft unions against what was perceived, by the summer of 1868, as the most immediate legal threat to their position: the proposal that they should be forced to separate their trade from their benefit funds.[24] Here an element of party division occurred. Some Liberals, such as Thomas Hughes, hailed societies which combined the two functions as the most laudable form of association, reducing the tendency to strikes and inculcating morally improving habits of collective self-help and self-government. Many Conservatives regarded such a mixture of functions with suspicion, and generally supported the idea of imposing some form of internal separation. Disraeli's views remained obscure for, in an almost comic series of evasions after he succeeded Derby as prime minister, he contrived to avoid meeting a deputation from the CAT.[25] His home secretary, Gathorne Hardy, was less

---

[19] Kettle, *Strikes and Arbitrations*, 21–2; Jaffe, *Striking a Bargain*, 253.

[20] W. H. Wood, *Trades Unions Defended* (1867), 9, 13.

[21] OSM FR 6–20 Feb. 1868, 25 June–9 July 1868, MRC MSS 78/OS/4/1/34.

[22] *Flint Glass Makers' Magazine*, 5 (Dec. 1866), 852.

[23] *Bee-Hive* (6 June 1868), 6.

[24] See Dronfield's warning to the TUC, *Bee-Hive* (6 June 1868), 5.

[25] CAT minutes, 15 Mar., 15 May 1868, Webb TU Coll. Section B (xviii), 89, 94–5.

reticent, and advised a cabinet colleague, Stafford Northcote, who wanted to know how to respond to his constituents' questions on the labour issue, that union trade and benefit funds should be kept apart.[26] There were several reasons for doing so. Some were put forward by employers undisguisedly to weaken the unions' industrial power, by preventing benefit funds being drawn on during stoppages. Others, such as those of Thring at the Home Office, were advanced on prudential grounds to protect members' rights to welfare benefits.[27]

Separation was the simplest of the many proposals put forward by employers to subject unions to stricter regulatory control and, as Applegarth foresaw, it was placed in the forefront of their schemes.[28] It is important, of course, not to overstate their coherence of aim. Most of the employers who gave evidence to the Erle commission confined themselves to defending the principle of the existing laws against intimidation, and the question of what legal status unions should hold was barely considered.[29] Employers' representative bodies had difficulty in achieving an agreed view, even where they thought the issue important enough to make the attempt. The inability of the Bradford chamber of commerce to arrive at a conclusion was shared by its counterparts in Manchester and Birmingham as well as the umbrella body, the Associated Chambers of Commerce. Discussions within the Sheffield chamber also revealed marked divergences of opinion.[30]

In a few cases, however, definite schemes were put forward, and these all favoured strong regulation. The most elaborate plan was submitted to the commission by the General Builders' Association (GBA), and was followed by a similar scheme drawn up by the master printers.[31] As well as pressing for the separation of funds, the builders' submission proposed that unions

[26] Northcote to Gathorne Hardy, 8 Sept. 1868, Gathorne Hardy MSS HA43 T501/271; Gathorne Hardy to Northcote, 10 Sept. 1868, BL Add MSS 50037, fo. 154; cf. Carnarvon's remarks, NAPSS, *Transactions, 1868*, 17.

[27] Undated (but by context *c.*1867–9) MS memorandum in OPC Bills and Memoranda (HT) 1875, xxiii–xxiv.

[28] Applegarth to Charles Williams, 16 Nov. 1867, Liverpool Trades Council (TC) MSS 331 TRA/2, fo. 57.

[29] RCTU 1st Rep. Q.3004; 3rd Rep. Qs.4375, 4699; 5th Rep. Qs.10,050, 11,734; 7th Rep. Q.14,536; 10th Rep. Q.19,079; 11th Rep., vol. ii, Appx.. D, 117.

[30] G. R. Searle, *Entrepreneurial Politics in Mid-Victorian Britain* (1993) 285; minutes of Manchester Chamber of Commerce, 28 Jan. 1867, 8 Apr. 1867, MCL M8/2/6; Birmingham Chamber of Commerce, council minutes 1866–72, 94; minutes of Sheffield Chamber of Commerce, 22 July 1867, SCL LD 1986/1. *Report of the Sixth Annual Meeting of the Association of British Chambers of Commerce* (1866), 85; *Report of the Tenth Annual Meeting of the Association of British Chambers of Commerce* (1870), 43.

[31] RCTU 11th Rep., vol. ii, Appx. L, 334–5; minute book of the General Builders Association, 1865–71, p. 90 (2 Aug. 1867); Price, *Masters, Unions, and Men*, 125; RCTU 10th Rep. Q.19,677.

should be brought within the law, with a government registrar purging their rules of 'anything illegal and impolitic'. All questions of wages, hours, and trade rules were to be dealt with by district courts of arbitration presided over by an independent umpire.[32]

Union responses included the traditional artisan resistance to interference, articulated by Richard Harnott of the stonemasons: 'if the Government of the country would leave matters as they stood, with the exception of giving them legal protection for the funds of their society, he thought they would do very well'.[33] There were also vague demands for legalization which might unwittingly have exposed unions either to separation of funds or more onerous supervision than they would have been willing to accept.[34] A very few, mainly, in Sheffield, sought extensive legal powers (see Chapter 5). There is no reason to doubt the importance which has been attached to the intervention of the Positivist lawyers at this point. In October 1867 Henry Crompton and Godfrey Lushington drafted the Trades Societies bill for the Conference of Amalgamated Trades as 'a declaration of principle'. They set out in legal language how unions might be declared lawful, and in a way that parliamentary opinion was likely to find acceptable. Unions would be allowed, if they wished, to take advantage of the Friendly Societies Acts, but would not become corporate bodies, nor would they be empowered to sue or be sued by their members.[35] This was as unrestrictive as any measure of legalization could conceivably have been. No alterations to union rules were required. Nor was there to be any interference in their internal management.

Factional squabbling within London trade unionism delayed total agreement on the bill until the end of October 1868. In June, however, the provincial trades at the first Trades Union Congress, held in Manchester, agreed that the proposed bill was an acceptable settlement. Pledges to support it were to be demanded of candidates at the forthcoming general election who solicited trade union votes.[36] Whether this intention was compromised by the secret agreement entered into between the Reform League secretary, George Howell, and the Liberal whip, G. G. Glyn, to provide electoral support for Liberal candidates, is questionable.[37] Although the

---

[32] RCTU 11th Rep., vol. ii, 699, Appx. L; cf. Price, *Masters, Unions, and Men*, 125.

[33] OSM FR 6–20 Feb 1868, MRC MSS 78/OS/4/1/34.

[34] RCTU 11th Rep., vol. ii, 59, 61, Appx.. D; *Report of the Trades Conference held at St Martin's Hall* (1867), 27, 18; RCTU 4th Rep. Qs.6645, 7464.

[35] ASE, monthly report, Nov. 1867, 41; ASCJ, monthly report, Nov. 1867, 231.

[36] *Bee-Hive* (31 Oct. 1868), 5; London TC minutes, 24 Oct. 1868, 29 Oct. 1868, BLPES M1061; *Bee-Hive* (13 June 1868), 6.

[37] Harrison, *Before the Socialists*, ch. 4; Leventhal, *Respectable Radical*, ch. 5.

Positivist E. S. Beesly later made sweeping allegations about the labour cause having been 'sold', in November 1868 he celebrated the amount of backing which the CAT's bill had received, claiming that 300 candidates were pledged.[38] Given to hyperbole, Beesly was not always a reliable source, but from early in 1868 there were many examples of test questions being put and pledges being obtained by branches of the CAT's constituent unions or by trades councils.[39] In some cases the questions were put by the Reform League's agents; undertakings were also obtained from Liberals who received League backing.[40] In Sunderland, a constituency targeted by the League, the Liberal candidate, E. T. Gourley, a shipowner, committed himself to leave unions 'to manage their funds as they pleased'.[41]

The 'Lib-Lab era in working class politics',[42] formalized by the Glyn–Howell arrangement, did not herald any willingness on the part of the amalgamated trades' leadership to compromise on the fundamental issue of autonomy. In December 1868 it was known that the Erle commission had begun to prepare its final report, and that the draft being discussed contained many of the building employers' proposals. Although the commission had long ceased gathering evidence, the CAT sent to the commissioners a terse statement of their views on the builders' submission. They may have felt strengthened by the outcome of the election, and especially by Mundella's success in ousting one of the members of the commission and a strident critic of unionism, J. A. Roebuck, from his Sheffield seat. Signed by Allan, Applegarth, Daniel Guile, Edwin Coulson, and George Odger, the CAT submission declared, 'Such legislation (*if we obeyed it*) would completely cripple our societies'. The working man chose to invest his money in subscriptions to unions, fully aware of the advantages and responsibilities involved:[43]

We protest against any attempt on the part of the State to dictate to him in the matter. We should regard it as an open declaration of war between the classes. Sorry as we should be to see such a challenge offered, we should firmly accept it.

---

[38] *Daily News* (2 Nov. 1868), 5.

[39] *Bolton Guardian* (25 Jan. 1868), 5; *Bury Times* (15 Feb. 1868), 3; *Birmingham Daily Post* (17 July 1868).

[40] *Cardiff Times* (7 Nov. 1868), 8; *Leeds Mercury* (23 Sept. 1868), 4; *Swindon Advertiser* (26 Oct. 1868); *Banbury Guardian* (29 Oct. 1868); *Hereford Times* (14 Nov. 1868), 2; *Brierley-Hill Advertiser* (12 Sept. 1868).

[41] *Sunderland Times* (10 Oct. 1868), 8; *Halifax Courier* (26 Sept. 1868), 6; *Oldham Standard* (22 Aug. 1868), 7; the CAT bill was supported by the Liberal press: *Daily Telegraph* (14 Nov. 1867), 6; *Daily News* (16 Oct. 1868), 4.

[42] Harrison, *Before the Socialists*, 209.

[43] RCTU 11th Rep., vol. ii, 336, Appx. L no. IX; cf. *Pall Mall Gazette* (5 Feb. 1868), 484; (14 Feb. 1868), 611.

Before the commission had reported, a non-negotiable limit, couched un-compromisingly in the language of class conflict, was placed upon the form that any future legislation could take.

THE ROYAL COMMISSION REPORT AND THE FREEDOM TO COMBINE

The draft final report, composed by James Booth at Erle's instigation, was in many ways the most far-reaching of the proposals to be discussed by the commission. Called to the bar in the year that the combination laws were repealed, Booth had been associated with the philosophic radicals, and his first official appointment was as a whig nominee on the Municipal Corporations commission in 1835.[44] He had recently retired from the Board of Trade where, from 1850 to 1865, he had been joint secretary during the period when the policy of free trade was consolidated. Of the same generation as Roebuck and Erle, he shared their utilitarian assumptions, and passages of his report echoed the confident, universalist sentiments of Bramwell and Lowe. He regarded unions as unjustifiable monopolies, which perpetuated anti-competitive fallacies and prevented individuals from pursuing their own best interests. His report was a sustained argument for applying what he called 'the general system of free trade' to the labour market. Insisting on the necessity for cheap labour, since the wages fund depended upon cheapness of production, Booth contended that low wages and long hours were preferable to starvation. Like Senior, he saw union restrictions on labour as likely to 'pauperise the rest of the community of labourers'.[45] No account was taken of the developments since 1860 in the debate on the labour question, and comparatively little use made of the voluminous evidence accumulated by the commission itself.

Since Booth developed his arguments from classical political economy, he could not completely deny the right of combination. Instead, he drew a distinction between temporary combination, and therefore strikes, which he was to a large extent willing to permit, and 'association', implying permanent forms of restriction upon the labour market, which he sought severely to limit.[46] Thus he proposed to impose heavier restrictions upon

---

[44] W. E. S. Thomas, *The Philosophic Radicals* (1979), 282.

[45] RCTU 11th Rep. cvii (para. 96), cviii (para. 99), cix (paras. 104, 106), cx (para. 108).

[46] On this distinction see Kahn-Freund, *Labour and the Law*, 228; on the parallel French example of 1864, see F. D. Longe, 'The Law of Trade Combinations in France', pt. 2, *Fortnightly Review*, n.s. 2 (Aug.–Sept. 1867), 299. Booth's views approximated to those

unions than on strikers themselves. The latter, as he had to admit, were doing no more than exercising their right not to bring a commodity to the market place at a particular time. But like the court in *Hilton v Eckersley*, he wanted to prevent men from surrendering their free will and binding themselves as to their future actions (though he dismissed at length the analogy between the restrictive rules of unions and those of the legal profession to which he belonged).[47] He was unconvinced by the arguments commonly advanced in the unions' favour: growth in size and wealth tended not to moderation and restraint but, as Martineau had contended, to a more complete and effective stifling of competition. Their claims to represent 'the trade' were especially objectionable. His hope was that, by subjecting them to legal and administrative controls, unions could be caused to revert 'to their ancient character of benefit clubs'.[48] Unions would be brought under the law by what was intended to produce a system of compulsory registration (submission to the process could be demanded by a single member). Trade and benefit funds would be separated. Rules such as those limiting apprentices, preventing the use of machinery, against piecework, or supporting workers in other unions when on strike, were to be void and expenditure to promote them forbidden. Strikes for these objects might well occur, but he hoped to cut off the means by which unions supported them.

Frederic Harrison warned Mundella that, if enacted, Booth's proposals 'would produce a *revolution*'.[49] With the precedents of 1828 and 1854 in mind, when an unreformed parliament had been forced to retreat from implementing not dissimilar measures of regulation, it was inconceivable that they would have passed the House of Commons. During discussions among the commissioners between December 1868 and February 1869, Booth's report was stripped of its more controversial assertions so as to achieve a document that a majority of them—Erle, Elcho, Gooch, Merivale, Booth, Roebuck, and Mathews—felt able to sign. In doing so, they removed the intellectual coherence of Booth's scheme and with it much of the theoretical basis for the restrictionist approach to legalization. That case was also severely weakened by the failure of the commission to demonstrate that trade unions had had a damaging effect on trade and industry—the question which had been directly posed by Creed and Williams early in 1867. The commission's appraisal of that controversy was

described by Leslie Stephen as characteristic of the 'old radicals', in 'The Good Old Cause', *Nineteenth Century*, 51 (Jan. 1902), 13–16.

[47] RCTU 11th Rep. cvi (paras. 92–3), cxi (paras. 116–20).
[48] Ibid. cxvii–cviii (paras. 153–6), cxv (144).
[49] Mundella to Leader, 3 Jan. 1869, Mundella MSS 6P/59/1.

hived off into a rather perfunctory and inconclusive statement by Herman Merivale, permanent under-secretary at the India Office and previously the holder of a chair of political economy. His failure to establish any firm connection between the loss of overseas markets and the actions of trade unions effectively extinguished that line of attack.[50]

Like Booth, the majority of the commission wanted to disallow rules 'framed in defiance of well-established principles of economical science'. Unions having such rules were not to be permitted to register to gain the benefits of the Friendly Societies Acts. But since union funds were now fully protected, as a result of Russell Gurney's Act, it was not clear why any union should wish to surrender its fundamental objectives to gain the small benefits registration would confer. Crucially, the commissioners drew back from making registration compulsory, which was the only way that restriction was likely to have any effect. Likewise with separation of funds: knowing that it could not be enforced, the majority attempted to encourage trade and benefit funds being kept distinct by granting the title 'First Class Trades Union Benefit Society' to any registered union which did so. The majority presumably hoped that ring-fencing welfare funds would be popular with individual members as a guarantee of solvency, and that such members might call upon their own unions to register. It was unclear what advantage, beyond the dubious imprimatur conferred, would accrue to any society that took this step. As Harrison commented to his fellow commissioner Lord Lichfield, the machinery of registration agreed by Erle and his colleagues 'will be a perfect dead letter—if not source of ridicule', a prediction confirmed by the comments of union secretaries when the report was published in March 1869.[51] 'Whatever the Commissioners may think,' Daniel Guile of the ironfounders told his members, 'they may rest assured that if we are only to legalize on these grounds we shall prefer to do as we have done in days gone by—remain illegal and abide by the consequences.' The flint glass makers insisted that such a scheme 'would either be secretly evaded or openly opposed'.[52] 'Unionists would not have [legal] protection at the price of allowing their funds and their actions to be under supervision', John Kane of the ironworkers told the second TUC, later in 1869.[53]

Since unions did not depend upon the law or the state for their existence,

[50] H. Merivale, 'Observations Appended to the Report', RCTU 11th Rep. cxxi–cxxv; Phelps Brown, *Origins of Trade Union Power*, 22–3.

[51] Harrison to Lichfield, 3 Feb. 1869, Anson MSS D615/P(P)/4/4/4.

[52] FSIF, Fifty-Ninth Annual Report, Jan.–Dec. 1868, vii; *Flint Glass Makers' Magazine* (Mar. 1869), 510.

[53] Kirk, *The Second Annual Congress of Trades Unions held … in the Odd Fellows' Hall, Upper Temple Street, Birmingham* (1869), 10.

and could continue to operate in defiance of both with little inconvenience to themselves, registration with onerous conditions attached was not likely to be an effective option.[54] This fact was acknowledged in the terms of Hughes and Harrison's counter-proposal for registration without any interference in unions' objects and internal arrangements (provided these did not involve anything actually criminal). They were joined by Lord Lichfield, who felt unable to support in the House of Lords any measure based on the majority's recommendations.[55] Lichfield's adhesion was important in reducing the impression that the minority proposals were partisan. Although he did not sign Hughes and Harrison's detailed minority report, disagreeing with much of the 'tone', he agreed with their approach to actual legislation and signed their short dissent, which summarized their recommendations. In the negotiations to secure Lichfield's signature, Harrison listed the points which were 'essential':[56]

1. Direct acknowledgement of some good in some unions.
2. Full repeal of the rule [i.e. common law of conspiracy] against trade combinations.
3. Unconditional Registration and no classes, with publicity.
4. Some modification of the molestation clause [i.e. of the 1825 Act].

Hughes, Harrison, and Lichfield's only condition for legal recognition was 'ample and real publicity', achieved by permissive registration under the Friendly Societies Act, which would carry no significant restrictions beyond the submission of rules and accounts, but would offer significant administrative advantages.[57] 'A real guarantee of publicity', Harrison assured Lichfield, 'will extinguish malpractices'.[58]

The willingness of unionists to engage their critics in open debate lent credibility to Harrison's argument. Following the example of T. J. Dunning's famous pamphlet of 1860, which was in part a response to Harriet Martineau, William Macdonald, secretary of the Manchester housepainters, published a reply to the criticisms levelled at unions by John Watts and W. S. Jevons.[59] Applegarth's Amalgamated Society of Carpenters and Joiners, to which both Mundella and the economist W. T. Thornton applied the epithet 'model trade union', was again an exemplar for its practice of sending copies of its annual report to the press for review

[54] Clegg, Fox, and Thompson, *History*, 46.
[55] Lichfield to Erle, 16 Mar. 1869, Bodl. MS Don c.71.
[56] Harrison to Lichfield, 3 Feb. 1869, Anson MSS D615/P(P)/4/4/4.
[57] RCTU 11th Rep. xxix–xxxi.
[58] Harrison to Lichfield, 26 Apr. 1869, Anson MSS D615/P(L)/6/18.
[59] Dunning, *Trades' Unions and Strikes*; W. Macdonald, *The True Story of Trades' Unions Contrasted with the Caricatures and Fallacies of the Pretended Economists* (1867).

and comment.[60] Harrison looked forward to a process of self-reform, whereby unions would be gradually transformed into 'peaceful and useful institutions', modifying their practices in the light of well-founded, disinterested criticism.[61] Much was made of the instances where they had shown themselves willing to do so. During the formation of an arbitration board in Bradford, Applegarth had caused a labourers' union to erase from its rule-book a 'ridiculous' regulation fining any man who worked too hard. Mundella persuaded the Nottingham stonemasons to drop their rule prohibiting the use of worked stone.[62] He prescribed self-reform as a moral duty consequent upon recognition and equal treatment by the law. In a public letter to the chairman of the Plymouth trades delegates he urged unions to do away with 'unwise and restrictive rules'.[63] It was the essence of the minority case that this should be voluntarily undertaken, with the encouragement of public opinion, rather then coercively, by law.

The underpinning for the counter-arguments in favour of legal regulation was supplied by Sir William Erle's *Memorandum on the Law of Trade Unions*, published in January 1869, in advance of the commission's recommendations. It was less an account of the state of the law than a contentious, and sometimes polemical, description of the principles which underlay it. Erle's testily expressed political sentiments have already been noted. He was concerned also to 'foster loyalty' to the common law in the face of attacks from those whom he represented as ill-informed lay critics. A lengthy passage sought to demonstrate that the rules of common law practically originated from the people, at the earliest stage of the law's development, and therefore rested upon popular consent. Furthermore, since the common law was in a perpetual state of renewal, it was a more appropriate mechanism for adjusting the changing relations between different groups in society than a statute, which was rigid and soon became outdated. Erle implied that the courts, rather than parliament, ought to have ultimate authority to adjudicate between the conflicting interests of employers and employed.[64]

The particular problem which Erle faced was to establish, and then to

---

[60] W. T. Thornton, *On Labour: Its Wrongful Claims and Rightful Dues. Its Actual Present and Possible Future* (1869), 195; ASCJ, monthly report, Apr. 1869, 68; *The Times* (1 May 1868), 9.

[61] RCTU 11th Rep. xl; Ludlow and Lloyd Jones, *Progress*, 214. The suggestion in C. G. Hanson, 'Craft Unions, Welfare Benefits, and the Case for Trade Union Law Reform, 1867–75', *Economic History Review*, 28 (1975), 243–59, that Harrison depicted unions as tending to become friendly and benefit societies is questionable; see the critical comment by P. Thane, *Economic History Review*, 29 (1976), esp. 619.

[62] RCTU 10th Rep. Qs 19,474, 19,476, 19,700; *The Times* (19 Feb. 1868), 10.

[63] *Western Daily Mercury* (Plymouth) (12 Aug. 1869), 3.

[64] RCTU 11th Rep. lxvi, lxxiii, lxxv, lxxvii.

justify, the grounds upon which the common law disapproved of combinations. He did so by presenting the common law as upholding, disinterestedly, a theory of free trade, founded upon the premise that:[65]

at common law every person has individually, and the public also have collectively, a right to require that the course of trade should be kept free from unreasonable obstruction.

He admitted that he could find no direct grant of such a right, but deduced its existence from records of actions for its violation. These led him to conclude that the common law had upheld free competition in the market for labour, as in other markets, during all periods. Any unreasonable obstruction to the free disposal of a commodity (as he regarded labour) was therefore unlawful, and on grounds which could not be attributed to modern class bias on the part of judges. His arguments nevertheless seemed to posit a harmony between political economy and the law.

Erle's thesis was attacked in two respects. It was exposed to the type of criticism of judicial legislation associated with Fitzjames Stephen. A review in the *Pall Mall Gazette*, whose content suggests Stephen's authorship, drew attention to what it alleged were the logical fallacies inherent in Erle's deductive method: a 'purely juridicial course of reasoning' was unsuitable to resolve contested social questions.[66] In a particularly savage dissection of Erle's reasoning, J. M. Ludlow—who may not have been pleased to see his *Progress of the Working Class* invoked as testimony to the beneficence of the unreformed parliament—attacked the 'extraordinary attempt to read modern political economy into our old common law, and to represent the latter as upholding "the right to a free course for trade" '. It was a historical absurdity, Ludlow contended, to attribute such an intention to the legal doctrines formed during a half-millennium of restrictive legislation (which the courts had supported) and long before the idea of labour as a commodity had been conceived.[67]

These critiques of Erle's memorandum foreshadowed wider responses to the two reports, and highlighted the fundamental theoretical differences between the majority and minority. The social theory expounded by Erle and the majority of the commission as being of universal applicablity was disputed in Hughes and Harrison's minority report. Substantially drafted by Harrison himself, the minority report has tended to be seen—particularly in the light of developments at the turn of the twentieth century—as

---

[65] Ibid. lxvii.
[66] *Pall Mall Gazette* (19 Mar. 1869), 943–4.
[67] *Spectator* (20 Feb. 1869), 234; but see Atiyah, *Freedom of Contract*, 112–30.

primarily an ingenious scheme to keep unions out of the law's reach. That aspect will be discussed more fully in Chapter 5. Perhaps of greater contemporary significance was the form of argument which the minority report invoked to attack Erle and Booth's case for restrictive legalization. Harrison's methodology had much in common with the historicist critique of classical political economy, which in the late 1860s began to inform approaches to the Irish land question.[68] In the first place, he challenged the majority report's deductivism: his report pointedly commenced with a section on 'conclusions from the evidence', leading to 'propositions containing the results of the evidence', in which optimistic findings about the nature of unionism were presented as arising directly from the testimony received. Social 'facts' were highlighted, while economic and moral objections to combination were sidelined as irrelevant 'speculative' abstractions.[69]

Those universalist abstractions were also attacked by reference to the historical development of labour law. Restrictions on the freedom to combine had been advocated by Erle and his colleagues in the name of free trade and individual competition. Harrison, on the other hand, described such restrictions as survivals of 'feudal' theories of labour, originating in a period when labour was regarded as a duty to the state, and when the individual labourer was denied the freedom to dispose of his labour as he chose—the very right which Erle claimed to be fundamental to the existing law. It was an infringement upon the freedom of labour to forbid men to agree jointly to place any condition upon the sale of their labour which they chose: 'There is no logical halting place between the old system of compulsion and that of entire freedom.'[70]

Harrison drew upon an historical trajectory outlined by F. D. Longe, whose analysis of the recent evolution of the law affecting combinations in France was intended to illuminate the parallel trends in England. Longe pointed to the iniquity and illogicality of perpetuating legal doctrines against combinations, dating from a pre-industrial economy, into the epoch of free competition, when the state had relinquished responsibility for fixing wages. The individual labourer was now left to fend for himself in conditions where capital had become concentrated, a surplus of labour existed, and the tendency of competition in the labour market was to force wages downwards, as he had demonstrated in his earlier critique of the wage fund theory. Those who sought to restrict the freedom of permanent association (i.e. by applying the doctrine of restraint of trade against

---

[68] Dewey, 'Celtic Agrarian Legislation', 30–43; Koot, *English Historical Economics*, 2, 32, 47–9.
[69] RCTU 11th Rep. xxxii, xli   [70] RCTU 11th Rep. lxi.

unions) weakened the ability of labour to protect itself, and helped to keep labourers 'in a state of abject dependence on their employers' of the sort which the Children's Employment commission, and later the Truck commission, brought to light.[71] Longe viewed labour as the victim of an incomplete historical process: the medieval guild idea had been supplanted by the forces of individualism, which in doing so had stripped away certain protections which labour previously enjoyed; the necessary countervailing force of a complete freedom to combine had yet to be conceded. Harrison worked these insights into his contention that freedom of trade and labour having been conceded to individuals, it was wrong to deny that freedom, unrestricted, to combinations.

In the context of the debate on the legality of unions and strikes, historicist modes of argument were not primarily directed towards sanctioning pre-industrial forms of social organization or restoring previously held historical rights. They were applied, instead, to discrediting policy prescriptions whose principles could be shown to derive from the coercive approaches to labour in earlier historical periods. Later in 1869, J. M. Ludlow did cite the precedent of medieval guilds to contradict the assumption that association was a novel product of nineteenth-century civilization. Habits of mutual relief and trade regulation could be shown to be deep-rooted; the stonemasons' controversial worked stone rule found an earlier analogy in a regulation of the craft guild of Bristol fullers against working on cloth which had been fulled outside the town.[72] In view of the remarkably close analogy between the two forms of association, it is perhaps surprising that the guild precedent was so little referred to by advocates of the case for legalizing unions.

One explanation for this is simply chronological: Ludlow's article and its inspiration, Toulmin Smith's edition for the Early English Text Society of the ordinances of the early English guilds, were not published until after the announcement, in July 1869, of the government's response to the commission reports. Only in the early 1870s, with the publication of the extended account by the German scholar and liberal, Lujo Brentano, did the idea of a lineage from guilds to trade unions as a positive characteristic begin to inform contemporary understanding of the organization of labour, and even then the comparison enjoyed only limited purchase. The analogy was more commonly invoked by critics, such as Lowe, to denounce the economic fallacies of unionism.

---

[71] Longe, 'Law of Trade Combinations in France', 213–19, 224–5, 303–9.
[72] J. M. Ludlow, 'Old Guilds and New Friendly and Trade Societies', *Fortnightly Review*, n.s. 6 (Oct. 1869), 390–1, 400, 406.

The medieval example of mutual association was not, anyway, especially helpful in advancing the legal argument which Harrison, Longe, and Lushington had erected. They emphasized the progressive, 'modern' trend towards permitting the freedom to combine. In some respects, their account of trade unionism was decidedly unhistorical, stressing discontinuities from earlier forms of association, a tendency which also encouraged the misleading view that conciliation and arbitration were recent innovations. Where an explicit parallel with the legal powers of the guilds was raised, in the case of the Sheffield metal-working trades, these advocates of legalization were anxious to distance themselves from it, joining in the depiction of William Broadhead and other Sheffield unionists complicit in outrages as 'criminals'. Indeed, one feature of the trade union campaign for equality and emancipation, focussed upon the protection of funds issue, was to sideline the sophisticated artisanal ideas of corporate control expounded by the Sheffield unionists.[73] In the wake of the outrages Sheffield was not, of course, an attractive model, and much of the minority report's argument about the nature of unionism involved drawing a distinction between the practices there and those of the amalgamated societies. Guild regulation was associated with localism, whereas the minority report was concerned to highlight the virtues of national organization. Most of all, the guild precedent was seen as being, historically, the accompaniment of theories of labour as an obligation to the state, albeit at a time when labour received some reciprocal protection. What distinguished the position of Ludlow, the foremost proponent of the guild analogy as a positive feature of unionism, from Harrison was the former's readiness to contemplate restrictions on the freedom to strike.

Harrison preferred to emphasize the link between the freedom to combine and the removal of state interference. In the past such 'meddling' had produced 'class' legislation, detrimental to the interests of labour, a contention later popularized by the historical economist and radical Thorold Rogers.[74] Hindrances to the freedom of association were an unwarranted and arbitrary interference by the state in the choices made by individuals. Unionism, Harrison asserted, was the 'exact correlative of competition', and he peppered his report with injunctions against the state taking sides in the decisions which individuals made as to whether competition or combination best served their own interests.[75] Association was therefore depicted as an outgrowth of individualism, and stood in contrast to the

---

[73] S. Pollard, 'The Ethics of the Sheffield Outrages', *Transactions of the Hunter Archaeological Society*, 7 (1957), 118, 122, 131; on the legal demands of the Sheffield unionists see Chapter 5, below.   [74] Koot, *English Historical Economics*, 69–71.
[75] RCTU 11th Rep. liv, xli, xxxvi, xl, xxxiv, xliii.

guild-type regulation of industry, deriving its authority from the state, of which the Cobdenite diplomat Robert Morier found examples in the history of the law of combinations in Prussia.[76] Harrison and other contemporary writers were elaborating an early version of what was conceptualized nearly a century later as 'collective *laissez-faire*': that is, 'allowing free play to the collective forces of society' while limiting the intervention of the law and the state to the margins of the relations between labour and capital.[77] Whether that concept represents a complete account of the relationship between the state and industrial relations in twentieth-century Britain—the context within which it has been frequently discussed—is open to question.[78] But as a description of the position developed by the minority report in 1869, it seems an effective one. It described a sort of half-way house between *laissez-faire* in its individualist form, when combinations were forbidden or severely restricted, and forms of collectivism in which the state itself protected labour and intervened in the 'private' area of the employment contract. Like Longe, Lushington suggested that the 'revolutionary theory of individualism', which he associated with 'advanced' Liberals, had done its work in freeing commerce from constraining laws, but a new phase of public policy was now required to free the voluntary, collective forces in society from restriction.[79]

Those forces found an enthusiastic and apparently impartial advocate in the comte de Paris, the exiled claimant to the French throne, whose treatise on the *Trades' Unions of England*, translated by Nassau Senior's son, appeared with an introduction by Thomas Hughes in March 1869. Although treated dismissively by the Webbs, the comte de Paris's book had a pronounced effect on contemporary opinion—more so than, for example, Brentano's undeniably more thorough, and subsequently better-known, researches.[80] The comte de Paris's account, which identified unionism with the success of English constitutional and moral values,[81] and contained an

---

[76] Morier's report, dated 28 Apr. 1867, was reprinted in RCTU 11th Rep., Appx. 159–65. Like Longe's account of France, Morier detected in the phases of opinion in Prussia an evolutionary trend towards a liberal freedom of association.

[77] Kahn-Freund, *Selected Writings*, 8.

[78] K. D. Ewing, 'The State and Industrial Relations: "Collective Laissez-Faire" Revisited', *Historical Studies in Industrial Relations*, 5 (1998), 1–31.

[79] G. Lushington, 'Workmen and Trade Unions', in *Questions for a Reformed Parliament* (1867) 48.

[80] Webb, *History*, 255n.; L. Brentano, 'The Growth of a Trades-Union', *North British Review*, n.s. 14 (Oct. 1870); J. Thompson, ' "A Nearly Related People": German Views of the British Labour Market, 1870–1900', in D. Winch and P. K. O'Brien (eds), *The Political Economy of British Historical Experience, 1688–1914* (2002), 93–6.

[81] For other examples, see Parry, 'The Impact of Napoleon III on British Politics', esp. 162–70; Harris, *Private Lives*, 220.

implicitly unfavourable comparison with the institutions of imperial France, had a powerful contemporary appeal. Gladstone told its author that the work confirmed his own 'cheerful view of the question of Trades Unions'.[82] Its conclusions amounted to an independent endorsement of the policy of the minority report, but couched in terms likely to appeal to whig–Liberal opinion. Following the Christian Socialists, the comte de Paris presented unionism as a positive application of the principle of association, with beneficial results both economically and morally. It was a product of— rather than, as critics had argued, a brake upon—political liberty and commercial prosperity. Unionism's defects could be remedied by exposure to the free press and public discussion which England enjoyed (and France did not). Full legalization would, the treatise claimed, 'add another stone to the edifice of English liberty'.[83]

DISCONNECTING LAW AND POLITICAL ECONOMY

Gladstone's meeting with George Potter's deputation of artisans early in 1868 had exemplified the idea, which lay at the heart of the minority report, that unwise or anti-social union practices should be met by persuasion and argument rather than by legal penalties or disabilities. He told the London craftsmen that many of their rules were damaging to themselves: restrictions on the employment of women, for example, harmed their own wives and daughters, while rules limiting output 'go to diminish the aggregate amount of the fund which constitutes the whole wages of the country'. Some craft restrictions upon labour were positively immoral, by 'refusing to make God's gifts go as far as He intended them to go'. Yet, as the previous chapter has indicated, the Liberal leader did not deny the unionists' right to combine to do any of these things, nor did he think their associations should be disadvantaged on that account.[84] This became a widely held position among Liberal politicians. Two such exponents were W. E. Forster and G. J. Goschen, representatives of the types of middle-class Liberal politicians assuming a leading role in Gladstone's first administration.[85] Those

---

[82] Matthew, *GD*, vii. 73 (24 May 1869); *Daily Telegraph* (14 Apr. 1869), 4; *Spectator* (24 Apr. 1869), 505.

[83] Comte de Paris, *Trades' Unions of England*, 23, 228, 198.

[84] *The Times* (19 Feb. 1868), 10–11; *Spectator* (22 Feb. 1868), 219; Matthew, *GD*, v. xli–xlii; vi. 575–6 (15 Feb., 18 Feb. 1868); Gladstone seems to have been unmoved by the critique of the wage fund theory contained in Fleeming Jenkin's, 'Trade-Unions: How Far Legitimate', *North British Review*, 48 (March 1868), which he read shortly before meeting the deputation.

[85] Forster in 3*H* clxxxv. 201 (8 Feb. 1867); Goschen in 3*H* clxxxv. 518 (18 Feb. 1867); J. Parry, *The Rise and Fall of Liberal Government in Victorian Britain* (1993), 228–9.

Liberals, such as Goschen, who had been involved in the campaign for the repeal of religious tests at the ancient universities, were receptive to the assertion, skilfully deployed by Harrison, that it was as foolish to attempt to enforce economic truth by law as it was to enforce religious truth.[86] Both the broad churchman Forster and the latitudinarian promoter of bills for tests repeal, J. D. Coleridge (who became solicitor-general in Gladstone's government), argued that economic error should not stand in the way of full legal recognition.[87]

Some political economists shared this aversion to the use of their science to justify laws hostile to unionism. Even so determined a critic of the 'pestilent principle of combination' as the Dumbartonshire calico printer and economic writer, James Stirling, believed that 'it is no good reason to outlaw men, that they are bad political economists'. G. K. Rickards similarly criticized the majority report's notion of the state operating 'an economic censorship'.[88] Mill's recantation of the wage fund theory was the most timely statement of this position—it appeared in the *Fortnightly Review* of May and June 1869 as Harrison's proposals were being brought before parliament. Whatever Mill's intentions may have been from the point of view of economic science, the policy conclusion was clear enough: the state's attitude towards trade unions, as Thring had previously observed, could no longer be determined by political economy.[89] Mill went on publicly to align himself with the supporters of Harrison's report, declaring in an open letter

whatever still remains objectionable in the rules or practices of any of the unions may be left to public opinion and to the general laws of the country, and constitutes no reason whatever why trades' unions should be outlawed and denied any of the legal facilities enjoyed by other associations established for inoffensive or useful purposes.[90]

Once political economy had been disconnected from the law, contemporaries could be reconciled to unrestricted legalisation. This might have appeared a paradoxical development at a time when the Cobdenite legacy was felt more strongly than ever.[91] After the general election of 1868, however, it had ceased to be credible to regard trade unionists as a threat to free trade or to retrenchment in fiscal policy; indeed, the sheer scale of their

[86] F. Harrison, 'The Trades Union Bill', *Fortnightly Review*, n.s. 6 (July 1869), 31.

[87] *Bradford Review* (21 Sept. 1867), 7; *Daily News* (19 Oct. 1867), 3.

[88] James Stirling, *Unionism* (1869), 53; G. K. Rickards, 'Thornton on Labour', *Edinburgh Review*, 130 (Oct. 1869), 414–15.

[89] Mill, *Collected Works*, ed. Robson, vol. v (1967), 646.

[90] *Bee-Hive* (26 June 1869), 5.

[91] A. Howe, *Free Trade and Liberal England, 1846–1946* (1997), 111–16; Matthew, *GD*, xliv; *Quarterly Review*, 123 (Oct. 1867), 365.

expenditure on welfare was seen as lessening the demands on the poor rate.[92] A member of Gladstone's Cabinet, the duke of Argyll, had argued in 1866 in terms similar to Longe that when workers combined 'for the restriction of their own labour against the effects of unrestricted competition', they were not only taking the action suggested by 'reason and experience' but also that 'which Parliament has indicated as the right course both by what it has itself done, and by what it has declined to do'.[93] Combination became not merely an undeniable right; it was a legitimate and even necessary form of self-protection, as the Irish historical economist Cliffe Leslie concluded in 1868.[94] Free trade, J. D. Coleridge suggested, was a 'misleading cry' to direct against such associations; it confused restrictions on the labour market by voluntary institutions with external interference by the state.[95] In line with these political pronouncements, the Liberal press overwhelmingly supported the proposals of the minority report, criticizing the majority for being 'led astray by a dogmatic creed' and by 'abstract' lines of thought.[96]

Those who invoked free trade theories to oppose the minority report had become, by the summer of 1869, very rapidly isolated as a small group of Manchester School radicals at odds with the much of Liberal opinion. At the Social Science Association Congress in the previous autumn, Edmund Ashworth, vice-president of the Manchester Chamber of Commerce, had been a lone voice in opposing the principle of arbitration.[97] James Nasmyth, the Manchester engineer celebrated by Samuel Smiles, gave evidence to the Erle commission on the same day as Mundella. He described how he refused to meet his men collectively, preferred individual saving to the mutuality of benefit societies ('I think it is better for every man to be his own benefit club'), and urged that society would benefit from a wider diffusion of 'the Robinson Crusoe feeling'. It was, Henry Crompton commented, an expression of the 'individualist' theory in its 'most naked and repulsive form'.[98] Edmund Potter, the calico printer, president of the Manchester chamber of commerce, and Liberal MP for Carlisle, criticized the minority

---

[92] Biagini, *Liberty, Retrenchment, and Reform*, 100–7, 173–5; Ludlow and Lloyd Jones, *Progress*, 212; Wood, *Trade Unions Defended*, 8.

[93] Duke of Argyll [George Douglas Campbell], *The Reign of Law* (1867), 411–13.

[94] T. E. Cliffe Leslie, 'Political Economy and the Rate of Wages', *Fraser's Magazine*, 78 (July 1868), 93; Koot, *English Historical Economics*, 49.

[95] *Daily News* (19 Oct. 1867), 3.

[96] *Daily News* (26 Mar. 1869), 4; (2 Apr. 1869), 4; *Daily Telegraph* (27 Mar. 1869), 5; (14 Apr. 1869), 4; *Morning Star* (15 Apr. 1869), 4; *Pall Mall Gazette* (29 Mar. 1869), 1041–2; *Spectator* (27 Mar. 1869), 381–2.

[97] NAPSS, *Transactions, 1868*, 587–8.

[98] RCTU 10th Rep. Qs.19,160, 19,167; Crompton, 'Arbitration and Conciliation', 628.

report as being opposed to free trade and competition; capital and trade needed to be 'unfettered' rather than subjected to the restrictions imposed by organized labour.[99]

All three Manchester critics had reduced or given up their business involvement by the late 1860s (Nasmyth having done so in 1856) and it is questionable how representative they were.[100] Their isolation was shared by the Social Science Association, which had reached the peak of its influence upon the labour question at its conference in July 1868 but very rapidly waned thereafter. It ceased to engage the younger Liberals who had played a crucial part in drawing up the 1860 report and had now either joined the backbenches or else found official employment. As the likes of Hughes, Ludlow, and Lushington melted away, the Labour and Capital committee of the SSA fell into the hands of a predominantly Unitarian group of economists, Frederic Hill, W. B. Hodgson, and Jevons. They redirected the SSA towards William Ellis's project of the 1850s for the elementary teaching of political economy, exposing the folly of strikes, and insisting on the unity of interest of capital and labour, in the belief that these truths offered the surest guarantee of rational progress.[101]

Uncompromising individualist critiques of unionism were now increasingly identified with Conservatives, such as Stephen Cave, who insisted along with Booth and Bramwell that free trade was 'the normal condition of mankind'. Stafford Northcote hailed piecework as enabling the elevation of the individual while deploring trade unionism, which operated 'through the class'.[102] Gladstone was careful to distance himself and his government from such dogmatic economic views. He told Walter Morrison, the Liberal MP for Plymouth and one of George Howell's wealthy backers during the 1868 election campaign, that the Manchester School's opinions on unions were 'extreme' and 'sectional'.[103] Nevertheless, the Webbs were convinced that the Liberal government was hostile 'to the very principles of Trade Unionism'.[104] Their conclusion was based upon the prevarication of

---

[99] E. Potter, *Some Opinions on Trades' Unions and the Bill of 1869* (1869), 5, 13, 45; *Colliery Guardian* (18 June 1869), 588; 3*H* cxcvii. 1370–2 (7 July 1869).

[100] Their views were at variance with the actual industrial relations practice of cotton employers in the 1860s, A. Howe, *The Cotton Masters, 1830–1860* (1984), 164, 176, 178.

[101] *Lectures on Economic Science, Delivered under the Auspices of the Committee on Labour and Capital of the National Association for the Promotion of Social Science* (1870); W. A. C. Stewart and W. P. McCann, *The Educational Innovators, 1750–1880* (1967), 328–9; Goldman, *Science, Reform, and Politics*, 229–31.

[102] Smith, *Disraelian Conservatism*, 33; NAPSS, *Transactions, 1869*, 82, 21.

[103] Gladstone to Morrison, 5 July 1869, Matthew, *GD*, vii. 91; Parry, *Liberal Government*, 245.

[104] Webb, *History*, 274–5; E. S. Beesly, *Letters to the Working Classes* (1870), 19–21; *Glasgow Sentinel* (10 July 1869).

Gladstone's home secretary, H. A. Bruce, and the opposition by Edmund Potter and the Leeds nonconformist newspaper proprietor, Edward Baines, to a bill introduced by Thomas Hughes and A. J. Mundella to carry out the recommendations of the minority report.

Hughes and Mundella's bill 'to amend the law relating to trade combinations and trade unions' embodied the principles of unrestricted legalization and of no 'special legislation'—meaning penal laws—directed against unionists. Promoted at meetings convened by local trades councils, who helped to organize the 106 petitions presented to parliament in its favour, the bill was the occasion for a rally at Exeter Hall, London, at the end of June 1869, attended by several Liberal MPs and chaired by Samuel Morley.[105] Opposing this mounting pressure was a group of employer MPs marshalled by Alfred Mault of the General Builders' Association and Sidney Smith, secretary of the London Shipbuilders' and Engineers' Association, who urged Bruce to use his influence to get the bill withdrawn. What the employers feared, as some of the less discreet among them admitted, was the bill going to a division and their being forced to explain to their constituents why they had opposed it.[106] Bruce appeared to place himself on the side of the bill's opponents by telling a subsequent unionist deputation that they should not press on with it but wait for the government to prepare its own measure.[107]

Bruce believed that a government bill alone would be regarded as a nonpartisan settlement of the issue, but he lacked the departmental resources within the Home Office to have a measure drawn up in the 1869 session. Henry Thring's appointment to the new Office of Parliamentary Counsel in February 1869, leaving no immediate replacement at the Home Office, deprived Bruce of his key legal adviser at precisely the moment when the reports of the Erle commission were published, compounding his department's already large legislative arrears.[108] Bruce's objection to the Hughes–Mundella bill was not, in fact, related to its concession of unrestricted legalization. But he failed to convince a unionist deputation of the government's neutrality. As the second reading approached, there was a developing sense

[105] See the CAT pamphlet, *Final Reports of the Royal Commission on the Working of Trades' Unions with a Copy of the Trades Union Bill* (1869), 46–8; *Leeds Mercury* (26 May 1869), 4; *Manchester Guardian* (17 June 1869), 4; *Sheffield Independent* (13 May 1869), 3; *Votes and Proceedings of the House of Commons, 1868–9*, 369–635; *The Times* (24 June 1869), 12.

[106] *Colliery Guardian* (18 June 1869), 588; (14 May 1869), 467; GBA Minute Book, 1865–71, 126–7 (21 Apr. 1869); GBA Committee Minutes, 1865–71, 131 (1 July 1869); PRO HO46/42, 4 June 1869; *Builders' Trade Circular* (18 Nov. 1869), 14.

[107] *Bee-Hive* (3 July 1869), 5.

[108] B. Harrison, *Drink and the Victorians* (2nd edn., 1994), 242–3; Bruce to Gladstone, 19 Oct. 1869, BL Add MSS 44086, fos. 44–5.

of unease among those MPs who took a special interest in keeping labour within the Liberal fold. This was alleviated only after the Cabinet decision on 3 July 1869 to support the second reading of the bill with a reservation as to the clause repealing the criminal provisions of the 1825 Act against intimidation, which was Bruce's concern. That enabled William Rathbone, the Liverpool merchant and MP who had received Reform League support in the 1868 election, to bring Applegarth, George Howell, and Henry Crompton together with Bruce to repair the breach which had developed between the government and the representatives of labour.[109] Rathbone's intervention had the intended effect of convincing Howell and Crompton that their lobbying had caused the government to change its position, whereas the cabinet had already resolved to support the bill.[110]

The government's decision was in fact largely dictated by the judgment in the case of *Farrer v Close*, delivered by the Court of Queen's Bench on the day that the cabinet met. From facts confusingly similar to those of *Hornby v Close*, this case reaffirmed that a trade union was not entitled to the special remedies of the Friendly Societies Acts against fraudulent officials.[111] That the case involved Applegarth's Amalgamated Society of Carpenters and Joiners made it one of peculiar political sensitivity. It had begun its progress through the courts in February 1867, when an action was brought by the president of the union's Bradford branch against the branch secretary, William Close (no relation, apparently, to the boilermakers' official), for misappropriating £40 of the society's funds. While admitting the facts as proven, the Bradford borough bench had thrown out the case on the ground that the ASCJ's rules disclosed that one of its main purposes was that of a trade union, and that consequently it was an illegal society.[112] This was an opportunity for the amalgamated societies to test the effect of *Hornby v Close*, for their rule-books were far less explicit about their objectives than those of the boilermakers had been.[113] If the ASCJ was unable to withstand judicial scrutiny, no union could.

The court, which had been unanimous in 1867, was now divided, with two judges (Cockburn and Mellor) upholding the decision of the Bradford

---

[109] BL Add MSS 44637, fo.77; Matthew, *GD*, vii. 90–1.

[110] Harrison to Beesly, 3 July 1869, Harrison MSS 1/15; Crompton to Howell, 3 Dec. 1875, Howell MSS LB7, fo. 821; Howell, *Labour Legislation*, 176.

[111] *Farrar v Close* (1869) 4 LRQB, 602; Matthew, *GD*, vii. 90n.

[112] *Bradford Review* (16 Feb. 1867), 8; (8 Feb. 1868), 4. In Hull the police court magistrate had refused to issue summons against a defaulting trustee of the ASCJ, *Hull News* (9 Feb. 1867), 4.

[113] ASCJ, monthly report, Feb. 1867, 26; May 1867, 97; Feb. 1868, 43; Mar. 1868, 81; July 1869, 152.

JPs and two (Hannen and Hayes) adjudging that the ASCJ should have been allowed the benefit of the 1855 Act. The decision against the union was carried only by the convention that, in a divided court, the senior judges should prevail. Both sets of judgments reflected the influence of the contemporary debate, Cockburn referring approvingly to the comte de Paris's treatise.[114] Both also expressed an uncertainty about the public policy issues involved and acknowledged that they could not readily be resolved by purely legal reasoning. The argument of the two junior judges echoed a recent legal commentary, which had questioned the doctrine in *Hilton v Eckersley* that certain contracts, although 'not violating any rule of law', might be void on the ground of public policy. Such a doctrine, the textbook editors complained, was likely to 'degenerate into the mere private discretion of the majority of the court' on matters open to differences of opinion.[115] This was precisely what occurred in *Farrer v Close*. Regarding himself as bound by the earlier judgment, Cockburn conveyed his unease at the position in which he was placed, and invited parliament to make any changes to the law which might be thought necessary. At the same time, he defended the policy of the law which held that a society which supported strikes was illegal. In doing so he illustrated why some critics thought this inappropriate territory for judges to enter. Cockburn decided that the ASCJ was not entitled to the benefits of the 1855 Act because the evidence of its practice, as opposed to the rather opaque provisions of its rule-book, showed that its funds were used to support strikes. Some strikes, he asserted, were for 'honest and just' objects but others were 'unreasonable' and 'tyrannical'. But he offered no indication of how a court might, from purely legal principles, distinguish between the two.

Sir James Hannen and Sir George Hayes—both recent appointments to the bench—questioned why strikes should be regarded as restraints of trade. The trade of an employer might well be restrained by a strike, Hayes reflected, 'but it must remembered that the men are traders as well as the employers'. It would be 'an odd way of promoting freedom of trade' to treat as illegal the attempt of men supported by their own savings to get the best price they could for their labour.[116] In the same month as this judgment was delivered, the Political Economy Club discussed the question of whether the rule of English law against contracts in restraint of trade was in accordance with sound economic policy. Bagehot, a member of the club, wrote

---

[114] *Farrar v Close*, 4 LRQB 608.
[115] J. W. Smith, *A Selection of Leading Cases* (6th edn., 2 vols., 1867), ed. F. P. Maule and T. E. Chitty, i. 350.
[116] 4 LRQB 617.

shortly afterwards that it was not, since individuals themselves were best placed to decide whether or not it was in their interests to trade.[117]

Another approach to the problem was supplied by Sir James Hannen, the youngest judge and 'well known as a Liberal in politics'.[118] His remarks in *Farrer v Close* became much quoted as an authoritative statement against judicial intervention in this contested area:[119]

By the expression that a thing is contrary to public policy, I understand that it is meant that it is opposed to the welfare of the community at large. I can see that the maintenance of strikes may be against the interest of employers, because they may be thereby forced to yield at their own expense a larger share of profit or other advantage to the employed; but I have no means of judicially determining that this is contrary to the interests of the whole community; and I think that in deciding that it is, and therefore that any act done in its furtherance is illegal, we should be basing our judgment not on recognized legal principles, but on the opinion of one of the contending schools of political economists.

A decade earlier, Lord Campbell had expressed unease about having to form a judicial view of the Wigan cotton masters' bond: a noted (and even notorious) legal biographer, Campbell reflected on how 'different generations of Judges, and different Judges of the same generation, have differed in opinion upon questions of political economy'.[120] Hannen may have known of Mill's recantation; he was clearly aware of the weakening of former economic certainties and acknowledged the unsuitability of judicial reasoning as a basis for restoring them.

Hannen's judgment formed the basis of the government's own position, and was alluded to by Bruce in the second reading debate.[121] Bruce committed the government to upholding the neutrality of the law in this area of economic policy. The Hughes–Mundella bill was withdrawn, on the promise that the Home Office would bring in a measure within these terms of unconditional legalization during the next session. Cheers recorded by a backbench diarist as the bill passed its second reading conveyed a palpable sense of relief that the House of Commons had successfully negotiated a delicate class issue.[122] Hostile employer-MPs were rescued from the

---

[117] *Political Economy Club*, vi. 90; 'The Trades Union Bill', *Economist* (10 July 1869), *Bagehot's Political Essays*, ed. N. St John Stevas (1974), viii. 34. Erle had anticipated this objection, based on the courts' earlier hostility to forestallers and regraters, by a reference to 'altered circumstances' (RCTU 11th Rep. lxix); cf. Hay, 'The state and the market in 1800'.

[118] E. Foss, *A Biographical Dictionary of the Judges of England* (1870).

[119] 4 LRQB 613.

[120] *Hilton v Eckersley* (1855) 119 Eng. Rep. 788

[121] 3*H* cxcvii. 1380 (7 July 1869).

[122] T. Jenkins (ed.), 'The Parliamentary Career of Sir John Trelawny, 1868–73', *Camden Miscellany*, 32 (1994), 368 (7 July 1869).

prospect of a division, but at the cost of relinquishing the 'restrictionist' position which had been their characteristic object throughout the previous two years. Bagehot reflected that the period of applying 'abstract doctrines' to the question was now past.[123] A leader in *The Times*, whose author is now identifiable as the academic Liberal, G. C. Brodrick, offered a classic account of the attitude of the Victorian state towards autonomous social institutions: 'True statesmanship will seek neither to augment nor to reduce their [trade unions'] influence, but, accepting it as a fact, will give it free scope for legitimate development.'[124]

It was impossible in practice to withold the benefit of friendly society legislation from a society like the Amalgamated Carpenters, which evidently devoted so much of its funds to welfare purposes. A flurry of MPs, anxious to be seen to redeem electoral pledges, put down motions to provide special protection.[125] Supported by the Cabinet, Bruce instructed the parliamentary counsel 'to draw a short Bill giving security to the property of Trades Unions, without entering upon debateable ground'.[126] Lack of legal assistance again proved an embarrassment, for Thring was unable to produce a draft at short notice. It was left to Rathbone personally to instruct (and presumably pay) a barrister, the academic radical R. S. Wright, to prepare the necessary measure, which enabled Bruce to face parliament with a substantial proposal.[127]

A temporary Act 'to protect the Funds of Trades Unions from Embezzlement and Misappropriation' was put in force for twelve months from August 1869. Rules laying down the terms on which their members were willing to be employed were not to prevent unions from enjoying the powers of the 1855 Friendly Societies Acts to protect their funds, should they choose to deposit their rules. Not only were union funds fully protected but, as Godfrey Lushington wrote anonymously in *The Times*, the law was relieved 'of the stigma which attaches to it from the open conflict among the Judges as to the everyday rights of workmen'.[128] Although members of the government were adamant that the temporary measure, hurriedly enacted, was not an attempt to recognize unions by 'a side wind', there was little doubt that it was a rejection of the recommendations of the

---

[123] *Bagehot's Political Essays*, viii. 35; for Bagehot's rhetorical tendency to characterize the classical school as 'abstract' see J. K. Ingram, 'Political economy', in *Encyclopaedia Britannica*, 9th edn., vol. xix (1885), 396–7.

[124] *The Times* (8 July 1869), 8; Harris, *Private Lives*, 181, 184.

[125] *House of Commons Notices of Motions, 1869*, 1617, 1632.

[126] Liddell to Hamilton (Treasury), 9 July 1869, PRO HO36/37, p. 93; PRO T13/8, p.125; Matthew, *GD*, vii. 93 (10 July 1869).

[127] E. Rathbone, *William Rathbone: A Memoir* (1905), 234; *Bee-Hive* (13 Feb. 1875), 1–2.

[128] *The Times* (19 July 1869), 9.

majority report.[129] Lord Chief Justice Cockburn, who saw in the temporary Act a response by parliament to his plea for a statement of policy, placed a broad interpretation upon the intention behind the measure when an embezzlement case concerning the Kidderminster Power Loom Carpet Weavers came before the Court of Criminal Appeal in January 1870.[130] Even though that society had not registered its rules, and had proceeded by the ordinary criminal law, Cockburn saw in the recent legislation an 'intimation' by parliament that all such unions, even though their rules might be in restraint of trade, should enjoy the protection of the law.

It fell to Tidd Pratt, in his last report as registrar of friendly societies, to record the legal and parliamentary transactions during the summer of 1869 that broke down the barrier—which he had for so long striven to uphold—against trade unions coming within the law.[131] Economic considerations had been severed from legal ones; objections grounded in political economy were no longer to stand in the way of the recognition of unions as lawful institutions.

---

[129] 3*H* cxcviii. 1070 (2 Aug. 1869).

[130] *R v Stainer* 11 Cox CC 488.

[131] Report of the Registrar of Friendly Societies in England, 1868 (*PP* 1868–9 lvi), 76–105 (dated 23 July 1869). Pratt objected to assuming the burden of registering trade unions, as provided for by the Hughes–Mundella bill: Pratt to Knatchbull Hugessen, 14 Apr. 1869, PRO HO45/8202.

5
Trade Unions Legalized

In July 1869 the Liberal government had committed itself to allowing trade unions a recognized legal status on one condition only, that their objectives were not actually criminal. The resulting Trade Union Act of 1871 removed the civil disabilities attached to unions and gave them a formally recognized status. At the time, and to an extent also in historical writing, the nature of this development was overshadowed by the controversial questions of criminal law (discussed in Chapter 6). These diverted attention from some crucial policy decisions taken within the Home Office to determine what form of corporate existence, if any, unions were to have, and what legal powers and liabilities should be conferred on them, to secure the objective which all parties claimed to espouse, of placing unions in a position of equality.

Although many contemporaries, including Gladstone himself, took an optimistic view of unions, and proclaimed the signs of improvement discernible among them, the official argument for legalization was not ultimately founded upon any of these hopeful expectations: rather, it was simply the recognition of an existing social fact. This position was adopted by Lord Stanley, soon to succeed as 15th earl of Derby. In a speech at the opening of a trades hall in Liverpool in October 1869 he brought Conservative thinking into line with the Liberal government's stated intentions. His own preference for reconciling capital and labour was co-operative proprietorship, but in the meantime he acknowledged the popularity of unions among working men as undeniable, and combination as something which 'Englishmen' regarded as 'morally their right'. The only control that could properly be imposed upon unionism was the public opinion of all classes in England, which favoured 'fair play and individual freedom'. If unionism failed to embody those principles, then it would fail.[1]

---

[1] *The Times* (6 Oct. 1869), 10; J. Vincent (ed.), *A Selection from the Diaries of Edward Henry Stanley, Fifteenth Earl of Derby (1826–93), between September 1869 and March 1878* (1994), 36–7.

CLUBS OR CORPORATIONS?

One way of giving unions a status in law was, as Thring had suggested in 1867, to confer on them full legal personality, by permitting them to register under the Companies Acts and to acquire the powers and liabilities of joint stock companies. Alternatively, legalization might take a more limited form, treating unions essentially as clubs, but allowing them to assume some of those characteristics of corporations which had been extended to voluntary associations through the Friendly Societies Acts.[2]

Both reports of the Erle commission favoured the latter option: the majority because, apparently, they never considered incorporation; the minority because they were determined to avoid it.[3] The two bills prepared by the unions' legal advisers, Crompton, Harrison, and Lushington in 1867 and 1869 conferred only limited corporate powers. Partial legalization envisaged unionism as resting on what the 1869 bill's promoters described as 'mutual voluntary agreement, not on any form of legal compulsion'— hence the absence of provisions enabling unions to proceed against their members, or be proceeded against, in matters of subscriptions and benefits.[4]

Within the contemporary trade union movement there were two strands of opposition to what was otherwise a generally agreed position. Some of the Sheffield metal trades demanded that union agreements with their members should be legally enforceable: the outrages inquiry commission was told that, deprived of a legal remedy, men might be driven to criminal means to enforce their contracts. Sir William Erle had previously raised this argument in his minority judgment in *Hilton v Eckersley*, and it was treated sympathetically by William Overend, the barrister who conducted the Sheffield inquiry.[5] The aims of the Sheffield unionists went beyond this for they sought to revive the guild-type regulations, enjoying the sanction of the state, which had been exercised by the Cutlers' Company until their repeal in 1814.[6] The Sheffield men's conception of unionism armed with legal powers to regulate trade was opposed to the voluntarism which underlay the more widespread support for a minimal form of legalization.

The issue was fought out during the general election campaign of 1868 in Sheffield when Mundella, who put forward his voluntary system of industrial conciliation, had the support of the Sheffield branches of the national

² D. Lloyd, *The Law Relating to Unincorporated Associations* (1938), 59, 84.
³ RCTU 11th Rep. lix–lx.
⁴ FSIF, annual report, Jan.–Dec. 1868, xii; cf. ASCJ, monthly report, Nov. 1867.
⁵ Pollard, *Sheffield Outrages*, Qs.2063–8; 13, 241–2, 15, 372a.
⁶ Pollard, 'The Ethics of the Sheffield Outrages', 137.

unions.[7] Both his opponents, the Conservative E. P. Price, and Roebuck, exploited the sense among the local societies in Sheffield that their interests were being overlooked and came out in favour of enforceable agreements— entirely opportunistically, for neither indicated any ideological disposition towards guilds as a form of industrial organization.[8] Nevertheless, Frederic Harrison and Henry Crompton took the matter seriously enough to write public letters warning the Sheffield unionists of the hazards to which they were exposing themselves. Their intervention persuaded William Dronfield, secretary to the Sheffield trades delegates, to retract his earlier opinions in favour of unions acquiring full legal rights.[9] With the defeat of Price and Roebuck, the Sheffield ideal was deprived of political support, and largely disappeared from the debate until briefly revived in 1875 by Lord Robert Montagu, the Conservative Irish Home Rule MP and convert to Roman Catholicism. Montagu, a critic of *laissez-faire* and freedom of contract arguments, favoured allowing unions legal powers to coerce their members as a means of protecting the trades which they represented from unrestricted competition.[10]

Among Scottish unions there was a more widespread and persistent demand for enforceability, though it derived from a less ambitious conception of the role of unionism than was the case in Sheffield.[11] Some Scottish unions kept their trade and benefit funds distinct, and benefits were treated as legally recoverable. In the Scottish courts, actions were successfully brought both for the payment of benefits and of arrears of subscriptions.[12] The Edinburgh Trades Council described the CAT's Trade Societies bill of 1868 as 'totally inadequate', a view shared by a meeting convened in Edinburgh in 1869 to consider the Hughes–Mundella bill.[13] A similar resolution, discussed by the Glasgow Trades Council, was rejected by only one vote. In February 1870, at a conference on trade union law organized by Edinburgh Trades Council, Charles Scott, an Edinburgh advocate, drew up a bill in opposition to the English proposals, permitting

---

[7] *Sheffield Independent* (5 Nov. 1868), 3.
  [8] *Sheffield Times* (7 Nov. 1868), 5; (10 Oct. 1868), 6; *Report of the Speeches of John A. Roebuck Esq together with Mr Roebuck's Answers to the Questions on Trades' Unions* (1868), 19.
  [9] Their letters, addressed to Applegarth, were reprinted in *Sheffield Independent* (21 Oct. 1868), 4; (13 May 1869), 3.
  [10] 3*H* ccxxiv. 1685–6 (10 June 1875); ccxxv. 652–6 (28 June 1875).
  [11] Evidence of John Proudfoot, RCTU 4th Rep. Q.8143.
  [12] *Reformer* (2 Jan. 1869), 8, (23 Jan. 1869), 8; (29 May 1869), 6; (19 June 1869), 7.
  [13] I. MacDougall (ed.), *Minutes of Edinburgh Trades Council 1859–73* (1968), 211; *Reformer* (15 May 1869), 3.
  [14] *Glasgow Sentinel* (29 May 1869); *Scotsman* (9 Feb. 1870), 3; (10 Feb 1870), 8; *Reformer* (12 Feb. 1870), 4, 8.

unions to sue and be sued as corporate bodies.[14] So marked did the division between Scots and English interests become that, reportedly, no Scottish delegates attended the third Trades Union Congress, held in London in 1871.[15] As in Sheffield, Crompton warned the Edinburgh trades that if they persisted in pressing their demands for unlimited legalization, with power to sue and be sued, they would be 'pulling the house down on their own heads'.[16]

Crompton and Harrison were concerned not simply that incorporation would expose unions to actions brought by members or outsiders. They regarded it as an inappropriately rigid form of legal status for voluntary associations. Apart from limiting the purposes for which unions could exist, incorporation presented a particular hazard by exposing them to liability for winding-up; a court could effectively break up a union against the will of its members. It was these drawbacks, of course, which recommended incorporation to writers such as Creed and Williams.[17]

Incorporation found its most energetic advocate in Edward William Cox, a serjeant-at-law and publishing entrepreneur who owned a string of periodicals including the *Law Times*, which he used as a platform for his schemes.[18] A relentless critic of the shortcomings of the bar, he turned his attention to the abuses of trade unions, devising a counter-proposal to the CAT's Trades Societies bill, which he criticized as 'tending to encourage the illegitimate exercise of the power that belonged to combination'.[19] Cox proposed to give all trade unions a corporate existence, based on the Companies Acts, requiring them to frame articles of association, defining —and limiting—their objects. An incorporated union could sue and be sued in its corporate name, and enter into contracts with employers on wages and conditions, allowing arbitration awards to be enforceable. Decision-making in unions was to rest with a council elected by the members, the union being 'liable in damages for injury done to any person in pursuance or in consequence of the votes or proceedings of the council'.[20] When the idea was discussed at the Bristol meeting of the Social Science Association, in 1869, G. J. Holyoake complained that Cox's plan would re-

[15] *Reformer* (18 Feb. 1871), 5.

[16] Letter from Crompton, 19 May 1869, *Reformer* (29 May 1869), 6.

[17] Creed and Williams, *Handicraftsmen*, 35; NAPSS, *Transactions, 1867*, 693–4; *Pall Mall Gazette* (19 Sept. 1867), 1014.

[18] On Cox see R. Cocks, *The Foundations of the Modern Bar* (1983), 64–77; C. C. Watkins, 'Edward William Cox and the Rise of Class Journalism', *Victorian Periodicals Review*, 15 (1982), 87–93.

[19] *Law Times*, 45 (10 Oct. 1868), 428.

[20] *Law Times*, 46 (13 Feb. 1869), 284; 47 (26 June 1869), 155; 47 (10 July 1869), 196; 48 (12 Feb. 1870), 290.

quire unions 'to observe rules prescribed by the law, and that would fetter their free action'. Cox described the objection as 'the very reason' for his scheme.[21]

Cox was elected Conservative MP for Taunton in 1868 and intended to bring in his bill as a private measure, but parliament never had the opportunity to debate it. The author of a standard manual on election law, Cox suffered an ignominiously premature termination to his political career when he was unseated on petition early in 1869. An outsider in public affairs, he found no one else to take up his bill in the House of Commons.[22] His ideas did resurface in a pamphlet circulated by an anonymous barrister as the Hughes–Mundella bill approached its second reading, critically itemizing the ways in which the bill shielded unions from being proceeded against or wound up.[23] It drew from Harrison a candid statement of the reasons for not bringing unions fully within the law.

Harrison discredited incorporation as a policy option by arguing that it would turn private interests into matters of public regulation. Unions owed their existence to the spontaneous activity of their members and not to the will of the state. Yet corporations were deemed to exist only by virtue of permission granted by the state, and their powers were limited to those specified in the articles of association approved by the official registrar. It followed that to incorporate unions would involve re-constituting them: 'You must provide a machinery for forming them, for regulating their life, and for winding them up.' This they would never submit to, and the attempt to enforce it would lead to 'interminable controversy', with the implied danger—which many of his readers would have recognized—that contested class questions would intrude upon politics. He presented his plan as offering the prospect of an equitable and defensible settlement. It would be wrong, for example, to allow unions to be wound up without allowing them to sue for subscriptions and, if their internal agreements became enforceable, the courts of law and equity would find themselves enforcing 'rules as petty and vexatious as those of a drinking club'. 'Unions', he insisted, 'are clubs which desire to manage their own affairs, and which neither the State nor the courts can manage for them'.[24]

---

[21] *Law Times*, 47 (16 Oct. 1869), 432; NAPSS, *Transactions, 1869*, 606–7; *Western Daily Press* (6 Oct. 1869).

[22] H. F. A. Davis, 'Trades' Union Legislation', *Law Magazine*, 28 (Feb. 1870), 318.

[23] [A Barrister], *Trades Unions Bill, 1869: Observations upon the Law Affecting Combinations and Trades Unions* (1869), 36–7, 47–8, 54–6.

[24] *Morning Star* (6 July 1869), 5.

DRAFTING THE GOVERNMENT BILL

Once the momentary political crisis of early July 1869 was resolved, the trade union question was removed from the Cabinet's concerns until January 1871, when Bruce was ready to bring his bill forward. Responsibility now reverted to the Home Office, where Bruce and Godfrey Lushington, who in October 1869 had succeeded Thring as Home Office counsel, had together formed the outlines of a measure by December.[25] J. D. Coleridge, the solicitor-general, was also involved but contemporaries believed, rightly, that Lushington undertook most of the preparation.[26] A former fellow of All Souls College, Oxford, and one of the mid-Victorian 'lights of liberalism', Lushington was, like Henry Crompton, his fellow Positivist, the son of a judge. Prior to his elevation to the bench, Lushington's father had been a radical MP and anti-slavery campaigner, and his influence might be detected in Lushington's campaigning zeal for 'free labour' in its collective form.[27] Since his involvement in the Social Science Association's inquiry into unions and strikes, Lushington had been publicly identified with the legal aims of the unions. His contribution in 1867 on labour law to the second volume of academic liberal reform essays presented an almost millenarian vision of the prospects for unionism after the franchise had been extended and unequal laws against working people eliminated. Once unions became recognized by the law and public opinion, their laudable characteristics—public-spiritedness, mutuality, and 'heroic struggles for the good of their order'—would be acknowledged, and 'society' would come to welcome every addition to their strength.[28] Such exuberant public expressions of the Comtist belief in a new moral order heralded by the legal and social emancipation of the working class, ceased with his appointment to the Home Office. Indeed, he became known for his scrupulous impartiality and rectitude. Lushington evidently kept his recent associates as advisers to the CAT in the dark about the progress of the department's deliberations.[29] With official position, moreover, came a

---

[25] Bruce to his wife, 8 Dec. 1869, in *Letters of Henry Austin Bruce* (2 vols., 1902) i. 293; E. H. Coleridge, *Life and Correspondence of John Duke, Lord Coleridge* (2 vols., 1904) ii. 200; Bruce to Gladstone, 30 Jan. 1871, BL Add MSS 44087, fo. 10.

[26] A. D. Murray (ed.), *John Ludlow: The Autobiography of a Christian Socialist* (1981), 302; Harrison, *Before the Socialists*, 289.

[27] Harvie, *Lights of Liberalism*, 167–8; S. M. Waddams, *Law, Politics, and the Church of England: The Career of Stephen Lushington, 1782–1873* (1992).

[28] G. Lushington, 'Workmen and Trade Unions', in *Questions for a Reformed Parliament* (1867).

[29] J. Pellew, *The Home Office, 1848–1914* (1982), 19–20; see E. S. Beesly's inaccurate speculations in *Letters to the Working Classes* (1870), 21n.

more guarded view of the likely results of legalization. He prefaced the Home Office's plan, in January 1870, with the observation:[30]

Any legislation, it is assumed, would be based upon the view that Trade Combinations are social institutions having large capabilities of being serviceable and likewise of being mischievous; and that these opposite capabilities are so blended that ... it is impossible for the law to assist what is useful without at the same time lending its sanction to abuses.

In future, the relation of the law towards them was to be 'one of neutrality'.

Lushington had already compiled for the Home Office's use an exhaustive memorandum which reviewed the statute and case law bearing upon trade unions and demonstrated that the law was neither impartial nor consistent. One of the lengthiest passages was devoted to an historical survey which sought to demolish Erle's assertion that 'since the earliest times' the common law had upheld a free course of trade. At All Souls, Lushington had been one of the young reformers who forced the implementation of a new requirement that fellows should be elected on the basis of an examination in jurisprudence and modern history. His response to Erle now drew upon the light which those two academic disciplines shed upon one another. To test the truth of Erle's thesis, he insisted that 'the only guide is history'. Lushington's researches demonstrated that, far from enforcing a consistent view of economic relations across all periods, judicial enunciations of the common law 'varied according to the philosophy, politics, and political economy of the period'.[31] It followed, then, that the obstacles to legalizing unions rested upon no universal principle.

Lushington discussed the position of trade unions as institutions under the heading of 'civil disabilities', suggesting the purely emancipatory sense in which he approached legalization. His scheme largely followed the argument of Harrison's minority royal commission report, by laying out a form of legalization which would remove the various disabilities to which unions were exposed, and enable them safely to enter into what he called 'subsidiary' contracts, such as acquiring premises or employing staff. At the same time, all their 'primary' contracts, such as rules laying down the terms on which members were to work, subscriptions, fines for violations of rules, and welfare benefits were to remain unenforceable and therefore irrecoverable. To contemporaries, this approach to the relations between unions and their members was perhaps the most controversial aspect of the eventual

---

[30] G. Lushington, 'Memorandum on the Proposed Trade Combination Bill' (21 Jan. 1870), 1 (OPC Bills and Memoranda (HJ) 1871, 805–20).

[31] G. Lushington, 'Law of Trade Unions' (27 Dec. 1869), 43 (OPC Bills and Memoranda (HJ) 1871, 747–804).

legislation, and the one which proved most vulnerable to criticism after 1871. It posed the most difficult problems in terms of achieving a solution which could be seen to be 'neutral'.

Lushington's plan, like the previous bills sponsored by the London trades, treated the good rules as equally unenforceable as the bad, a difficulty which Thring had tried to address in 1867, when he suggested that members should be allowed to recover welfare benefits at law. Since then, the unions' successful resistance to separation of their trade and benefit funds had made it practically impossible to give members rights to benefits. If unions were liable to be sued for benefits, they had to be given the reciprocal power to recover subscriptions, but those subscriptions might be applied to support objectives highly averse to the 'public good'.[32] But the argument against making welfare benefits recoverable ultimately rested on the understanding that a union's primary purpose was the regulation of trade. So long as its funds were liable at any time to be applied to strikes, a union's solvency as a welfare provider could never be guaranteed and no legal entitlement to welfare benefits could prudently be created.

Lushington's memorandum disposes of the speculation that legislators were misled by the 'labour lobby'—and Harrison's minority report in particular—into believing that unions were evolving into friendly and benefit societies and therefore qualified to enjoy the legal 'privileges' accorded to those societies.[33] Many objections might be laid against the Home Office's policy of limiting the legal liabilities to which unions were exposed, but this is one of the least credible of them. Lushington was under no misapprehension as to the primary purposes of a trade union, as his discussion of internal contracts showed. And far from overlooking the evidence of potential union insolvency, which has been held to have undermined the unions' case, Lushington addressed it directly. It was the basis for one of his recommendations, that the provisions of the Joint Stock Companies Acts and the Friendly Societies Acts should not apply to unions because of their inability to fulfil the requirements placed upon those two forms of association. If the amalgamated unions were brought under the Companies Acts there was a real possibility that, on the basis of the evidence to the Erle Commission supplied by the government actuary showing that their reserves were inadequate to meet future liabilities, a judge could impose a winding-up order.[34] Incorporation in these circumstances was inappropri-

---

[32] Lushington, 'Law of Trade Unions', 50.

[33] Hanson, 'Craft unions', esp. 247; cf. the remark of the earl of Morley, who spoke on Home Office matters in the House of Lords, that unions did not wish to be treated as friendly societies, 3*H* ccv. 1918 (1 May 1871).

[34] Lushington, 'Proposed Trade Combination Bill', 7–8.

ate for two reasons: a union was not a commercial insurance company; and, being a voluntary association, a union had access to resources unavailable to a joint stock company by way of levies of members when a financial crisis arose, and this offered the best prospect of liabilities being met.

A more manifestly weak point in Harrison's minority report lay in its promises of publicity, through voluntary registration, and the security that this was supposed to offer the public for the conduct of unions. Lushington agreed with Harrison that 'nothing would so much tend to improve the character of Trade Unions as publicity and regularity in their proceedings', but differed from him in regarding registration as likely to be worthless in bringing this about.[35] If registration carried a serious obligation to submit to scrutiny, unions would simply not register; conversely, a simple requirement to deposit rules and accounts would represent a negligible check against malpractice. As the defiant expressions of the union secretaries had shown, their societies did not need even the limited corporate rights which registration would confer since, like the gentlemen's clubs of London, they held property through trustees. Although summary remedies against fraud were useful to them, their funds were already protected by other means. Lushington's conclusion, that there should be no registration, was overruled, presumably by Bruce, and possibly on the ground that parliament, by approving the principle of the civil provisions of the Hughes–Mundella bill, had been assured that such a system would be put in place.

On the question of accountability to the public, Lushington considered that 'with a Trade Union ... the great danger is infringement of the Criminal Law', by which he meant violence and intimidation carried out in the course of a strike, and this priority was generally shared by contemporaries.[36] Posterity, after the Taff Vale judgment in 1901, was more interested in the question of whether legislators in 1871 had considered the possibility of attaching civil liabilities to unions. Writing in 1901, Lushington insisted that the judgment was contrary to the intention of those who framed the 1871 Act: 'at the time it was not dreamt of'.[37] The possibility of making unions financially responsible for their actions was never addressed in the proceedings of the Erle commission, in the parliamentary debates, or in Lushington's own memoranda, though thirty years earlier Archibald Alison had suggested that unions might be proceeded against through their office-holders, an idea that resurfaced following the Sheffield outrages.[38]

---

[35] Ibid. 8–9.   [36] Ibid. 11.

[37] G. Lushington, 'Trade Unions and the House of Lords', *National Review*, 33 (Dec. 1901), 562.

[38] SCCL (1837–8), Qs.1967–8; *Pall Mall Gazette* (19 Sept. 1867), 1013; *Daily News* (24 Dec. 1867), 4.

Lichfield, Hughes, and Harrison's dissent to the Erle commission's final
report reaffirmed the liability of individuals for their actions, though E. W.
Cox had objected that an individual would not be worth suing and proposed, by incorporating unions, to make them liable to civil actions for
torts.[39]

Cox's contention had been borne out by a case in 1868. An action was
brought in Chancery by the Springhead Spinning Company, which owned
a mill near Oldham. The company sought an injunction restraining the
president and secretary of the Oldham spinners from publishing placards
and placing advertisements in the press, exhorting prospective hands to
stay away from the firm while its own workforce was on strike. Damages for
loss of profits, estimated at £178 per week during the course of the strike,
were also sought.[40] The bill of complaint filed against the two officials
admitted the difficulty of recovering damages from an organization having
numerous members but no legal personality. It made the case for an injunction to prevent further damage being done precisely because of the
inability of 'these working men'—stereotypical men of straw, one of whom
reputedly kept the paperwork of the Oldham spinners' union in the lining
of his hat—to make recompense.[41] Although an interim injunction was immediately granted by Sir Richard Malins, neither the union nor the police
were able to restrain crowds of up to 5,000 who gathered to jeer the handful
of strikebreakers.[42] When Malins finally delivered judgment, on 31 July
1868, the dispute had been settled through the mediation of the Anglican
incumbent of the parish in which the mill was situated, and the proceedings
for damages were dropped.[43]

That an employer had no effective remedy in such a case was pointed out
by the anonymous barrister who attacked the Hughes–Mundella bill, and
also by the capital and labour committee of the Social Science Association
which in March 1870 proposed that union funds be liable for indemnifying
anyone wronged in 'person, earnings, or property' by the actions of a union.
A year later the same committee complained in a memorial to the Home
Office that the Trade Union bill made no such provision.[44] By then the
Social Science Association carried no political weight on this issue and the

[39] RCTU 11th Rep. xxxi (para. 4); *Law Times* 47 (10 July 1869), 196.
[40] *Springhead Spinning Company (Limited) v Riley* (1868) 37 Law Journal Reports
Chancery, 889; Orth, *Combination and Conspiracy*, 133.
[41] Bill of Complaint, 30 Mar. 1868, PRO C16/528/S92; on Riley, *DLB*, vii. 9.
[42] *Oldham Chronicle* 25 Apr. 1868, 5; 20 June 1868, 5; 27 June 1868, 5.
[43] *Law Times* (31 Oct. 1868), 466; *Spectator* (8 Aug. 1868), 928–9; E. S. Beesly in ASCJ,
monthly report, Sept. 1868, 241–2.
[44] [A Barrister], *Trades Union Bill*, 35; NAPSS, *Sessional Proceedings, 1869–70*, 259; ibid.,
1870–71, 348.

Home Office ignored its representations. While Lushington was not quite accurate in his recollection that no one had considered civil liability in 1871, it was not promoted by any significant political or industrial interests, and was not a specific consideration in the decision to perpetuate an essentially extra-legal status for unions.

Incorporation still found adherents, though for reasons largely separate from the question of civil liability. As a result of an incident in the drafting process this option was nearly imposed upon the Home Office. Early in January 1870, shortly after Lushington's plan had been prepared, Tidd Pratt, the long-standing registrar of friendly societies, died.[45] There was now an opportunity for a radical reappraisal of official policy towards voluntary associations. In an article which drew directly upon Lowe's views on company legislation—so much so that it is hard to believe that he did not have a hand in it—*The Economist* proposed that the various privileges attached to friendly societies should be swept away, along with the existing system of registration. Instead, all clubs and societies should be entitled to become corporate bodies like joint stock companies. One advantage of replacing a system which favoured certain sorts of association with a neutral procedure of incorporation open to all would be, the article pointed out, to remove many of the problems of dealing with unions. A legal status could be provided for them without any suggestion of conferring special rights or privileges.[46]

Shortly before the article appeared, the unexpected discovery had been made that the right of appointment to Pratt's office lay not, as was assumed, with the Home Office but with Lowe, as Chancellor of the Exchequer.[47] Lowe had been silent on trade unions since autumn 1867, and now approached the status of voluntary associations as a critic of 'paternal interference' by the state through mechanisms such as those which favoured friendly societies. In February 1870 he announced that Pratt's place was not to be filled, and Treasury officials immediately set about dismantling the friendly society registry, preparing dismissal notices for the clerks and announcing savings of £1,500 a year in salaries.[48]

As Lowe set about breaking up the existing apparatus of regulation, the Home Office formally requested the Treasury to instruct the Office of the

[45] Hughes to Ludlow, 10 Jan. 1870, CUL Add 7348/20, fo. 1; Harrison to Beesly, 13 Jan. 1870, 18 Jan. 1870, Harrison MSS 1/16.

[46] *Economist* (15 Jan. 1870), 64.

[47] Lushington to Ludlow, 12 Jan. 1870; Forster to Ludlow 12 Jan 1870, Ludlow MSS Add 7348/20, fos. 2–3; Bruce to Gladstone, 14 Jan. 1870, BL Add MSS 44086, fo. 89.

[48] 3*H* cxcix. 156 (10 Feb. 1870); cf. Lowe's evidence to the Northcote Commission, Royal Commission on Friendly Societies 3rd Rep. (*PP* 1873 xxii), Q.28,237; Treasury minute, 28 Feb. 1870, PRO T1/6988A/14555/3907.

Parliamentary Counsel to draw up a Trade Union bill.[49] Lowe's influence was felt also at this stage, for the Office of the Parliamentary Counsel had been established at his instigation to ensure that legislation prepared on behalf of government departments was subject to Treasury supervision in respect of any financial implications. Accordingly any trade union measure would have to conform to the Treasury's overall arrangements for the civil service and to take account of the abolition of the friendly societies registry. The resulting draft prepared by Thring's assistant, Henry Jenkyns, and printed on 1 June 1870, departed in critical respects both from the minority report and Lushington's briefing documents. By registration unions would be accorded a full corporate status in terms lifted verbatim from the 1862 Companies Act. Recognized as a corporate entity, a union could be proceeded against in its registered name or be wound up in the same way as a joint stock company. An incorporated union was not, however, to be enabled to use the law to force members to comply with trade rules, nor could it recover subscriptions or fines from them. But implicitly a member was enabled to proceed against his union to recover benefits, a one-sided arrangement which embodied Lowe and Thring's earlier objectives.[50]

Even the mid-Victorian Treasury could not withstand the political pressure mobilized by the powerful friendly society lobby in and out of Parliament, and Lowe was forced to stand down. His proposed legislation to reorganize the registration of friendly societies was withdrawn. Responsibility for voluntary associations was restored to the home secretary, the wider issues relating to friendly societies being referred to a royal commission chaired by Stafford Northcote. In the meantime, the friendly society registry remained in temporary operation.[51] With the defeat of Lowe, the Home Office could revert to Lushington's earlier plan. The Treasury's intervention was of significance, however, for it demonstrated that legislators directly confronted the issue of full incorporation, and deliberately rejected it. As has been noticed elsewhere,[52] the 1871 legislation followed the wording of the Joint Stock Companies Act in several places, but omitted the crucial provisions for creating and winding up corporate bodies.

---

[49] A. F. O. Liddell to secretary of the Treasury, 9 Apr. 1870, PRO HO36/37, 241.

[50] 'Draft of a Bill for amending the Law relating to Conspiracy and Trade Societies', OPC Bills and Memoranda (HJ) 1871, 825–36.

[51] PRO T1/7236/17272(1)/17540.

[52] N. McCord, 'Taff Vale Revisited', *History*, 78 (1993), 247.

ENACTMENT AND OPERATION

When the bill was introduced in Parliament, in February 1871, Bruce acknowledged that it followed the recommendations of the minority report. Trade unions were no longer to be unlawful on the ground that their objects were in restraint of trade. They were to be given the opportunity to acquire 'qualified civil rights' enabling them to hold property and to have summary remedies against dishonest officials, in return for registering their rules and accounts with a public officer. Agreements between unions and their members relating to their terms of employment, subscriptions to union funds, and entitlement to benefits were to remain unenforceable.[53] These essential points were unaltered during the passage of the bill through parliament.

The actual effect of all this on unions and their activities was minimal: they were protected from the effects of hostile legal doctrines, but were left in other respects undisturbed. Hence George Odger's acknowledgement that it was 'a good and liberal Bill', and the TUC's resolution approving its general effect.[54] It was thus a defeat for those who had sought to use legal regulation to impose far-reaching alterations to union policies and structures. Not that such advocates pressed the point. The *Colliery Guardian*, representing the views of the Mining Association, complained that 'the whole scheme is, unfortunately, marred by the unions being enabled, if they think fit, to keep, as they now are, comparatively out of arm's reach of the law'.[55] Stephen Cave, formerly under-secretary at the Board of Trade under the Conservative administration, was apparently briefed by the General Builders' Association, and led the attack on the bill, while Sir George Elliot, a Conservative colliery owner, moved hostile amendments.[56] Neither succeeded in making a political issue out of their objections. Describing the bill as a 'reasonable solution', *The Times* supported the compromise which allowed unions 'to continue to be independent of the law'.[57] Even some employers' associations took this line, including the Associated Chambers of Commerce, in which Mundella played a prominent part, and the Sheffield and Glasgow chambers.[58] Having failed to arouse other employers, the *Colliery Guardian* admitted at the end of March 1871, 'we

[53] *The Times* (16 Feb. 1871), 5; 3*H* cciv. 266–7 (14 Feb. 1871).
[54] *The Times* (8 Mar. 1871), 5.
[55] *Colliery Guardian* (24 Feb. 1871), 202.
[56] 3*H* cciv. 2034 (17 Feb. 1871); *House of Commons Notices of Motions, 1871*, 456–7.
[57] *The Times* (17 Feb. 1871), 9; (1 Apr. 1871), 9.
[58] Association of British Chambers of Commerce, *11th Annual Report* (1871), ix; Sheffield Chamber of Commerce Minutes, LD 1986/1, p. 198 (9 Mar. 1871); *Appendix to the Reports of the Select Committee of the Commons on Public Petitions, 1871*, 103–4.

entertain no fundamental objections' to the bill.[59] Thereafter the energies of organized employers were diverted to the more controversial criminal provisions.

This consensus meant that the Home Office avoided any sustained parliamentary scrutiny of the measure. Since registration was not compulsory, no obligation was placed on the unions to publicize their rules-and accounts; indeed, unregistered unions need not even have rules or keep accounts. An amendment to require registration was opposed out of hand by Bruce, prompting the mover to complain that 'no reason had been assigned against it'.[60] Bruce's reticence concealed a recognition that, whether or not registration was desirable, the state was incapable of enforcing it. The conditions attached to registration were not onerous beyond the submission of a rule-book, a list of the names of the officers, and annual accounts—one of the few practical restrictions placed on unions was to limit their landholdings to one acre.[61] Elliot's amendment to require that rule-books should provide that, in all matters relating to 'the operations and funds of the union' decisions 'shall be arrived at by ballot', was never put to the vote.[62]

Bruce predicted that unions would have no objection to registering. Hoping to exploit his reliance on their co-operation, members of the TUC refused to register in protest at the criminal provisions of the 1871 legislation. If the Criminal Law Amendment bill was 'thrust upon us', Howell warned, the 'leading societies of the kingdom will refrain from Registration and thus render inoperative the entire Act'.[63] By the end of 1871 the TUC's determination remained solid, only two unions having registered.[64] But they had taken Bruce too much at his word, and assumed that the Home Office attached more importance to registration than, as Lushington's confidential memorandum had shown, was actually the case. Failure to register did not weaken Bruce's resolve on the criminal questions at issue. The only parties injured by the policy of non-co-operation were Liberal apologists for the unions, who had always contended that the openness with which they were willing to conduct their affairs was a guarantee that their

---

[59] *Colliery Guardian* (31 Mar. 1871), 340.

[60] 3 *H* ccv. 815–16 (28 Mar. 1871).

[61] A. Offer, *Property and Politics, 1870–1914* (1982), 80; for an unsuccessful request by Manchester and Salford Trades Council, 22 Dec. 1875, that the restriction be relaxed, see PRO HO45/9396/50218/2.

[62] *House of Commons Notices of Motions, 1871*, 457–8; the Railway Companies Association discussed the introduction of a provision for ballots, United Railway Companies Committee Minutes, 2 Mar. 1871, PRO RAIL 1098/2.

[63] Howell to Auberon Herbert, 22 Mar. 1871, Howell MSS LB6, fo. 229.

[64] Howell to Hodgson Pratt, 2 Dec. 1871, Howell MSS LB5, fo. 509; *Pall Mall Gazette* (16 Jan. 1874), 218.

power would not be abused. Among them was Mundella who vainly urged registration upon the TUC at Nottingham in 1872.[65]

Some unions objected to registering on the traditional ground that any such submission to official scrutiny was 'inquisitorial'. The persistence of this sentiment, and particularly the objection to making their financial state publicly known, probably explains why several long-established craft unions, including the flint glass makers, brushmakers, stonemasons, cordwainers, and cabinet-makers, failed to register even after the repeal (in 1875) of the contentious criminal legislation.[66] A majority of the 252 unions who had registered by the end of 1876 were founded in the 1870s.[67] They were the 'new' unions, products of the economic boom in the early years of the decade, often in trades where no tradition of union membership existed, and where the sanction of a government official might be presented as a guarantee to prospective, and possibly sceptical, members that their contributions were secure. The Amalgamated Society of Railway Servants, founded in 1871, was among the first to register.[68] More followed suit when it became clear, as Howell candidly advised a provincial official, that 'I cannot conceive that it will in any way hamper your actions'.[69] Indeed, so benign was the regulatory regime found to be that, by 1873, the TUCPC asked the Home Office to make technical changes to the registration procedure to meet the convenience of some of the larger societies who had found it advantageous to register.[70] Yet the absence of so many unions from the register ensured that data on their scale and objectives in the possession of governments after 1871 was scarcely more comprehensive than in the late 1850s, when Tidd Pratt first complained of the dearth.

TRADE REGULATION OR WELFARE PROVISION?

Having effectively ensured that unions would be free from executive interference, the 1871 settlement ensured that judges could not interfere in their internal affairs. It did so in a way that reflected the assumption stated in

[65] *Nottingham Daily Express* (11 Jan. 1872).

[66] W. P. Roberts, *The Trade Union Bill, 1871: A Letter* (1871), 5; A. E. Musson, *The Typographical Association* (1954), 342; *Bee-Hive* (18 Mar. 1871), 3.

[67] Reports of the Registrar of Friendly Societies in England, 1876 (*PP* 1877 lxxvii), Appx. R.

[68] Reports of the Registrar of Friendly Societies in England, 1871 (*PP* 1872 liv), 20; *Bee-Hive* (3 Feb. 1872), 4; P. Bagwell, *The Railwaymen: The History of the National Union of Railwaymen* (1963), 53.

[69] Howell to D. Stott, 5 July 1875, Howell MSS LB9 fo. 274.

[70] Howell to Lowe, 29 Aug., 29 Oct. 1873, Howell MSS LB8 fos. 140, 190; Winterbotham to Howell, 3 Oct. 1873, PRO HO136/10, p. 197.

Lushington's memoranda, that the provision of welfare was not the unions' primary purpose. Section 4 of the Act, which prevented courts from enforcing most contracts which unions entered into, perpetuated the extralegal status of union activities. The justification was, as Coleridge put it, that otherwise 'the Court of Chancery would be called upon to enforce strikes'.[71] Public opinion, one Sheffield newspaper explained, would never consent to trade union secretaries suing members in the county courts and distraining their goods and chattels.[72]

What was left unsaid was that members were deprived of a remedy against their union to recover welfare benefits. It was a subject on which both the Home Office and the TUC were notably sensitive. Reminded by the building employers in March 1871 that 'by virtue of this clause, trade unions are left in possession of very great coercive powers over their members', Bruce replied that men joined unions knowing that they were primarily trade, not benefit societies, and consented to the conditions of membership. Mault, who had very much the better of the exchange, doubted the degree of 'consent', forcing Bruce into an explicit admission: 'That is simply the present condition of things. We do not interfere in such matters one way or other.'[73] One dissident unionist, Mark Hayler Judge, president of the Wokingham branch of the ASCJ, who repeatedly embarrassed his executive by interventions in the press and at public meetings, presented a petition to parliament in 1871 urging that welfare benefits offered by trade societies should be legally recoverable.[74] His interruption to the proceedings of the TUC meeting in London caused Odger to bring the discussion to an abrupt close, pleading 'the lateness of the hour'. Judge's interventions were no more welcome at the Home Office, and Bruce declined to meet him.[75]

Actions were brought against union officers by disgruntled members claiming that they had been deprived of benefits to which they were entitled. They reinforced a sense that the compromise of 1871 had sacrificed individual rights and treated the welfare aspect of unionism as secondary to their purely industrial functions. In a case brought against William Allan, general secretary of the ASE, at Newcastle county court in 1873 by a member who sought to recover benefit for an injury sustained at work, the

---

[71] 3*H* cciv. 2045 (17 Feb. 1871).
[72] *Sheffield Daily Telegraph* (8 Mar. 1871).
[73] *Builders' Trade Circular* (16 Mar. 1871), 7.
[74] *Appendix to the Reports of the Select Committee of the Commons on Public Petitions, 1871*, 18.
[75] *South London Advertiser* (4 Mar. 1871, 25 Mar. 1871, 1 Apr. 1871); *The Builder* (19 Apr. 1873), 313.

union's solicitors did not attempt to answer the claim. They successfully argued, as union lawyers had done before 1871, that the court had no jurisdiction in the matter.[76] 'Each member is entirely at the mercy of the executive of his particular society', Mark Judge complained. When the apparent injustice was raised in parliament, Coleridge's brisk response betrayed a defensiveness: men who joined unions did so 'at their peril'.[77] The wording of the section was unambiguous and judges subsequently called upon to interpret the Act showed, in this period, no inclination to find ways round it. In 1874 a claim against the Scottish masons for accident benefit came before the lord justice clerk, Moncreiff, who had been lord advocate in Gladstone's administration. Admitting the case was one 'of considerable hardship', he nevertheless offered a well-informed account of the policy behind the 1871 Act. It would have been 'a singular thing' if the courts had been empowered to enforce trade rules, and though the welfare provisions of unions were 'meritorious and laudable', the two objects were 'so mixed up' that it was impossible to discriminate between the two.[78] In 1880, Sir George Jessel, formerly one of Gladstone's law officers, dismissed a claim for reinstatement by a member of the Journeyman Hatters expelled for transgressing trade rules on the ground that it was 'the manifest intention of the legislature' that he should not interfere.[79]

Yet if judges proved willing to leave unions to manage their own affairs, criticisms by organized employers, particularly after the return of a Conservative government in 1874, made the TUCPC nervous that the 1871 compromise was vulnerable to renewed challenge.[80] Hence Howell's protest against an innocuous government proposal in 1874 to repeal the Trade Union Act and re-enact it in a composite measure covering all voluntary associations.[81] A subsequent TUC deputation to the Chancellor of the Exchequer, Stafford Northcote, secured an undertaking that the legislative distinction between trade unions and friendly societies would be

---

[76] *Newcastle Daily Journal* (21 Dec. 1872); *Newcastle Daily Chronicle* (24 Mar. 1873), 3; *Law Journal* 8 (29 Mar. 1873), 185; cf. OSM FR 30 Jan. – 13 Feb. 1873, MRC MSS 78/OS/4/1/42; *Capital and Labour* (24 June 1874), 396.

[77] *The Builder* (19 Apr. 1873), 313; 3*H* ccxv. 221 (27 Mar. 1873); *Bee-Hive* (5 Apr. 1873), 2.

[78] *M'Kernan v United Operative Masons' Association of Scotland* (1874) Sessions Cases 4th scr. i. 460; cf. *Manners v Fairholme and Others* (1872) Sessions Cases 3rd scr. x. 520.

[79] *Rigby v Connol* (1880) 42 LTNS, 141; cf the comments of Sir Henry James, another law officer in Gladstone's first administration, in *Yorkshire Miners' Association v Howden* AC [1905], 275.

[80] *Capital and Labour* (25 Nov. 1874), 914; (1 Mar. 1876), 155; Iron Trades Employers Association, *The Piece-Work Question and a Report as to the Financial Position of the Amalgamated Society of Engineers* (1876).

[81] Howell, *Labour Legislation*, 352–3; *Bee-Hive* (20 June 1874), 8; (27 June 1874), 3, 7; Murray, *Ludlow*, 289–90.

maintained.[82] Further challenges from Scottish unions, some of whom had petitioned against the 1871 measure, were also repelled: motions at the Congresses held at Liverpool and Glasgow, in January and October 1875 respectively, that unions should be empowered to sue and be sued by their members were defeated.[83] Not all the Scottish unions supported the idea, however, and the English officials were unanimous against it, stressing that the primary object of unions was to protect labour rather than to provide and guarantee benefits.[84]

Probably unknown to the TUC, an attempt to reopen the status of unions was made by Ludlow, the newly appointed registrar of friendly societies, in a confidential paper circulated within the relevant government departments early in 1876. He disliked the severance of trade union from friendly society legislation, regarded the existing character of unions as 'transitory', and constantly advocated that they seek to develop less class-bound, 'broader' forms of association.[85] An anomaly in the definition of a trade union in the 1871 Act provided him with an opportunity to redraw the boundaries. In a section which had been considerably amended (though without debate) during its parliamentary passage, a union was defined as a combination which, if the Act had not been passed, would have been deemed to have been unlawful by reason of having purposes in restraint of trade. Any society seeking registration had effectively to demonstrate, for example, that its rules provided for strikes and would therefore be treated by the courts as 'illegal'. A well-informed commentator believed that the reason for this negative definition was simply to draw a line between unions and friendly societies for the purpose of registration.[86] It had the effect, though, of disqualifying from legal recognition certain types of association concerned with regulating working conditions such as Sunday Rest Associations and the Early Closing Association. Since they did not offer welfare

[82] Howell to Guile, 13 June 1874, Howell MSS LB7, fo. 501; Harrison to Howell, 22 June 1874, Howell MSS; *Bee-Hive* (21 Nov. 1874), 3–4; *The Times* (19 Nov. 1874), 6; (20 Nov. 1874), 12; H. F. A. Davis, *The Law and Practice of Friendly Societies and Trade Unions* (1876), 206.

[83] *Reformer* (18 Mar. 1871), 8; *Appendix to Public Petitions, 1871*, 116, 136, 149; *House of Commons Votes and Proceedings, 1871*, 241; MacDougall (ed.), *Edinburgh Trades Council*, 314. A. T. Innes, 'The Paradox in the Law of Trade Unions', *Law Magazine*, n.s. 4 (1875), 409–13, and 'The Common Law Status of Trade Unions', *Journal of Jurisprudence*, 18 (1874), 181, pointed out that unions had never been forbidden under Scots law, raising the question as to why their contracts should be treated as unenforceable.

[84] *Liverpool Daily Post* (20 Jan. 1875), 7; *North British Daily Mail* (13 Oct. 1875), 3.

[85] RCTU 11th Rep., vol. ii, Appx. E, 124 (5 July 1867); *Bee-Hive* (12 Aug. 1871), 2; J. M. Ludlow, 'Proposed Legislation in Reference to Companies and Friendly Societies', *Law Magazine*, n.s. 4 (1875), 130–1

[86] Guthrie, *Law of Trade Unions*, 11.

benefits, they could not register as friendly societies; but because they did not use the strike weapon they were not in restraint of trade and consequently fell outside the Trade Union Act.

In seeking permission from the Treasury to use his discretionary powers to allow such bodies to register under the Friendly Societies Acts, Ludlow suggested that those trade unions which offered welfare benefits might also come within that ambit. Possibly he had in mind the amalgamated societies, for even before 1871 the Court of Queen's Bench had been divided as to whether the ASCJ's rules were actually illegal. An even stronger example of an association standing on the boundary between trade union and friendly society legislation was the Amalgamated Society of Railway Servants (ASRS). Founded with the assistance of the brewer and Liberal MP, M. T. Bass and other progressive employers such as Thomas Brassey and Samuel Morley, the ASRS was established on the model of existing friendly societies for railwaymen, and promoted improvements in working conditions without resort to strikes.[87] Its avoidance of strikes in some ways mirrored the strategy of the Short Time Committee, which in 1872 turned away from industrial conflict to achieve reduced working hours, and instead promoted parliamentary agitation for factory legislation. Ludlow had doubts (confirmed by the opinion of the Crown law officers) whether his predecessor, the temporary registrar A. K. Stephenson, had acted correctly in permitting the railwaymen to register as a trade union under the 1871 Act.[88]

Ludlow contended that the 'best' of the trade unions were those which offered friendly benefits, since the latter acted as 'a strong check upon violent action', and he aimed to encourage the trend by blurring the statutory distinction between a trade union and a friendly society.[89] Administrative change might hasten a process which he had been urging upon the amalgamated societies, with limited success, for over two decades. On this occasion, his objectives were thwarted not by what he had once termed the labour movement's instinctive 'tory' opposition to innovation,[90] but by departmental considerations in Whitehall. His plans were briskly dismissed by the Board of Trade, whose permanent secretary, T. H. Farrer, did not disguise his impatience with Ludlow's meddling in areas likely to create confusion with the Companies Acts and charities legislation. The Home Office opposed any encroachment upon the territory of the Trade

---

[87] S. Cordery, 'Mutualism, Friendly Societies, and the Genesis of Railway Trade Unions', *Labour History Review*, 67 (2002), 270–2.

[88] Reports of the Registrar of Friendly Societies in England, 1874 (*PP* 1875 lxxi), 33–8.

[89] Memorandum as to the Granting of Special Authorities under the Friendly Societies Act 1875, 13 Jan. 1876, PRO T1/7559A/19735, 6–7n.

[90] RCTU 11th Rep., vol. ii, Appx. E, 124.

Union Act.[91] Instead, an amending Act (1876) was brought in, which as well as implementing many of the minor administrative changes requested by the TUCPC, broadened the definition of a trade union so as to encompass the societies identified by Ludlow as being of ambiguous standing. The effect was to confirm the registration, as trade unions, of such associations as the railway servants.[92] Although unsuccessful in his wider ambitions, Ludlow was one of the few contemporaries to probe what was meant by a 'trade union' in the 1870s legislation, and to try to use legislation to divert unionism into a particular channel. Intended by the Home Office simply as a descriptive means of distinguishing unions from other forms of association, the definition was interpreted in a more restrictive sense by the courts a generation later.[93]

'COLLECTIVE *LAISSEZ-FAIRE*'

Ludlow had achieved official position too late to have any influence upon the fundamental shape of the Liberal government's settlement. He was passed over as a possible member of the Erle commission, and his contribution to its proceedings was limited to a written submission buried in the appendices.[94] Consequently his prescriptions for full legalization coupled with compulsory arbitration and the eventual outlawing of strikes and lockouts—a far more radical departure from existing practice than Harrison's plan—were never fully discussed. Like the French writer who in 1867 contrasted the 'brutal English formula of the strike' with the French preference for co-operation, and the petitioners of the Prussian Popular Union who insisted that repeal of laws against combination in Prussia must not lead to 'wasteful strikes as in England', Ludlow was a critic of strikes and lock-outs as 'public nuisances', damaging to both parties engaged in them.[95] He rejected the policy of removing both the law and executive government from industrial relations. By contrast, Gladstone breezily accepted 'that friendly strife which must always go on between the capitalist and labourer'.[96]

---

[91] Liddell to Treasury, 24 Feb. 1876, Farrer to Treasury, 5 Feb., 22 Feb. 1876, PRO T1/7559A/19735.

[92] PRO HO45/9396/50218/1a; Reports of the Registrar of Friendly Societies, 1875 (*PP* 1876 lxix), 27–8.

[93] Clegg, Fox, and Thompson, *History*, 414; Webb, *History*, 615–25.

[94] His submission, 5 July 1867, is in RCTU 11th Rep., vol. ii, Appx. E, 123–6.

[95] H. Collins and C. Abramsky, *Karl Marx and the British Labour Movement* (1965), 126; RCTU 11th Rep., Appx. 163 (Morier's report on Prussia); Ludlow and Lloyd Jones, *Progress*, 210.

[96] *The Times* (19 Feb. 1868), 10.

Indeed, some saw recourse to strikes to resolve market conflicts as a healthy sign. In 1867 Lushington hoped that, by giving unions a recognized legal standing, contests between employers and workers would be 'reduced to simple industrial disputes'—meaning strikes and lock-outs—and would cease to be 'class feuds'.[97] The latter was the dangerous form which English observers often perceived such conflicts to assume elsewhere in Europe; the French observer, Hippolyte Taine, was equally impressed by the way in which industrial conflict in England was contained within the boundaries of the market.[98]

The Edinburgh advocate Alexander Taylor Innes, a Liberal in politics, perceived that what was done in 1871 reflected a national model of industrial relations consonant with England's standing within Europe as the country of free trade. What Innes described as English ideas of freedom of industry, freedom of contract, and freedom of association left employers and employed collectively to bargain as they chose, and when that bargaining broke down, to resort to strikes and lock-outs at will. Wasteful though this was, it was a 'self-working and self-contained' mechanism that cured itself, and was less dangerous than any type of legislative interference which might be favoured by a mass electorate to regulate the market.[99] 'Collective *laissez-faire*', as this system came to be known in the mid-twentieth century, entailed an acceptance that unions were 'fighting organizations', as Thomas Hughes complained in 1873; they felt no responsibility for what was 'fair or just' to either employers or the community at large in the pursuit of their material ends. Thus Hughes regarded unionism as far inferior in conception to co-operation which, like many contemporaries, he favoured as the route to a 'juster, and nobler, and gentler life'.[100]

By the early 1870s Hughes had become disappointed at the failure of the newly legalized unions to represent the brotherhood, altruism, and good citizenship which he had detected in their early development. That their leaders were associated with the campaign for Church disestablishment further increased his alienation from them.[101] Other contemporaries were more willing to see the outcome of the arrangements devised in 1871 as a successful integration of unions into the mainstream of national life. Just as

[97] Lushington, 'Workmen and Trade Unions', 57; cf. A. Toynbee, *Lectures on the Industrial Revolution in England* (1884), 199.

[98] H. Taine, *Notes on England*, trans. W. F. Rae (1872), 293.

[99] A. T. Innes, 'Trade-Unionism: Its Limits and Its Future', NAPSS, *Transactions, 1874*, 919–21.

[100] T. Hughes, 'Problems of Civilization', *Macmillan's Magazine*, 28 (May 1873), 85–9; Parry, *Democracy and Religion*, 31.

[101] Parry, *Democracy and Religion*, 100, 337; Biagini, *Liberty*, 243.

twenty years earlier Hughes had seen hopeful signs in the engineers' dispute of 1852, so another generation regarded the long strike in the South Wales coalfield in 1873 as signifying the strength of popular 'patience and moderation', marshalled by 'responsible' leaders. 'The Hallidays, the Normansells, the Macdonalds, the Arches give hope for the future', the Christian Socialist clergyman Llewelyn Davies told the Church Congress in October 1873.[102] His sentiments were echoed by the historical economist Thorold Rogers. While regretting the frequency of strikes as 'a barbarous means of adjusting matters in controversy between professing Christians', Rogers paid tribute to the good order with which the South Wales dispute was conducted, not least because proper notice was given by the strikers and therefore no contract was broken. And he acknowledged that unionism, now 'a recognized branch of our social system', had improved the condition of 'British workmen'.[103]

While this process of integration predated the Trade Union Act, and was not dependent upon it, self-evidently any measure which unambiguously secured union funds, insulated them from legal hazards or the threat of winding-up, and made it easier for them to acquire premises, facilitated permanence. It helped to legitimize the position of the unions and their officers, and to that extent could open the way for them to play a part in a system of collective bargaining or joint regulation. When legal disabilities were removed, the Lanarkshire miners were emboldened to demand from their employers the setting up of boards of arbitration and conciliation in recognition of the men's equal standing within the industry.[104]

Although this might point to an official intention to promote the involvement of unions in the collective regulation of industry, it is important to emphasize that those in the Home Office responsible for drawing up the legislation recognized that any such outcome, even if desirable, was beyond their control. All the provisions of the legislation were, as Lushington observed, potentially double-edged and legislators were powerless to discriminate between those aspects of unionism which they might wish to encourage, and those which might appear less welcome. Legalization might indeed bring additional institutional security to institutions committed to negotiation and arbitration; it could, and did, provide equal security to associations which used their strength to promote unilateral regulation. Those unions which offered welfare benefits might be more prone to moderation than purely 'strike' societies; yet friendly benefits also operated as a

---

[102] *Authorised Report of the Church Congress held at Bath, 1873* (1873), 32, 38, 42.
[103] J. E. T. Rogers, 'Strikes', *British Quarterly Review*, 58 (Oct. 1873), 347, 376.
[104] Harrison, *Independent Collier*, 168.

lever to enforce collective solidarities in favour of some end which might be perceived as undesirable. Likewise the centralization of union administration might enable an executive to control its branches; it might also be a more effective way of enforcing craft rules.

Collective bargaining existed before 1871, and was not essentially dependent upon legal change for its development; conversely, unilateral regulation persisted long after the 1871 Act took effect, and might indeed be encouraged by the type of legal facilities now enjoyed by unions. In some industries recognition of unions was extended in the years immediately after the 1871 Act was passed, but this was more a result of the economic upturn than of changes to the law. When the economic boom of the early 1870s ended, wage reductions were imposed by employers without troubling to consult their former partners, and some unions disintegrated.[105] Mere legalization could not guarantee their survival in the face of adverse economic conditions and employers unwilling to deal with them. Central support for the institutions of joint regulation was confined to moral endorsements by politicians, who also lent their services as arbitrators, and such symbolic acts as the conferring of a knighthood upon Rupert Kettle, in 1880, 'for his public services in establishing a system of arbitration between employers and employed'.[106]

Where collective agreements became established, the idea of incorporation was revived, for how could unions otherwise be held to their side of bargains? Employers sometimes cited this as a reason for refusing to enter into collective bargaining: the South Wales coalowners at first declined to meet the miners' delegates because the union could not be legally bound by any agreement reached.[107] Although the 1871 Act had specifically rendered such contracts unenforceable, Kettle considered ways of enabling proceedings to be taken against both parties to arbitration settlements, whether organized employers or workers, in some form of corporate capacity. His was a more narrowly economistic application of Ludlow's ideas. If strikes and lock-outs could be done away with, unions could develop into 'great joint stock labour insurance companies', selling the labour of their members to employers for fixed periods while using their funds to support members during periods of unemployment. By 1872 he had come to favour full legalization and enforceable contracts.[108] Another county court judge,

---

[105] R. Church, *The History of the British Coal Industry*, iii (1986), 664, 658. [106] *DNB*.
[107] RCTU 3rd Rep. Q.4329; Select Committee on Dearness and Scarcity of Coal (*PP* 1873 x), Q.5360.
[108] R. Kettle, *Masters and Men* (1871), 30; R. Kettle, 'On Boards of Conciliation and Arbitration between Employers and Employed, and what is Required to give them Further Success', NAPSS, *Sessional Proceedings*, 4 (1871), 184; *Colliery Guardian* (11 Oct. 1872), 396.

Thomas H. Terrell, who had experience of the South Wales coalfield, developed the suggestion in a pamphlet published in 1873. He favoured incorporation, giving unions a legal responsibility for carrying out agreements entered into on behalf of their members.[109]

Despite their enthusiasm for formalization in industrial relations, union officials did not take up Terrell's ideas, which gained no support when he addressed the Amalgamated Miners' conference in 1873.[110] There were attempts by employers to get round the problem by demanding financial bonds as security that arbitration awards would be adhered to, as the Oldham master spinners demanded in 1872, or else restitution for the cost of a stoppage, as the Durham coalowners claimed in 1873.[111] Neither carried legal force and in practice the implementation of agreements depended upon, as before, collective moral pressure, and the ability of union executives to keep their members in line. In the absence of corporate status, the matter of redress for civil injuries was also left to informal remedies. One litigant tried his hand at a legal action against a union's branch officials shortly after the 1871 Act came into force but, like the Springhead Spinning Company, found that proceedings against individuals were almost worthless. The plaintiff, a foreman, was awarded exemplary damages of £300 against branch members of the Yorkshire glass bottle makers' society, to which he belonged; they had 'blacked' him and forced him out of employment, after he was alleged to have violated the society's trade rules. Nearly four years later, he had not received a penny, and had been unemployed for seventeen months. Only through the intervention of a Sheffield clergymen did he finally obtain £80 by way of a 'friendly' settlement.[112]

By the virtually seamless way in which it set the seal on unions as recognized institutions, the Trade Union Act might be accounted a highly effective instalment of the Gladstone administration's programme of emancipatory reform. To Bagehot, it was 'a characteristically English measure' since, while alleviating 'many practical evils', it lacked any sort of theoretical completeness.[113] Having earlier advocated incorporation,

---

[109] T. H. Terrell, *Capital and Labour: A Plan for their Reconciliation* (1873), 39; *Bee-Hive* (9 May 1874), 2.

[110] *Cardiff Times* (5 Apr. 1873).

[111] *Oldham Chronicle* (13 Jan. 1872), 8; *Durham Chronicle* (20 June 1873), 7; (19 Sept. 1873), 2.

[112] *Purchon v Hartley and others*, *Law Times* (19 Aug. 1871); *Leeds Times* (19 Aug. 1871), 3; *Rotherham and Masbro' Advertiser* (19 Aug. 1871), 5; (14 Nov. 1874), 5; (13 Mar. 1875), 8; *Sheffield Independent* (13 Mar. 1875), 7; *Sheffield Daily Telegraph* (12 Mar. 1875), 3; Glass Bottle Makers of Yorkshire Trade Protection Society EC Minutes (1869–75), 193, 464–5, 490.

[113] 'Trades Union Bill', 18 Feb. 1871; *Bagehot's Political Essays*, ed. Stevas, viii. 39.

Bagehot naturally regarded the form of status conferred on unions as rather anomalous and incomplete. But as a description of a settlement which, in practice, changed very little and adapted the law to existing social facts, his was a generally fair appraisal. He perhaps understated, though, the ideological underpinning of the scheme, in ideas of state neutrality, non-intervention, free trade, and voluntarism as an appropriate solution to the problem of combinations in an age of minimal government. The settlement also reflected the unions' own positive attachment to those approaches to market issues.[114] In 1894 unionists who defended the voluntarist principles of the Act, described it as a hard won 'charter of Trade Union freedom', as if it had had to be extracted from a reluctant government.[115] Yet its essential 'Englishness' way well have been represented by the state's unwillingness to challenge artisan traditions of independence. Those responsible for the legislation showed no inclination to do anything other than to treat unions as private clubs, and to accept whatever disadvantages which allowing them to remain in that comparatively unregulated form might entail. They nevertheless hoped that by exposing unions to publicity, and the morally bracing force of public opinion, those characteristics of self-restraint and group discipline, which had impressed observers of unionism since the 1850s, might be developed and extended.

[114] McKibbin, 'Why was there no Marxism in Great Britain?', 31; Biagini, *Liberty*, 85, 101, 139.
[115] Royal Commission on Labour, 5th Rep. (*PP* 1894 xxxv), 146 (report by William Abraham, Michael Austin, James Mawdsley, and Tom Mann).

6

The Criminal Law Amendment Act, 1871

Parliamentary opinion in 1871 insisted that the criminal law should be strong enough to ensure that those individuals or groups of individuals who chose not to belong to unions or take part in strikes would be protected from being coerced, by physical acts, abuse, or personal harassment, into doing so. The majority of the Erle Commission had recommended preserving the penal section of the 1825 Act, with its vague and all-embracing prohibitions against 'threats', 'molestation', and 'obstruction'. Others regarded this as unsustainable, and believed that the 1825 Act should be repealed. In that case a question remained as to what alternative protection, if any, ought to be put in its place. Was the existing criminal law sufficient to punish the intimidation which commonly occurred in trade disputes? If not, where should the line be drawn as regards acts which inevitably lay on a very indistinct borderline of crime? And if certain acts of intimidation and molestation were to be punishable, should this be in the context of trade disputes and union organization alone, or should such a penal law apply to all social relations?

When the Gladstone government's measure was introduced in February 1871 the Home Office circulated to the press a summary of its content and implications.[1] Lushington's authorship may be inferred from the similarity in form and content to his internal memoranda. The 1825 Act was to be repealed, but in order to punish 'the improper means for effecting the purposes of a Trade Union' its penal provisions against violence, threats, intimidation, molestation, and obstruction were to be re-enacted. This announcement encouraged later commentators to assume that what was proposed was merely a codification of previous law. That was not the case: instead of leaving the definition of such offences to be worked out by judges, as had been the case in the period after 1850 when courts had placed increasingly broad constructions upon them, they were to be defined, and limited, by Parliament. Yet even this intended benefit, from the unions' point of view, was overshadowed by the Home Office's extraordinary acknowledgement that the bill created (or rather perpetuated) 'special' offences confined to trade disputes which, moreover, though applying to employers and employed alike, were 'not likely to be committed by employers'.

---

[1] *The Times* (16 Feb. 1871), 5.

Whether the announcement about the criminal provisions—which concealed the practical effect of some of the immunities to be conferred—was couched in such uncompromising terms in order to reassure parliamentary opinion and ensure the safe passage of the measure legalizing unions, cannot be known. It did reflect the strong belief among proponents of a broad freedom to combine, that it should not be taken as a licence for the physical coercion of individuals who chose to remain outside the combination. It also suggested that the Home Office had either not anticipated, or chosen to disregard, the TUC's likely response. Meeting in London in March 1871, the third congress of the unions deplored the proposed measure as one 'which presupposes criminal intentions or tendencies on the part of English workmen as a class'.[2] Bruce's only concession was to hive off the criminal provisions into a separate bill, enacted in June 1871 as the Criminal Law Amendment Act (CLAA). Such a gesture was insufficient to prevent a trade union agitation for the Act's repeal.

IMMUNITY FROM JUDGE-MADE LAW

The rhetoric of the labour laws agitation depicted the CLAA as an oppressive law directed against unionists. There was another, less well understood aspect to the government's approach to the criminal law, illustrated by Lushington's observation, in 1873, that the CLAA was 'intended to be an Act to relieve from pains and penalties'.[3] Informed by the advanced theories of the freedom to combine developed during the debates of the 1860s, the CLAA attempted to withdraw the criminal law from the ground which it had occupied as a result of the series of judicial decisions after 1850. In particular, the Home Office sought to remove any criminality that might attach to strikes, or threats of strikes, as a result of extended applications of the law of conspiracy.

Thring had identified the need to extinguish the common law rules against labour conspiracies as the first priority of any scheme to address the unions' 'reasonable' complaints against the law.[4] Providing such immunity, however, raised technical problems for the draftsman because of the obscurity as to precisely what those rules were, and where they originated. Lushington, following F. D. Longe, took the common law rules to rest on

---

[2] *Bee-Hive* (18 Mar. 1871), 3.
[3] PRO HO45/9326/18243/30a (7 Feb. 1873); see also Thring's comment, p. 203 below.
[4] See his undated [*c.*1867–9] MS memorandum, OPC Bills and Memoranda (HT) 1875, xx–xxii.

very slender foundations, and found the most extensive application of them set out in Sir William Erle's memorandum for the royal commission.[5] Erle had asserted that the joint use of molestation or obstruction, short of violence, to coerce either another workman or employer in the pursuit of his trade was a conspiracy at common law, since the law secured to individuals the right to a free course of trade. On the basis of Erle's account of the law, the CLAA sought to prevent this rule being applied against strikers in future. It defined those physical actions which were to constitute molestation or obstruction and declared that no acts other than these were to be punishable 'on the ground that such act restrains or tends to restrain the free course of trade'.[6] The CLAA was intended to eliminate the scope for judicial intervention, an objective to which Lushington attached particular importance.

Characteristically, Lushington analysed the law of conspiracy in terms of a long historical process, which commenced with the emancipation of individuals from 'the legislative power of Judges'. Subsequently combinations, alone, were exposed to this judicial power, which was gradually circumscribed by confining its application to exceptional instances 'established by precedent'. More recently, as he claimed to detect in the observations of those whom he designated the more 'liberal' nineteenth-century judges, there was a trend to confine conspiracy to acts which would be crimes if carried out by individuals.[7] Accordingly, the immunities intended to be granted by the bill were simply the fulfilment of an existing trend towards curbing the legislative power of the courts; and a statute would, he assumed, put an end to the uncertainty about the rights of combinations to which the variety of judicial pronouncements had given rise.

Petitions and deputations from employers, including the Glasgow, Birmingham, and Halifax chambers of commerce, unsuccessfully pressed that offences such as 'molestation' and 'obstruction' should be undefined, leaving the courts to interpret them in a very broad sense, as they had in the past.[8] Under the CLAA strikers, provided they steered clear of the physical acts defined in the statute, were thought to be protected from the common law. The previous distinction between the legitimate and illegitimate objects of a combination was now removed. Lushington described that earlier

---

[5] Lushington, 'Law of Trade Unions', 16–18 ('The Common Law Doctrine as to Molestation') OPC Bills and Memoranda (HJ) 1871.

[6] 34 & 35 Vict. c. 32, s. 1.

[7] Lushington, 'Law of Trade Unions', 35–7 ('The Common Law Doctrine of Conspiracy').

[8] *Builders' Trade Circular* (16 Mar. 1871), 6; *Birmingham Daily Post* (11 Mar. 1871), 5; *Appendix to the Reports of the Select Committee of the Commons on Public Petitions, 1871*, 103.

concept, which underlay the 1825 Act, as 'unquestionably a relic of the feudal principle of class-subordination', forbidding men to combine to interfere in matters held to be within the sole prerogative of the 'master'.[9] In Lushington's view, men should be permitted to withold their labour for whatever reason they chose. Issues about the organization of work—such as how many apprentices should be employed in a workshop—were already, in daily practice, bargained between the two parties, and the law, which was practically inoperative, should acknowledge the fact.

Lushington also criticized the recommendation of the majority of the Erle commission that strikes against individuals—non-unionists or an objectionable foreman, for example—should continue to be prohibited. This had become a key point of difference between the utilitarian theorists of the majority and the younger Liberal writers whose ideas had been absorbed into the minority report.[10] Booth thought it more important to protect the individual being struck against than to preserve the rights of those striking against him; falling back on a pragmatic argument, he considered that the non-unionist, standing alone, was less able to protect himself and on that ground the law should put its weight behind him.[11] To Harrison, Dicey, Longe, W. T. Thornton, and others, a prohibition of strikes against objectionable individuals would embody the objectionable principle of coerced labour. What right did an individual have to force others to work with him, if they chose not to, and were not under contract to do so? And by what right could an employer claim the services of men not contracted to him, if they decided not to work alongside other men in his employment whom, for whatever reason, they found objectionable?[12] Hence Lushington's seemingly paradoxical conclusion that maintaining the (ineffective) criminal ban on such strikes was 'contrary to the principle of freedom of labour'.[13]

What an earlier generation had denounced as 'dictation', and wished to treat as a crime, now came to be seen—at least by those making policy—as no more than the legal right of individuals acting jointly to stipulate conditions for the sale of their labour.[14] When he met George Potter's deputation of artisan unionists in 1868, Gladstone himself had conceded that strikes against non-unionists were the exercise of 'a very extreme right' which, like

---

[9] Lushington, 'Memorandum on proposed Trade Combination Bill', 2.

[10] See W. E. J. McCarthy, *The Closed Shop in Britain* (1964), 186–98.

[11] RCTU, 11th Rep. p.c (para. 55).

[12] Longe, 'Law of Trade Combinations in France', 300; cf. Dicey, 'Legal Boundaries of Liberty', 5–6; RCTU 11th Rep. lxi; Thornton, *On Labour*, 180, 333.

[13] Lushington, 'Memorandum', 3.

[14] See Llewelyn Davies's observation, *Authorized Report of the Church Congress, 1873*, 30.

the right of a landlord to turn out all his tenants for whatever reason he chose, could not be denied but ought not to be used.[15] His later moral reproof, in 1874, to the Aston Hall colliers for striking against non-unionists, and his implied support for his colliery manager's threat to evict the strikers from their cottages if they persisted with their demand, is well known.[16] Less familiar—because the Home Office did not advertise it, nor Parliament debate it—was the fact that his government's labour legislation aimed to decriminalize strikes against non-unionists or anyone else strikers might object to, thus enabling unionists to enforce what became later known as the 'closed shop'.

The CLAA also carried out Thring's recommendation of four years' earlier and eradicated the effect of the post-1860 case law (described in Chapter 1) by limiting the definition of 'threats' to threats of violence.[17] The Webbs' description of the CLAA as re-enacting the court decisions of the 1850s and 1860s 'in a codified form' was highly misleading.[18] Not only were strikes against objectionable individuals to be legalized, but so too were threats to that effect: ultimata to employers, and specifically those demanding the dismissal of fellow workers, backed by the threat of strike action, were no longer punishable. Employers, and in particular the master builders who had been most energetic in bringing prosecutions during the 1860s, were to be deprived of the assistance of the criminal law in curbing autonomous regulation in the workplace, though they persisted in trying to bring it to bear.

Within days of the CLAA coming into force, a shop steward of the stonemasons was convicted by the Bolton justices for demanding that another mason should pay a fine imposed upon him by the lodge, coupled with the threat of a walkout if he refused to pay.[19] The higher courts had previously upheld the criminality of such ultimata; now the conviction was quashed on appeal by the recorder of Bolton, who affirmed that under the CLAA threats had to be ones of violence.[20] Bruce described the original decision of

---

[15] *The Times* (19 Feb. 1868), 10; cf. the analogy with landlords and tenants, *Companion to the Newspaper*, 12 (1 Dec. 1833), 177.

[16] *The Times* (10 June 1874), 12; Matthew, *GD* viii. 499n.

[17] 3*H* cciv. 265 (14 Feb. 1871); Orth, *Combination and Conspiracy*, 140; Fraser, *History*, 47.

[18] Webb, *History*, 280; followed by G. D. H. Cole, 'Some Notes on British Trade Unionism in the Third Quarter of the Nineteenth Century', in E. M. Carus-Wilson (ed.), *Essays in Economic History*, iii (1962), 216.

[19] *Bolton Chronicle* (12 Aug. 1871), 3; OSM FR 20 July–3 Aug. 1871, MRC MSS 78/OS/4/1/39.

[20] Trades Union Congress Parliamentary Committee, *The Criminal Law Amendment Act: A Memorial* (1872), 12–6.

the Bolton magistrates as 'absurd' and 'quite contrary to the spirit' of his legislation.[21]

SPECIAL OR GENERAL LEGISLATION?

That 'spirit', according to Bruce's critics—referring to the penal sections of the statute—constituted 'special' or 'class' legislation. Their complaint was that the various acts of annoyance defined as punishable by magistrates were made so only when done 'with a view to coerce' a 'workman', for example, to leave his work or join a combination, or else to force a 'master' to do or not to do certain specified things. Some commentators denied that the Act was 'special', since any person could be convicted (and many were) of the offences stated. Those offences were 'special', however, because they applied only to the circumstances of employment or union relations. Workmen who wished not to join a union or a strike, or employers who wished to resist some demand by a combination, were given protection against certain named acts which the criminal law did not offer to persons in other circumstances who might be 'molested' in the same way. Persons could, therefore, be penalized for doing certain things to achieve the objects of a combination (whether of workmen or employers), which would not be criminal if done to forward some other objective.[22] As the Home Office's statement made clear, the object was to identify, and punish, offences peculiar to collective labour.

The 'special' legislation issue had been in contention since 1869, when Harrison's minority report recommended that all vestiges of the combination laws, including the summary provisions against intimidation in the 1825 Act, should be swept away. Unionists, like other citizens, should be answerable to the general criminal law alone. It was a view supported by Mill along with a number of advanced Liberal MPs,[23] and was embodied in the Hughes–Mundella bill of 1869, which provided no summary remedies at all against threats or molestation. That bill left those who were intimidated by trade combinations to seek whatever remedy the general criminal law might supply. Opposition came from employers who feared that it would deprive 'free labour' of any useful protection. Bruce himself believed, as he told a unionist deputation in June 1869, that the general

---

[21] Ibid. 20; Bruce to Gladstone, 21 Nov. 1871, BL Add MSS 44087, fo. 34.

[22] Orth, *Combination and Conspiracy*, 140–1.

[23] See Mill's comments in his review, 'Thornton on Labour and its Claims', pt. ii, *Fortnightly Review*, n.s. 5 (June 1869), *Collected Works*, v. 660.

criminal law was inadequate to reach certain acts commonly committed by organized workers, instancing 'hissing and hooting at a man working contrary to the union's rules'.[24] This concern had led to the Gladstone Cabinet's reservation about the 1869 bill.[25]

In his advice to Bruce, Lushington tried to promote the policy of the 1869 bill. He sought to demonstrate that the general criminal law relating to offences against the person, malicious injury to property, libel, riot, and the power of Justices to demand sureties for the maintenance of the peace was, 'if vigorously put into execution', sufficient to deal with the problem of intimidation.[26] The only area of doubt proved to be the practice of rattening, where this involved simply hiding the tools of dissidents, rather than damage to them: the former constituted neither larceny nor malicious injury to property. Other than this, he urged—against Bruce's previous statements in parliament—that no new law was necessary. Lushington had, of course, dismissed the recommendation of the majority of the Erle commission that the 1825 Act, and the judicial constructions placed upon it, should be left intact: the offences were 'vague' and 'unsafe' to leave in the hands of JPs.

Both Harrison and Thring had floated an alternative approach, which was dismissed by Lushington with perhaps insufficient consideration. Harrison's report had acknowledged that there might be a deficiency in the protection that the general criminal law afforded to persons subjected to harassment:[27]

If it be alleged that certain forms of physical injury and personal annoyance are common with picketers—such as threats of violence, hustling, dogging, hooting, bonneting, and the like—which are not cognizable as offences by the statute law, we think the statute law should be amended, so that all citizens should be protected against physical molestation.

Thring had considered that the general criminal law needed strengthening in three such areas: first to punish the use of threats of violence to force another person to do, or not to do, something against his will; secondly, to punish the use of 'insulting words or gestures in public with a view to bring a person into contempt or ridicule'; and finally, to prevent 'the persistent watching or dogging of a person' in such a way as to 'inspire terror'.[28] Some of these actions bore a resemblance to the offences of criminal intimidation, insult, and annoyance described in the Indian Penal Code where, crucially,

[24] *Bee-Hive* (3 July 1869), 5.
[25] 3*H* cxcvii. 1381 (7 July 1869)
[26] Lushington, 'Law of Trade Unions', 11–14; 'Proposed Trade Combination Bill', 5.
[27] RCTU 11th Rep. lviii.
[28] Thring undated [*c.*1867–9] MS memorandum, OPC Bills and Memoranda (HT) 1875, xxii–xxiii.

they were not made criminal simply because they were done to further the cause of trade combinations, but applied to all circumstances and protected all citizens.[29] In what was to prove a considerable miscalculation, Lushington (who was not a criminal lawyer) ruled out such an extension to the general criminal law as too all-embracing, without apparently considering the Indian precedent.

Lushington made perhaps a bigger misjudgement when he came to discuss Bruce's preferred option, a replacement for the section in the 1825 Act punishing intimidation in trade disputes. He rehearsed the difficulties in the way of drawing up a safe form of words to define the offence, but rather casually observed of the matter of principle involved, 'I see no reason against a penal enactment applying to Trade Combinations, provided that such an enactment is required for the public welfare.'[30] His misplaced confidence in what proved the most contentious point was partly explicable by his own role in drawing up the CAT's own Trades Societies bill. That contained a clause punishing violence and threats of violence in trade disputes. Although it therefore perpetuated 'special' or 'class' offences, the bill had been endorsed by the bulk of the trade union movement and was the subject of the test questions put to candidates during the 1868 general election. MPs had not been pledged to oppose special legislation, for this demand had come only with Harrison's report early in 1869. Even as he was drafting the report, Harrison himself had not at first insisted on it as a condition for Lichfield's adhesion, specifying merely that there should be 'some modification' of the 1825 Act. Unlike the other Positivists, Lushington seems to have cultivated few personal links with unionists and he failed to grasp how far, and how rapidly, union opinion had moved during 1869. By August, at the second Trades Union Congress held at Birmingham, 'special legislation' was denounced and a resolution carried, on George Howell's motion, that any legislation on trade unions should embody 'the entire repeal of combination laws'.[31]

The Home Office was more directly aware of a hardening of opinion in an opposite direction. In January 1870 a riot at Thorncliffe Colliery near Sheffield, in which striking miners ransacked cottages occupied by blacklegs, was seized on as renewed evidence to associate unionism with violence. J. T. Delane, the editor of *The Times*, promised the South Yorkshire magistrates of the paper's support if the local authorities, whose pleas for

[29] W. Theobald (ed.), *The Legislative Acts of the Governor General of India in Council from 1834 to the End of 1867*, iii. 624 (s. 503).

[30] Lushington, 'Proposed Trade Combination Bill', 6.

[31] Kirk, *Second Annual Congress of Trades Unions*, 9–10.

assistance had been rejected by the Home Office, were driven to taking 'severe measures against the unionists'. A leading article used the riot to question the recent optimistic claims made on behalf of unionism. While the 'more skilful and intelligent' unionized craftsmen might be in a position to deal with dissidents in peaceful ways by refusing to work with them, workers in occupations where the supply of alternative labour was potentially limitless, were likely to resort to violence. Thorncliffe undermined claims by 'the working men and their amateur advocates' that unions were voluntary associations bound together by purely moral sanctions.[32] Although the circumstances of the riot were less discreditable to the union than *The Times* made out—the colliery owners had been intransigent in insisting on dealing with the men individually, while the officers of the South Yorkshire miners had urged restraint on the men and offered arbitration[33]—the episode was a damaging one for those who had depicted an 'improvement' in the character of unionism. Furthermore, a recurrence of outrages—a murder and a gunpowder explosion—in the Manchester building trade provided another occasion for Alfred Mault of the General Builders' Association to remind the Home Office that 'the worst phase of unionism is by no means extinct'.[34] Cumulatively, such incidents reinforced the underlying assumption throughout the Home Office's deliberations that, whatever the claims of passivity and respectability made on behalf of the well-established craft associations, strikes in practice frequently spilled over into forms of physical molestation.

Bruce cited his own knowledge of intimidation in the South Wales coalfield as an illustration of the need for additional legal protection for non-strikers.[35] In 1850, as stipendiary magistrate in Merthyr Tydfil, he had brought in troops against striking miners who were harassing blacklegs.[36] His more recent experience was as a landowner deriving mineral royalties from collieries, and as a trustee of the Dowlais ironworks, which employed over 8,000 workers. According to his fellow trustee, works manager, and close friend, G. T. Clark, there were no unions at Dowlais, but the works made extensive school provision, had a savings bank, a reading room, and a sick fund.[37] Bruce's social reforming interests, dating back to his earlier

---

[32] *The Times* (27 Jan. 1870), 7; Delane to Wharncliffe, 26 Jan. 1870, Wharncliffe MSS WhM 464; PRO HO45/8370; F. Machin, *The Yorkshire Miners* (1958), 369–75.
[33] Wharncliffe to Normansell, 8 Feb. 1870, Wharncliffe MSS WhM 464.
[34] Mault to Bruce, 22 Oct. 1869, PRO HO45/8301; PRO HO45/8428; *The Times* (9 May 1870), 14.
[35] 3*H* cxcvii. 1382 (7 July 1869).
[36] Bruce to Home Office, 28 Mar. 1850, PRO HO45/3134.
[37] RCTU 5th Rep. Q.10,050.

Christian Socialist associations, were of an interventionist kind—he was long-standing supporter of measures to outlaw payment by truck—and he viewed the clause against molestation as a form of protective legislation to meet a recognized social evil.[38] Manchester School politicians defended a special measure as necessary to uphold the independence of the individual workman, and therefore promote their version of free labour. Bruce never used this language. He knew that an unobstructed market for labour was something the law could not practically achieve. In Merthyr Tydfil, he pointed out to the building employers, 'thousands' of Irishmen were willing to work in the pits on terms which the Welsh colliers declined, but no Irishman would dare go underground and there was nothing the law could effectively do to protect them.[39] But parliament, he told the TUC, would not consent to legalizing unions without providing for the punishment of offences 'which they all knew were sometimes committed by trades unionists'.[40]

Bruce's humiliating general election defeat in Merthyr Tydfil in 1868 foreshadowed the difficulties he encountered in dealing with the union question. One of the most democratic constituencies, the Merthyr electorate had been vastly extended in 1867 and was dominated by miners. Among other reasons, he attracted their hostility because of his partiality towards the coalowners over mines regulation, and his insensitivity towards popular radicalism.[41] In 1871 he showed no sympathy with the TUC's contention that, by penalizing offences committed by strikers, the CLAA amounted to 'class legislation'. He told Birmingham's Liberal MPs, who had taken up the complaints of Birmingham Trades Council, that it was no more class legislation than the Merchant Shipping Act, which made punishable acts committed by shipowners, or the Mines Regulation Acts, which likewise placed obligations on colliery proprietors. The Truck Act could equally be held to presuppose 'criminal intentions on the part of the employer'. No one supposed that these protective statutes cast a moral aspersion upon those who were likely to commit the offences made punishable by them. Why then should the criminal clauses of the government's bill be felt as a stigma by unionists?[42]

The CLAA might be seen as 'class legislation' from another standpoint.

[38] For the parallel with the CD Acts, see Biagini, *Liberty*, 159–61.
[39] *Builders' Trade Circular* (16 Mar. 1871), 6.   [40] *Bee-Hive* (11 Mar. 1871), 6.
[41] I. G. Jones, *Explorations and Explanations* (1981), 208–14; B. Ll. James (ed.), *G. T. Clark* (1998), ch. 4.
[42] G. Dixon to T. Wilkinson, 14 Mar. 1871, in Birmingham Trades Council Minutes (1869–73), i. 93. A decade earlier factory masters had complained at being 'stigmatized' by protective legislation passed by a landed parliament, Searle, *Entrepreneurial Politics*, 275.

George Melly, the Liverpool businessman and Liberal MP for Stoke, sought the opinions of one of his working-class constituents, a collier and prominent New Connexion Methodist, who had recently been elected as labour representative on the Hanley school board. Melly's correspondent complained that the activities of the men during strikes were punished, but the 'most oppressive and repulsive form' of molestation practised by the masters—blacklists—escaped.[43] Bruce's answer was that both sides were now free to circulate blacklists, though in practice it was a more effective and more common tactic for employers to use than it was for the men.[44]

Finally, the CLAA was held to be 'class legislation' because it made minor acts of violence and threats of violence, which in other circumstances might have resulted in a fine or binding over, punishable by imprisonment with hard labour simply because they were committed to further the objects of a trade union or a strike. 'If I knock a man down because he is a knobstick, I can have three months prison', William Crawford of the Durham miners commented; 'if I knock a man down merely as a man, I may have a 5/- fine'.[45] Under the CLAA magistrates were deliberately not given the option of imposing fines, which were thought to be a worthless punishment in combination cases as unions or strikers collectively were likely to pay them on behalf of the defendants.

The great majority of convictions under the CLAA, as under section 3 of the 1825 Act, were for physical acts of intimidation. Some 30 per cent of known convictions were for violence (assaults, stone-throwing, and the like), and nearly 40 per cent were for threats of violence (how seriously these were meant might, of course, be disputed). But for the fact that they were done with a view to one or more of the purposes specified in the CLAA they would have been dealt with by fines or by binding over those involved to keep the peace.[46] The pattern of offences reinforced Bruce's stance, that there were very few convictions 'to which any reasonable man could object'.[47] What Bruce took to be a clinching argument against the TUC's demands for repeal could, however, cut both ways. It might equally be asked, as the TUCPC did, why such undeniably criminal acts should not be tackled under those provisions of the criminal law 'such as are applied to other subjects of the realm'?[48]

---

[43] William Mayer to Melly, 25 Feb. 1871, Melly MSS 920MEL/22/4405.
[44] *Bee-Hive* (11 Mar. 1871), 6; Bruce to Herbert, 8 July 1873, in S. H. Harris, *Auberon Herbert: Crusader for Liberty* (1943), 148.   [45] RCLL 2nd Rep. Q.506.
[46] H. Crompton, 'The Government and Class Legislation', *Fortnightly Review*, n.s. 14 (July 1873), 31
[47] Bruce to Gladstone, 21 Nov. 1871, BL Add MSS 44087, fo. 34.
[48] TUCPC, *The Criminal Law Amendment Act: A Memorial*, 1.

THE CLAA AND PICKETING

The most controversial practical aspect of the CLAA concerned its effect upon picketing. The legality of picketing had been highly contested since Bramwell's charge in the tailors' trial in 1867. His declaration that, for all practical purposes, the practice was unlawful had very tangible effects—more so, arguably, than *Hornby v Close*—upon the ability to wage success-ful strikes. As a direct result, pickets were withdrawn during a dispute in Nottingham and the Lace Makers' Society had to accept defeat; in Liverpool, warrants were brought against the office-bearers of the Operative Bricklayers' Society to force them to withdraw pickets; at Leeds Assizes in August 1868 a number of masons were convicted on a conspiracy indictment for shouting 'bah, bah' at non-strikers.[49] Trades councils were formed, or revived, in Bradford, Edinburgh, and Oldham to respond to the legal threat posed by the conviction of the tailors' leaders.[50] So stringent was the law considered to be that when Elcho proposed a recommendation in the royal commission report explicitly outlawing picketing, it was rejected, apparently on the ground that it was unnecessary.[51]

As the majority were finalizing their report, the position of pickets was placed in a new light by a case heard by Sir Robert Lush at the Central Criminal Court in January 1869. Members of the East End Ladies Shoe-makers' Society were indicted for conspiring to use means forbidden by the 1825 Act (threats, intimidation, and molestation) against men seeking em-ployment from an individual master shoemaker who had refused to abide by an existing code of rules and a price list regulating the trade. Like the tailors, the striking shoemakers had picketed a workshop, but unlike the earlier case, the evidence showed the pickets to have been 'civil, and their demeanour perfectly respectable'. They were acquitted after Lush (who had presided over the conviction of the Sheffield masons a year earlier) had addressed the jury in terms which drew a distinction between physical in-timidation and purely moral suasion. Pickets had a right to persuade 'in a peaceable manner' but they must not abuse their fellow workmen in any

---

[49] *Nottingham Journal* (10 Aug. 1867), 2; *Liverpool Mercury* (28 May 1868), 3; (29 May 1868), 6; (30 May 1868), 5; OSM FR 6–20 Aug. 1868; MRC MSS 78/OS/4/1/34 (*R v Sheridan and Others*).
[50] Minutes of Bradford Trades Council, 13 Aug. 1867, Bradford RO 56D 80/1/1; *Oldham Chronicle* (25 July 1867), 7; MacDougall, *Minutes of Edinburgh Trades Council*, 192.
[51] C. J. Kauffman, 'Lord Elcho, Trade Unionism and Democracy', in K. D. Brown (ed.), *Essays in Anti-Labour History* (1974), 203; see RCTU 11th Rep. xxii (paras. 71–2); Harrison to Lichfield, 22 Mar. 1869, Anson MSS D615/P(P)/4/4/4.

way, such as by hooting or shouting at them.[52] He approved their acquittal, as he privately told Erle, 'though what they did was a great annoyance and injury to the master'.[53]

In his review of Thornton's work on labour questions, later in 1869, Mill took a view which was broadly similar to Lush's account of the law. Mill argued that it was unreasonable for unionists and strikers to be prevented by law from expressing 'in an impressive manner' their disapproval of those who chose not to join them. But these expressions of social pressure should not be permitted 'to extend to an infringement, or a threat of infringement, of any of the rights which the law guarantees to all—security of person and property against violation, and of reputation against calumny'.[54] Picketing stood 'on the border' between what should be allowed and what should not; its legitimacy, in Mill's view, depended on the facts of each case, that is whether 'the language or gestures used' in a particular instance threatened an infringement of an individual's personal security. Like Lush, he was willing to punish pickets if they resorted to 'hooting' and 'offensive language' but, crucially, only by the ordinary criminal law as would apply in all other circumstances.

Within the Home Office Lushington acknowledged that picketing was essential, and by implication legitimate, for carrying out successful strikes. In practice, though, picketing forced all those who continued to work 'to run the gauntlet certainly of observation, and generally, also, of taunts, ridicule and abuse'. Where the pickets constituted a crowd, including strikers' wives, the effect might be menacing; the very fact of bringing together in large numbers strikers and non-strikers was likely to lead to breaches of the peace.[55] These, however, could be dealt with by the general criminal law. His concerns differed from those of either Senior or Bramwell. Senior had objected to picketing because it obstructed the free operation of the market; Bramwell because it limited the exercise of individual free will. During the drafting of the 1871 legislation, the Home Office's objective was a more limited one of preserving public order, perhaps the closest parallel being the contemporary moves to curb the involvement of crowds in parliamentary elections.[56] As counsel for the Stockton bricklayers, in their appeal to the Court of Queen's Bench in 1866, Coleridge had argued that

---

[52] *R v Shepherd and others* (1869) 11 Cox CC, 325; *St Crispin* (16 Jan. 1869), 29; (13 Mar. 1869), 149–51; H. Crompton, *The Labour Laws Commission* (1875), 16–17.

[53] Lush to Erle, 18 Jan. 1869, Bodl. MS Don. c. 71.

[54] Mill, *Collected Works*, v. 660.

[55] Lushington, 'Law of Trade Unions', 22.

[56] J. Vernon, *Politics and the People: A Study in English Political Culture, c. 1815–1867* (1993), 9, 158.

the 1825 Act 'aimed at preventing personal violence and breaches of the peace'.[57] This was not altogether accurate, as Peel had clearly intended the statute to go further than this. But it was on this basis that Coleridge, as a law officer, stiffened Bruce's determination to press ahead with a measure. Bruce's later statements echoed Coleridge's view of what the law should do: the government's object was 'simply to prevent violence and the approach to violence', as indicated by the new definition of a 'threat'. Gladstone recorded the gist of Bruce's statement to the Cabinet about the bill in similar terms: 'Principle to prevent violence; & in all economic matters the law to take no part'.[58]

The problem of defining the offences which Bruce had in mind exercised the draftsmen over several months and delayed the introduction of Bruce's bill.[59] The molestation clause, which attempted to narrow the definition of that term to include only physical acts, was evidently the focus of intense discussion, and at one point the parliamentary draftsman, Henry Jenkyns, expressly distanced himself from the content.[60] There was to be an offence of 'molestation' if someone, 'with five or more other persons', beset the home or place of work of some other person with a view to coercing them for certain purposes connected with combinations. On 28 January 1871 the cabinet reduced 'five persons' to 'two' and subsequently, following consultations between Bruce and Coleridge, the offence was enlarged to include 'watching' as well as 'besetting'.[61]

Having already proved so malleable in the drafting stage, the watching and besetting clause was exposed to alteration in its parliamentary passage as organized employers mobilized to tighten the law.[62] An amendment by Edmund Potter, on behalf of the National Association of Factory Occupiers, to make watching and besetting an offence by one man acting alone was defeated in the Commons, but was carried in the Lords by the Conservative peers Cairns and Derby.[63] By the time the Lords amendment came back to the Commons, Derby recorded 'something like a panic' spreading among the 'upper and middle classes' as a result of the Paris Commune and its threats to religion and property. Reports of the mobbing

---

[57] *Wood v Bowron* (1866) 10 Cox CC 347

[58] *Builders' Trade Circular* (16 Mar. 1871), 6; Matthew, *GD*, vii. 440 (28 Jan. 1871).

[59] *The Times* (8 July 1870), 6.

[60] OPC Bills and Memoranda (HJ) 1871, 855 (23 Jan. 1871).

[61] BL Add MSS 44616, fo. 21; Bruce to Gladstone, 30 Jan. 1871, BL Add MSS 44087, fo. 10.

[62] *Sheffield Independent* (6 Mar. 1871), 3; Minutes of Oldham Cotton Spinners and Manufacturers Association, 21 Mar. 1871; Home Office to Joseph Clegg, 28 Mar. 1871, PRO HO136/1, p. 161.

[63] 3*H* ccv. 979 (30 Mar. 1871); ccvi. 781 (15 May 1871).

of cotton mills during a lock-out at Oldham, which marked the beginning of a renewed short-time movement, gave the picketing question a sudden immediacy.[64] As Liberal party discipline faltered, economic interests asserted themselves and several Liberal employers voted against the government to carry the Lords' amendment.[65] Birmingham chamber of commerce, which had lobbied the Home Office to make the bill more restrictive, drew satisfaction that the CLAA 'more effectually protects the workmen in their individual independence' than the government's original bill had done.[66]

Supporters of the Lords' amendment, who included Elcho, believed that they had thereby prohibited picketing in any form. Bruce always denied this, though he sometimes found it convenient to blame the amendment for excesses in the implementation of the new law. Numbers were not the crucial issue for 'watching and besetting' was an offence only when done with the criminal intent to 'coerce', and everything turned on what 'coercion' meant. Bruce insisted that there must be overt acts 'exceeding the mere moral influence which one man might exert over another'—the test which Sir Robert Lush had applied in the shoemakers' trial.[67] An insistence that the crime depended on the intention to coerce, however, undermined the argument against the Lords' amendment, for one person might as effectually coerce another as two (and this may explain why, in 1875, when the CLAA was replaced, the amendment was not reversed). Nevertheless, if 'coercion' was interpreted in the way Bruce described, peaceful picketing was lawful when 'conducted peaceably and inoffensively', as he told the secretary of Greenock Trades Council set up in his Renfrewshire constituency to oppose the CLAA.[68]

In the absence of a decision from the higher courts as to the meaning of the statute, there was no guarantee that the courts of summary jurisdiction would follow what Bruce stated to be the Home Office's intention. In January 1872 John Turk, an engineer but not a union member, was sentenced to two months' hard labour by the Hammersmith police court magistrate for having walked up and down the road near the foundry where he was striking for the nine hours demand, handing out leaflets containing a temperate appeal to potential strikebreakers not to take work in the firm.[69]

[64] Vincent (ed.), *Derby Diaries*, 79–80 (6 May 1871); *Standard* (19 June 1871), 4; *Daily News* (4 May 1871), 3.

[65] 3*H* ccvii. 288 (19 June 1871); *Bee-Hive* (15 July 1871), 5.

[66] Birmingham Chamber of Commerce, half-yearly report (27 July 1871), 4.

[67] 3*H* ccvii. 282, 285 (19 June 1871).

[68] Bruce to Allan, 3 Apr. 1872, in *Bee-Hive* (20 Apr. 1872), 6.

[69] *Hammersmith Defence Fund: Report and Balance Sheet* (1872), 4.

That an artisan was subjected to the indignity of having his head shaved, and was put to work on a treadmill, created a particular sense of outrage, and the TUCPC hoped to take the case to the highest courts to obtain a definite ruling on the state of the law. Subsequent appeal proceedings were mishandled by the local defence committee, who accepted an offer to drop the case when it came before Middlesex sessions in April 1872.[70]

Convictions such as those of Turk drew support for the TUC's arguments from Liberal MPs such as W. V. Harcourt and Auberon Herbert, for whom the CLAA was, like Bruce's drink trade licensing proposals, another product of Gladstone's 'grand-maternal Government'.[71] It was a piece of over-protective legislation which criminalized large bodies of otherwise law-abiding citizens, and produced miscarriages of justice, on doubtful grounds of expediency. Harcourt was impressed by the evidence of plainly wrongful convictions; Herbert by a belief that 'molestation' was defined too stringently, depriving men of their ordinary civil rights.[72] They were supported by Liberal MPs such as Mundella, George Dixon, George Melly, and William Rathbone, who were anxious to respond to signs of labour alienation from the Liberal party.[73]

Howell's controversial attempt in 1872, with Harcourt's assistance, to repeal the 'watching and besetting' section of the CLAA (rather than attempt to repeal the whole Act) to prevent further convictions of peaceful pickets, came at a time when relations between the TUCPC and the Liberal leadership were at a low ebb. It is hard, therefore, to see the proposed amendment to the CLAA as evidence of the TUCPC's quiescence, for the choice of Harcourt, one of the Gladstone administration's most persistent critics, as the bill's promoter was in itself a provocation to ministers. But the bill was bound to fail. Bruce's opposition to it was a response to a dominant view in Parliament that any demand for repeal or amendment of the CLAA was, in practice, a demand for licence by organized workers to terrorize those who chose to make their own terms with employers.

Having achieved nothing, Howell's tactics were exposed to attack both from principled critics and personal enemies, who saw him (or were enabled to present him) as failing to carry out the TUC's policy of total repeal.[74] He was open to criticism for a tactical error. But what he was not

[70] Memorandum on TUCPC activity 1872, 43, Howell MSS; Howell to Kane, 30 Apr. 1872, LB6, fo. 411.
[71] B. Harrison, *Drink and the Victorians*, 194.
[72] Ibid. 254; *Glasgow Herald* (25 Aug. 1873), 4.
[73] *Nottingham and Midland Counties Daily Express* (10 Jan. 1872).
[74] Harrison, *Before the Socialists*, 294–8; Leventhal, *Respectable Radical*, 156–64. The transactions are recapitulated in L. L. Witherell, 'Direct Parliamentary Representation of Labour and the Controversy of 1872', *Parliamentary History*, 12 (1993), 143–63.

doing was compromising the trade union practice of picketing, whether out of a corrupt allegiance to the Liberal party, class collaboration, or else a willingness to see workplace militancy curbed by law, as has been variously suggested.[75] By following Harcourt's advice to concentrate on the 'watching and besetting' section, Howell was seen to be compromising, or at least deferring, the 'class legislation' issue, which for the Positivists, with their ambitions for the social incorporation of the working classes, was paramount. Their personal attacks on Howell in turn gave an opportunity for his personal enemy Edwin Coulson and rival George Shipton, on behalf of the London Trades Council, to attempt to wrest the leadership of the campaign away from the TUCPC.[76] Whatever they were, these were not the voices of an outraged 'rank and file'; the 'jealousies and rivalries' at work among the aspirants to leadership were transparent to an outside observer and to newspaper correspondents at the Leeds TUC, in January 1873, when Howell's handling of the campaign was debated.[77]

The 1872 fiasco highlighted how central the picketing issue was to many union secretaries, and how misleading it is to suggest that they were lukewarm in opposing the CLAA. Indeed, from the very publication of the bill, it was they who sustained the objections to the legislation in the face of much apathy among their memberships. Their institutional priorities impelled them to seek changes to the law: the executive of the ASCJ justified expenditure to secure repeal because of the legal costs of fighting prosecutions.[78] Those who were identified with pacific industrial policies were no less resolute in their opposition. 'The builders could hardly do without some sort of "picketing"', George Houseley, the secretary of the Manchester Order of Bricklayers, told the London TUC, 'for whether they had Arbitration Courts or not, strikes would be sure to occur.'[79] Howell, who from the first had attacked the Home Office measure as 'a blow at certain practices inseparable from Trades Unions', told a demonstration in

---

[75] Allen, *Sociology of Industrial Relations*, 132–4; Burgess, *Origins of British Industrial Relations*, 102; Price, *Masters, Unions, and Men*, 126.

[76] London Trades Council Minutes, 7 May, 16 May, 11 June, 21 June, 25 June 1872; Leventhal, *Respectable Radical*, 149.

[77] A. Herbert to Lady Florence Herbert, 17 Jan. 1873, in Harris, *Auberon Herbert*, 145; *Leeds Mercury* (16 Jan. 1873), 7; *Dundee Advertiser* (17 Jan. 1873); *The Times* (16 Jan. 1873), 7; cf. J. Zeitlin, ' "Rank and Filism" and Labour History', *International Review of Social History*, 34 (1989), 94.

[78] ASCJ, monthly report, May 1872, 75; June 1875, 92; cf. FSIF, 62nd Annual Report, Jan.–Dec. 1871, iv.

[79] *Sheffield Daily Telegraph* (11 Mar. 1871), 3; Crawford of the Durham miners, an exponent of conciliation and strong critic of union branches who reneged on collective agreements, described the CLAA as 'villainous' and an attack on 'the rights and liberties of Trades Unionists'. *Durham City and County News* (30 June 1871), 8; (1 Sept. 1871), 8.

Bradford that picketing was 'the great bone of contention': trade unionists claimed the right to be able to approach and persuade strikebreakers.[80] While publicly criticizing Howell, Frederic Harrison was privately willing to admit to Harcourt that the amendment, for which he had denounced Howell, 'removes the main injustice of the late Act, the interference with innocent "picketing" '.[81] If the Harcourt bill had been worse than the Act it was amending, as the London Trades Council contended, it is difficult to see why employers in building and engineering should have lobbied against it so strongly.[82] To them, Howell's supposedly abject compromise went to the heart of the industrial issue at stake.[83]

Refusing to repeal or amend the Act, Bruce maintained that if it was being wrongly applied to peaceful pickets, unions should appeal and obtain authoritative decisions to clear away doubts and promote uniformity of interpretation of the statute by magistrates. This shifted the onus and expense of clarifying the law onto the TUC. It also prolonged the uncertainty because no authoritative ruling was obtained until the trial of the London cabinet-makers (*R v Hibbert*) at the Central Criminal Court on 4 and 5 May 1875, after Bruce and the Liberals had left office. That such a long interval elapsed before a case arose was in itself an indication of how few prosecutions there had been simply for peaceful picketing. Even then the outcome lent itself to differing constructions. Five striking members of the Alliance Cabinet-Makers' Association were indicted for conspiring to commit offences under the CLAA, specifically, 'watching and besetting with a view to coerce'. For several weeks they had picketed the shop of an employer who had unilaterally imposed a system of individual bargaining on his workforce.[84] Declining an offer by the prosecutors to drop the charges in return for an apology and the withdrawal of the pickets, the men stood trial in order to test the law.[85] No instances of physical molestation or disorder were brought to light, despite the investigations of two private detectives whom the firm employed, and the facts were broadly similar to those heard

[80] *Bee-Hive* (25 Feb. 1871), 2; *Sheffield Independent* (28 Feb. 1871), 6; *Bradford Evening Mail* (10 June 1872), 3.
[81] Harrison to Harcourt, 6 June 1872, Bodl. Harcourt MS dep 203, fo. 117; *Bee-Hive* (28 June 1872).
[82] *Builders' Trade Circular* (30 May 1872), 5; (20 June 1872), 5; *Western Daily Press* (7 June 1872), 1.
[83] Harcourt's bill actually went further than the 1875 Conspiracy and Protection of Property Act, which retained the 'watching and besetting' sub-section, but with a proviso: see below, Ch. 9.
[84] See the shorthand notes of the trial reprinted in Central Criminal Court (*R v Hibbert*) (*PP* 1875 lxi).
[85] *The Times* (3 June 1875), 3.

in the 1869 trial of the London shoemakers. The charge to the Old Bailey grand jury by Russell Gurney, the recorder of London, was the fullest explanation of the CLAA since it had come into force. Speaking of the pickets, Gurney observed that the main purpose of 'the watchers' was to inform 'all comers' who had been attracted to the workshop by newspaper advertisements that there was a strike 'and to endeavour to persuade them to join in it'. 'All this is lawful', Gurney stated, 'so long as it is done peaceably.' He followed Lush's distinction in the shoemakers' trial between force and intimidation and purely moral suasion. The jury were directed to consider whether the pickets had obstructed access to the firm's place of business, whether anything was done calculated to intimidate those passing to and fro, 'or whether there was an exhibition of force, calculated to produce fear in the minds of ordinary men'.[86]

Although Gurney's charge explicitly permitted peaceful persuasion of the type which the cabinet-makers had used, they were convicted at the subsequent trial and sentenced to one month's imprisonment.[87] Sir Anthony Cleasby's summing up applied a more stringent definition of 'coercion' than either Lush or Gurney had used. In particular he dwelt not upon the coercion suffered by other workers seeking employment (of which there was no evidence) but rather on that exercised upon the employers by the implicit threat of economic loss engendered by the pickets, a consideration which Lush had dismissed in the earlier case of the shoemakers but which had been paramount in the Wolverhampton trials twenty-five years earlier.

When the Conspiracy and Protection of Property Act, which among other things repealed the CLAA, was enacted in the summer of 1875, copies of Russell Gurney's charge, which had been printed as a parliamentary paper, were circulated to all courts of summary jurisdiction to illustrate how the new Act was to be interpreted.[88] This prudent step, intended to avoid a repetition of the injustices associated with the CLAA, places both Acts in a new perspective: the 1875 Act was to be understood in the light of an exposition of the measure it replaced. In other words, nothing was to be permitted after 1875 which had not been intended to be allowed in 1871.

---

[86] Central Criminal Court (Charge of the Recorder) (*PP* 1875 lxi), 2–3.
[87] *R v Hibbert and Others* (1875) 13 Cox CC 82.
[88] Circular to Clerks of Petty Sessions and Borough Justices, 30 Aug. 1875, PRO HO158/4, p. 18. See also the historical observations by D. F. Schloss on 'peaceful persuasion by pickets' (7 May 1903), PRO LAB2/1481/CL&S/L749.

CLASS LEGISLATION AND THE REPEAL CAMPAIGN

Bruce regarded himself as unlucky that the enactment of the CLAA coincided with a strike wave unmatched in scale since that of 1853. The public order imperative came into play almost immediately, following complaints from the German consul that strikebreakers brought in from Germany had been assaulted and insulted during the nine-hours strikes in the North-East in the summer and autumn of 1871. In response the Home Office urged the local authorities in Newcastle to punish the offenders and prevent any recurrences, and this produced a crop of convictions.[89]

Bruce was further undermined by miscarriages of justice, such as the Bolton and Turk cases, and by overly harsh sentencing, though both were predictable consequences of his insistence upon placing the administration of the statute in the hands of courts of summary jurisdiction. Even the royal commission appointed after Bruce left office to investigate the law, and which broadly defended the CLAA, nonetheless admitted in a piece of magisterial understatement that 'in their desire to give full effect to a salutary law', its administrators 'may have been led to strain it too far'.[90] During the passage of his bill Bruce had resisted the TUC's requests that jurisdiction be removed from unpaid justices, his only concession being that in Scotland jurisdiction would be confined to sheriff courts.[91] His answer to complaints when harsh decisions accumulated in England was that these would cease once magistrates became more familiar with the law. Instances of maladministration did not persuade him that there was a case for any 'alleviation' of the Act.[92]

A succession of cases involving the imprisonment of women defendants failed to weaken Bruce's resolution. The Home Office regarded the individuals as properly convicted, since in each instance a breach of the peace was involved and the defendants were plainly not involved in acts of peaceful persuasion. Seven wives of strikers, from among a crowd several hundred strong who shouted and banged kettles on the arrival of blacklegs, were sentenced to one week's imprisonment during the South Wales coal dispute, in August 1871.[93] A widowed washerwoman, in poor health,

---

[89] H. Winterbotham to mayor of Newcastle, 27 Oct. 1871, PRO HO34/26, pp. 270–2; E. Allen et al., *The North-East Engineers' Strikes of 1871* (1971), 136, 140.

[90] RCLL 2nd Rep. 23.

[91] *The Times* (9 Mar. 1871), 12.

[92] C. B. Adderley, reporting a conversation with Bruce, *Potteries Examiner* (2 Mar. 1872); Bruce to Matthew Allan (Greenock Trades Council), 3 Apr. 1872, *Bee-Hive* (20 Apr. 1872), 6; Bruce to Gladstone, 5 July 1873, BL Add MSS 44087, fo. 92.

[93] *Western Mail* (15 Aug. 1871), 3; (16 Aug. 1871), 2.

dragged from a crowd mobbing the flax mills in Leeds during the nine-hours strike in April 1872, was put to hard labour for fourteen days in Armley gaol.[94] Sixteen women, mainly agricultural labourers' wives, from Ascott-under-Wychwood, Oxfordshire, were imprisoned *en masse* in May 1873 by the Chipping Norton bench for periods of seven to ten days' hard labour. They allegedly used threats of bodily harm against two labourers brought in by farmers to take the places of men on strike—the women were said to have brandished sticks and, by one account not gone into at the trial, bundled the two young men over a gate—but the sentence was grossly disproportionate to whatever the women had done, which their defenders insisted was, at worst, 'larking'. What was disturbing to the government about the Chipping Norton case, which became notorious, was not the fact of convictions having taken place: Lord Selborne, the lord chancellor, considered that evidence provided sufficient proof of an offence. Instead, he criticized the magistrates' handling of the incident, suggesting that they would have done better to concentrate on those of the defendants who had been most culpable rather than incarcerating a large group of individuals whose role was peripheral. The result, he complained, was to create sympathy for the law breakers (who were commemorated as the Ascott martyrs) and to neutralize the exemplary effect of criminal proceedings.[95]

Even allowing for the bad convictions, it might be said that some of the contemporary platform and published rhetoric directed against the CLAA —an attempt to 'put artisans back into the feudal ages', 'an angel of death to working men'—seemed disproportionate to the Act's effects.[96] After all, the peak of the mid-Victorian phase of union growth came in 1874, when the CLAA was in force.[97] Much of the momentum for the agitation derived from the very successes of organized labour in the early 1870s. It gained strength from the spread of the amalgamated miners in previously unorganized coalfields in Lancashire, the Midlands, and Wales, and was articulated in the corresponding network of provincial labour newspapers forming the *Examiner* syndicate.[98] Those penalized under the CLAA were mainly the unskilled, the unorganized, and, as the Liberal MP G. O.

---

[94] *Leeds Evening News* (10 Apr. 1872), 3; (11 Apr. 1872), 4; (23 Apr. 1872), 3.

[95] *Oxford Chronicle* (24 May 1873), 5; (31 May 1873), 7; *The Times* (26 May 1873), 12; (2 June 1873), 7, 8; Selborne to Marlborough, 4 June 1873, Chipping Norton Magistrates: correspondence respecting the sentence passed (*PP* 1873 liv), 1–2. For responses to the action of the Ascott women see K. Sayer, *Women of the Fields* (1995), 128–35.

[96] *Oldham Chronicle* (22 July 1871), 7; *Potteries Examiner* (17 Feb. 1872).

[97] Clegg, Fox, and Thompson, *History*, 47.

[98] A. Jones, 'Workmen's Advocates', in J. Shattock and M. Wolff (eds), *The Victorian Periodical Press* (1982), 297; Harrison, *Independent Collier*, 6.

Trevelyan pointed out, the unenfranchised.[99] From an analysis of the known cases, the miners' leader Alexander Macdonald reckoned that under 10 per cent of those convicted were actually trade unionists, the rest being non-unionized strikers, strikers' wives, and sympathizers.[100]

Some of the disparity between rhetoric and result can be attributed to the strength of what Howell and others described as the 'sentimental grievance'.[101] This followed the precedent of the parliamentary reform agitation in the mid-1860s when, it has been contended, the concern 'to vindicate the moral character of the "people"' against Lowe's allegations of venality came almost to overshadow the practical issue at stake.[102] The rhetoric of 'stigma' crowded out discussion about what, precisely, campaigners thought strikers ought to be permitted to do to prevent others taking their places. Most of the impetus behind the demonstrations, public meetings, petitions, and representations to MPs derived from the moral arguments against a penal statute directed against working people.[103] The agitation was sometimes strongest where no prosecutions had occurred.[104] This trend was most pronounced in Scotland, where the Glasgow Trades Council appointed an executive committee to co-ordinate activities parallel to the work of the TUCPC in England. Its highly efficient campaign, which included the publication of a series of Glasgow Tracts for Trade Unionists and the organization of large demonstrations at Edinburgh, Glasgow, and Dundee, impressed a correspondent from the *New York Herald* who interviewed the campaign secretary, Andrew Boa, a stonemason promoted to clerk of works.[105] But the executive omitted to fulfil its instruction to collect and publish 'full and reliable reports of prosecutions successful and unsuccessful under the Act'.[106] Only four Scottish cases resulted in convictions up to the time of the last demonstration at Dundee in January 1874, and sentencing by the sheriffs was conspicuously more lenient than in England.

The campaign broadened the TUC from its origin as a sectional pressure group: as one Liberal paper commented, the delegates of 700,000 unionists

[99] *Dundee Advertiser* (5 Jan. 1874).

[100] *Glasgow Sentinel* (24 July 1875).

[101] *Bradford Evening Mail* (10 June 1872), 4; Mundella to Leader, 11 Mar. 1871, Mundella MSS 6P/61; cf. A. Anderson, 'The Political Symbolism of the Labour Laws', *Bulletin of the Society for the Study of Labour History*, 23 (1971), 13; R. Q. Gray, *The Labour Aristocracy in Victorian Edinburgh* (1976), 154.

[102] Biagini, *Liberty*, 260.

[103] Associated Carpenters and Joiners of Scotland, 12th Annual Report, 1873, 2, MRC MSS 78/C&JS/4/1/1.

[104] *Bradford Evening Mail* (10 June 1872), 3; *Kidderminster Shuttle* (29 June 1872), 6.

[105] *Labour League Examiner* (6 June 1874), 2.

[106] *Glasgow United Trades' Council, 1872-3*, 6.

attending the Leeds TUC represented, through their wives, children, and the 'dependent' workmen who worked alongside them, possibly a majority of the 'industrial population'.[107] Campaigners regarded the CLAA as a challenge to the identities of working men as producers, citizens, and even, following the prosecutions of strikers' wives, as heads of families. They dwelt on the 'insult', 'stigma', and sense of exclusion implied by the Act: it was both 'derogatory to the character of trade unionists' and a 'direct insult to the whole industrial order'.[108] A carpenter told a meeting in Bolton that there was no justification for a special law directed against trade unionists, since they were 'as peaceable, as intelligent, as skilled and as patriotic subjects as any in the nation'.[109] To the politically Conservative Manchester and Salford Trades Council, the CLAA was 'exceptional' because it inflicted 'pains and penalties upon one class of Her Majesty's subjects'.[110] At the first conference of the West of England and South Wales Labourers Union, the corresponding secretary contended that the CLAA denied the right of his members 'to be treated as citizens of the state'.[111] 'Woe to England's Manhood if it submits to clerical persecution of workmen's wives and children', a banner proclaimed at the London Trades Council rally 'to protest against the Criminal Law Amendment Act, and other class-made laws which favour employers and punish workmen': the slogan referred to the incarceration of the Ascott-under-Wychwood women by parson magistrates at Chipping Norton.[112]

It is as a denial of equal citizenship, rather than in terms of any practical effect upon trade union activity—of which there is very little evidence—that the CLAA is best understood. Where the CLAA undermined the intended effect of the Trade Union Act, it was because the latter sought to be integrative, while the CLAA, by defining offences committed only by wage earners, created a sense of class cleavage. It thus weakened the objective of those Liberals who, in the previous decade, had urged franchise extension to prevent a popular agitation assuming a class character.[113] In the industrial sphere, Mundella regarded the CLAA as equally damaging, for it undermined the formal equality between capital and labour upon which his schemes for conciliation were founded. Far from the CLAA being a useful disciplinary mechanism to underpin the formalization of industrial rela-

---

[107] *Daily Telegraph* (16 Dec. 1873), 5

[108] *The Times* (8 Mar. 1871), 5; *Reformer* (1 Apr. 1871), 4.

[109] *Bolton Chronicle* (18 Nov. 1871).

[110] *Sixth Annual Report of the Manchester and Salford Trades Council* (1872), 15.

[111] *Western Daily Press* (16 July 1873).

[112] *Bee-Hive* (7 June 1873), 9.

[113] E.g. W. E. Forster in 1865, cited in Steele, *Palmerston*, 222.

tions, he saw it as standing in the way of mutual trust, creating suspicion and resentment which obstructed attempts to persuade the men to accept rational alterations to the organization of work.[114]

When the CLAA was repealed some of Bruce's strongest critics acknowledged, in private, that the CLAA would not have been an inherently unjust law if it had been fairly administered.[115] It would have been less exposed to the 'class legislation' complaint if it had been framed in a different form. Later developments vindicated Bruce's judgement that there had been a gap in the English criminal law relating to threats of violence and various types of social annoyance: his error was to assume that a remedy for this deficiency could, after 1867, be confined to the circumstances of working people acting in combination.[116] It is hard to dispute the contemporary assessment that the CLAA was 'a truly miserable bungle'.[117] That 'bungle' was compounded when the intervention of a judge, in the gas stokers' case of December 1872, demolished the protections against the common law which lay at the heart of the CLAA, and left the Liberal attempt to settle the union question in ruins.

---

[114] Sheffield Chamber of Commerce Minutes, 24 Jan. 1874, LD 1986/1, pp. 337–8.

[115] Beesly to Crompton, 8 Sept. 1875, Beesly MSS; Crompton to Howell, 6 Sept. 1875, Howell MSS; cf. Harrison to John Morley, 19 Apr. 1873, Harrison MSS 1/56; Mundella to Leader, 30 May 1873, Mundella MSS 6P/63/4.

[116] J. F. Stephen, *A History of the Criminal Law of England* (3 vols., 1883), iii. 320–1; cf. Harrison, *Drink and the Victorians*, 256–7.

[117] Crompton, 'The Government and Class Legislation', 29.

7

The Gas Stokers' Case and the Freedom to Strike

'With a statute only eighteen months old to guide him, what did the Judge go wandering through his musty old books for?', George Odger complained following the imprisonment of five gas stokers for conspiracy after an unsuccessful strike in London in December 1872.[1] Whether the law laid down by Sir William Brett in *R v Bunn and Others* (the gas stokers' case) was founded upon 'musty' old law or was the product of modern judicial creativity provided a subject for legal debate. Whatever its basis, Brett's ruling has been described as 'one of the most momentous English court decisions of the nineteenth century'.[2] Strikers, whether trade unionists or not, who had been promised that 'common or judge-made law would be swept away', found that a completely unexpected judicial intervention had 'turned the whole flank of the legislation of 1871'.[3]

The case's significance is well-established in the legal historical literature,[4] though rather less so within the labour history tradition. In the latter, the case has sometimes been presented as if it were an extreme instance of the CLAA's oppressiveness. This view served the rhetorical purpose of implying that the Liberal government's legislation was responsible for the indictment of the stokers.[5] A number of new issues were raised by the case: the judge's handling of the trial and his sentence on the stokers; the revival of the law of conspiracy in labour cases; the limits of the freedom to strike where the safety of the public was endangered; and the inequality of the Master and Servant Act, whose alteration was now added to repeal of the CLAA in the TUC's programme, agreed at Leeds in January 1873.[6]

---

[1] *The Times* (10 Jan. 1873), 3.
[2] Kahn-Freund, *Labour and the Law*, 230.
[3] George Dixon MP to a deputation of Birmingham trade unionists; report in Birmingham Trades Council Minutes (1869–73) i. 97; 3*H* ccxvii. 1535 (4 Aug. 1873).
[4] Rubin, 'Historical Development', 323–4; Orth, *Combination and Conspiracy*, 142.
[5] See e.g. Harrison, *Before the Socialists*, 297.
[6] *Bee-Hive* (25 Jan. 1873), 3.

THE LONDON STOKERS' STRIKE

For a generation the Home Office had treated strikes as private matters between employers and their workers, with whom government should not interfere except when violence arose. When the immunities written into the CLAA to secure the freedom to strike had been drawn up, no consideration was given to two issues: first, the damage to the public caused by strikes in essential services (though the Erle commission had discussed banning strikes among railway engine drivers after a series of stoppages in 1867); and second, the position of strikers in breach of contract, which was thought to be settled by the Master and Servant Act of 1867.[7] These problems surfaced when state employees took part in the strike wave of 1871–3. Strikes of Post Office telegraphists in 1871, though not put down by law, were speedily suppressed.[8] In November 1872 six divisions of the Metropolitan Police refused to go on duty until PC Goodchild, who had been dismissed for acting as secretary to a 'most mischievous association' which sought increases in police pay to meet the higher cost of living, was reinstated. Their strike was met with prosecutions and imprisonment under a special Act regulating the police.[9] Press alarm at the prospect of central London being left unguarded on a Saturday night prompted a suggestion that employment in vital services could not be regulated by the ordinary conditions of the labour market. One paper suggested that those employed by the government in 'the services required for the protection of society' should receive more than the market rate of wages, 'but on the understanding that the labourer if he comes to us must forfeit his rights of combination, and his liberty of striking'.[10]

A separate issue arose when essential workers were in private employment. In August 1872 a strike by bakers raised the question of the rights of the community 'when threatened by a strike which affects its very existence'.[11] Troops were brought in to gather the harvest in Berkshire and Oxfordshire during the agricultural labourers' strikes in August and September 1872, but following protests by London Trades Council the neutrality of the executive government in labour disputes was reaffirmed. The War Office's regulations were altered to prevent such use of troops in

[7] RCTU 11th Rep. xxiii, cv.
[8] See files in GPO archives POST30/215/E274/1872. No evidence has been found to support the account in H. G. Swift, *A History of the Postal Agitation* (1900), 87–8, that a conspiracy indictment against the leaders of the postal workers was being prepared late in 1873.
[9] PRO MEPOL3/131, special report, 29 Nov. 1872.
[10] *Morning Advertiser* (21 Nov. 1872), in PRO MEPOL2/148.
[11] *Spectator* (31 Aug. 1872), 1097.

future.[12] Even when, in October 1872, a 'simultaneous strike' by gas stokers threatened production from one London supplier, the Home Office turned down a request from the employers for assistance: 'The Secretary of State cannot in any way interfere in the dispute between the Company and the men in their employ.'[13]

Gas lighting made London, in the eyes of contemporaries, 'the most illuminated capital city in Europe'.[14] Since the security of persons and property was thought to depend upon the illumination of the capital's streets, a strike by stokers potentially carried both considerable inconvenience and possible danger to the public. Though not regarded as skilled, the stokers possessed dexterity as well as a great deal of strength and endurance. New men took several months to reach the levels of productivity achieved by the regular teams of stokers. Moreover, only very limited quantities of gas could be stored so sudden interruptions in the manufacturing process would very rapidly affect consumers. A mixture of autocratic and paternal management strategies were adopted by the companies to secure a disciplined, regular workforce tied to contracts which generally required a week or even a month's notice of termination. Recurrent attempts to develop machinery to charge the retorts showed the anxiety of the companies to reduce their dependence upon the stokers.[15]

The gas companies' vulnerability to concerted action by the men increased during the early 1870s. A large area of central London had become dependent upon a single source of supply as a result of the expansionist policy followed by the largest company, the Gas Light and Coke Company (GLCC) or Chartered Company as it was sometimes known. Between 1869 and 1872 it acquired five other companies and consolidated a monopoly from Pimlico to the City, closing smaller gas-producing works and concentrating production at Beckton, East London, which, when it opened in 1870, was the largest and most modern plant of its kind in the world. Although subject to Board of Trade dividend and price control, the GLCC came under increasing attack from the Metropolitan Board of Works and the City of London Corporation. The company was accused of being over-capitalized and inefficient, providing both a poor quality and an expensive service to the public, the Beckton works having failed to achieve the predicted economies of scale.[16]

---

[12] Webb, *History*, 332; War Office to George Shipton, 25 Nov. 1872, *Bee-Hive* (30 Nov. 1872), 5.

[13] H. Wintherbotham to H. Chubb, 28 Oct. 1872, PRO HO136/7, 471–2.

[14] See L. Nead, *Victorian Babylon: People, Streets and Images in Nineteenth-Century London* (2000), pt. ii ('Gas and Light').   [15] E. J. Hobsbawm, *Labouring Men* (1964), ch. 9.

[16] S. Everard, *History of the Gas Light and Coke Company, 1812–1949* (1949), ch. 15;

Labour market conditions in 1872 enabled the stokers, like other previously unorganized groups, to form a union and begin a movement for wage increases and to abolish Sunday labour. Taking advantage of the companies' unpopularity with consumers, supporters of the stokers, notably the radical Lloyd Jones, urged them to win public sympathy for their cause. A claim to be relieved from working on Sundays was well adapted to appeal to the consciences of gas company shareholders, many of whom were known to be 'ladies and clergymen seeking a safe, steady return on their capital'.[17] Initially the stokers' movement followed the example set by the Amalgamated Society of Railway Servants which, backed by middle-class patrons, sought to achieve their aim of shorter working hours by appeals to the travelling public rather than by strikes.[18] Not only was this method regarded by its advocates as morally superior to the threat of a strike, it also had a greater chance of success—earlier strike movements among both railwaymen and gas workers had been defeated. It was also less likely to endanger the objective of forming durable associations to protect previously unorganized groups of unskilled or semi-skilled workers. Significant gains were achieved by the stokers without the use of strikes: fourteen out of twenty-five gasworks in London were induced to end Sunday work, and wage increases were also conceded.

In the gas industry, as on the railways, the companies responded by weeding out known activists. The railwaymen dealt with this by setting up a victimization fund to support those deprived of their jobs. Henry Broadhurst of the stonemasons recommended such a tactic to the stokers' union, warning them not to endanger their fledgeling association by striking on behalf of those who were victimized, but to support them until they found other work. Instead, a meeting of the stokers' union delegates on 1 December 1872, held in secret to prevent the companies from anticipating the contingency, agreed on a strike throughout London on the following day to secure the reinstatement of the sacked men.[19] The flashpoint

---

S. Hughes, *The Construction of Gas Works* (1880), 82; J. F. B. Firth, *The Gas Supply of London* (1874), 37; T. H. Farrer, 'Industrial Monopolies', *Quarterly Review*, 131 (Oct. 1871), 482; cf. T. L. Alborn, *Conceiving Companies: Joint-Stock Politics in Victorian England* (1998), 168.

[17] *Journal of Gas Lighting* (5 Nov. 1872), 924–5; for the numbers of women and clergy shareholders, see *PP* 1867 lviii. 585.

[18] Cordery, 'Mutualism, Friendly Societies, and the Genesis of Railway Trade Unions', 272.

[19] The circumstances of the strike are documented in the Gas Stokers Defence Committee, *The London Gas Stokers: A Report by the Committee* (1873), which contains the trial proceedings (see also *R v Bunn* (1872) 12 Cox CC 316–51); *Journal of Gas Lighting* (5 Nov. 1872), 924; (3 Dec. 1872), 997; (17 Dec. 1872), 1025–43; *The Times* (4 Dec. 1872), 5; (5 Dec.), 3; (6 Dec.), 10; (7 Dec.), 9; (11 Dec.), 8; Everard, *Gas Light and Coke Company*, 244–5; *PP* lvii esp. Qs. 310, 1342–3; and the records of the London gas companies in the London Metropolitan Archives

occurred on the following morning when the shifts changed at Beckton. All 500 men gathered to confront the superintendent and threatened to strike unless a delegate who had been discharged was reinstated (which the superintendent agreed to do under duress). They also demanded that victimized men at another company's works in Fulham be given their jobs back. When the superintendent claimed to be unable to interfere in the other company's affairs, they walked out, as did men at all but one of the other fourteen gasworks in London.

The stokers' delegates seem to have expected that the companies would cave in, so as not to incur the public odium of depriving London of artificial light in the middle of winter. At Beckton the men waited nearby expecting to be called back. The trial judge took that fact as indicative of their belief that they could exercise irresistible force upon their employers and, therefore, strong evidence of the strikers' coercive intent. A less hostile construction was that the stokers had merely wished to remind the companies that they were indispensable, and were fully prepared to return to work immediately without inconveniencing the public.[20] Instead, the companies, who had made secret plans to link their mains and supply one another in the event of a strike, toughed it out. Resorting to the tactic successfully used to break stokers' strikes in 1834 and 1859, the companies brought in unskilled labour as replacements. Although the strike led to a dimming of street lighting—arriving in London on the second day, the earl of Derby found 'some confusion and a great deal of alarm'[21]—a limited supply was maintained. This gradually increased, albeit at very considerable cost (which the GLCC later tried to pass on to London's gas consumers) since it took 2,000 new men to carry out the work formerly done at Beckton by the 500 strikers.

The gas companies had little difficulty in fixing the blame for the interruption of the gas supply upon the stokers. Instead of turning on the companies, consumers responded to appeals for economy and stockpiled candles, while the strikers themselves received little support from workers in other trades whose livelihoods in the approach to Christmas were threatened by the loss of gaslight in their workshops. That many of the stokers' leaders were reportedly Irish did not increase solidarity. Moreover, those who had helped the stokers' attempts at unionization regarded their walk-

esp. minutes of the Commercial Gas Co. B/CGC/8, 172–3; Gas Light and Coke Co. B/GLCC/32/1, 208–226; Imperial Gas Light and Coke Co. B/ImpGLC/28, 146–7, 152, 169–70; B/ImpGLC/76, 254–6, 263, 278, 300–1, 314; London Gaslight Co., B/LGLC/5 (11 Dec. 1872); Phoenix Gas Light and Coke Co. B/Ph.G/III/20, 430; South Metropolitan Gas Light and Coke Co. B/S.MetG/III/7/1, 295, 304–7, 311.

[20] F. Harrison, 'Misrepresentation of Strikes', *Bee-Hive* (18 Jan. 1873), 1–2.
[21] *The Times* (8 Jan. 1873), 11; MS Derby diary, 3 Dec., 4 Dec. 1872.

out as 'mistaken and ill-judged', correctly predicting that it was likely to bring about the destruction of the union. The strike crumbled within days. Facing destitution, strikers pleaded to be allowed to return to work but many companies, the GLCC being the most obdurate, refused. Blacklists were circulated to prevent the stokers getting work with other companies.

THE STOKERS' TRIAL

Like railway companies, the gas conglomerates were no strangers to litigation and they readily turned to the law to punish the men. Early in the strike several of the companies took out summonses against strikers, who had all left work without notice, and secured convictions with terms of six weeks' hard labour under section 14 of the 1867 Master and Servant Act, which treated 'aggravated' breaches of contract as criminal offences. The most systematic use of the Master and Servant Act was made by the GLCC. Its secretary J. O. Phillips (known as 'the Bismarck of Gas' on account of his aggressive expansion of the company) arranged for summonses to be taken out against all 500 Beckton men, as well as those who had struck at the company's other works. Only twenty-three Beckton men and two from Bow Common were actually brought to trial, all but one of whom received six weeks' hard labour; those proceeded against included known union delegates. In addition, on the advice of the GLCC's solicitors, summonses for conspiracy were taken out against 'the ringleaders'. Two of these, described by the company as 'the principal mutineers', absconded in terror and rewards were offered for their apprehension. By this time the strikers were defeated, but the legal process was continued with vigour and expedition.[22] On 19 December 1872 five gas stokers employed by the GLCC at Beckton were tried at the Central Criminal Court on ten counts of conspiracy, the deputy-recorder of London and Liberal MP, Sir Thomas Chambers, having described the men's action as a 'revolt'.[23]

As well as provoking the recurrence of older forms of language to describe industrial conflict, the stokers' walk-out led to a revival of legal doctrines which regarded strikes as an improper coercion of employers. Sir William Brett, the trial judge, divided the counts of conspiracy for which they were indicted into two types. One was for conspiring to interfere with the free will

---

[22] Gas Light and Coke Co., Minutes of Court of Directors, 6 Dec. 1872, 13 Dec. 1872, LMA B/GLCC/32/1; Imperial Gas Co., Minutes of Committee of Works, 4 Dec. 1872, LMA B/ImpGLC/76; *The Times* (7 Dec. 1872), 9.

[23] *R v Bunn* (1872) 12 Cox CC, 316; *The Times* (17 Dec. 1872), 10.

of the gas company in the management of its business by the use of improper threats and molestation (by which was meant, threatening a lightning strike to force the company to do something which it would not otherwise have been willing to do); the second was for conspiring to commit an offence under the Master and Servant Act by breaking their contracts. Those counts which were framed upon the first type of conspiracy were the most contentious since they were based upon the common law and not upon any statute. As the defence solicitors pointed out, if the men were convicted on those counts, any combination to induce an employer to do something he might not otherwise want to do could constitute a criminal conspiracy.[24]

Brett rejected the argument of the defence counsel, Douglas Straight, that the 1871 legislation had extinguished the common law offences, and directed the jury:[25]

if there was an agreement among the defendants by improper molestation to control the will of the employers, then I tell you that would be an illegal conspiracy at common law, and that such an offence is not abrogated by the Criminal Law Amendment Act.

The stokers were not, however, found guilty of this common law conspiracy but were convicted for a conspiracy to commit a statutory offence by simultaneously breaking their contracts. For the latter they were sentenced to twelve months' imprisonment (four times the maximum laid down by the Master and Servant Act for aggravated breaches of contract) in spite of the jury's recommendation for mercy.

Brett was acting strictly within his powers since a conspiracy to commit a statutory offence was a misdemeanour, for which the punishment was up to two years' hard labour. In his summing up to the jury he had acknowledged that the workers employed by the gas companies were under no contractual obligations to the public, and the effect on the public formed technically no part of the offence. But the danger and inconvenience to inhabitants of the capital was a fundamental issue both in the evidence against the men and the sentence which he passed. 'The first and most obvious effect would be to set the whole of the thieves of London to work', a police court magistrate commented at an earlier stage of the proceedings.[26] Counsel for the GLCC, H. S. Giffard (later Lord Halsbury) did not omit to stress this point in his opening address.[27] One commentator suggested that the trial exposed a weakness of the *laissez-faire* policy towards strikes:

[24] *The London Gas Stokers. A Report* (1873), 13.
[25] 12 Cox CC 331–3, 340.
[26] *Journal of Gas Lighting* (17 Dec. 1872), 1,041.
[27] *The Times* (20 Dec. 1872), 11.

where the public was threatened, the right to strike should be curtailed, but at the same time employers should be obliged to recognize and deal with the men's unions to resolve differences.[28] Even the stokers' defence committee, though sharply critical of the companies, was at pains not to justify the strike.[29]

'In passing sentence of punishment', Brett later told the Home Office in explanation of his severity, 'the disregard of public safety is always a main element'. In his view, the very degree of organization of the strike showed that the men were intelligent and capable of knowing the consequences of their action. The secrecy with which they carried out their resolution simultaneously to strike was proof, in his view, that they were aware that they were doing wrong. Brett was strongly impressed that one of the delegates spoke of the resolution as 'a secret that he would not tell his father if he rose from the grave'—an echo of the oath which had led to the transportation of the Dorchester labourers nearly forty years previously.[30]

Brett's handling of the trial contributed to a discernible shift in trade unionist attitudes towards the judiciary. The idea that judges were hostile to combination is such a commonplace that it is worth emphasizing the strength of popular confidence in the judiciary before the gas stokers' trial. Unions did, of course, want to be protected from what William Allan of the engineers had called, in 1868, 'judge-made law', and the leader of the boilermakers complained that the Court of Queen's Bench which decided *Hornby v Close* had been unduly influenced by a hostile public opinion.[31] But the comte de Paris observed that the British delegates to the congress of the First International at Lausanne declined to support a motion censuring the *Hornby v Close* decision, on the ground that it was 'a point of law' and therefore beyond politics.[32] Indeed, after the unfavourable judgment in *Skinner v Kitch*, also in 1867, a Bolton stonemason, who later became prominent in the campaign against the CLAA, insisted that 'the prevailing opinion of working men in this country is that, for integrity and impartiality in the administration of the law as they find it, our judges stand unrivalled'.[33] A marked theme of popular radicalism in this period was its deep attachment to the rule of law.[34] It was the middle-class Positivist, E. S.

---

[28] 'The Limitations on the Right of Striking', *Spectator* (7 Dec. 1872), 1, 544–5.

[29] *The Times* (21 Dec. 1872), 5; Broadhurst to Ludlow, 29 Dec. 1872, Ludlow MSS Add 7348/1, fo. 21.

[30] W. B. Brett to Home Office, 25 Jan. 1873, PRO HO45/9326/18243/24.

[31] *Bee-Hive* (17 Oct. 1868), 5; (9 Mar. 1867), 6.

[32] *Trades' Unions of England*, 231; *The Times* (7 Sept. 1867), 10.

[33] *Bee-Hive* (1 June 1867), 7.

[34] Biagini and Reid, *Currents of Radicalism*, 5, 11.

Beesly, who alleged that judges were on the side of the employers, while the bitterest, most sarcastic personal attack on Sir William Erle's report had been from the pen of the Christian Socialist lawyer, J. M. Ludlow.[35]

While judges were sometimes outspoken in their views, they were careful to ensure that trials should be seen to be fair, and their sentencing of men whose previous characters were in the main exemplary was usually merciful. Cresswell's refusal to permit a rushed trial of the Preston strikers in 1854, and Bramwell's unwillingness to imprison the tailors in 1867, have already been noted. The senior judges had also been anxious to refute the misconception that the law failed to protect union funds against theft. Bramwell summed up strongly against the secretary of the Birmingham lodge of the stonemasons, indicted in July 1868 (at a time when the masons were denounced on all sides for their restrictive trade policies) for embezzling society funds, and sentenced him to nine months' hard labour.[36] Unionist invective against unfavourable judgments tended as a result to be directed against the vindictiveness of employers in bringing prosecutions, the bias of shopkeeper juries, the harsh sentencing of magistrates, whether unpaid or stipendiary, or the improper interference of the police in matters between the men and their employers. The acquittal of the London shoemaker pickets in 1869, following Lush's favourable summing up, had inspired George Odger with the hope that trade unions would in future receive 'fair play' from the courts.[37]

Brett broke with a number of these conventions. He had not been seen to ensure that justice was done to the poor and uneducated men brought before him by a wealthy and powerful company employing leading counsel. He refused defence requests for a postponement to the next sessions even though briefs for defence counsel had not been prepared until the night before the trial. This prevented evidence from being gathered to show that the companies themselves customarily dismissed men at a moment's notice when demand was slack. Brett's summing up, which some alleged was unduly influenced by a vengeful public mood, was held to lack impartiality. He was accused of inventing an *ex post facto* offence, of which the men could not conceivably have known. And most of all, he disregarded the jury's recommendation for mercy and passed a sentence more severe than any that had been imposed on non-violent combined action perhaps since the trial of the Dorchester labourers.

These points were made in an uncompromising memorial for clemency,

---

[35] *Bee-Hive* (21 Sept. 1867), 5.
[36] OSM FR 9–23 July 1868, MRC MSS 78/OS/4/1/29.
[37] *Bee-Hive* (16 Jan. 1869), 1.

drafted by George Howell on behalf of the Gas Stokers Defence Committee and forwarded to the Home Office. The petition, which did not adopt the usual form of a remorseful solicitation for mercy, conveyed the animosity felt towards the judge.[38] Elsewhere, in a visceral attack, John Morley denounced the sentence as 'truly scandalous', passed to appease public, and specifically middle-class, prejudice.[39] At protest meetings trade unionists and plebeian radicals complained that it was 'oppressive and vindictive', and 'cruel', and attacked Brett by name as a political partisan: he had sat as a Conservative MP and had been promoted to the bench under the Conservative government in 1868.[40]

There was sufficient level of protest to cause Liberal MPs, as recipients of resolutions from public meetings in their constituencies, to press for official intervention.[41] One such, the Rochdale MP Thomas Bayley Potter, was privately informed by Gladstone that, although the prerogative of mercy could not be exercised politically, the case was being investigated within the Home Office.[42] Bruce had declined to meet a deputation from the defence committee, and failed, contrary to normal practice, to acknowledge the memorial on behalf of the men (it was 'so offensive that it could not be noticed') but he had forwarded it to Brett for comment.[43] Before, it seems, that Brett's reply was received, the Cabinet endorsed a decision—which could not but be regarded as political—to remit eight months of the men's sentences. Gladstone reported to the queen that 'many considerations', which 'did not in any degree impugn either the law laid down by the Judge or even the soundness of the judgment', enabled the Cabinet to make the recommendation.[44] Those 'considerations' included the jury's recommendation for mercy and the fact that the law had been vindicated 'so far as the public were concerned'. Brett's comments on the case, when they finally arrived, did not concede anything to the defence committee's memorial and he left it to the Home Office to find any extenuating circumstances in the men's favour.[45]

[38] *The London Gas Stokers*, 42; *The Times* (8 Jan. 1873), 11; draft of memorial, Howell MSS LB12, fos. 189–97.

[39] *The Times* (8 Jan. 1873), 11; J. Morley, 'The Five Gas Stokers', *Fortnightly Review*, n.s. 13 (Jan. 1873), 138.

[40] *The Times* (21 Dec. 1872), 5; (23 Dec. 1872), 5; (10 Jan. 1873), 3; (22 Jan. 1873), 9.

[41] Winterbotham to J. J. Grieve MP, PRO HO136/8, p.372; Charles Foster MP to the secretary of Walsall Trades Council, 15 Jan. 1873, in *Walsall Free Press* (18 Jan. 1873); *Midlands Advertiser* (8 Feb. 1873); J. Newton, *W. S. Caine MP* (1907), 53.

[42] Gladstone to T. B. Potter, 15 Jan. 1873, Matthew, *GD*, viii. 271.

[43] Mundella to Leader, 2 Feb. 1873, Mundella MSS 6P/63/12.

[44] Gladstone to the Queen, 22 Jan. 1873, Bodl. MS Film 597 (CAB41/5/2); Matthew, *GD*, viii. 273 (22 Jan. 1873).

[45] W. B. Brett to Home Office, 25 Jan. 1873, PRO HO45/9326/18243/24.

As Brett pointed out, there was no petition from the men themselves, and only after further intrigues, in which Thomas Hughes acted as an intermediary between the Home Office and the men's solicitors, was a reasonably penitent plea for mercy obtained from the prisoners in Maidstone gaol. The Home Office treated this as sufficient to act on, and the remissions were announced at the beginning of February 1873. The duration was carefully chosen to preserve the principle that a sentence for a conspiracy to commit a statutory offence might exceed that for the offence itself—not because the principle was supported, but that it was for Parliament, not the Home Office, to alter it.[46] No gratitude was expressed at the breakfast organized by Maidstone Trades Council to celebrate the men's release, in April 1873, an occasion which, like the contemporary campaign on behalf of the Tichborne Claimant, signified a palpable ebbing away of popular respect for the administrators of the law.[47]

REFORM OF THE LAW OF CONSPIRACY

Brett's ruling showed that the protections written into the CLAA had proved insufficient to shield strikers from the common law. He instructed the jury that the gas strike was a conspiracy at common law, not because it attempted to restrain the free course of trade—which the draftsman of the CLAA assumed was at the root of the common law doctrines against combination—but because it constituted an unjustifiable interference with the free will of the employers in the conduct of their business. The strikers' threat to leave London in darkness unless their demands were met was an obstruction of the free will 'of persons of ordinary nerve and courage';[48] and though not one of the offences defined as molestation in the CLAA, it was held to be a criminal conspiracy at common law when carried out by several persons acting in combination. As Brett explained to the Home Office, he found the law for this in Erle's decision in the Wolverhampton tin-plate workers' case (*R v Rowlands*), where the threats against the manufacturer were held to create such alarm in his mind as to force him to alter the mode of carrying out his business, and especially in Bramwell's charge in the London tailors' trial (*R v Druitt*) which ruled that an agreement by a

---

[46] 'The Humble Memorial of John Bunn ...' (received 30 Jan. 1873); G. Lushington, 'Memorandum on the Course taken in Regard to the Sentence Passed on the Gas Stokers' (4 Feb. 1873) PRO HO45/9326/18243/28 and 30; Howell, *Labour Legislation*, 248–9.

[47] *Bee-Hive* (18 Apr. 1873), 4; McWilliam, *Popular Politics in Nineteenth-Century England*, 69.

[48] Brett to Home Office, 25 Jan. 1873, PRO HO45/9326/18243/24.

number of men to coerce the liberty of another man's mind was a criminal conspiracy.[49]

When he introduced his measures in 1871, Bruce had criticized the effects of the judge-made doctrines of conspiracy, citing with approval the critical observations of Bentham and Fitzjames Stephen.[50] After the gas stokers' case, the Home Office sought the opinion of the government's law officers to establish what the position now was, and whether the law needed to be changed to ensure that strikers would not in future be exposed to criminal proceedings for conspiracy. In addition the law officers were asked for an opinion as to whether the common law of conspiracy as a whole should be 'retained, amended or abolished'.[51]

The Home Office's concerns were linked to a wider debate, initiated by writers such as Fitzjames Stephen, Frederic Harrison, R. S. Wright, and Vernon Harcourt, which had its origins in the tailors' trial of 1867. Ought judges to be free to use the law of conspiracy to declare that acts committed by several persons in combination were criminal, which were not punishable by an individual acting alone? Perhaps the most influential commentator, and certainly the most persistent, was Stephen, recently returned from India where he had been legal member of the viceroy's council. Impressed by the example of the Indian Penal Code, Stephen was energetically promoting the codification of the English criminal law,[52] and he seized the opportunity presented by the gas stokers' case to advertise the benefits which 'all classes' had in codification. Following the passage of parliamentary reform he had sought to enlist the political force of enfranchised labour in support of the cause. Of all members of the community, he noted, trade unionists were those most directly exposed to the obscurity of the common law. His aim in England, as in India, was to promote strong government by ensuring that the criminal law was 'knowable'. Within days of the stokers' conviction, he went into print with an account, derived from his textbook commentaries, showing how Brett's ruling was an example of a doctrine 'devised exclusively by the Judges out of their own heads', to enable them 'retrospectively' to punish acts done for any purpose of which they happened to disapprove. He thus confirmed the defence committee's allegation that the men could not have known that they were committing an offence.[53]

[49] Ibid.
[50] 3H cciv. 260, 262–3 (14 Feb. 1871).
[51] Request for Law Officers' Opinion, 7 Feb. 1873, PRO HO45/9326/18243/30a.
[52] Smith, *James Fitzjames Stephen*, 73–83; E. Stokes, *The English Utilitarians in India* (1959), 278–83; J. F. Stephen, 'Codification in India and England', *Fortnightly Review*, 12 (Dec. 1872), 649; cf. Stephen's comments on R. Kettle, 'The Law of Conspiracy in its Modern Application', NAPSS, *Sessional Proceedings, 1873–4*, 88–9.
[53] *The Times* (25 Dec. 1872), 9 (reprinted from the *Pall Mall Gazette*).

Stephen was not condoning the stokers' strike. Quite the reverse: he suggested that by introducing the anomaly of the common law into the trial, the object of criminal justice had been undermined. It had created a sense of injustice, which overshadowed the men's actual offence—the breaking of their agreements in circumstances which threatened public safety—for which it was proper that they should be punished, though he considered the sentence to be excessive. It was the duty of the men to give proper notice before leaving their employment, but this moral lesson of the trial had been been lost.

To Stephen, Brett's direction also showed the difficulty facing legislators who sought to create exceptions to the common law: 'The real fact is that the common law is so vague that it is impossible to make intelligible exceptions to it. To try to do so is like trying to scoop a hole in quicksand.'[54] Many of the common law conspiracies, as he demonstrated in one of his articles on the subject in the *Pall Mall Gazette*, had been evolved by judges to meet deficiencies in particular areas of law (frauds, for example). Those offences would need to be defined before the common law could be swept away. But the prospects of implementing his preferred solution, an English penal code like that drawn up for India, were remote, and in the meantime he lent his support to an immediate amendment of the law to reverse the effect of Brett's ruling. Stephen believed that Brett's interpretation of the law was probably correct: the doctrine applied in the gas stokers' case rested technically upon the 'extremely shadowy' branch of the law of conspiracy 'which treats as conspiracies combinations for the purposes of injuring individuals by means other than fraud'. On the other hand, Stephen believed that any value the doctrine might have was outweighed by the dangers produced when its result was to undermine a statute which had been passed to settle a bitter and potentially dangerous controversy. In 1871 Parliament had agreed to legalize strikes; in the light of the recent trial there needed to be an amending statute to make parliament's intention 'effective and thorough-going'.[55]

Another writer with an interest in criminal codification, the secularist academic radical R. S. Wright, published in May 1873 a treatise on *The Law of Criminal Conspiracies and Agreements*, which also promoted the cause of law amendment. Wright had held government employment as secretary to the truck commission and then as draftsman of a criminal code for Jamaica commissioned by the Colonial Office.[56] Although his treatise surveyed the

---

[54] Ibid.   [55] *Pall Mall Gazette* (17 Apr. 1873), 1420–1.
[56] M. L. Friedland, 'R. S. Wright's Model Criminal Code', *Oxford Journal of Legal Studies*, 1 (1981), 326.

law of conspiracy as a whole, it necessarily focussed upon the question of unions and strikes since 'the most prominent characteristic of the law of criminal combinations in the present century is its extended application to combinations of workmen'.[57] He extended the historical argument which F. D. Longe had earlier propounded,[58] that the textbook cases of conspiracy against workmen before 1800 were not conspiracies at common law, but conspiracies for purposes prohibited by the statutes then in force regulating wages: once the statutes regulating wages were repealed, the grounds for treating workers' combinations as criminal conspiracies were removed also. Parliament had therefore been acting under a misapprehension in 1825 when it sought to restore the common law against labour combinations, since those combinations never had been conspiracies at common law but conspiracies to violate statutes which were now no longer in force. It followed that the decisions against combinations since 1825 were in fact newly created law, and an unwarranted assumption of legislative power on the part of the judges.[59]

It was an indication of the movement of contemporary opinion that a critique of Brett's charge by Frederic Harrison convinced *The Times* that a case had been made out for amending the law.[60] Whether this was likely to happen depended on the law officers' opinion, which was drawn up by Coleridge, Jessel, and Charles Bowen (who had worked with Wright on the truck commission), and presented to the Home Office in May 1873.[61] Their opinion reflected the conclusions of Stephen and Wright, though they preferred Wright's particular view that the doctrine enunciated by Brett was 'of very modern origin'—so modern, in fact, as to be unaffected by the 1871 Act. Although the doctrine had never been fully discussed on appeal, they warned that it was consistent with the language of other judges in recent rulings, and like Stephen they considered that there was every likelihood that other judges would follow it. They recommended further legislation to prevent Brett's ruling making any further inroads upon the criminal law.

The law officers drew back from supporting Stephen's ambitious plans to 'amend or codify' the law of conspiracy as a whole—desirable though they regarded that as being 'on abstract principles'. There were certain instances, such as those identified by Stephen, where the existing law was valuable. Furthermore, there were examples of where it was clearly

[57] R. S. Wright, *The Law of Criminal Conspiracies and Agreements* (1873), 12.
[58] Longe, *Law of Strikes*, 13–14, 23, 29, 33–4.
[59] Wright, *Law of Criminal Conspiracies*, 50, 88; Orth, *Combination and Conspiracy*, 40–1.
[60] *The Times* (24 Mar. 1873), 7, 9; Harrison's letter was repr. as *Workmen and the Law of Conspiracy* (Tracts for Trade Unionists, 2, 1873).
[61] 9 May 1873, PRO HO45/9326/18243/30b.

appropriate that a heavier punishment should be imposed on persons acting in combination than in those cases where a crime was committed by an individual. Since the 'chief evil' of the law of conspiracy was 'its obscurity in reference to questions that occur between employers and employed', the law officers were content that an amending statute should be confined to restoring the freedom to strike.

In opposition to this broadly liberal thrust, Harry Bodkin Poland, a seasoned criminal lawyer who conducted prosecutions for the Crown and advised the Home Office on criminal matters, presented Bruce with an extended dissent, contending both that Brett's ruling was correct and that it should not be altered. Strikes remained 'legal if used for legitimate purposes', which he believed the gas strike was not. His was a restatement of the long-standing argument that the courts should be left to determine what was 'legitimate'. In terms similar to Tomlinson's in 1831, he valued the elasticity of the common law of conspiracy which, like the law of libel, 'must be left to be administered by Judges of learning and good sense and by Juries imbued with the spirit of the times'.[62]

One of those judges, Sir Robert Lush, offered the Home Office yet another view, based on a case that had recently come before him at Glamorgan spring assizes in March 1873. An indictment for conspiracy framed in similar terms to that used against the gas stokers, alleging a conspiracy to molest their masters to coerce them to alter their mode of carrying on business, was brought against a number of South Wales miners at the Plymouth ironworks. The men had determined not to work with some non-unionists and walked out when the manager refused to remove the non-unionists from the coalface. Lush told the grand jury that this was not a criminal offence. No act of physical molestation described in the CLAA was shown to have occurred, and the strikers had merely done what they had a right to do, namely to dictate the terms on which they were willing to work.[63]

Lush's interpretation of the law was exactly that intended by the Home Office in 1871. It seems to have reinforced Bruce in the view that Brett's ruling was not likely to be followed by other judges and that, contrary to the advice of the law officers, an amending Act to protect strikers was not an urgent necessity.[64] Bruce could, anyway, fall back on the argument that the TUCPC had no reasonable grounds to demand restorative legislation until

---

[62] Poland's Opinion, 9 May 1873, PRO HO45/9326/18243/30b.
[63] *South Wales Daily News* (8 Mar. 1873), 3; (10 Mar. 1873), 3; (12 Mar. 1873), 2–3; Lush to Bruce, 21 Mar. 1873, PRO HO45/9326/18243/31.
[64] 3*H* ccxvi. 608 (6 June 1873); ccxvii. 1542 (4 Aug. 1873).

an authoritative decision had been obtained from the court of appeal. But he did not at first oppose an attempt by Harcourt, on behalf of the TUCPC, to bring in an amending bill during the last days of the parliamentary session. Harcourt's bill would, Bruce told Gladstone, 'remove the main grievances of the workmen' and though 'very objectionable in many particulars', it was 'capable of amendment'.[65]

Bruce's principal objection was that the bill confined itself to reversing the effects of the gas stokers' case. Harcourt wanted to ensure that strikers could not be prosecuted for conspiracy unless they did something which was in itself indictable, or else punishable under the CLAA (violence, threats, intimidation, or molestation): that is, labour conspiracies must be linked to crimes. Such immunities from the law of conspiracy were limited to acts 'done for the purposes of a trade combination'.[66] Bruce now made it a condition of government support that the bill should reform the law of conspiracy as a whole.[67] Government amendments were introduced to extend its principles to all types of conspiracies, a move which involved defining those common law offences which it was considered necessary to retain.

Such an extension opened the way for Conservative peers led by Cairns to wreck the measure in the Lords. Cairns could now argue that it was too late in the session to attempt a wholesale revision of an important area of the criminal law: the judges had left London to go on circuit and could not be brought together to give their collective opinion, as was customary when such major changes were proposed. As the bill returned to the Commons it simply restricted penalties for conspiracies under the Master and Servant Act to the maximum permitted by the statute. Since this was an acknowledgement that combinations to break contracts of employment were criminal conspiracies—a highly contested proposition—it placed strikers in a worse position than before.[68] The bill was withdrawn and the government was accused of having contributed to the loss of 'the only popular measure of the session'.[69]

Bruce's decision to insist on a change which would be likely to imperil the measure is at first puzzling. It was at odds both with the advice of the law officers in May 1873, that the 'chief issue' which required remedying was the impact of the law upon strikers. Personal antagonisms between the law

---

[65] Bruce to Gladstone, 6 July 1873, BL Add MSS 44087, fo. 92.
[66] *The Law of Contract of Masters and Servants, and the Law of Conspiracy* (Tracts for Trade Unionists, 4, 1873), vii.
[67] 3*H* ccxvi. 1890 (7 July 1873); ccxvii. 1533 (4 Aug. 1873).
[68] *Pall Mall Gazette* (7 Aug. 1873), 10.
[69] *Law of Contract of Masters and Servants* (1873), xv; *Bee-Hive* (9 Aug. 1873), 4.

officers and Harcourt, who did not adopt a conciliatory approach towards the administration's difficulties, may partly explain Coleridge's opposition in parliament to a bill substantially carrying out his own recommendations as attorney-general.[70] In the government's weakened parliamentary position after its defeat on the Irish University bill, Bruce and Coleridge may also have wanted to avoid being seen to be making concessions to the mounting external pressure. A Conservative writer criticized the London Trades Council's demonstration in Hyde Park at the beginning of June as an attempt to overawe parliament and one which would be ultimately damaging to the prospects of the Liberals, who faced secessions from their own whig 'right'.[71] Those secessionists were not likely to seek an accommodation with a popular agitation which, after the imprisonment of the Ascott-under-Wychwood women by the Chipping Norton bench in May 1873, also directed its fire against clericalism and landlordism.[72]

A new consideration, not raised in his advice to Bruce, was now introduced by Coleridge in correspondence with Harcourt to explain the government's position: 'I cannot admit the *right* of one class more than another to have the law dangerously and loosely altered for them.'[73] To invoke an argument against 'class legislation' perhaps came oddly from Coleridge, as one of those responsible for the CLAA. It did, however, reflect a new concern among legislators as the labour laws campaign became more strident. In May 1873 the issue had been whether or not Brett's ruling was likely to be followed and whether, in practice, an amending measure was needed. By July, when some commentators had begun to refer to Harcourt's bill as giving 'exceptional exemptions' to strikers, a larger principle was introduced into the argument. This was the moment when some politicians began to perceive a danger that the balance might be shifting away from severity towards 'privilege', which the attempt to implement a general reform of conspiracy was intended to avert.[74] Bruce and Coleridge thought 'exceptional' legislation a greater danger than the cost of perpetuating, until the next parliamentary session, an acknowledged grievance.[75]

---

[70] See the exchanges in 3*H* ccxvi. 574, 593–4, 599, 605 (6 June 1873).

[71] 'The Trade Unionists in Hyde Park', *Saturday Review* (7 June 1873), 734–5.

[72] *Oxford Chronicle* (7 June 1873), 6.

[73] Coleridge to Harcourt, 10 July 1873, Bodl. Harcourt MS dep 204, fo. 39; Coleridge, *John Duke, Lord Coleridge*, ii. 95–6.

[74] On this point see Dicey, *Law and Opinion*, 476.

[75] *Saturday Review* (28 June 1873), 837–8.

MASTER AND SERVANT

A third issue faced by the Home Office as a result of the stokers' trial arose from the imprisonment of the strikers' leaders either for conspiring to commit a breach of the Master and Servant Act or for actually breaking their contracts. Trials arising out of the annual hirings of skilled workers in the Staffordshire Potteries had, in September 1872, led to a renewal of the trade union agitation against an unequal contract law: the gas stokers' strike forced it onto the TUCPC's agenda.[76] While Elcho's statute of 1867 had moved towards treating breaches of contracts of hiring as civil wrongs, it had done so incompletely, hostile amendments by coal and iron employers having rendered proceedings under it a muddle of civil and penal remedies. In certain instances breaches of contract by workers could still be punished by fines or imprisonment with hard labour.[77]

Those of the stokers imprisoned for individual breaches of contract had been convicted under section 14 of the 1867 Act which empowered magistrates to impose penalties of up to three months' hard labour in 'aggravated' cases. This provision had been directed at such instances as an engine man leaving his post and causing the flooding of a mine, and similar acts imperilling the lives of other men or the property of the employer. Breaches of contract by agricultural labourers, placing livestock or crops at risk, were particularly likely to be treated as 'aggravated'. During 1872 and 1873, 152 and 141 persons were imprisoned for 'aggravated' breaches.

Ordinary breaches of contract were dealt with under Section 9 of the 1867 Act. This, too, subjected workers to penal sanctions in certain circumstances if they broke agreements with their employers. Magistrates could impose a fine of up to £20 if compensation was inadequate to rectify the damage done by the workman in breach of contract. If the fine or compensation was not paid, or if an order requiring a workman to fulfil his contract was not complied with, a term of imprisonment could be imposed. That sanction was applied to hundreds of persons in the early 1870s, while thousands annually were fined. The judicial statistics did not indicate whether those convicted were masters or servants, but the indications from press reports and a sample of cases gathered by a royal commission in 1874 were that the latter formed the overwhelming majority.

Lushington added the question whether the 1867 Act should be 'retained, amended or repealed' to those on which the Home Office sought the

---

[76] *Potteries Examiner* (7 Sept., 14 Sept., 21 Sept. 1872).

[77] Steinfeld, *Coercion*, 203–4; Simon, 'Master and Servant', 185–6; Kauffman, 'Lord Elcho', 194–6.

law officers' opinion. He described Elcho's Act as 'practically though not in form one sided' since employers were rarely if ever likely to be imprisoned under it. It was anomalous, since recent policy had been to limit the circumstances in which debtors could be subject to imprisonment. And it was exceptional, because such sanctions were not applied to other contracts. Against these considerations had to be weighed the immense damage which might result from breaches of contract by workmen, and their inability to make adequate recompense.

Since the law officers declined to give an opinion on this point, describing the issue of the Master and Servant Act as 'a matter of policy only' rather than one of law, the Home Office could not devolve responsibility for deciding between the two contending positions.[78] On the one hand, there was the argument from principle that breaches of the labour contract should be treated no differently from other agreements. In 1867 Lushington had subscribed to this view, which had been advanced during the debates on Elcho's bill by Henry Fawcett, a member of the select committee which had investigated the old law in 1866.[79] Frederic Harrison's critique of the inequality of the Act of 1867, pointing out that breaches of commercial contracts by capitalists could have quite as disastrous effects as those of employment contracts by workers, was adopted by the TUCPC as the first of its series of 'Tracts for Trade Unionists'.[80] A lecture in Glasgow by W. A. Hunter, professor of law at University College, London, and later an advanced Liberal MP, attacking the Master and Servant Act as being founded upon 'an ancient and discredited policy' towards labour, was published by the Scottish CLAA Repeal Association in its parallel series of 'Glasgow Tracts for Trade Unionists'.[81] Howell described the TUC's demand, that breach of contract between master and workmen should be a purely civil matter, as 'thoroughly in accord with the whole tenor of recent legislation'.[82]

The TUC's interpretation of legislative policy accorded with that laid down by the whig-Liberal politician George Cornewall Lewis nearly a generation earlier. Lewis depicted the progress of civilization as moving towards equalizing the legal rights of all subjects, the 'personal freedom of

[78] PRO HO45/9326/18243/30B.
[79] Lushington, 'Workmen and Trade Unions', 37; Goldman, *The Blind Victorian*, 162–3; 3*H* clxxxvii. 1610 (4 June 1867).
[80] *The Times* (5 Apr. 1873), 9; F. Harrison, *Imprisonment for Breach of Contract, or, The Master and Servant Act* (Tracts for Trade Unionists, 1, 1873).
[81] W. A. Hunter, *A Lecture on the Criminal Laws Affecting Labour* (Glasgow Tracts for Trade Unionists, 4, 1874), 7–13.
[82] Howell to Gladstone, 12 July 1873, BL Add MS 44439, fo. 156.

the working classes' being the 'characteristic mark of modern civilized societies'.[83] In practice, however, the transition described by Lewis was far from complete. His own purpose in elevating it to a central position in public policy had been to counter proposals for state protection to labour propounded by tory paternalists. As a home secretary in the late 1850s he did nothing to remove the blatant inequality of the old Master and Servant law. Many instances of what has been termed 'class law', discriminating against the working classes, were perpetuated after franchise extension in 1867.[84] The closest parallel to the continuing class inequality of the Master and Servant Act was the difference in the law's treatment of wealthy and small debtors. As a select committee which reported in July 1873 pointed out, the former were enabled by bankruptcy law to obtain discharge from their debts, while poor debtors continued to be liable to imprisonment, despite the statute of 1869 which nominally ended imprisonment for debt. Their imprisonment, like that under section 9 of the Master and Servant Act, was not technically for the debt itself but for the failure to carry out an order of the court.[85]

On these grounds Harry Poland again urged the Home Office that no change was necessary. He disputed the allegation that 'mere' breaches of labour contracts were treated criminally and therefore exceptionally. Proceedings under section 9, even where they resulted in imprisonment, were no different from proceedings ordered by magistrates for enforcing the payment of poor rates. Moreover, Poland saw no objection to subjecting to criminal sanctions those 'aggravated' breaches which resulted in injury to persons and property.[86]

In a seminal twentieth-century analysis, criminal sanctions against breaches of employment agreements were depicted as 'mainly propping up small and backward enterprises' so that, by the mid-1870s, 'the most wealthy and influential sections of the capitalist class' thought the Act of 1867 no longer worth preserving. The judicial statistics suggest that its penal provisions were used predominantly in agriculture, small workshop trades, or where production involved sub-contractors, such as the butty-masters, and in that sense it was 'the weapon of the small master'.[87] Yet

[83] G. C. Lewis, 'Legislation for the Working Classes', *Edinburgh Review*, 83 (Jan. 1846), 70-1.

[84] P. Johnson, 'Class law in Victorian England', *Past and Present*, 141 (1993), 147-69.

[85] Select committee to inquire into the subject of imprisonment for debt by county court judges (*PP* 1873 xv), vi; G. R. Rubin, 'Law, Poverty, and Imprisonment for Debt', in G. R. Rubin and D. Sugarman (eds), *Law, Economy, and Society, 1750-1914* (1984), 247.

[86] Poland's Opinion, 12 May 1873, PRO HO45/9326/18243/30b.

[87] Simon, 'Master and Servant', 190, 191, 199.

convictions brought by the heavily capitalized gas companies accounted for one-fifth of all those imprisoned under section 14 in England and Wales during 1872. These statistics suggested both that the increasing complexity of production processes caused some large employers to seek the assistance of a penal contract law, and that the dependence of an urbanized community upon vital services might create a public argument for retaining such a law.

The 1867 Master and Servant Act's most vocal defenders were not small masters but the representatives of an organization of large employers. The National Federation of Associated Employers of Labour arose out of a joint meeting of the Iron Trades Employers Association and the National Association of Factory Employers, convened in April 1873 in response to Harcourt's motion on the law of conspiracy and master and servant, and Mundella's bill to repeal the CLAA.[88] About fifty employers were present, claiming between them to employ a million workers—roughly the number represented at the TUC. With head offices in Manchester, and connections with veterans of the Anti-Corn Law League, the NFAEL deployed free trade arguments to defend the sanctity of contracts, which the lifting of penal sanctions would, in their view, undermine. For how else could men without property be kept to their agreements? Theirs was fundamentally an ideological attack on the TUC's programme, though many of the NFAEL's constituents believed that a penal contract law served their own economic interests.

Bruce was among the coalowning MPs who had stifled reform of Master and Servant law in 1867. He had argued for the retention of penal sanctions not simply for breaches of contract which threatened physical injury to persons or property, but also to punish walk-outs by small groups of men which threw hundreds of others out of work and exposed employers to enormous and irrecoverable losses.[89] His own close association with the South Wales iron and coal industries predisposed him against compromise in the 1870s. As a recipient of coal royalties, he shared the difficulties faced by the colliery owners during the early 1870s through 'the agitation of the labour markets, and the irregular working of the colliers, consequent upon the unfortunate use they make of their high wages'.[90] William Menelaus, the manager of the Dowlais works of which Bruce was a trustee, was present at the founding meeting of the NFAEL and later asserted that penal

---

[88] Minutes of the Leeds and District Association of Factory Occupiers, MS 200/58, p. 52 (1 May 1873); TUCPC, *The Plot Discovered, or Conspiracy amongst the Masters* (1873); *Colliery Guardian* (25 July 1873), 118.

[89] 3*H* clxxxvii. 1609 (4 June 1867).

[90] Bruce to Gladstone, 24 Dec. 1872, BL Add MSS 44087, fo. 86.

sanctions were necessary for discipline.[91] In parliament Bruce was adamant against any alteration to the 1867 Act, claiming that it was a great improvement on its predecessor of 1823.[92] When the radical MP Hinde Palmer moved the omission of section 14 on the annual renewal of the 1867 Act, Bruce cited the fact that 'the public generally approved' of the imprisonment of the stokers as evidence of the justice and necessity of maintaining the penal provisions.[93]

Invoking public support for the stokers' conviction reflected the part which the strike wave of the early 1870s played in generating what contemporaries identified as a Conservative 'reaction'. The public as consumers were affected by strikes to a previously unparalleled extent, and Bruce was responsive to the resulting shift of opinion. In doing so, however, he did not distinguish between the grounds of public safety upon which the gas stokers' strike appeared to justify the maintenance of a penal contract law, and the private convenience which such a law represented for certain types of employers and consumers.

Just as he refused to acknowledge that the CLAA was 'class legislation' so Bruce also dismissed the claim that the Master and Servant Act was 'unequal'. Avoiding the questions of principle raised by the TUC and jurists, he relied upon the judicial statistics in a rather clumsy attempt to answer the law's critics and to depict repealers as irrational zealots. Shortly after the imprisonment of the Ascott-under-Wychwood women, he declared that the CLAA 'did not operate in the case of the working classes with that exceptional severity which some appeared to suppose', and cited evidence that the number of convictions was falling. He defended the continuation of imprisonment for breach of contract on the ground that in 1866, under the old law, 1 in 7 of those convicted were imprisoned, whereas by 1872 the proportion had fallen to only 1 in 27.[94] His secretary, Albert Rutson, berated Frederic Harrison for making 'such a fuss about the law of conspiracy, by which he [Rutson] says not a dozen men are punished in the year'.[95]

Recognizing Bruce's fundamental hostility, Howell approached Gladstone directly. Since his interventions on the labour question during the 1860s, Gladstone had not taken any significant part in the development of ideas and policy on the subject. Treating the issue as a purely departmental one, he declined to meet the TUCPC, and agreed only to receive a written statement of their grievances. Howell accompanied these with a

[91] RCLL 1st Rep. Q.562; see also p. 215 below.
[92] 3*H* ccxvi. 610 (6 June 1873).
[93] 3*H* cxvii. 1,251–2 (29 July 1873).
[94] 3*H* ccxvii. 459 (16 July 1873); ccxvi. 610 (6 June 1873).
[95] Harrison to John Morley, 21 Aug. 1873, Harrison MSS 1/56.

covering letter, whose content he omitted from the TUCPC's published version of his correspondence with the Liberal leader. In it Howell confided his anxiety lest the government should face the electorate before making some concessions to labour and urged that his old Reform League contact, James Stansfeld, now a minister, should be consulted in the hope that some compromise of the sort achieved in July 1869 could be engineered.[96] Not taking the hint, Gladstone merely forwarded the correspondence to Bruce, who had already ruled out any hope of alleviating the Master and Servant Act and the CLAA, and was not willing to expedite improvements to the law of conspiracy.[97] Gladstone's refusal to accord political significance to the TUCPC's concerns, and to remove them from Bruce's sole departmental responsibility, ensured that at the end of the parliamentary session none of the central demands agreed by the TUC at Leeds had been conceded, and the legality of many strikes remained in doubt.

[96] Howell to Gladstone, 28 June 1873, Howell MSS LB8, fo. 84 (copy); Gladstone to Howell, 1 July 1873, BL Add MSS 44542, fo. 132; Howell to Gladstone, 12 July 1873, BL Add MSS 44439, fo. 152; Howell to Gladstone (covering letter), 14 July 1873, BL Add MS 44439, fo. 163 and Howell MSS LB8, fo. 103 (copy).

[97] Bruce to Gladstone, 6 July 1873, BL Add MSS 44087, fo. 92.

8

Reforming Labour Law, 1873–1874

It is now well established that Robert Lowe, who replaced Bruce on 8 August 1873, prepared a comprehensive settlement of the TUC's grievances during his brief tenure at the Home Office. Although Lowe's nineteenth-century biographer quoted contemporary rumours that he had drafted a bill reforming the labour laws, it was not until the appearance of a modern life that Lowe's radical approach to the question was brought to light; and only with the publication of correspondence and cabinet minutes in the *Gladstone Diaries* was the existence of a government plan confirmed.[1] In view of Lowe's attacks on unions during the parliamentary reform debates, however, the TUCPC had good grounds for regarding his arrival as increasing the obstacles in their way.[2] One of his first official acts, rejecting petitions for the mitigation of the severe sentences of between nine and six months' imprisonment passed on three London joiners convicted of conspiracy after assaulting a fellow worker whom they believed to have been a strikebreaker, was described by the London Trades Council as evidence of his 'haughty, heartless and vindictive policy towards the working classes'.[3] At a rally against the CLAA organized by Edinburgh Trades Council, on 23 August, Lowe was identified 'as one of the most bitter enemies to all legislation on their behalf'.[4]

[1] A. P. Martin, *Life and Letters of Robert Lowe, Viscount Sherbrooke* (2 vols., 1893) ii. 388–9; J. Winter, *Robert Lowe* (1976), 304–5; Matthew, *GD*, viii. 394, 417 (27 Sept., 26 Nov. 1873); M. Curthoys, 'The Home Office and Trade Union Legislation, 1871–6' (seminar paper, Oxford, 1979); idem, 'Trade Union Legislation, 1871–6' (Oxford D.Phil. thesis, 1988), ch. 7; McKibbin, 'Why was there no Marxism?', 28; J. Spain, 'Trade Unionists, Gladstonian Liberals, and the Labour Law Reforms of 1875', in E. Biagini and and A. J. Reid (eds), *Currents of Radicalism* (1991), 123–5; Hoppen, *Mid-Victorian Generation*, 607.

[2] Howell to W. H. Wood, 14 Aug. 1873, Howell MSS LB8, fo. 133.

[3] 14 Aug. 1873, PRO HO138/5; London Trades Council Minutes, 2 Sept. 1873. The case, which had been brought by the employers' association, was an example of how an indictment for conspiracy could magnify the punishment for a relatively minor offence. See *The Times* (9 May 1873), 11; (12 June 1873), 16; Central Association of Master Builders Minutes, 28 Apr. 1873, LMA A/NFB.1/A1/1.

[4] *The Scotsman* (25 Aug. 1873), 5.

A CONTEXT FOR CONCESSION

Every member of the cabinet was sent copies of the resolutions passed at the Edinburgh demonstration. These demanded, on behalf of 'the industrial classes of Scotland', the total repeal of the CLAA and the criminal clauses of the Master and Servant Act, and ending of the use of the law of conspiracy in labour disputes. A resolution was passed calling for support to be given only to those parliamentary candidates who pledged themselves to give effect to the demands.[5] They were sufficient to alarm Lowe who, within three weeks of taking office, reversed Bruce's entrenched attitude of indifference towards the labour laws' agitation. Lowe's warning to Gladstone that the demonstration represented a manifestation of working-class power echoed his predictions in the previous decade that under an extended franchise the organizational power of unions would be directed to political objects.[6] In 1866–7 his fellow Adullamite, Elcho, had addressed the inequalities of Master and Servant law in an attempt to avert the politicization of the unions; similarly Lowe now found the demonstrators' argument against engrafting criminal liabilities upon civil contracts hard to resist—'if the principle is right why is it restricted to labour contracts?'.[7]

Lowe's apprehension of class conflict was acute and Gladstone, while encouraging him to investigate how the controversy might be resolved, hinted that his colleague's apprehensions were overdone.[8] Lowe was not alone, however, in attaching deeper significance to the summer's campaign. While some London papers viewed the gala atmosphere of the trades council's Whit-Monday demonstration as evidence primarily of the general spread of prosperity, all noted the emphasis on class bias in the administration of justice, a theme promoted by the advocates of the Tichborne Claimant, whose trial for perjury had begun in April.[9] In May 1873 the London demonstrators, marshalled by former PC Goodchild, the policeman dismissed for striking, included two of the released gas stokers, who carried a banner proclaiming 'This is our reply to (in) Justice Brett'. Others criticized the role of unpaid justices of the peace. The marchers heard George Odger's denunciation of 'tyrannical and partial law-making' conclude with a demand for the appointment of a minister of justice with power to dismiss judges.[10] Although Odger's animus against the legal system may

[5] *Repeal of the Criminal Law Amendment Act: Trades' Demonstration* (1873), 4.
[6] R. Lowe, *Speeches and Letters on Reform* (2nd edn., 1867), 52.
[7] Lowe to Gladstone, 29 Aug. 1873, BL Add MSS 44302, fo. 152; Kauffman, 'Lord Elcho', 192–8.   [8] Gladstone to Lowe, 3 Sept. 1873, Matthew, *GD*, viii. 382.
[9] *The Times* (3 June 1873), 6; *Daily Telegraph* (3 June 1873), 2; *Daily News* (3 June 1873), 4.
[10] *Bee-Hive* (7 June 1873), 9.

have been heightened by his own impending bankruptcy following a failed libel action,[11] the manifesto received general assent. Legislators were reminded that the 'general tranquillity' of the country derived not from their own wisdom or statesmanship but from the recognition among working men and their unions of the benefits of law and order; but unionists demanded that those laws and their enforcement be fair and impartial.

The *Daily News*, which backed Harcourt and others of Gladstone's Liberal critics, regarded it as a 'serious social phenomenon' that the law had come to be so widely regarded as reflecting the interests of the classes which enforced it. This theme was taken up at length by a more overtly anti-Gladstonian metropolitan paper, the *Pall Mall Gazette*, which reflected on how the impartiality of the rural magistracy had been undermined by its administration of justice during the agricultural labourers' strikes.[12] Fearful of the political dangers if the working classes ceased to recognize the neutrality of the state, it accused the government of treating their disaffection from both the law and existing political parties with insufficient seriousness. More dangerous than labour candidates, who were rarely likely to secure election, was the prospect that working-class electors 'will sullenly and ostentatiously allow their votes to remain unused'.[13]

By the autumn recess, as Lowe began to work on his plan, class cleavage and estrangement became occasional themes of political speculation and initiative. At the end of August the Labour Representation League used the Blackburn demonstration against the labour laws to launch its campaign of targeting winnable constituencies, and was encouraged by the subsequent success of labour candidates in municipal elections.[14] Rather more attention was paid to the emergence of the national employers' federation, whose proceedings had been tentative and secretive until news of its objectives and membership found its way into the newspapers in December.[15] While it is open to question whether, industrially, the NFAEL represented a counter-attack against unions rather than an attempt to restore what its members took to be an earlier form of reciprocal relations, contemporary commentators, noting its clandestine origins, tended to view the federation as having sinister political implications.[16] Some feared that the quarrels between capital and labour would spill over into politics, with the result

---

[11] *Pall Mall Gazette* (20 June 1873), 9.

[12] *Daily News* (3 June 1873); Parry, *Liberal Government*, 272.

[13] 'The Liberal Party and the Working Classes', *Pall Mall Gazette* (18 June 1873), 1; 'Chipping Norton Magistrates', ibid. (27 May 1873), 5; 'Paid and Unpaid Magistrates', ibid. (30 May 1873), 1.   [14] *Blackburn Times* (23 Aug. 1873), 3; *The Times* (18 Nov. 1873), 5.

[15] *The Times* (13 Dec. 1873), 5; (16 Dec. 1873), 10; (18 Dec. 1873), 11.

[16] See the leader in *The Times* (16 Dec. 1873), 9.

that the 'old-fashioned vertical cleavage according to diversity of taste and opinion' which divided the political community would give way to a horizontal stratification in which the interests of the rich and poor were pitted against each other.[17] A nervousness crept into press comments that the continental pattern of class antagonism in politics, which the British had prided themselves on avoiding, was now developing at home. In the 'new' politics, as the *Pall Mall Gazette* writer envisaged them, 'a candidate would be asked, not whether he is for or against household suffrage in the counties, or for or against the 25th clause of the Education Act, but whether he is for capital or for labour'. Such a development, the paper suggested, would undo the legacy of Peel, whose action in repealing the corn laws had saved the nation from a political conflict turning on a social issue which divided producers and consumers.[18]

These apprehensions suggest why some politicians, and not necessarily those exposed to direct electoral pressure, came to recognize that a solution to the labour laws controversy had become an urgent necessity. One response was the programme promoted by the Birmingham manufacturer and radical candidate for Sheffield, Joseph Chamberlain. Like other critics of the government, he considered the 'discontent and irritation' felt towards the law by a large portion of the population was 'no trifling matter' and he brought the unionist demands within his radical 'quadrilateral' of free church, free land, free schools, and free labour.[19] The latter—by which he meant the repeal of laws unfairly restricting the freedom of organization—would, he predicted, be the first to be conceded, not least because the law of conspiracy had few active defenders.[20] To Salisbury, reviewing Chamberlain's manifesto, such a prospect heightened propertied fears of union aggression and encouraged the formation of a league of capitalists.[21] While Salisbury appeared to welcome the coalescence of capital, W. E. Forster, a member of Gladstone's cabinet, warned of its dangers when he spoke as president of the economy and trade department at the British Association meeting held in Bradford in September. Replying to a paper by the chairman of the Halifax chamber of commerce, William Morris, who argued that the remedy for union power lay in a counter-combination of

---

[17] *Saturday Review* (7 June 1873), 735; *Spectator* (20 Dec. 1873), 1604.

[18] *Pall Mall Gazette* (29 Dec. 1873), 2257.

[19] 'Class Legislation' (23 Sept. 1873), in C. W. Boyd (ed.), *Mr Chamberlain's Speeches* (2 vols., 1914), i. 31.

[20] J. Chamberlain, 'The Liberal Party and its Leaders', *Fortnightly Review*, n.s. 14 (Sept. 1873), 298–9; H. W. McCready, 'The British General Election of 1874', *Canadian Journal of Economic and Political Science*, 20 (1954), 169.

[21] 'The Programme of the Radicals', *Quarterly Review*, 270 (Oct. 1873), in P. Smith (ed.), *Lord Salisbury on Politics* (1972), 306.

'the superior power of capital' of the sort represented by the NFAEL, Forster feared that both sides would then compete to use the law and legislation in its own interests. Denying that the threat of unions was as great as Morris supposed—strikes might be more frequent and last longer than in the past but they posed fewer threats to order—Forster argued against trying to uphold laws which restricted the freedom to combine. Furthermore, in protecting men who chose not to join combinations, it was wrong to stretch the law beyond what it could rightly or effectively do. Having introduced the government's ballot bills, Forster was familiar with the arguments about protecting individuals from undue influence, and contended that in an industrial context men should be protected from physical violence of various sorts 'but it is no use attempting to protect them against persuasion or even against moral intimidation'. The side against whom the law was used would regard such an attempt as an 'interference with their reasonable liberty'.[22] Both Forster and Chamberlain, like Mundella, regarded laws which undermined popular consent to the administration of justice as a greater danger than the economic activities of unions.

Forster's was the first public statement by a member of the government to acknowledge that the legislation of 1871 might be open to review. He was followed by Bright, recently restored to the cabinet; at the end of September, prompted by Harcourt, he expressed to Gladstone his anxiety about the controversy.[23] In an address to his Birmingham constituents Bright spoke of the possibility of concession on all three of labour's demands in a way that that would be just to all classes of the community. Shortly afterwards Coleridge identified to his Exeter constituents the law of master and servant, and conspiracy, as subjects which would be cleared up in the coming session. On the promotion to the judicial bench first of Jessel then of Coleridge himself, Gladstone replaced them as government law officers with the two lawyers in the Commons most closely associated with the TUC, Henry James and Harcourt. Seeking re-election at Taunton following his appointment, James reaffirmed his support for reform.[24] Harcourt told an Oxford audience that placing 'the legal rights of the wage-earning class on a more equal footing' would be a fitting conclusion to the reforms of the Liberal ministry.[25]

[22] *The Times* (22 Sept. 1873), 7; (20 Sept. 1873), 10 (Morris).
[23] Gladstone to Lowe, 27 Sept. 1873, BL Add MSS 44542, fo. 189.
[24] *The Times* (23 Oct. 1873), 5; (31 Oct. 1873), 7; (13 Oct. 1873), 8.
[25] *Oxford Chronicle* (13 Dec. 1873), 7.

When meetings of the Cabinet resumed early in October, Lowe was given sanction to draw up substantial proposals.[26] Lowe presented his argument as one entirely of principle: practical consequences were not discussed, and at no point did he refer to 'unions', 'strikes', or 'picketing'. Instead, he spoke in general terms of rights and remedies, of 'irritation and discontent among the working classes', and of the consideration which he emphasized as fundamental to all his recommendations: 'If we are ever to have peace on these questions it must be by eschewing class legislation.'[27]

First, the law of conspiracy was subjected to Lowe's scrutiny. It was objectionable that conspiracy could transform a minor statutory offence punishable by summary jurisdiction into a misdemeanour, heard before a higher tribunal with power to inflict heavier penalties. It was even more objectionable that conspiracy could transform an action which was not an offence at all when committed by an individual into a misdemeanour when agreed to (without even being actually committed) by more than one person. Lowe had earlier praised Stephen's general arguments for rendering the criminal law into a 'simple, rational, and intelligible system'.[28] He now repeated the substance of Stephen's complaint about the obscurity of the law of conspiracy, and the enormous discretion it gave judges to create crimes out of virtually anything done with a joint intent of which they happened to disapprove.[29] Although the issues discussed by Lowe were those raised by the trial of the gas stokers, he was careful not to limit his proposals to reversing that case. Thus he shared Coleridge's objection to Harcourt's bill that it proposed to alter the law solely as it affected trade offences. The latter was 'class legislation'. Instead, Lowe aimed to reform the law on general principles 'applicable to the whole community'. Conspiracies to commit minor offences would be abolished, as would conspiracies which made crimes of actions not in themselves unlawful. In the latter types of conspiracy, as criminal lawyers had pointed out during the debates on Harcourt's bill, certain exceptions might need to be preserved in order to fill gaps in the law. As a rule, however, Lowe wanted to confine the offence of conspiracy to its principal useful function, 'the power to punish a crime where the proof of its commission is defective'.[30]

---

[26] Matthew, *GD*, viii. 396 (3 Oct. 1873); R. A. J. Walling (ed.), *The Diaries of John Bright* (1930), 357 (4 Oct. 1873).
[27] Confidential memorandum on (1) Law of Conspiracy; (2) Masters and Servants, 1867; (3) Criminal Law Amendment Act 1871, 28 Oct. 1873, printed 7 Nov. 1873, BL Add MSS 44621, fos. 130–3.   [28] R. Lowe, 'Criminal Law Reform', *Edinburgh Review*, 121 (1865), 135.
[29] BL Add MSS 44621, fo. 131.   [30] Ibid.

The Master and Servant Act of 1867, Lord Elcho's legislative gesture to the working classes, was dissected and found to be full of procedural anomalies. All were shown to be oppressive to labour. The statute was a 'legislative curiosity', whose penal remedies for breaches of contract Lowe found 'monstrous'. He proposed its complete repeal, leaving county courts to adjudicate in disputes about contracts to buy and sell labour as a purely civil matter. Employment agreements would become contracts like any other, acknowledging labour's claim, advanced since the 1840s,[31] to be treated on equal terms with capital.

Master and Servant offered many parallels with public policy questions with which Lowe had previously engaged. Assisting Harcourt's researches earlier in 1873, Stephen recalled the 'great controversy in India in Maine's time about punishing breaches of contract connected with the cultivation of indigo'.[32] That controversy turned on the question of whether the cultivators of indigo ('ryots'), who had received advances for their crops, should be subject to a penal contract law. Its similarities to the arguments about the Master and Servant Act were pointed out by G. O. Trevelyan, the Liberal MP, in a speech to his Hawick constituents in November 1873 supporting the TUC's programme.[33] They were familiar also to Lowe, who had been for fifteen years (1853–68) an Indian law commissioner.

The Indian Penal Code drafted by Trevelyan's uncle, T. B. Macaulay, narrowly restricted the circumstances in which breach of contract might be treated criminally. Sections 490–2 of the code, eventually enacted in 1860, punished with imprisonment breaches of contracts to convey travellers— abandoning them in uninhabited wastes, for example—or to attend to helpless persons.[34] Submitting their draft in 1837, Macaulay and his colleagues endorsed the belief of 'the great body of jurists' that mere breach of contract ought not to be an offence. Such powers would be an instrument of oppression in the hands of bad masters; good masters, in the existing state of the labour market, would never have difficulty in finding replacements if their employees deserted them.[35] As a result, the law enacted in India was, to a significant degree, less severe than that applied in England under the Master and Servant Act of 1823, and remained so even after Elcho's reform.

Yet there remained the question of how the propertyless were to be made

---

[31] Frank, 'Trade Unions and the 1823 Master and Servant Act', 43.
[32] Stephen to Harcourt, 7 June 1873, Bodl. Harcourt MS dep 204, fo. 33.
[33] *Newcastle Daily Chronicle* (26 Nov. 1873), 3.
[34] W. Theobald (ed.), *The Legislative Acts of the Governor General of India*, iii. 615–17.
[35] A copy of the penal code prepared by the Indian Law Commissioners (*PP* 1837–8 xli), 115–16.

to keep to their undertakings. During the 1860s European planters agitated for an extension to the exceptional circumstances provided for in the Indian code so that ryots who defaulted on their obligations could be punished. Like British workmen, ryots who failed to carry out their agreements were supposed to be incapable of paying damages commensurate with the losses incurred by the employer or planter. As legal member of the governor-general's council in India, Maine opposed the mixing of criminal and civil remedies and, to avert the planters' demands for a penal contract law, looked for other legal means of giving security to the planters that ryots would fulfil their engagements. He proposed a machinery for the specific performance of indigo contracts, enabling the courts to order the ryots, on pain of imprisonment for disobedience, to carry out their agreements.[36] It was a form of 'forced' labour and met with objections from London on the ground that it would be oppressive. Maine responded that this came strangely from a government which upheld the policy of the Master and Servant Act of 1823. The objection was even more curious given that Elcho's Act of 1867 actually created specific performance as a remedy in labour contract cases.[37] In 1866 Lowe was a signatory to the report of the Indian law commissioners which decided against introducing any extraordinary remedies for enforcing specific performance against the ryots.[38] By 1873 he was arguing that the principle defended and applied in relation to Indian cultivators should now be extended to British operatives.

In order to do so, Lowe drew up upon Maine's famous historical maxim. 'The truth is', Lowe asserted:[39]

our law regarded labour as a matter of status, not of contract, and regulated wages and employments, and that this is a relic of that system. It would be very impolitic, now that attention has been drawn to this Act, to enter into a contest with the working classes in a matter in which they appear to be so entirely in the right.

The same historical trajectory was drawn upon by W. A. Hunter, who described the Master and Servant Act as a survival of the legislative policy of the pre-free trade era, before the relationship of employer and employed was seen as one of contract: 'Slowly, step by step, we have been coming to see that labour is a commodity, like others, to be bought and sold.'[40] Like Hunter, Lowe presented repeal of the Master and Servant Act as an

---

[36] East India (Indigo Commission) (*PP* 1861 xliv), pp. xli–xlii; M. E. Grant Duff, *Sir Henry Maine: A Brief Memoir of his Life* (1892), 89, 166.
[37] G. Feaver, *From Status to Contract: A Biography of Sir Henry Maine* (1969), 81.
[38] East India (Contract Law) (*PP* 1867–8 xlix), 4, 92; Grant Duff, *Maine*, 176.
[39] BL Add MSS 44621, fo. 131.
[40] Hunter, *Lecture on the Criminal Laws*, 14.

acknowledgement by the law of these changed conditions, the case being strengthened by the fact that a penal remedy found no direct parallels in the law of either France or America. To prove his point, he instituted inquiries through the Foreign Office to establish whether in 'the leading European countries' there was any difference in the manner of enforcing the labour contract as distinct from other contracts, and whether any instances existed of criminal liabilities being incurred for breaches of the labour contract. Replies from consular staff reinforced Lowe's impression of British peculiarity.[41]

Lowe denied the argument for making contract violation a criminal offence in extreme circumstances, that a worker breaking his contract might do huge damage to property which he had no resources to compensate. First, to make a person 'pay in person because he cannot pay in purse' was at odds with the policy of abolishing imprisonment for debt. Secondly, other forms of contract could be broken with equally disastrous results. Like Frederic Harrison, he asked why, if workmen were to be imprisoned for breaking their agreements, should other contractors not face the same sanction? Finally, he doubted whether the threat of imprisonment was necessary to keep men to their contracts. The working classes had as great an interest as anyone in contractual fidelity; they had no reason to perform 'wanton damage to property'. Like Maine, who insisted that trust in fellow men was fundamental to modern assumptions about contracts, Lowe contended that 'The machine of society could not work for a day if nothing could be relied on except the dread of punishment to keep it in motion.'[42] Lowe's comment was a repetition of one of his statements made during the personally formative experience of carrying through limited liability legislation; his approach to the contract question, presuming a fundamentally optimistic view of men's inherent willingness to carry out private obligations, was a further example of his break from earlier, retributive models of economic behaviour.[43]

Lowe's approach to the CLAA was equally sweeping. He had no sympathy with those who protested against the existence of an Act which protected workers and employers from the 'tyranny of the majority', nor did he acknowledge (if he knew) that there were instances where it had plainly

[41] Liddell to under-secretary, Foreign Office, 10 Nov. 1873, PRO HO34/33, p. 360; Master and Servant (Law of Foreign Countries) (*PP* 1875 lxii); cf. Steinfeld, *Coercion*, 244n.

[42] BL Add MSS 44621, fo. 132; cf. S. Collini in A. Diamond (ed.), *The Victorian Achievement of Sir Henry Maine* (1991), 89.

[43] For a discussion of Lowe's approach to limited liability, see Hilton, *Age of Atonement*, 258–62; on his belief that imprisonment for debt was incompatible with the commercial spirit see Rubin, 'Law, Poverty, and Imprisonment for Debt', 250.

been harshly applied. What he found objectionable was that the CLAA's protection was limited to the relations of employers and workers. Every member of the community should be free from the sorts of annoyances which the CLAA prohibited. The point was illustrated by the case of Lady Burdett Coutts who, on inheriting her fortune, was pestered for eighteen years by a suitor, an insane, bankrupt barrister, who persistently dogged her movements. It was a matter of notoriety that the criminal law offered her no redress.[44]

Lowe's solution was to make the offences enumerated in the CLAA apply generally, rather than only to the circumstance of unions and strikes. It was the approach to dealing with social annoyances which had originally been proposed by Thring in the late 1860s, and had been offered as a compromise by Frederic Harrison in 1869, but was rejected as impractical by Lushington during the drafting of the 1871 legislation. Again, the Indian Penal Code offered a precedent, for section 503 of the code prohibited intimidation, insult, and annoyance in all circumstances.[45] In 1869 Thomas Brassey had suggested a variant of the Indian provision as a way of avoiding objections to 'special' legislation and the idea attracted other adherents, including Mundella, Crompton, and Harrison, as the CLAA controversy wore on. Indeed, it came to be seen as a remedy for the peculiarity of English law that there were no specific penalties for the types of physical harassment and intimidation described in the CLAA and which, for example, R. S. Wright's model criminal code provided for the colonies.[46] A general enactment on the lines of the Indian code would remove the stigma of a penal law directed against a class, while also meeting the complaint of those who protested that, if the CLAA were simply repealed, individuals would lose protection against physical harassment. The TUC had always maintained that if the ordinary criminal law was inadequate to meet physical coercion, it should be strengthened. Lowe took them at their word, while giving magistrates the option of imposing a fine, in the hope of ensuring that there would be no more martyrs to summary justice.

Lowe's need to establish whether his plan would appease the promoters

---

[44] BL Add MSS 44621, fo. 132; E. Healey, *Lady Unknown: The Life of Angela Burdett-Coutts* (1978), 54; cf. J .F. Stephen, *A History of the Criminal Law of England* (3 vols., 1883), iii. 320.

[45] Theobald, *Legislative Acts*, ii. 624.

[46] *Pall Mall Gazette* (9 July 1869); T. Brassey, *Trades' Unions and the Cost of Labour* (1870), 61; *House of Commons Notices of Motions, 1871*, 455; cf. *Journal of Jurisprudence* (Mar. 1874), 126, and a speech by W. A. Hunter, *Aberdeen Daily Free Press* (6 Nov. 1873); Mundella to Leader, 30 May 1873, Mundella MSS 6P/63/41; H. Crompton, 'The Government and Class Legislation', *Fortnightly Review*, 14 (July 1873), 32; Harrison to J. Morley, 21 Aug. 1873, Harrison MSS 1/57; *The Times* (1 July 1875), 12; RCLL 2nd Rep. Q.1178 (Wright's code).

of the labour laws agitation caused him to become, rather oddly, the first minister to invite the TUC to contribute to the policy-making process.[47] On the day after he had completed the memorandum, and before it was circulated to the Cabinet, he let it be known that he would be willing to receive a TUC deputation. Approach was indirect and secretive, Thomas Hughes acting as the intermediary. Howell immediately saw its significance and in a flurry of letters informed fellow TUCPC members and provincial unionists of 'a bold stroke for us' and imminent legislation. He urged Bright to carry the work of repeal to a successful conclusion and breakfasted with Mundella in preparation for the 'delicate and important' interview with Lowe.[48] Hughes, who introduced the deputation, presented the unions' case in terms which coincided with, and suggested some prior knowledge of, Lowe's opinions. Trade unionists sought only 'to be placed under the same conditions as other citizens'. They had no wish to be exempted from the ordinary law; as regards protection against intimidation, they believed that 'the law might very well be made general'.[49] Up to a point this was a fair statement of the views of the TUCPC. Howell in his opening statement asked only for equal treatment and Macdonald emphasized that working men were as committed to upholding contracts as any other section of the community.[50] But when Lowe raised the matter of picketing, the TUCPC's arguments took a different form and it proved less easy for the deputation's Liberal sponsors, who anxiously interjected when the discussion entered sensitive territory, to keep the unionists within a framework of demands for strict legal equality. On picketing, the issue in contention was whether, or how far, the act itself should be curtailed by law. Howell, who insisted that the TUC did not excuse acts of violence to persons or property, was adamant:

we do not consider 'picketing' an offence against the law; we do not consider it morally wrong or at all unlawful in any sense of the term. 'Picketing' seems to be very much misunderstood. The object of it is simply to give information to workmen brought from distant parts of the country when strikes take place; and the fact of 'picketing' does not imply, in the remote sense, coercion.[51]

---

[47] R. M. Martin, *TUC: The Growth of a Pressure Group, 1868–1976* (1980), 30.

[48] Howell, *Labour Legislation*, 323; Howell diary, 29 Oct., 3 Nov. 1873, Howell MSS; Howell to Lowe, 29 Oct. 1873; to Bright, 29 Oct. 1873; to Macdonald, 1 Nov. 1873; to Prior, 3 Nov. 1873, Howell MSS LB8, fos. 190, 195, 202, 206; Howell to Harcourt, 1 Nov. 1873; to Owen, 1 Nov. 1873; to Turner, 16 Nov. 1873, Howell MSS LB7, fos. 309, 312, 323.

[49] *Trades' Union Congress Parliamentary Committee: A Special Report of the Deputation to the Home Secretary* (1873), 3.

[50] Ibid. 5

[51] Ibid. 4.

Lengthy contributions by Daniel Guile of the ironfounders and George Odger on behalf of the shoemakers indicated that, speaking as unionists, they regarded this as the matter of primary importance. They deployed an equality argument concerning the practical effect of the CLAA, though not one which Lowe was willing to acknowledge: the law interfered with the most effective method available to the men to enforce a strike, picketing, while employers could apply their own favoured counter-measure, blacklisting strikers, with impunity.

It required the intervention of Mundella to reformulate their objectives in a form more likely to be acceptable to Lowe. On occasions unionists had been convicted for actions which would not have been crimes when committed by other citizens and would not conceivably be regarded as crimes even if there were a general enactment against intimidation and annoyance. Lowe's idea for a general measure had some application to this point. Magistrates would be obliged to be more even-handed if a generally applicable law was in place: if they convicted a picket for calling 'bah!' after a blackleg, magistrates they would have to treat in the same manner someone who, for example, abused a parliamentary candidate for his political opinions. In particular, a general law was likely to make magistrates more cautious about inferring criminal intent than they had been in their administration of the CLAA. The latter, referring solely to trade offences, tempted the law's administrators to interpret the fact of a strike as evidence of coercion.[52]

'We left a good impression, now we all feel that the Government will do something next session', Howell reported to an officer of Bristol Trades Council, Macdonald expressing similar confidence in a speech to the Miners' National Association conference.[53] With all the signs that the TUC was on the verge of a breakthrough, the NFAEL sought to put the case for preserving the existing law. Lowe was not immediately co-operative, requesting a written statement of their views before deciding to meet them.[54] After a date was finally fixed, for 11 December, to coincide with the NFAEL's inaugural conference, Lowe postponed the meeting, preventing many of the intended delegates from attending. A deputation, led by two Liberal MPs and manufacturers, Edmund Potter and Sir Thomas Bazley, finally obtained a hearing at the Home Office on 13 December. The employers' printed memorial, replying to the TUCPC deputation, repro-

[52] See the example given by Mundella, ibid. 7.
[53] Howell to Thomas, 6 Nov. 1873, Howell MSS LB7, fo. 318; *Bee-Hive* (22 Nov. 1873), 9.
[54] Liddell to Bazley, 28 Nov. 1873; to Whitworth, 6 Dec. 1873; to Whitworth, 10 Dec. 1873: PRO HO136/10, pp. 235, 256, 267.

duced many of the conventional arguments which Lowe's cabinet memorandum had dismissed as dangerous fallacies. By appearing before him in person they exposed themselves to a decidedly hostile cross-examination. In one exchange, Lowe contradicted the employers' attempt to maintain that the CLAA was not exceptional legislation, and trapped one into saying that it was a necessary balance to the Trade Union Act (and therefore 'special').[55] Many of the federated employers were survivors of the Anti-Corn Law League. A generation later they now found themselves presented as defending class privilege and compromising the neutrality of the state in favour of special economic interests. Their sense of Lowe's determination on the CLAA, and their own failure to dissuade him, was conveyed by a Home Office clerk's note of a subsequent communication by them (which has not survived) to the department: 'Federation of Associated Employers—President—Criminal Law Amendment Act—Begs reconsideration of opinion expressed.'[56]

THE EMPLOYERS AND WORKMEN BILL

By the time the NFAEL met Lowe, the Cabinet had already discussed Lowe's paper and given him authority, on 26 November, to draw up a bill, which was to be ready for the next session of parliament.[57] His plan was accepted by a Cabinet still divided over the education controversy and anxious to find non-religious issues to reunite around.[58] On 27 November Lowe met Henry Thring, the parliamentary draftsman, and two days later the Home Office formally requested that a bill be drawn up embodying Lowe's verbal instructions.[59] Thring, who had worked with Lowe at the Board of Trade in preparing limited liability legislation, played a significant part in shaping the plan, a reflection of his earlier familiarity with the subject and of the mutual confidence which existed between him and Lowe.

[55] See Lowe's exchange with Robinson of the engineering employers, reported in *National Federation of Associated Employers of Labour: Report of an Interview on 13 December 1873* (1874), 8.

[56] Home Office register of in-letters, miscellaneous, 12 Jan. 1874, PRO HO46/55; Robinson contended that the CLAA *penalized* all persons who committed the offences described, which was correct, but Lowe's point was that it *protected* only certain categories of persons, RCLL 2nd Rep. Q.269.

[57] Gladstone to the queen, 26 Nov. 1873, Bodl. MS Films 597 (CAB41/5/41); Matthew, *GD*, viii. 414 (21 Nov. 1873), 417 (26 Nov. 1873), 419 (1 Dec. 1873).

[58] Parry, *Democracy and Religion*, 386.

[59] Liddell to secretary of the Treasury, 29 Nov. 1873, PRO HO34/33, p. 307; Lowe described such a session with the draftsman in his evidence to the Select Committee on Acts of Parliament, *PP* 1875 viii, Q.1506.

Lushington, at the Home Office, seems to have been sidelined. Thring's explanatory paper setting out the objects of the Employers and Workmen bill, as Lowe's scheme was provisionally entitled, was completed on 26 December, but was not printed until 28 January 1874, when it was accompanied by a draft of the bill itself.[60] Lowe's plan was therefore finally produced four days after Gladstone's sudden dissolution, though before it had become apparent that the government would be defeated at the polls.

In two respects the actual bill drawn up was less ambitious than Lowe's original ideas. This was partly the result of comments put before the Cabinet by the lord chancellor, Selborne, and partly also a consequence of drafting considerations raised by Thring himself. Selborne wanted to preserve the principle that agreements to commit acts not in themselves illegal might constitute criminal conspiracies. It was obvious, he contended, that there were certain acts which the law did not punish if committed by an individual but which, on account of the resulting element of 'wrong or mischief to individuals or society' were properly punishable as a conspiracy when undertaken by several persons acting jointly.[61] Such instances as offences against public morality had already been instanced by Stephen, and Lowe himself had acknowledged that there would need to be exceptions to his proposal for complete abolition of this type of conspiracy. The contentious issue of what those exceptions should be had led to the failure in the 1873 session of Harcourt's bill, and remained for Lowe and the draftsman to resolve.

Discussion between Thring and Lowe reduced the extent of change further still. Thring's priorities were limited to practical legislative considerations, and were less concerned with the pure points of principle which interested Lowe. Thring's input, however, went somewhat beyond the restricted role prescribed by the later theory of the draftsman's office: that the department initiating legislation had the last word on policy matters, while the draftsman had final responsibility for 'matters of form or law'.[62] In defining the issue, Thring did not look beyond the limited aims of removing the grievances of unions and strikers, and of restoring the intention of the draftsmen in 1871. He described the purpose of Lowe's bill in terms

[60] H. Thring, 'Employers and Workmen Bill: Memorandum', and 'Draft of a Bill to Restrict the Law of Conspiracy in its Application to the Relations of Employers and Workmen, and to make Better Provisions with Respect to such Relations, instead of the Master and Servant Act, 1867, and the Criminal Law Amendment Act, 1871', in OPC Bills and Memoranda (HT) 1874, 421–38.

[61] Memorandum by Selborne, 31 Oct. 1873, appended to Lowe's memorandum, BL Add MSS 44621, fo. 133; Matthew, *GD*, viii. 417.

[62] H. S. Kent, *In on the Act: Memoirs of a Lawmaker* (1979), 45. I am indebted to the late N. C. Rowland CBE for drawing my attention to this source.

which Lowe himself would not conceivably have used: it proposed 'to better the position of trade unions, and is supplemental to the legislation of 1871 in favour of those bodies'. In itself this was a rather inaccurate statement, for immunities to strikers need not be confined to trade unionists, and abolition of a penal contract law benefited all workers. But it disclosed rather bluntly those interests which Thring believed the bill was primarily intended to appease. The Act of 1871 had '*intended* to relieve the members of trade unions *wholly* from the [liability to] indictment for conspiracy' and the new bill proposed 'to fulfil in its integrity the first promise of the Legislature in 1871'.[63] So whereas Lowe had pointed to the anomalies of the law of conspiracy as a whole, Thring concentrated on the departmental objective of restoring the Home Office's original intentions, which he himself had helped to lay down.

The divergence of approach became more apparent when Thring set out two available drafting options. The first, which approximated to Lowe's, involved codifying the law of conspiracy, listing those elements which were thought necessary to preserve and omitting those parts which applied to strikes. An alternative, which did not involve reforming the whole area of law, was simply to exclude strikes from the existing law of conspiracy. Thring favoured the latter, more limited option, even though it conflicted with Lowe's fundamental aim of dealing with the subject in a broad and general way. Any proposal to reform the law of conspiracy as a whole underestimated, in Thring's view, the difficulty of describing exhaustively all those parts of the law which it was necessary to retain. In its passage through Parliament, such a measure would be exposed to 'endless amendments', as had been the experience at the end of the session of 1873. 'In short', Thring concluded, 'to deal with the law of conspiracy by enumeration could only be done successfully as the concluding operation of an English criminal code', something which he considered unlikely to be achieved in the near future. He was sceptical about the alleged ease with which an English code might be drawn up, and in an anonymous article published almost contemporaneously with his work on Lowe's bill he countered Stephen's advocacy of codification with the observation that less spectacular expedients might produce more immediately useful legislative results.[64]

Thring's solution to the difficulty which had arisen from the gas stokers' case was to frame a clause specifically 'to legalise strikes and lock-outs and

---

[63] Thring, 'Memorandum' (1874), 1–2. .

[64] Ibid. 2–3; H. Thring, 'Simplification of the Law', *Quarterly Review*, 136 (Jan. 1874), 55; H. Thring, *Practical Legislation, or, The Composition and Language of Acts of Parliament* (1877).

all acts done in furtherance of strikes and lock-outs'. His proposed form of words anticipated the definition of a trade dispute, later dubbed by labour lawyers the 'golden formula', on which the later freedom to strike was founded. It effectively provided that anyone taking part in a strike or lock-out was to be protected from the law of conspiracy unless they did, or agreed to do something, which was in itself a crime.[65] Within Lowe's terms this was class legislation, and was the sort of approach which he and Coleridge had wanted to avoid in meeting the TUC's demands. Dicey and other twentieth-century writers, following Coleridge, regarded an exemption from the law of conspiracy confined to trade combinations alone as giving strikers a favoured position. Yet, paradoxically, that limited change to the law, which invited accusations of 'privilege', was dictated by Selborne's legal conservatism, and Thring's legislative caution.

Selborne's comments on the Master and Servant Act resulted in a second retreat from the strict principle of Lowe's plan. The chancellor wanted to retain the power to punish breaches of contract by persons engaged in service, where there was a wilful and malicious intent to injure life or property. Thring agreed that 'if society is to be secure some breaches of contract must be penal'. There were instances where breach of duty amounted to something more than the breach of a private agreement between an employer and a worker, and might 'place society in peril' and therefore be properly treatable as crimes. A police strike on the eve of a Fenian insurrection, or a strike of turncocks to deprive London of its water were two possible examples.[66] He therefore proposed that abandonment of duty where 'the immediate probable consequence' would be either to endanger human life, or to deprive a place of policing, lighting, or water supply, or to expose property worth not less than £100 'to immediate destruction', was to be punishable by imprisonment.

Since, by referring to breach of duty, it applied to employers as well as workers, Thring contended that the penal clause was not 'special legislation'. It was, however, an acknowledgement that the gas stokers had been rightly imprisoned. Although formally they were under no contractual obligations beyond those to their employer, their abandonment of duty was potentially so threatening to the security of society that it was proper to view it as analogous to, though not punishable with the same severity as, a mutiny. Thring insisted on the danger to society as being the sole ground for treating contract breaches criminally.

---

[65] Thring, 'Memorandum' (1874), 3; Wedderburn, *The Worker and the Law*, 520–1.
[66] Thring, 'Memorandum' (1874), 6.

In other respects Thring's bill simply carried out Lowe's ideas. The Master and Servant Act was to be repealed, leaving ordinary breaches of the labour contract to be dealt with by the civil process before county courts or, in small cases, Justices of the Peace. The only remedy on either side was the payment of damages—unlike Elcho's Act, there were to be no fines or specific performance—and these were to be enforced by distress, if need be, but not by imprisonment if there were not the means to pay. The Cabinet had agreed that the CLAA should be made general, and Thring effected this by repealing it and replacing it with a clause punishing the 'molestation' of 'any person', molestation being the various acts described in the Act of 1871. The essential criminal intent was, however, redefined: in place of the ambiguous 'intent to coerce', which had been at the root of the contentious convictions under the CLAA, Thring defined the essence of the offence as the intent 'to seriously annoy' or 'to alarm'.[67]

Lowe and Thring between them were the effective originators of the settlement effected by the Conservative government in 1875. Lowe took an unexpectedly prominent part in the later debates, to the extent that some observers raised questions about the true authorship of the measures introduced by Disraeli's administration.[68] An outburst by Harcourt in July 1875 was attributed to irritation that the Conservative administration had stolen the credit for its predecessor's achievement.[69] In a response to Disraeli's self-congratulatory Mansion House speech on Conservative social legislation in 1875, Hartington alleged that the Conservatives had benefited 'from the materials which had been accumulated at the Home Office' by the previous home secretary.[70] A generation later, the rumours resurfaced during a debate on trade union law, when a Liberal MP, W. C. B. Beaumont, whose father had sat in the parliament elected in 1874, paused 'to remind the House of what I believe was the origin' of the labour legislation of 1875:[71]

It was drafted originally by a Liberal Government, when Mr Lowe was Home Secretary, and was left in a pigeon-hole at the Home Office when Mr Gladstone suddenly dissolved Parliament in 1874. The following year it was fished out and was introduced by a Conservative Government by Mr (now Lord) Cross, and no doubt the Conservative Government claimed very great credit therefrom as friends of the working man.

---

[67] Thring, Draft employers and workmen bill, clauses 4, 5, and 6.
[68] *The Scotsman* (5 July 1875).
[69] *Bee-Hive* (17 July 1875), 2.
[70] 3*H* ccxxvi. 653 (6 Aug. 1875).
[71] 4*H* cviii. 279–80 (14 May 1902).

As Beaumont recognized, establishing Lowe as the true author of the settlement in 1875 opened the way for a reconsideration of the long-held view that Gladstonian Liberalism was unable to accommodate the legal demands of the trade union movement. Indeed, it has more recently been contended that a campaign organized round the demand for equal legal rights for employers and workers, and successfully linked by its parliamentary supporters 'to the grand theme of nineteenth-century liberalism—civil and legal emancipation', was one that 'the liberal establishment, in both its "Whig" and "Liberal-Conservative" variants, could not ultimately ignore'.[72] As an overview, this explains the terms in which a concession to the TUC's campaign could be made by a Liberal government, though it begs the question why the demands were resisted in the first place or why, having been regarded almost with derision by members of the government in May and June 1873, those demands were so rapidly conceded.[73] Both sides in the labour laws controversy invoked arguments for equality, and it was by no means self-evident that the TUCPC's version of them should prevail. Harcourt at first dismissed the idea that the CLAA was 'special legislation', and few Liberal MPs were willing to acknowledge the justice of the TUC's complaint. Bright, as Howell recalled, angrily rejected it earlier in 1873. Nor did Liberal backbenchers or ministers readily perceive the inequality of the Master and Servant Act. Most property holders intuitively regarded a demand for the repeal of penal sanctions as being one of 'superficial fairness' only.[74] Like the European planters in India, they believed that formal equality would simply enable one side to walk away from their obligations with impunity, a sentiment which was reinforced by the strike wave which peaked in 1873.

Lowe's appeal to purely legal principles circumvented this practical objection by disconnecting the terms of his plan from their possible economic consequences. In doing so, he repeated the tactic which he had employed in pushing through limited liability, by drawing freely upon doctrinaire arguments to justify a predetermined course of action—in this instance, for the purpose of stemming what he feared was becoming a dangerous class controversy.[75] It represented a considerable retraction of his views in 1867 on the legal position of combinations. He had recently undertaken a 'brazen' somersault, in the case of Irish land tenure, to preserve

---

[72] Spain, 'Trade Unionists', 114–15, 120.

[73] Cf. Harrison, *Before the Socialists* (new edn., 1994), introduction, li–lii.

[74] *Economist* (30 Aug. 1873), 1048.

[75] For Lowe's earlier use of doctrinaire arguments see B. Hilton, review of J. Winter, *Robert Lowe*, in *Historical Journal*, 19 (1976), 1036–7; and for his later use of 'the modern myth of free labor' to justify the change, see Steinfeld, *Coercion*, 215.

the Union with Ireland; he now repeated that feat, to forestall the emergence of class politics.[76]

Lowe was confident that collective action alone could not artificially raise the rewards of labour: as chancellor of the Exchequer, he had warned that unjustifiably high wages in a particular industry would either encourage foreign competition, or attract other workers, and operatives would 'infallibly be beaten down' to their former wage levels.[77] He was less confident that imbalances in the post-1867 political system could so readily correct themselves and this anxiety, prompted by the labour laws rallies in the summer of 1873, drove him to seek a resolution. Here his standing as, in Frederic Harrison's tribute, a 'scientific jurist' was crucial.[78] For while his position during the franchise debates seemed to distance him from the mainstream of academic Liberalism, there were always strong affinities between the two positions and these increased with the post-1867 intellectual drift into anti-democratic scepticism.[79] Thus, as Dicey had warned that the persistence of laws restricting liberty represented a danger in the hands of a democratic electorate, so Lowe contended that perpetuating inequalities would encourage the numerically dominant class to legislate in its own interest. 'It was very important to teach the working men', Lowe said during the 1875 debates, 'to consider that they were not a class apart from the rest of the country'—a remarkable statement from a political figure whose political rhetoric in 1866–7 was widely thought to have achieved the opposite result.[80] While unionists were founding their campaign upon arguments for freedom of contract and equality before the law, he saw the opportunity to integrate labour within a framework of universally applicable laws. The exigencies of what Thring styled 'practical legislation' prevented Lowe from carrying this out in its purest form, an 'exceptional' provision to protect strikers being seen as the only feasible option to deal with the problem of conspiracy. Dicey later contrived to obscure the issue really at stake, when he depicted the settlement as evidence of a 'preference for collective action' enacted by men who were 'very far from accepting the Benthamite ideal of free trade in labour', either unaware of, or unwilling to acknowledge the inconvenient fact that, the real author was the figure whom he hailed as 'the last of the genuine Benthamites'.[81]

---

[76] Steele, *Irish Land*, 306.

[77] *The Times* (27 Sept. 1872), 6.

[78] *The Times* (1 July 1875), 12.

[79] On Harrison's admiration for Lowe see Harrison, *Before the Socialists*, 126; cf. Harvie, *Lights of Liberalism*, 123–4.   [80] 3*H* ccxxv. 1342 (12 July 1875).

[81] Dicey, *Law and Public Opinion*, 266, 271, 253; for a discussion of usages of that epithet see Thomas, *Philosophic Radicals*, 1–11.

9
'The Workmen's Victory'?

THE GENERAL ELECTION OF 1874

The Webbs described the tone of the TUC, meeting at Sheffield shortly before the general election in January 1874, as one 'of bitter anger' against the Gladstone government, and speculated:[1]

It will be a question for the historian of English politics whether the unexpected rout of the Liberal party at the election of 1874 was not due more to the active hostility of the Trade Unionists than to the sullen abstention of the Nonconformists.

Neither factor is now thought to have been decisive in the Liberal defeat except in the negative sense that the activities of both groups drove disaffected propertied Anglicans towards Conservatism.[2] Labour's loyalty to the Liberal party in fact remained remarkably strong both before and during the election.[3] Rumours in unionist circles that Lowe had 'distinctly pledged himself', encouraged the Sheffield Congress to pass a resolution whose terms, rather than condemning the government, gave it an opportunity to redeem itself in the coming session.[4]

The Cabinet's position was spelt out by Forster in a speech at Bradford at the beginning of the election campaign. Responding to written test questions put to him by Bradford trade unionists, he acknowledged that the CLAA was 'badly framed', and should be repealed. Instead of 'exceptional legislation' directed against workmen in their relations with employers, the offence of molestation and annoyance should apply 'in all affairs of life . . . punishing all classes exactly alike'. The criminal portions of the Master and Servant Act should be repealed, except in cases where breaches of contract threatened public safety; capitalists who relied on criminal enforcement of the labour contract were 'leaning on a broken reed'. It was too complicated to re-make the entire law of conspiracy, but it should be amended so that the men's 'power of combination' could not in future be taken from them by

---

[1] Webb, *History*, 286–7.
[2] Parry, *Liberal Government*, 272.
[3] Biagini, *Liberty*, 162–3.
[4] *Newcastle Daily Chronicle* (1 Jan. 1874), 3; *Dundee Advertiser* (5 Jan. 1874; 20 Jan. 1874); *Glasgow Sentinel* (10 Jan. 1874); *The Times* (14 Jan. 1874), 12.

the courts.[5] On the following day Stansfeld made a similar statement at Halifax, adjudged by the secretary of the Halifax Workingmen's Association, which had considered running its own candidate, as a 'real sound explanation' worthy of union support. Frederic Harrison, their intended candidate, treated the pronouncements as a guarantee that the government had adopted the labour programme.[6]

Liberal candidates responded to this lead, and the available evidence suggests that, where the question was actually raised, they overwhelmingly pledged themselves on the three points.[7] At Hull, the two successful Liberal candidates committed themselves at a meeting of trade unionists. Among those who spoke in the candidates' favour was John O'Neill, for thirty-two years a member and officer of the local branch of the boiler-makers, who recalled his imprisonment in 1863 under the 1825 Act (described in Chapter 1) for an action which the CLAA ceased to make an offence.[8] Even some of those Liberal candidates who were initially evasive or outright hostile proved susceptible to pressure. Edward Baines, whose defeat at Leeds was brought about by the intervention of a radical temperance candidate pledged to the unionist programme, moved towards conceding repeal.[9] The most notable about-turn was made by Sir Thomas Bazley at Manchester. Having sponsored the NFAEL deputation to Lowe in December 1873, he made only a guarded reference to the CLAA in his election address but after meeting a deputation of trade unionists was forced to accept their entire programme. Following his humiliating recantation five leading union officials took out a newspaper advertisement urging trade unionists to support the two Liberal candidates, a move which may have assisted him to scrape home for the third seat behind two Conservatives, though his Liberal partner, Jacob Bright, who had supported CLAA repeal from the start, was forced out.[10]

After the election, concerned to explain the vigour of popular toryism, some observers pointed to a trend among Conservative candidates to pledge themselves to the TUC programme.[11] Throughout the manufacturing districts, Frederic Harrison claimed, 'Conservative candidates, rather

---

[5] *Bradford Observer* (29 Jan. 1874), 5–9.

[6] *Halifax Courier* (31 Jan. 1874), 6; (7 Feb. 1874), 6; Kent, *Brains and Numbers*, 113.

[7] A sample of the provincial press turned up 44 Liberal candidates pledging support (of whom 30 were elected), while 6 opposed or declined to give a definite response. For examples from South Wales see R. Wallace, *'Organise! Organise! Organise!'* (1991), 227–9.

[8] *Eastern Morning News* (2 Feb. 1874), 2

[9] J. Vincent, *The Formation of the British Liberal Party, 1857–68* (1972 edn.), 159–61; *Leeds Mercury* (29 Jan. 1874), 5; (2 Feb. 1874), 5.

[10] *Manchester Guardian* (31 Jan. 1874), 8, (4 Feb. 1874), 1; *Bee-Hive* (14 Feb. 1874), 2.

[11] E. S. Beesly, 'The Workman's New Friends', *Bee-Hive* (21 Mar. 1874), 1.

more often and distinctly than the Liberal candidates, have supported the measures desired by the workmen.'[12] Harrison's statement was at variance with what he had written during the campaign itself: it should perhaps be read as a contribution to the debate within Liberalism about the failure of the Gladstone administration. Pressure groups on the Liberal 'left', who considered that their interests had not been sufficiently attended to, had strong motives for emphasizing their role in the electoral defeat.[13] Conversely, the importance of Conservative pledges has been asserted so often as an indication of the likely disposition of the new majority in the House of Commons towards the TUC's demands, that it is perhaps surprising to find that examples are not at all numerous.[14] Since the labour laws were not at the root of party division, one would expect to find some Conservatives in borough constituencies occasionally making a commitment. At Oldham a Conservative candidate, J. M. Cobbett, who had been the first MP to take up the cause of Master and Servant Act reform in 1864, had already pledged himself at a by-election in 1872.[15] One of the successful Conservative candidates for Norwich, the lawyer John Huddleston, told a deputation of trade unionists that he had helped Elcho to reform the Master and Servant Act in the face of opposition from Manchester School MPs, and agreed to support repeal of the 1867 Act's criminal clause. He also favoured putting the law of conspiracy on a statutory basis, but carefully avoided the CLAA, claiming rather implausibly not to have heard of it. He was not alone among Conservatives prepared to contemplate Master and Servant law reform, but distinctly evasive when confronted with the trade union question.[16]

In the north of England numerous Conservatives supported statutory limitation of factory hours, as W. R. Callender, the Manchester tory, impressed upon Disraeli. There is much less evidence of an inclination to acknowledge the trade unionists' demands for changes to collective labour law.[17] In his election address Callender made no reference to a pledge on the

[12] F. Harrison, 'The Conservative Reaction', *Fortnightly Review*, 15 (March 1874), 303; cf. his comment to John Morley, 10 Feb. 1874, Harrison MSS 1/57.

[13] F. Harrison, 'Workmen and the Elections', *Bee-Hive* (31 Jan. 1874), 1; Parry, *Democracy and Religion*, 396..

[14] Webb, *History*, 290; Spain, 'Trade Unionists', 126–7; the sample of the provincial press which identified 44 Liberal pledges produced 10 pledges from Conservatives (only 5 of whom were elected), and an equal number opposed (of whom 6 were elected).

[15] *Oldham Chronicle* (1 June 1872), 6; in 1864 Cobbett sat as a Liberal.

[16] *Norwich Chronicle* (1 Jan. 1874), 2; *Retford Times* (7 Feb. 1874), 6; *Rochdale Observer* (7 Feb. 1874), 7.

[17] W. R. Callender to Corry, 16 Feb. 1874, Disraeli MS 122, fo. 11; Smith, *Disraelian Conservatism*, 188–9.

union question, and made only an ambiguous reference in his address to his working men constituents: both he and his Conservative counterpart at Salford, who had also reportedly made a pledge, were more obviously responsive to the popular protestantism (and therefore Conservatism) of the leadership of the Manchester and Salford Trades Council.[18] At Blackburn the Conservatives, who supported the Fifty-Four Hours bill, declined to be pledged on union law, a pattern repeated at Preston, where both candidates conceded only a limited amendment to the CLAA (apparently to reverse the Lords' amendments).[19] Sandon, who recalled a Conservative tradition of promoting protective legislation, similarly avoided committing himself on the questions put by the Liverpool Trades Council.[20] Where an opportunity arose at Leeds to exploit Baines's awkward position, the Conservative candidates either chose not to, or thought it not in their interests to do so, and resolutely opposed the trades council's demands.[21] There is little evidence to alter the view that the successes of popular toryism in the northern boroughs were the result of the party's position on licensing and denominational education, and the tradition of restricting factory hours, rather than upon a handful of sometimes ambiguous, and unadvertised, pledges to support union rights. The only pointer to the future was that at least one Conservative candidate recognized Forster's solution as one which both parties might be able to support.[22]

None of the Conservative leadership is known to have made a commitment, and the example commonly cited is almost certainly a misidentification. E. S. Beesly reported that among 'the great many' tory members who had pledged themselves was ('if I am not mistaken') Richard Assheton Cross, appointed home secretary in Disraeli's administration.[23] It would have been highly significant if Cross, as has been asserted, was 'induced to swallow the entire unionist dose'; on the basis of Beesly's remark, inferences have been drawn about Cross bringing 'fresh thinking' to bear on the problem and the new government being committed to concession.[24] There are, however, a number of grounds for doubting this version of events. Cross's county constituency, South-West Lancashire, was not, as the Webbs thought, one 'in which the trade unionists were dominant'.[25] No Liberal opponents went to the polls against him, so Cross and his Conservative partner were under no pressure to give an undertaking. Cross

[18] *Manchester Guardian* (31 Jan. 1874), 8; Joyce, *Work, Society, and Politics*, 323–4.
[19] *Preston Herald* (31 Jan. 1874).
[20] *Liverpool Daily Courier* (30 Jan. 1874), 5.   [21] *Leeds Mercury* (28 Jan. 1874), 7.
[22] *Wakefield Herald* (31 Jan. 1874), 5.   [23] *Bee-Hive* (21 Mar. 1874), 1.
[24] Harrison, *Before the Socialists*, 302; Fraser, *Trade Unions and Society*, 144, 165, 194; Roberts, *Trades Union Congress*, 80.   [25] Webb, *History*, 291n.

had spoken in favour of the CLAA during the 1871 debates, and as a representative of Lancashire business Conservatism he had no affinity with the tory radicalism of Callender, sharing Derby's suspicion of the 'semi-socialist ideas' of the New Social Movement project.[26] Although he favoured a more positive Conservative programme of social and administrative reform, this did not initially embrace the issues of civil disabilities which the TUC espoused. Only one reference has been located to Cross's views on the labour laws during the 1874 election campaign. Addressing the Southport District Conservative Working Men's Association, on 29 January, he attacked Joseph Chamberlain's 'quadrilateral', alleging that 'free labour', as Chamberlain and the TUC defined it, 'aims at depriving the individual of freedom of contract'.[27] His sentiments followed those of a *Quarterly Review* article which appeared in the same month and was recommended to Conservative candidates by Disraeli's secretary as a statement of his party's position. Written by a Conservative barrister, it argued that the repeal of the existing laws would undermine individual freedom: 'what they [trade unionists] seek is not freedom but privilege'.[28]

Another candidate by the name of Cross was returned for a Lancashire manufacturing constituency, and he did swallow 'the unionist dose'. John Kynaston Cross, a millowner, stood as a Liberal for one of the two Bolton seats. At a public meeting attended by unionists he read out extracts from Forster's speech, and then gave positive responses to the test questions put by the trades council, which had been energetic in pushing repeal since the wrongful conviction of the masons' shop steward in the town in 1871.[29] The episode was widely reported and it seems probable that Beesly—like other London-based writers—confused the two men. J. K. Cross's victory reflected the continuing strength of the Liberals in the northern boroughs, a trend which also returned the radical, libertarian lawyer, Charles Hopwood, who became one of the members of the new parliament most active in promoting the TUC programme.[30]

---

[26] 3H ccvii. 283 (19 June 1871); Vincent (ed.), *Derby Diaries*, 91 (7 Oct. 1871); Smith, *Disraelian Conservatism*, 195.

[27] Cross MSS Lancs RO DDX 841 (newscuttings), *Liverpool Daily Courier* (30 Jan. 1874), 7.

[28] J. H. Fyfe, 'The Despotism of the Future', *Quarterly Review*, 136 (Jan. 1874), 200; Smith, *Disraelian Conservatism*, 188.

[29] *Bolton Chronicle* (31 Jan. 1874), 7, 8; *Bolton Evening News* (29 Jan. 1874), 3, 4; (31 Jan. 1874), 3; the Webbs may have been misled by the Bolton Trades Council's delegate to the TUC who described the assurance obtained from 'Mr Cross', *Liverpool Daily Post* (21 Jan. 1875), 6.

[30] Parry, *Democracy and Religion*, 400–1; *Stockport Advertiser* (30 Jan. 1874), 7.

THE COCKBURN COMMISSION

The parliamentary majority of the new Conservative administration was founded not upon numerous undertakings to appease the unionists, but if anything on an inclination to resist them.[31] Thus the incoming home secretary, R. A. Cross, inherited a legislative settlement drawn up by his departmental predecessor which neither he nor most of his party's supporters had much desire to promote. He always claimed that his decision in March 1874 to appoint a royal commission, seen by the TUCPC as a delaying tactic, was dictated by the fact that he found insufficient material at the Home Office to guide him in preparing legislation.[32] His version of events is suspect on two counts. Insofar as a bill was actually in print, there was too much material than was politically convenient. Secondly, before Cross was even appointed, the new administration had determined upon an inquiry. Cairns, the Lord Chancellor, who had opposed the temporary protection to union funds in 1869, introduced the Lords' amendments to the CLAA in 1871, and ensured the loss of Harcourt's conspiracy bill in 1873, agreed with Derby soon after the government was formed that the matter should be referred to a commission, a ploy that had already been floated by some Conservative candidates anxious to avoid pledging themselves.[33] Cairns's idea seems to have been to vest the subject in a commission with a strong judicial element, and with terms of reference limited to the practical working, rather than the philosophy of the existing law, thus excluding the TUC's fundamental grounds of objection. As county magistrates, Derby and Cross were both aware that there had been contradictory decisions under the CLAA: two such cases had recently come before them at the Lancashire quarter sessions, and in both they quashed the convictions.[34]

While the purpose of the commission may not actually have been delay— Cross regretting that the TUCPC, in making the allegation, 'should have so entirely misunderstood the intentions of the Government'[35]—that was the result. Nearly two months elapsed between the commission's appointment

[31] *The Scotsman* (29 Jan. 1874), 4; cf. Halifax to Gladstone, 12 Feb. 1874, cited in J. Morley, *The Life of William Ewart Gladstone* (3 vols., 1903), ii. 494.

[32] F. J. Dwyer, 'The Rise of Richard Assheton Cross and his Work at the Home Office, 1868–80' (Oxford B.Litt. thesis, 1954), 123.

[33] Vincent (ed.), *Derby Diaries*, 164 (16 Feb. 1874); Cross was not offered the Home Office until 18 Feb.; *Huddersfield Daily Chronicle* (3 Feb. 1874), 3.

[34] *Potteries Examiner* (18 Oct. 1873); OBS Monthly Reports, Sept. 1873, 1,276–7; Nov. 1873, 1,292, MRC MS 78/oB/4/1/4; OSM FR 20 Nov. – 3 Dec. 1873, MSS 78/oS/4/1/47; *Liverpool Daily Post* (26 Nov. 1873), 4 (letter from Albert Crompton on the Garston case); MS Derby diary, 23 Jan. 1874.

[35] A. F. O. Liddell (Home Office) to Howell, 24 Mar. 1874, PRO HO136/10, 512.

and its first sitting. It adjourned in July 1874 having failed to complete its inquiries by the end of the parliamentary session, the secretary resigning in August (he was reinstated in October) after a squabble with the Treasury over cuts to the clerical budget.[36] By the time the last evidence was heard, in December, the commission had managed just eleven sittings, many of them sparsely attended by the commissioners themselves. The chairman, the lord chief justice, Sir Alexander Cockburn, and the other senior judge, Montague Smith, along with the recorder of London and Conservative MP Russell Gurney, took part in only three sessions.

In the judges' absence the sittings were dominated by three opponents of the TUC. Some of the sittings were chaired by Winmarleigh, a Conservative landowner in Lancashire and parliamentary representative in the 1850s of the National Association of Factory Occupiers. His questions sought to bring out that the Master and Servant Act was fair between both parties: if a master failed to pay a damages award he, too, would be liable to imprisonment.[37] On other occasions the chair was taken by E. P. Bouverie, a whig defector from Liberalism, and Roebuck, whose defeat of Joseph Chamberlain at Sheffield symbolized the failure of radicalism at the general election. They both subjected unionist witnesses to searching and unfriendly scrutiny with the aim of discrediting the assertion that the CLAA was exceptional, disputing the analogy with employers' blacklists, and demonstrating that most convictions under the Act had been justifiable.[38]

The TUCPC's boycott of the proceedings meant that the case against the existing law was weakly and unconvincingly put. The two commissioners whom Cross had induced to take part to balance its composition, Thomas Hughes and the miners' leader, Alexander Macdonald, arranged for a handful of unionist witnesses to appear, but the latter made a poor impression. George Shipton, secretary to the London Trades Council, chose to dwell on a Master and Servant case, which proved on further inquiry not to be the iniquity which he had suggested. The testimony of Andrew Boa, of the Scottish CLAA repeal campaign, was fatally undermined by his failure to produce any examples to support his assertion that the courts had blocked proceedings against masters who operated blacklists.[39] Henry Crompton's diffident testimony as the final witness, at the personal invitation of the commission, was evidently reluctant and possibly undertaken only out of courtesy to the lord chief justice.

---

[36] PRO HO46/54, 6 Aug. 1874, 20 Aug. 1874, 17 Oct. 1874.
[37] RCLL, 2nd Rep. Q.181.
[38] RCLL 2nd Rep. Qs.10–20, 502, 512, 556, 901.
[39] RCLL 2nd Rep., 7; Qs.37–41, 71n.

Instead the commission provided a forum for the federated employers to reopen an argument which, only weeks' earlier following their exchanges with Lowe, appeared to have been lost. Having in February 1874 launched their journal *Capital and Labour*, edited by a professional writer, W. H. S. Aubrey, and committed 'to set labour wholly free', the NFAEL was ready to challenge the TUC's position. Their president, John Robinson, a Manchester engineer, immediately approached the new home secretary to press the Federations' contention, which Lowe had dismissed, that the CLAA was not exceptional legislation.[40] Evidence to the commission from organized employers emphasized that the laws were useful to them, and essential for the running of their businesses. Those involved in managing large-scale ironworks, in particular, where a few men could bring a large operation to a standstill and in extreme cases ruin plant and raw materials, were emphatic about the need to retain penal sanctions for contract breaches.[41]

Deterrence was also the ground on which employers in cotton, engineering, shoemaking, tailoring, and, most of all building, justified the CLAA, for they alleged that it curbed picketing and made strikers more cautious in their tactics. Having petitioned parliament in opposition to any mitigation of its provisions, the master builders insisted that the Act underlay the comparative industrial peace within the industry, and that its repeal would open the way to renewed disharmony.[42] Though ordinarily disposed to treat the employers' views uncritically, the majority of the commissioners referred with polite dismissiveness to the proposition that the CLAA had produced a palpable change in the character of industrial relations. Macdonald seems to have arranged for counter-testimony by union witnesses from coalfields where conciliation and arbitration had, as in the building trade, recently been established. William Crawford of the Durham miners insisted, 'I do not think the Act [the CLAA] has changed the customs or practices of our men one iota.'[43]

Running throughout the commissioners' report, signed on 17 February 1875, was a reversion to the arguments for legal intervention and control

[40] *Capital and Labour* (25 Feb. 1874), 1, 4; Home Office to J. Robinson 27 Mar. 1874, HO136/10, 522; RCLL 2nd Rep. Q.269.
[41] RCLL 1st Rep. Q.287, 513, 752–3.
[42] See the evidence of the Liverpool and Leeds master builders, RCLL 2nd Rep. Qs.87–9, 99, 340, 351.
[43] RCLL 2nd Rep., 20; Qs.109–15, 292, 441; Q.468 (Crawford). The building employers' testimony is the basis for the contention that the CLAA helped to discipline the 'rank and file' into accepting the formalization of industrial relations, see Price, *Masters, Unions, and Men*, 127; and, from a different standpoint, as establishing the necessity for the Act, Biagini, *Liberty*, 157.

previously urged by the majority of the Erle commission. For Roebuck, who was never reconciled to the eventual shelving of the majority report of the previous inquiry, this was an opportunity to reopen the issues. Thus the Cockburn commission report reprinted with a favourable gloss one of its precursor's most tendentious passages, to the effect that free competition in the relations between labour and capital, as in all other areas of trade, was the proper object of public policy.[44] From this premise their overall conclusion was in favour of leaving the two statutes substantially as they stood.[45]

Their recommendations on the Master and Servant Act have been well described as 'an elaborate rationalization for keeping the act's main provisions as they were'.[46] On the one hand they endorsed the principle—and hardly anyone did not—that ordinary breaches of contract should be matters for civil proceedings. But they retreated from carrying the principle through. They contended rather implausibly that the 1867 Act already embodied the principle, though acknowledging the awkward anomaly of fines, which they agreed to abolish. But they were not yet willing to accept that remedies for breaches of the labour contract should be like those for any other contracts. Prison needed to be kept not far in reserve otherwise workers, having insufficient property to pay damages awards, would simply break their contracts with impunity. Imprisonment was to remain for those who failed to pay damages awards, even where there was no proof of ability to pay (as was required in small debt cases). In other words, as Macdonald critically observed in his brief dissenting report, imprisonment was to remain as 'a punishment for poverty'.[47] On section 14 of the 1867 Act (imprisonment for 'aggravated' cases) they were divided. Some favoured dealing with such cases civilly, with heavy imprisonment (up to six months) in the event of failure to pay compensation; others that it should be retained, but with the option of trial by jury. A divided recommendation on this point presumably ensured the adhesion of Thomas Hughes, who had critically questioned employer witnesses, and possibly Russell Gurney, who was regarded as a progressive law reformer.

There was no concession, however, to the arguments against the CLAA, which were depicted as being 'of a very shadowy and insubstantial character'. That the Act was exceptional was no sufficient argument against it, for 'nowhere but in the labour market is free competition sought to be prevented by unwarrantable means'. The only change admitted was that defendants should in future be allowed the option of trial by jury.[48]

[44] RCLL 2nd Rep. 20–2.   [45] *The Times* (23 Feb. 1875), 9.
[46] Steinfeld, *Coercion*, 210.   [47] RCLL 2nd Rep. 10–11, 28.
[48] Ibid. 22.

THE 'NEW' LAW OF CONSPIRACY

Apart from a section of Henry Crompton's testimony, witnesses before the Cockburn commission were not questioned about the law of conspiracy, a matter which the commissioners presumably thought too recondite to lend itself to inexpert discussion. While the commission was sitting, however, developments in that area of law disproved Bruce's confidence in 1873 that Brett's ruling in the gas stokers' case would not be followed by other judges. Indeed, with the formation of the NFAEL there was now an organization dedicated to defending the law of conspiracy,[49] and whose supporters were willing to use it. Seven conspiracy indictments are known to have been brought between 1872 and 1875, including those against the London cabinet-makers, the gas stokers, the colliers at the Plymouth ironworks, and the London carpenters noted in previous chapters.[50] Some were conspiracies to commit crimes and did not raise contentious points of law: as in the pre-1867 cases (discussed in Chapter 1), conspiracy indictments were used to bring defendants before a higher tribunal for the purpose of inflicting greater punishment or to make an example of ringleaders. Proceedings against the cabinet-makers' pickets in 1875 (described in Chapter 6) were instigated by Peter Graham, a member of the NFAEL's council, while the Newmarket Farmers' Defence Association was behind an indictment brought against a group of agricultural labourers for conspiring to intimidate non-unionists during the lock-out in East Anglia in 1874. Their trial at Suffolk assizes was redolent of the old pattern of legal paternalism. Having pleaded guilty, the labourers were dismissed without sentence, though not before the venerable Sir Fitzroy Kelly had terrified them with a warning of the term of imprisonment which he was empowered to impose. This was followed by advice against being led astray by 'foreign agitators', by which Kelly meant union organizers from outside the county.[51]

Less theatrical but more legally remarkable were the indictments for common law conspiracies. As appeals to quarter sessions had confirmed, it was not possible to bring summary proceedings under the CLAA in cases of non-violent workplace ultimata. Even before the gas stokers' case, there was a temptation for aggrieved employers to try to revive common law remedies. The unsuccessful indictment of the South Wales miners, tried before Sir Robert Lush in 1873, originated in advice from a Merthyr Tydfil

[49] *The Trades Union Congress Parliamentary Committee and the National Federation of Associated Employers of Labour* (1873), 20.

[50] A further example, brought by an anti-union employer in the Devon lace trade, broke down during the committal proceedings, *Barnstaple Times* (2 Nov. 1874).

[51] *Bury and Norwich Post* (4 Aug. 1874), 6.

solicitor at a time when managerial control at the Plymouth ironworks was, according to press reports, being systematically undermined.[52] Two further cases which came before the courts in 1874, however, confirmed the extension to the law of conspiracy which Brett had set in train.

One was brought against Thomas Halliday, president of the Amalgamated Association of Miners (AAM), and hung over him as he unsuccessfully contested Merthyr Tydfil in the general election. The case was raised at the general election by some Liberal candidates, who pointed out that Conservative obstruction in the House of Lords had blocked conspiracy law reform and left the way open to prosecutions.[53] Along with seven other AAM officers he appeared at Manchester assizes in March 1874 indicted for conspiring to induce Cornish blacklegs to break their contracts with a firm of Burnley coalowners who had tied the new, non-union colliers to one-year agreements. Although the AAM officials were not convicted, as the jury failed to reach a verdict, in the course of legal argument Sir Richard Amphlett confirmed that the CLAA had failed to abrogate the common law. He also ruled that a combination to persuade men to break their contracts was a criminal conspiracy.[54] In a further case at the next Manchester assizes in August 1874 Sir Charles Pollock, like Amphlett a very recent appointment to the bench, pushed the law even further. Ten members of the Manchester and Salford Coarse Spinners' Association were indicted for conspiring to procure the discharge of a spinner who belonged to a rival union by striking to force his dismissal. Pollock laid down that, while one man could decide not to work with an objectionable individual, 'if a body of men . . . went and said to their employers, "If you do not dismiss that man we won't work for you", then the law said that was not a legal act.'[55] The latter, in particular, was regarded as very doubtful law, but as the spinners were discharged without sentence there was no occasion for an appeal, and an emphatic reversal of the intention of the 1871 legislation went unchallenged.[56]

[52] RCLL 2nd Rep. Q.1104; *Colliery Guardian* (27 Sept. 1872), 341; *Merthyr Express* (12 Oct. 1872); *Merthyr Telegraph* (27 Sept., 4 Oct. 1872); *South Wales Daily News* (1 Oct. 1872); *Cardiff Times* (22 Feb. 1873); see also p. 180 above.

[53] *Oldham Standard* (31 Jan. 1874), 7.

[54] *The Colliers' Strike and Lock-Out at Burnley: Report of the Trials of the Miners' Officials for Conspiracy* (1874); *The Times* (21 Mar. 1874), 11; RCLL 2nd Rep., Appx. 4 (c), 106.

[55] *Charge of Conspiracy and Intimidation against Members of the Manchester and Salford Coarse Spinners' Association, tried at the Manchester Assizes, August 4th, 1874, by Baron Pollock* (flysheet in Howell Collection); *The Times* (6 Aug. 1874), 11 (*R v Collinge and Others*); both Amphlett (a former Conservative MP) and Pollock had been elevated to the bench in the last days of the Gladstone government.

[56] H. Crompton, *The Law of Conspiracy* (1875), 5.

Responsibility for the passage of the royal commission's report which addressed the objections to the law of conspiracy seems to have rested with Cockburn, who had taken the chair when Crompton voiced criticisms of its effects on strikers. This was the aspect of the controversy on which judges might be expected to have a pronounced view. During Halliday's trial, Amphlett had been concerned to refute the idea that conspiracy was an oppressive class law. It protected the poor as much as the rich: 'Just conceive the state of society if you allow rich men to combine together to injure poor men.'[57] The passage on conspiracy in the Cockburn commission's report likewise sought to refute some of the 'specious' arguments levelled against the common law, and a rationale was offered for its attitude towards combinations. The common law made offences of combinations to effect wrongful purposes, which if done singly would be no crime, because of their 'more formidable and aggravated character' when many persons joined together to do so. Numbers transformed a private wrong into a threat to the community, and therefore a crime, and warranted the use of the state's powers of repression.[58]

The report's substantial recommendation, however, was that the law of conspiracy should be altered to restore the immunity intended in the CLAA. Assuming that Pollock's ruling in the spinners' case was a correct statement of the law, then the law should be altered. The CLAA's immunity should be extended to prevent any court in future from holding, as Brett and Pollock had done, that a strike was a conspiracy on the grounds that the object was 'to force or control the action or will of a master or workmen', which of course every strike or lock-out sought to do. It was a less comprehensive immunity than that proposed by Harcourt, for it would not prevent the courts from discovering some other new ground on which a strike might be regarded as a criminal conspiracy. It did, however, follow the view of Harcourt and Thring that any change to the law of conspiracy should be confined to cases which arose between employers and workers.

While restoring strikers' immunities in one direction, the Cockburn commission's report raised a new threat to them from another. The suggestion that numbers might turn a private wrong into a crime raised an issue about strikers who broke their contracts. Supposing that breach of contract were treated as a civil wrong only, might its commission by several persons acting with joint intent transform it, by Cockburn's definition of a conspiracy, into a crime? The majority of the commissioners believed it would, and recommended that no alteration in the law should render strikers immune

[57] *The Times* (21 Mar. 1874), 11.
[58] RCLL 2nd Rep. 25.

from prosecution for conspiracy if they jointly broke their contracts. This was not simply to apply to instances like the gas stokers, where there was a direct effect upon the public, but was intended to penalize all collective breaches: strikers would have to take care to give proper notice to be safe from prosecution.

THE CONSERVATIVE SETTLEMENT

When Cross introduced his legislation in June 1875 it was evident that, as regards both the Master and Servant Act and the law of conspiracy, he preferred to be guided by Lowe's plan than by the Cockburn commission's recommendations. Recognizing the striking resemblance to his own bill, Lowe praised Cross's speech 'loudly and publicly', and later congratulated Cross for having 'emancipated his mind boldly and freely from a mass of prejudice'.[59] What led Cross to the same conclusion as his predecessor in office? As has been argued above, the outcome cannot be explained simply as the carrying out of Conservative electoral pledges, but was much more likely to have represented the adoption of a pre-existing departmental plan, as the contemporary rumours mentioned in the previous chapter alleged. But how Cross came to adopt much of Lowe's proposals remains unclear, for the lack of Home Office papers cannot be supplemented by drafting materials. Thring and Jenkyns were swamped by the great pressure of legislation in 1875, and outside counsel were commissioned to help relieve the burden of preparing government bills. The instructions given to those outsiders, which may never have been written down, have not been preserved.[60] Some inferences may, however, be drawn from public reactions to the Cockburn commission report.

Cross later acknowledged that, although many of the recommendations of the commission were 'thrown overboard' by himself, its function had been to contribute to the 'ripening' of public opinion.[61] The report provoked a critique by Henry Crompton—rushed into print as soon as the official report appeared—which Howell believed to have been influential with the Home Office.[62] Unlike Macdonald's own brief dissent to the

[59] Vincent (ed.), *Derby Diaries*, 222 (11 June 1875); 3*H* ccxxv. 658 (28 June 1875).
[60] H. Jenkyns to Treasury, 3 Aug. 1875, PRO T1/7469/16412/12272, citing the labour bills as one of the reasons for payments to additional counsel.
[61] *The Trade Unionist* (23 Oct. 1875), 69.
[62] Howell, *Labour Legislation*, 366; Howell MSS LB7, fo. 829, draft article on the labour laws agitation; copies were received at the Home Office, PRO HO136/12, p. 174; HO46/57, 1 Mar., 8 Mar. 1875; Cross cited it, 3*H* ccxxiv. 1673 (10 June 1875).

commission report, Crompton's paper was a penetrating analysis of the commissioners' methods and assumptions, and fulfilled the same role as Frederic Harrison's minority report to the Erle commission. Crompton brought two distinctive insights to bear. Both professionally, as a clerk of assize, and by upbringing as the son of a distinguished common lawyer, Sir Charles Crompton (who as late as 1855 had held trade unions to be criminal conspiracies), he had an especially acute perception of the failure of judges to 'comprehend the ideas and views of the working-classes'. Yet he also possessed a deep personal reverence for the higher courts and the men who presided over them. He believed that judges genuinely sought to be impartial, but that their misconceptions of industrial matters led them into a false position when the respective rights of labour and capital were in contention.

In a series of articles addressed to members of the agricultural labourers' union, Crompton tried to impress upon them that in most respects the law protected the poor as much as the rich. It was in their interests that the law should be as strong as possible and the authority of its administrators upheld. Equally, though, the unfairness in labour cases needed to be addressed.[63] He was accordingly vehement in his criticisms of the principles which underlay the Cockburn commission report, highlighted by its unreflecting use 'of the old legal-economical language' about unrestricted competition being in the best interests of all. He instanced the commissioners' refusal to recognize the inequality of the relationship between masters and individual servants, their one-sided concern with employers' interests while regarding manual workers as morally unequal in contract matters, and their casual endorsement of exceptional penal laws against workers' breaches of duty which did not apply to similar negligence among other classes of the community. He exposed the oppressiveness of Cockburn's recommendation to criminalize combined breaches of contract: for many workers an immediate strike was the only means of resisting arbitrary acts of 'tyranny and unkindness' in the workplace.[64]

Crompton's second line of criticism concerned the report's deficiencies as a work of investigation, and here he brought to bear his findings as an observer of contemporary industrial trends. Despite its remit, the commission had done little to look into the instances of injustice or the severity of punishments administered. Relying on the unsupported assertions of employer witnesses, the commission made no attempt to gather systematic

---

[63] See his series of articles on 'Our Criminal Justice', in *Labourers' Union Chronicle* (26 Dec. 1874 – 23 Jan. 1875), reprinted as a booklet in 1905.

[64] Crompton, *Labour Laws Commission*, 9–11, 15, 20.

evidence on the rise of 'minute' contracts (that is, contracts terminable at a moment's notice on either side) in major industries. By failing to do so it overlooked the practical evidence that working men were decreasingly willing to enter into contracts—though they were perfectly willing to abide by them—as a result of the failure of the law to treat each side equally.

Another Liberal jurist, W. A. Hunter, scrutinized what he called the 'complex organization of labour argument' of the large iron manufacturers, who insisted on the need for a penal contract law to keep key workers at their posts. He accused such employers of using the law to supply their own deficiencies in management. If certain men were so vital, why did the employers not take more care to employ reliable individuals, obtain character references, pay them well, and keep others in reserve? Instead, they chose to depend on itinerant, casual workers vulnerable to intemperance, and disciplined them by the threat of the criminal proceedings which were rarely taken for fear of the ill-will caused.[65]

While the radicalism of Crompton's critique of the legal fiction of equality in labour contracts was antithetical to Cross's own stated views, no one could have read Crompton's or Hunter's discussion of the evidence without concluding that in places the commission's report was a deeply flawed document. The evidence on the Master and Servant Act had been in the public domain since October 1874 and, in advance of the commissioners' own report, the findings were analysed within the Home Office.[66] Such moves suggested a willingness to proceed independently of the commissioners' recommendations, a view reinforced by an important contact which Cross is known to have had in the spring of 1875 with A. K. Rollit, a Conservative solicitor and steamship owner from Hull.

Rollit later became a leading exponent of constructive urban Conservatism and welfare capitalism;[67] his significance in 1875 lay in his demonstration of how a concession could be accommodated within a 'modern' form of business Conservatism. He had for some time urged that the Master and Servant Act could 'safely' be repealed, leaving breaches of labour contracts to be dealt with by civil remedies, and he put this solution personally to Cross.[68] After their interview, Rollit elaborated his ideas in an open letter, which appeared on the same day that Cross put his own scheme before the Cabinet. Before any details of Cross's bills were made public, Rollit

[65] W. A. Hunter, *The Master and Servant Act, 1867, and the First Report of the Royal Commission* (1875), 7–9.

[66] PRO HO46/55 (register of in-letters), 10 Dec. (law officers), 16 Dec. (Home Office counsel) 1874.

[67] Offer, *Property*, 223–4.

[68] *Eastern Morning News* (3 Feb. 1874).

confidently predicted to a meeting of Hull Conservatives that the issue 'would be approached in a broad and liberal spirit' and 'would establish the fame and popularity of the Cabinet upon the most lasting footing'.[69] It is hard to avoid the conclusion that he was given ministerial encouragement to test the waters. If so, the reaction was immediately favourable. A leading article from the Conservative *Sheffield Daily Telegraph*, which was forwarded to the Home Office, applauded the idea from a business standpoint. Placing contracts on a civil basis was not a concession to organized labour but a recognition that 'in these railroad times labour is a floating commodity' like any other, a fact which should be recognized by the law.[70]

Rollit was also sensitive, in a way that the Cockburn commission had not been, to popular objections to the tribunals which heard Master and Servant cases and to the stigma of criminality which attached to the existing proceedings. The commission had ruled out transferring jurisdiction to county courts on the practical grounds that those courts were held less frequently than petty sessions, while the fees charged to litigants in county courts were higher. Rollit's idea was to declare explicitly that all proceedings would be of a purely civil nature, and to limit jurisdiction to stipendiary magistrates or county court judges or their registrars, thus eliminating unpaid justices of the peace. There would be a clear demarcation between ordinary breaches of contract and very exceptional cases which warranted a criminal remedy. An alteration to the general criminal law, rather than a special measure relating to employers and workers, would deal with those extreme instances of breach of duty where loss of life or actual damage to property were involved. No less than any other members of the community, Rollit insisted, the working classes regarded such breaches of duty as criminal, but they justifiably objected when penal sanctions were directed against themselves alone. The similarity to Lowe's views was obvious. J. E. Davis, a former stipendiary magistrate in Stoke and Sheffield, and recently appointed Home Office legal adviser to the Metropolitan Police, had also proposed that a strict line be drawn between the civil and criminal aspects of the question,[71] and this was embodied in the eventual legislation, which divided the issues into two separate bills.

Parliamentary considerations also affected Cross's options. As the Act of 1867 was annually renewable, the government could not avoid a decision in the summer of 1875 as to whether it should remain in force. So long as it

[69] A. K. Rollit, *The Master and Servant Act: A Letter to the Right Hon. R. A. Cross MP* (1875) (reprinted from the *Eastern Morning News* (26 May 1875); *Hull Packet* (28 May 1875), 8.

[70] *Sheffield Daily Telegraph* (31 May 1875), 3; PRO HO46/57, 5 June 1875; *Bee-Hive* (12 June 1875), 7.

[71] RCLL 1st Rep. Q. 418, 439; 2nd Rep. Q.315.

was, the Home Office would be exposed to pressure from radical MPs every time a bad instance of imprisonment occurred: one arose shortly after the publication of the commission's report.[72] Such complaints were hard to resist in the face of the commission's own apparent acceptance, however qualified, of the principle of civil remedies. These considerations helped to overcome opposition from Carnarvon and Salisbury when Cross put his proposals to the Cabinet at the end of May. Having recoiled in 1867 at the prospect of household suffrage, they now baulked at the abolition of a penal law to enforce labour contracts.[73] Carnarvon raised doubts, and 'the more considered it was, the more difficult it seemed to become': Gathorne Hardy noted an unusually long discussion over the difficulty of dealing with the subject on 'sound principles'. But both Carnarvon and Salisbury came round to the view that a settlement was unavoidable.[74] Nor could there be any retraction, even in the face of competing demands for parliamentary time. Once Cross had announced, in June, the government's intention to repeal the Master and Servant Act, it was impossible to allow months to elapse during which individuals were likely to be imprisoned for breaches of contract.[75]

While repeal of the Master and Servant Act proved difficult for some Conservatives to accept, once they had done so it was the easiest part of the legislation to present to the party and to parliament. The previous reform, in 1867, had been accomplished with the support of a Conservative government. It also enabled trade unions to be kept very much in the background, as Cross intended them to be, though the change to the contract law obviously removed a practical obstacle to strikes. Master and Servant was placed at the forefront of the settlement, which took the title of Thring's draft of 1874, the Employers and Workmen bill.

Cross adopted a view of labour contracts which was, in relation to the legal practice of the time, advanced. It surprised even Crompton by its radicalism, and won Lowe's admiration for adopting a principle that had been embodied in Thring's bill.[76] For Cross, like Lowe and Thring, rejected the remedy of specific performance, except with the agreement of the worker

---

[72] See P. A. Taylor on the case of Luke Hills, a carter, imprisoned for three months by Cuckfield magistrates for being unable to pay damages following a simple breach of agreement, the terms of which were anyway in question, 3*H* ccxxii. 1485 (9 Mar. 1875), 1610–1 (11 Mar. 1875); ccxxiii. 102–4 (19 Mar. 1875)

[73] See Winmarleigh's continued doubts, 3*H* cxxvi. 40–1 (26 July 1875).

[74] Carnarvon diary, 26 May, 29 May 1875, BL Add MS 60907; Vincent, *Derby Diaries*, 219–20 (26 May, 29 May); Johnson (ed.), *Gathorne Hardy Diary* (1981), 238 (30 May 1875).

[75] As Cross impressed upon Derby, 22 June 1875, Derby MSS 920DER(15) 16/2/5.

[76] H. Crompton, 'The Workmen's Victory', *Fortnightly Review*, n.s. 18 (Sept. 1875), 402; J. E. Davis, *The Master and Servant Act, 1867* (1868), iv; Steinfeld, *Coercion*, 53–7, 214–16.

proceeded against. Such a remedy had been inserted in the 1867 Act at J. E. Davis's suggestion and was frequently used by local courts to order workers back to their employment. To practitioners like Davies and Rollit, who had also sanctioned it, specific performance seemed a reasonable replacement for imprisonment, and an alternative to damages which might not be paid and which a worker might prefer not to have to pay. To legal theorists like Lowe, however, specific performance amounted to forced labour, and a 'vestige of slavery', oppressive in the same sense that had led to its rejection as a remedy against the Bengal ryots. 'An order for specific performance means that a man is slave for the remainder of his term', W. A. Hunter claimed.[77] It had led to a spectacular case of oppression when a skilled metal-worker named Cutler was repeatedly proceeded against under the 1867 Act. He was subjected to three months' imprisonment to force him to carry out a five-year engagement he had entered into with an employer, who refused to increase his wages during the economic boom of the early 1870s. When the case was put before the Cockburn commission by a union official, the judges, Cockburn and Smith, were at pains to show that, despite appearances, the law had been neither harshly nor unjustly applied. Its rationale was, in their view, the reasonable one of enforcing agreements that had been freely entered into.[78]

Under Cross's measure a worker could, if he wished, and by agreement with his employer, return to his employment as an alternative to paying damages, but could not be compelled to do so. He stood to forfeit sureties, and undergo debt proceedings if they were not paid, if he reneged upon an agreement to return. Providing such a remedy suggested the legacy of what has been described as 'a hierarchical, disciplinary model of service', and the procedures have been shown to grant powers to the courts not available in other types of contract disputes.[79] Imprisonment remained as a sanction of final resort but, following Liberal amendments, it came only after a number of procedural stages had been passed and only, as in small debt cases, if the defaulter could be shown to have the means to pay but refused to do so.[80] Despite these qualifications, contemporaries were impressed by the fact that an essentially civil procedure was created, as signalled in the preamble

[77] Hunter, *Master and Servant Act*, 14.

[78] RCLL Qs.32–6, 76; the case of *Cutler v Turner* 9 LRQB (1874) 503, is discussed in Steinfeld, *Coercion*, 61.

[79] S. Deakin, 'The Contract of Employment: A Study in Legal Evolution', *Historical Studies in Industrial Relations*, 11 (spring 2001), 24–9; W. Steinmetz, 'Was there a De-juridification of Individual Employment Relations in Britain?', in *Private Law and Social Inequality in the Industrial Age* (2000), 282–93.

[80] Steinfeld, 217–18.

which, following Rollit's suggestion, emphasized the object to extend the powers of county courts in employment disputes.[81]

Those breaches of contract which threatened life or property or which created 'a general public danger to the state, or a large body of the community', were dealt with in Cross's Conspiracy and Protection of Property bill.[82] Wilful breaches of contract, where the probable consequence was to endanger life or valuable property, such as allowing a furnace to melt down or an engine to run out of control, were to be punishable. So too were breaches of duty in the vital services of gas and water vindicating, as some pointed out, the convictions of the gas stokers in 1872. Here Cross was less bold than Lowe for he did not share Lowe's insistence that punishments should apply to breaches by all contractors rather than simply those in contracts of service and hire. Lowe's attempt to insert the clause which Thring had drawn up was resisted within the Home Office by Lushington, on the ground that it 'almost indefinitely extends the range of the criminal law'. The only concession, to reduce the appearance of class bias, was a change of wording so that it referred to all persons, rather than just employers or workmen.[83]

The aspect of Cross's bills which attracted virtually no attention when they were introduced was a sweeping change to the law of conspiracy. The Conspiracy and Protection of Property bill provided that combined action undertaken 'in contemplation or furtherance of a trade dispute between employers and workmen' could not be indictable as a conspiracy unless the act was a crime if committed by one person alone. This was another direct appropriation, with some rewording, of Thring's draft. For the Conservative administration, which had stifled a restorative measure when in opposition in 1873, it marked a very significant change of view. Following Harcourt, Lowe, and Thring, Cross now comprehensively blocked off any future attempts by judges to bring strikers within the common law of conspiracy. The lord chief justice's proposals for treating joint breaches of contract as criminal conspiracies were disregarded, an immunity which came to be seen by some jurists as a dangerous precedent once other forms of association adopted the tactic of deliberately breaking agreements in order to secure their ends.[84] Cairns avoided addressing this point, which

---

[81] 38 & 39 Vict. c. 90 preamble.
[82] 3H ccxxiv. 1676 (10 June 1875).
[83] 3H ccxxv. 662 (28 June 1875), ccxxv. 1341–4 (12 July 1875); Conspiracy and Protection of Property bill, Mr Lowe's amendment, 28 June 1875, Request for Law Officers' Opinion, 1 July 1875, PRO HO45/9384/45462; Steinfeld, *Coercion*, 220–2.
[84] Dicey, *Law and Opinion*, 268, on the analogy with organized rent strikes by agricultural tenants (in the case of the Irish Land League).

went unchallenged. It could be argued that the extreme cases of joint contract breaches which Cockburn had cited in justification of his wider proposal were now met by the penalties in the case of vital services and threats to life and property. Moreover, Cockburn had not answered another objection, which was crucial in the context of the debates of 1875, where all arguments turned upon procedural equality between capital and labour. His recommendation would have treated strikers as criminal conspirators, because they were many, while an individual employer who locked out all his workers without notice would not be exposed to criminal proceedings, because in most cases he was acting alone.

Unlike Lowe and Thring, Cross tried to avoid dealing with the CLAA, with the exception of incorporating the Cockburn commission's recommendation for allowing trial by jury. This in itself was an indication that neither Cross nor his colleagues felt themselves to be answerable to electoral pledges on the matter. It also shows that they did not bring any new perspective to bear on the problems raised by the CLAA beyond a belief that it should be upheld. That confidence was sustainable because there was no great flood of petitions to parliament demanding repeal—only three have been located—and the Home Office received only four resolutions from trades councils and public meetings. Even these took a much milder form than eighteen months earlier; while most insisted that no legislation would be acceptable which did not repeal the CLAA, they were mitigated by expressions of approval for the rest of the bills.[85]

On the picketing question Cross was able to point to Russell Gurney's charge to the grand jury in April 1875 at the committal of the London cabinet-makers as evidence that all reasonable acts were permitted under the existing law. Gurney had specifically said that pickets who confined themselves to peaceful persuasion were acting lawfully, carrying out the view that the Cockburn commission, of which he had been a member, had also advanced.[86] There was therefore no justification for touching the CLAA. The difficulty then became that in the subsequent trial Sir Anthony Cleasby seemed to describe the law more restrictively than Gurney had done, and the pickets were convicted and imprisoned. Were they convicted because they had gone beyond peaceful persuasion, or because, even though peaceful, Cleasby had held that picketing in itself was unlawful because it coerced an employer by depriving him of a supply of labour?

---

[85] *Votes and Proceedings of the House of Commons, 1875*, 478, 505, 651; *Bee-Hive* (19 June 1875); (17 July 1875), 5; *The Times* (18 June 1875), 12; (25 June 1875), 8; (28 June 1875), 7; PRO HO43/123, 113 (26 June 1875), 114 (28 June 1875); *Reading Observer* (26 June 1875).

[86] RCLL 2nd Rep. 23–4; see p. 160 above.

Henry Selwin-Ibbetson, parliamentary under-secretary to the Home Office, insisted that the cabinet-makers had been convicted because their activities had 'amounted to something more than peaceful persuasion'. Cross, apparently on the authority of a report on the case drawn up for the Home Office by the solicitor-general, denied that there was any inconsistency between Gurney and Cleasby's interpretations of the law.[87] The issue was of particular concern to the Amalgamated Engineers, who were threatened by employers seeking to reverse the nine hours gains, won in the North-East through picketing. The ASE complained that if they were deprived (as Cleasby's ruling seemed to imply) of the right to persuade others not to do what they thought to be wrong, it 'would end in social serfdom', and they organized their own deputation to Cross, independently of the TUCPC, to obtain clarification. He undertook that if judges failed to carry out Gurney's charge, then he would bring in a declaratory bill.[88]

At the end of June 1875 Lowe opened up the other question of 'general' as against 'special' criminal legislation. He moved for the repeal of the CLAA, replacing it with a version of the clause drawn up by Thring in January 1874 punishing intimidation. In a letter to *The Times* Frederic Harrison seized on Lowe's amendment—which was actually reviving the proposal of Harrison's minority report in 1869—as the solution to the controversy.[89] The TUCPC was at first uncertain of whether to support it, and the Cabinet determined to resist it except for minor verbal changes suggested by the law officers.[90] Harrison, Mundella, and Crompton were present when the TUCPC was eventually persuaded that the clause represented 'the recognition of a principle for which we have long contended'; the Cabinet was induced to consider Lowe's proposal only after concerted Liberal pressure in the division lobbies, and on being reassured that Conservative backbenchers were willing to support the change.[91]

Although Lowe's principle was accepted by the government, Thring's wording was not, and the final form of words was that devised by Cairns, who introduced it at the Lords stage.[92] In substance there was little

---

[87] 3H ccxxiv. 583 (13 May 1875); ccxxv. 676 (28 June 1875); PRO HO46/57, 'Law Officers', 3 June 1875.
[88] ASE, monthly report, April 1875, 26–7; *Glasgow Sentinel* (10 July 1875).
[89] *The Times* (1 July 1875), 12.
[90] Howell to Prior, 2 July 1875, Howell MSS LB9, fo. 267; Law Officers' Opinion, 2 July, PRO HO45/9384/45462; Carnarvon diary, 3 July, 7 July 1875, BL Add MSS 60907; Vincent, *Derby Diaries*, 228 (3 July 1875).
[91] *The Times* (6 July 1875), 5; Richmond to Hardy, 15 July 1875, Cranbrook MSS T501/257, cited in Smith, *Disraelian Conservatism*, 216–17; Spain, 'Trade Unionists', 130.
[92] Carnarvon MSS PRO30/6/72, p. 223; 3H ccxxvi. 165 (29 July 1875); *House of Lords Sessional Papers, 1875*, iii; *Journals of the House of Lords*, cvii (1875), 380–1.

difference between the two. Both made the protection apply to everyone. They also replaced the controversial criminal intent 'to coerce' and removed references to 'molestation and obstruction' and 'threats'. Cairns's version also included the option of a fine and of trial by jury. In other respects, however, Cairns's clause closely followed the wording of the CLAA (to the extent of retaining the Lords' amendment of 1871) and this was, perhaps, the real point at issue. At the very last stage of discussion Cross, stiffened by the presence of Gathorne Hardy, a former Conservative home secretary notably unsympathetic to unionism, insisted that he would not 'shrink from the provisions laid down in that Act [CLAA]'.[93]

The later Conservative claim to have legalized peaceful picketing rested upon a proviso added to the watching and besetting sub-section. Attending at a person's house or workplace 'in order merely to obtain or communicate information' was not to be deemed 'watching and besetting'. The purpose was to clarify the confusion which had arisen between Gurney's charge and Cleasby's ruling: the proviso was intended to confirm Gurney's interpretation of the CLAA, a point which was reinforced by the decision to circulate his charge to all the courts of summary jurisdiction who were to administer the new legislation.[94] Later in 1875, addressing the Edinburgh Conservative Working Men's Association, Cross described the intention of the section on picketing as being 'not to change the law but to explain it'.[95] Only in the twentieth century, when the inequality of the Master and Servant law was long forgotten but the picketing issue still resonant, was a minor, and in fact far from unambiguous, aspect of the 1875 legislation elevated into its essential characteristic. It was a further paradox that the picketing clause was the one aspect of the settlement which was not intended to be a departure from the existing state of things.

WITHDRAWING THE CRIMINAL LAW

Contemporaries were surprised by the rapidity and comprehensiveness of the settlement, labelled by Crompton as 'The Workmen's Victory'. It seemed the more remarkable since external pressure for such a concession

---

[93] 3H ccxxvi. 716 (7 Aug. 1875); *The Times* (9 Aug. 1875), 9.

[94] 38 & 39 Vict. c. 86, s. 7. A Liberal amendment, explicitly to permit watching and besetting where the purpose was 'peaceably to persuade', was rejected on the ground that it 'was clear peacefully persuading was not illegal, and there could be no object in inserting the words in the bill', 3H ccxxvi. 715 (7 Aug. 1875).

[95] *The Trade Unionist* (23 Oct. 1875), 69. For a detailed contemporary analysis of what was done in 1875 see Davis, *Labour Laws*, ch. 6; Orth, *Combination and Conspiracy*, 143–5.

had so greatly diminished. As unionism receded during 1874–5, with the defeats of the agricultural labourers and the amalgamated miners who had been in the forefront of the earlier expansion, the labour laws campaign itself lost force. The Hyde Park rally on the release of the cabinet-makers in May 1875 was the only significant demonstration since January 1874. In the provinces, and markedly in Scotland, the campaign fell into abeyance, the *Scotsman* observing a 'quietness about matters as to which not long ago there was so much noise'.[96] The TUC, meeting at Liverpool in January 1875, while passing the usual resolutions for repeal, was given over to recrimination about the campaign's failures, and no fresh initiatives were planned. By July 1875 Howell was complaining that there were 'signs of flagging and of schism' within the TUC, in the face of press reports of separate initiatives by the northern unions and of proposals for federation among the larger societies, frustrated at the power exercised by local bodies.[97]

This actually helped the passage of Cross's measures in two ways: it avoided the appearance of direct concession to overwhelming union pressure and, in consequence, reduced the possibility of the federated employers mobilizing in response. The NFAEL, which had been brought into being to counteract the activity and successes of the TUC, was taken by surprise at the extent of the changes proposed and was unable to organize a counter-attack. It faced the further difficulty that Conservative opinion as indicated by the *Standard*, which had welcomed the report of the Cockburn commission as the probable basis for legislation, now described Cross's opening speech as having 'laid down a basis which no party can openly reject'.[98] The NFAEL's journal *Capital and Labour* alternated between indignation at what it saw as rivalry between the two parties to strike a popular pose, and grim satisfaction that the principles of equality were merely those for which it had always contended.[99] Cross helped to dampen controversy by refusing to admit reporters when he received a deputation from the TUCPC in May 1875, and there were no press reports of a deputation to him from the NFAEL in June.[100] Compared to earlier phases of the agitation, there was little lobbying by organized employers, and hostile amendments in the Lords proposed by Winmarleigh were withdrawn

---

[96] *The Scotsman* (25 Feb. 1875), 4.

[97] Howell to R. S. Wright, 21 July 1875; to editor of *Daily News* (10 July 1875), Howell MSS LB9, fos. 285, 275.

[98] *Standard* (26 Mar. 1875), 4; (14 June 1875), 4.

[99] *Capital and Labour* (30 June 1875), 327–8; (14 July 1875), 361; (21 July 1875), 379; (28 July 1875), 397; (4 Aug. 1875), 417.

[100] The NFAEL deputation was on 24 June, *Capital and Labour* (1 Mar. 1876), 156.

without discussion. Sheffield chamber of commerce, which in 1866 had helped to trigger the process of inquiry, discussed the bills but decided that interference would be inadvisable 'in consequence of all parties in the House of Commons being united on the subject'.[101]

This unanimity was in line with the view expressed by one Lancashire Conservative at the general election, that MPs should not try to derive party advantage from the subject of labour law, but should remove it from 'the arena of party politics, and settle it on a fair and lasting basis'.[102] In 1876 Sir John Huddleston, briefly Conservative MP for Norwich before his elevation to the judicial bench, impressed upon trade unionist defendants in a picketing trial that the new laws were the product of 'anxious deliberation on the part of all parties', in consultation with representatives of the men and the two workingmen MPs (the Lib-Labs Burt and Macdonald); as the men themselves had had a hand in framing the law, they should now abide by it.[103] Liberals were naturally anxious to claim a share in the outcome— after all, it was they who were more numerously pledged to the electorate— and Mundella, anxious to keep the alliance with labour in good repair, highlighted the role of the Liberals in shaping the eventual legislation.[104] Lowe, however, acted independently of the TUCPC and of radical backbenchers. His approach, like Cross's, was bipartisan in the sense that it aimed to place the fundamental principles of the settlement above party.[105] Competition between the parties in the division lobbies turned on issues of how forms of words could be rendered most neutral and equal, and not on how each could most favour labour. Above all, it was an exercise in demonstrating the efficiency of parliament in addressing the claims of labour when those claims were presented in the form of demands for strict equality and freedom of contract.[106]

Disraeli did try to give the settlement a party complexion in his private correspondence once the likely success of Cross's bills became apparent.[107]

---

[101] Sheffield Chamber of Commerce Minutes, 8 July 1875, LD 1986/1, p. 384; cf. G. Alderman, *The Railway Interest* (1973), 61.

[102] *Manchester Courier* (3 Feb. 1874), 3 (address of J. P. Chamberlain Starkie).

[103] *R v Bauld* (1876) 13 Cox CC 287.

[104] During the 1875 debates Mundella recounted his own parliamentary activity and achievements at length to the editor of the *Sheffield Independent*, mentioning any praise he received from grateful trade unionists: see the extracts in W. H. G. Armytage, *A. J. Mundella* (1951), 150–2. Mundella's version of events is followed in Spain, 'Trade Unionists', 130–3.

[105] 3*H* ccxxiv. 1668 (10 June 1875); ccxxv. 1358 (12 July 1875).

[106] Hence the descriptions of both parties' eagerness to achieve a settlement, Howell to Knight, 14 July 1875, Howell MSS LB9, fo. 281; *Saturday Review* (17 July 1875), 67; cf. Davis, *Labour Laws*, 102.

[107] See the letters to Lady Bradford and Lady Chesterfield, 29 June 1875, cited in Smith, *Disraelian Conservatism*, 215–17. For a discussion of Disraeli's role see R. Shannon, *The Age of*

His claims, though, to have been Cross's only backer in the Cabinet during the discussions as to whether to press ahead with a radical form of legislation do not find support in the admittedly sparse records of Cabinet diarists. In the only reference to a prime ministerial input, at the crucial Cabinet on 29 May, Derby noted Disraeli favouring postponement. Nor did Disraeli have any discernible role in the government's approach when the peaceful picketing question surfaced in the last stages of the bill's passage. Those details were settled between Cairns and the law offices without Cabinet involvement; Disraeli's celebratory missives to Lady Bradford and Lady Chesterfield were, anyway, written when the government still hoped to avoid dealing with the CLAA at all.

More significant in winning acceptance for Cross's plan was a clarification of the terms of the debate during 1874–5. The central questions in contention turned upon the circumstances in which it was proper that actions by workers, unaccompanied by violence, should be treated as crimes. As the employers' evidence to the Cockburn commission came under scrutiny, it was apparent that what they were seeking to preserve was a penal (that is to say, public) remedy for what were—setting aside exceptional instances of wilful breaches threatening life and property—essentially infringements of private interests, most obviously economic losses sustained as a result of strikes without notice. Although the commissioners proclaimed the neutrality of the state as between capital and labour,[108] they did not challenge the claims of employers to use penal sanctions for private ends. Indeed, Cockburn's justification for numbers transforming a private wrong into a criminal conspiracy was an explicit removal of the boundaries between the two. In a political context, this was a potentially harmful step to take, for the result was bound to be that disputes between employers and workers would be drawn into the sphere of parliamentary concerns. While Cross was preparing his legislation Sir Edward Watkin, the railway promoter, raised in the House of Commons the question of whether a resolution at a conference of mining unions for a simultan eous, nationwide stoppage was a criminal combination; Alexander Macdonald immediately responded by asking whether the lock-out by the South Wales Mineowners' Association was similarly unlawful.[109]

Withdrawing the criminal law from the bargaining between organized

Disraeli, 1868–1881 (1992), 213–15, and B. Hilton, 'Disraeli, English Culture, and the Decline of the Industrial Spirit', in L. Brockliss and D. Eastwood (eds), *A Union of Multiple Identities* (1997), 51.

[108] RCLL 2nd Rep. 15; Harris, *Private Lives*, 140.
[109] 3*H* ccxxiv. 388–90 (10 May 1875).

workers and employers has been seen to be, and was intended to be, a further instalment in the mid-Victorian project of taking the market out of politics.[110] Trade unionists, or indeed any employees acting in combination, were no longer under the stigma of having a criminal law directed against forms of social annoyance committed by them alone. By the CPPA they were now under the same law which applied to the rest of the community; or rather, the rest of the community might now be punished for offences which had previously been punishable only in the context of employment relations. Yet, as the Liberal journalist Leonard Courtney warned, the new statute could never be a final settlement of the picketing issues, since its lawfulness depended on the individual circumstances, and each case could be decided only by reference to a jury.[111] Huddleston's account of the law during the trial of pickets involved in the engineers' dispute at Erith in 1876 showed that the line could still be drawn very strictly, though its effect depended upon the ability to enforce it.[112] That difficulty continued to exercise the Home Office in the early twentieth century, when the definition of unlawful picketing 'remained as unclear as ever'.[113]

During the trial of the Erith pickets the prosecution commented that the law was not only lenient, but exempted workmen from charges to which other persons were liable.[114] Of all the changes made in 1875, the immunity from the law of conspiracy was the least discussed during its parliamentary passage, and yet potentially the most contentious. By 1876 employers were already regretting its loss, both the NFAEL and the Central Association of Master Builders regarding it as the most 'unwise' aspect of the settlement.[115] A case arose in the Nottingham building trade in 1876 which illustrated both 'the terrorism to which the unions resort', and the legal power which the employers had lost.[116] A firm of builders' merchants, who had been in dispute with the slaters' union over the employment of non-society men and apprentices, received demands from the local council of the building unions for the payment of considerable fines and the discharge of the men to whom the slaters objected. Though this was done, a further dispute arose and more fines demanded, and when these were not paid in full the firm was 'blacked' throughout the city and found its business severely

---

[110] McKibbin, 'Why was there no Marxism?', 29.

[111] *The Times* (17 July 1875), 11.

[112] *R v Bauld and Others* (1876) 13 Cox CC 287, 290–1; G. Howell, 'Picketing and Intimidation', *Contemporary Review*, 30 (Sept. 1877), 618–20.

[113] J. Morgan, *Conflict and Order: The Police and Labour Disputes in England and Wales, 1900–1939* (1987), 148–53, 160, 179–81, 185.

[114] 13 Cox CC 289.

[115] LMA A/NFB.1/A1/1, p. 193, 15 Feb. 1876; *Capital and Labour* (1 Mar. 1876), 156.

[116] *Capital and Labour* (16 Feb. 1876), 123; (1 Mar. 1876), 155.

damaged. On receiving legal advice that, as a result of the Conspiracy and Protection of Property Act of 1875, no indictment could be laid against the organizers of the action 'for conspiring to injure, oppress and ruin them [the merchants] and illegally interfere with their trade', the firm's solicitors passed the papers to Home Office.[117] Selwin-Ibbetson, the parliamentary under-secretary and one of those responsible for introducing the 1875 bills, was evidently surprised that legislation for which he was responsible had had that effect. Remarking that the case was one 'of great tyranny', he sought Lushington's comments.

Lushington summarized the departmental view of what the withdrawal of the criminal law meant, and in doing so re-stated his own longstanding opinion. The Act of 1875 undoubtedly prevented any criminal proceeding under the law of conspiracy: 'But is this to be regretted? There may be many acts which deserve moral reprobation to which it would be inexpedient to extend the criminal law.'[118] This was really a reformulation of the approach which Thring had set out eight years' earlier, before either the Junta or the TUC had drawn up their demands. Strikes (and lock-outs) were bound to occur, and however at variance with political economy, or oppressive of individual liberty, or foolish, or unjust, and provided only that they were pursued by non-violent means, they ought not to be treated as crimes.

[117] J. and A. Bright to Cross, 24 Mar. 1876; opinion of H. B. Poland, 29 Feb. 1876, PRO HO45/9406/54064.
[118] Ibid., Lushington's docket, 4 Apr. 1876.

Conclusion: Combination and the Liberal State

For nearly half a century after the repeal of the Combination Acts the liberty to combine continued to be restricted—in theory, if not much in practice. Governments and the courts admitted the impolicy of an outright ban on combination. But they were unwilling to recognize unions or to remove the penalties for strikes, or threats of strikes, in all instances: to do so would be to sanction conditions placed upon the sale of labour which might be deemed 'arbitrary', 'tyrannical', or 'foolish'. Such conditions were improper encroachments upon the prerogatives of the masters, and were contrary to the broader policy that markets should operate free from obstruction. In the 1860s the case for perpetuating legal restrictions and administrative controls upon combinations was elaborated in the majority report of the royal commission on trade unions. The commission's dominant intellectual forces, Sir William Erle and James Booth, drew upon the view of combinations propounded a generation earlier by writers such as Nassau Senior and Harriet Martineau. They assumed an identity of aim between the law and classical political economy; treated combination as analogous to the commercial policy of protectionism; and expected that if artificial structures of combination were eliminated, wages and conditions of employment would naturally be determined by individual bargaining. Their priority was to secure competition within the labour market, and to assimilate labour to the general policy of free trade, as they understood it. To this end, combination was to be subjected to strict legal control.

One theme of the preceding chapters has been the disintegration of this position. Damaged by the contemporary assaults on classical economic theory during the late 1860s, the case for legal restriction upon unions and strikes was fatally undermined by the general reaction against policy prescriptions founded upon deductive categories of thought. Empirical evidence indicated that the position which favoured legal restriction conceptualized labour market relations in ways that bore little relation to the actual practice of collective bargaining and its outcomes. Nor could it plausibly account for the development and expansion of trade unions, brought scientifically to light by the inquiries of the Social Science Association. Historical critiques exposed the 'feudal' roots of the legal doctrines against combination which the majority of the Erle commission sought to uphold, and reinforced the argument that those laws were unequal, punishing working people for acts which would not be treated criminally if done by other citizens. Such inequalities were unlikely to be sustainable in the new conditions of household suffrage.

Instead, the legislation of the 1870s brought about the unrestricted legalization of unions and the 'decriminalisation of labour law', which for practical purposes protected the freedom to strike.[1] The settlement was founded upon the ideas of a younger generation of Liberal theorists, who regarded legal restrictions upon the freedom to combine as survivals of 'old class law', exemplified by the law of conspiracy. The middle class, Frederic Harrison observed in 1868, had successfully swept away those 'class' laws which affected itself, emancipating capital from restrictions upon trade and commerce, but 'the parts which reach down to the depths of society have still to be examined and recast'.[2] The argument for coercing labour into conformity with the system of free trade was now turned on its head: freedom of trade and labour, Godfrey Lushington commented in an internal Home Office memorandum, had been secured to individuals earlier in the nineteenth century, but that freedom had yet to be fully extended to those who chose to act collectively.[3] There was an echo of the argument which supporters of limited liability had invoked in the previous decade.[4]

Advocates of unrestricted legalization insisted that labour could not be regarded as free unless working people were permitted to combine to place whatever conditions which they chose upon the sale of their labour. There should be no limitation on that collective freedom; whether the object of a strike or a trade union was reasonable or not was immaterial. Even the royal commission on the labour laws, whose dominant outlook was hostile to the exercise of collective power, acknowledged the force of this argument, and did not attempt to revive the Erle commission's recommendation that strikes against individuals should be punishable. 'Labour being free,' the Cockburn commission concluded in 1875, 'we think that men ought to be at perfect liberty, when not under contract, to agree among themselves not to work for a particular master, or with a particular workman who may be obnoxious to them.'[5] An account of the freedom to combine as an extension

---

[1] Deakin and Morris, *Labour Law*, 9; RCTU 11th Rep. liii–liv, lvii, lxi; G. Lushington, 'Workmen and Trade Unions', 54; Lushington, 'Law of Trade Unions', 49–50.
[2] F. Harrison, *Order and Progress* (1875), 227; cf. Lushington, 'Workmen and Trade Unions', 48, 57
[3] Lushington, 'Law of Trade Unions', 47 (OPC Bills and Memoranda (HJ) 1871).
[4] Hilton, *Age of Atonement*, 261.
[5] RCLL, 2nd Rep. 22, 27.

of the freedom of contract, nascent in J. R. McCulloch's writings in the 1820s, was thus brought—in the eyes of its advocates—to its logical conclusion. Within the dominant evolutionary perspective, the legislation was seen to complete the removal of 'feudal' restraints upon labour. Hence the economic historian Arnold Toynbee's reflection in 1881 upon the recently enacted laws: 'The workman had at last reached the summit of the long ascent from the position of a serf, and stood by the side of his master as the full citizen of a free state.'[6]

It was, perhaps, paradoxical that historicist critiques of classical political economy and the law produced an outcome in which, as a legal history of trade unionism comments, 'contract was put in the centre of things'.[7] In the case of Irish land tenure, historicist intellectual currents contributed to precisely the opposite results: the rehabilitation of custom, the limitation of contract, and the sanctioning of state intervention between landlord and tenant.[8] The example of India, which countered universalist approaches to land tenure, led to a very different conclusion when applied to the TUC's grievances: the utilitarian legacy of British rule in India exposed how incompletely labour law in Britain itself embodied the principle of equality both in regard to contracts and to protection from intimidation. Edmund Potter, the Manchester School propagandist, assumed that he was introducing an argument fatal to unionism when he insisted, at the Social Science Association's meeting in 1860, 'that labour must be considered as a mere purchaseable article, like all other commodities'. He was perhaps surprised that it was a conception which many of his opponents were willing to embrace.[9] The Chartist solicitor W. P. Roberts, who had resisted Master and Servant prosecutions on the ground that employment agreements should be treated like any other contracts, agreed with the proposition put to him by Potter in 1866, that in legal terms labour was 'an article to buy and sell'.[10] Toynbee saw it as a symptom of progress that questions of wages should become treated like the price of coal and cotton.[11] Emancipated from the subordinate status to which coercive laws had consigned them, democratically equal citizens would be free to bargain collectively, and the legitimacy of their doing so would be readily acknowledged.[12]

[6] A. Toynbee, *Lectures on the Industrial Revolution*, 196.
[7] Orth, *Combination and Conspiracy*, 154. The transition from the Master and Servant model of employment law was, in practice, incomplete: S. Deakin, 'The Contract of Employment: A Study in Legal Evolution', *Historical Studies in Industrial Relations*, 11 (2001).
[8] Dewey, 'Celtic Agrarian Legislation', 39.
[9] NAPSS, *Trades' Societies and Strikes*, 595, 605 (Fawcett), 612 (Dunning), 617 (Ludlow).
[10] Select Committee on Master and Servant (*PP* 1866 xiii), Q.2229; Simon, 'Master and Servant', 199.   [11] Toynbee, *Lectures*, 199.
[12] Cf. Stedman Jones, 'Some Notes on Karl Marx', 126.

To the Webbs, reflecting on the position later in the century, the emphasis upon contract in the arguments for law reform in the 1870s was both a disagreeable feature of the settlement, and a contradictory one. 'The insistence upon the Englishman's right to freedom of contract was, in fact, in the mouths of staunch Trade Unionists, perilously near cant', they tartly observed.[13] Unionism necessarily limited individuals' freedom to make separate bargains with an employer.[14] To Liberal advocates of unrestricted legalization this was no bad thing. Accounts of the workings of the labour market revealed that the absence of combination among working people did not lead to the free operation of supply and demand; rather, it allowed employers unilaterally to impose whatever terms they chose. This was the foundation of Harrison and F. D. Longe's attacks on classical wage theory. To them, combination was a necessary counterbalance to capital in a labour market which the state—properly, in their view—declined other than in marginal instances to regulate. Indeed, throughout this period the freedom to strike was viewed as an essential corollary to the withdrawal of the state from fixing wages. The duke of Argyll's account of combination as an expression of the human tendency towards association, and a natural form of voluntary self-defence by labour to mitigate competition in circumstances where the state had relinquished that task, became the established view.[15] Combination's legitimately protective effect was noted by the young academic Liberal barristers appointed to investigate the incidence of payment by truck. Their report, in 1871, found that such degradation did not occur 'where the working classes are thoroughly organized in trades unions or other bodies'; protective legislation became necessary where combination did not exist.[16]

The distinction between protection for labour enforced by law, and that which was carried out by the voluntary will of individuals choosing to act collectively, was crucial to refuting those, such as Potter and Lowe, who attacked unionism as a form of protectionism. Proponents of unrestricted legalization insisted that trade unions and strikes were entirely compatible with the *laissez-faire* state, and were indeed a logical consequence of it. By the late 1860s Liberal opinion grew impatient with an identification of free trade with an extreme form of social atomism. Echoing Gladstone's private

---

[13] Webb, *History*, 280; Burn, *Age of Equipoise*, 111.

[14] J. E. T. Rogers, 'Trades' Unions', *British Quarterly Review*, 46 (Oct. 1867), 509.

[15] See the citation of Argyll in Howell, *Conflicts*, 132–3, and T. H. S. Escott, *England: Its People, Polity, and Pursuits* (1885), 156; cf. Haldane's comment in 1888, M. Freeden, *The New Liberalism* (1978), 61.

[16] Report of the commissioners appointed to inquire into the truck system (*PP* 1871 xxxvi), p. xx.

opinion, the Liberal *Daily Telegraph* insisted that 'in Mr Potter's sense of the term, free trade never did exist, never will exist, and never could exist'.[17]

By legalizing trade unions, the state implicitly recognized the anti-competitive objectives which they pursued. To that extent, custom and collectivity were now sanctioned. But unions were endowed with no legal powers other than those required to assist them to own and protect property. They ceased to be discriminated against by the law, but their trade rules remained legally unenforceable: the demands of the Sheffield artisans were emphatically rejected. A former law officer in the Gladstone government, Sir George Jessel, later observed that to have made union rules enforceable at law 'would have reduced a certain portion of the workmen to a condition of something like slavery or serfdom': each would have been compelled, by law, to work in the particular way that union rules might decree.[18] Lord Moncreiff, who had served as lord advocate in Gladstone's administration, explained that prior to the 1871 legislation the courts declined to enforce union rules on the ground that 'nobody has a legitimate or legal interest to compel performance of them'—that is, the interest of the 'trade' was not acknowledged legally to exist in matters affecting an individual's right to dispose of his labour as he chose—and parliament had emphatically reaffirmed that position.[19] Unions might, of course, enforce their objectives as effectively by other, lawful, means at their disposal, and this was well understood.

Previous writing on this subject has rightly emphasized the Liberal government's determination to prevent intimidation and to protect from physical coercion individuals who chose to bargain alone in the market. Their Conservative successors were equally resolute on these points. Yet official opinion was not squeamish about the tendency to sacrifice individuals to collectivities, so long as no physical force was involved. Members' rights to benefits were left to whatever internal procedures unions might have in place. Dissidents could be struck against, and perhaps driven from employment. How far union membership itself was in practice voluntary was not scrutinized too closely, except to ensure that no one was physically forced to participate. Even then it was recognized that the law was often powerless to deal with the types of physical threat which an individual might encounter. Governments limited themselves, as far as possible, to upholding reciprocity between the various parties involved. If a union could not to sue its members for subscriptions and fines, then members

---

[17] *Daily Telegraph* (8 July 1869), 4; Matthew, *GD*, vii. 91.
[18] *Rigby v Connol* (1880) 42 LTNS 141.
[19] *M'Kernan v United Operative Masons' Association* (1874) *Sessions Cases*, 4th ser. 1. 458.

could not be permitted to proceed against a union; unionists might 'black' non-unionists but, equally, employers (could and very frequently did) circulate blacklists to keep known unionists out of employment. Neither was to be punished for doing so. The legal solutions adopted would inevitably produce some unattractive outcomes. These could be curbed only by the gradual influence of public opinion.

The minority report of the Erle commission, drafted by Frederic Harrison, gave legal form to this social collectivism. His report defined official policy, and determined the ways in which Liberals understood the union question, until the early twentieth century at least. The achievement of the Positivists in formulating the legal settlement is well established and, if anything, re-emphasized in the preceding narrative.[20] They were far from being isolated, embattled lobbyists for labour. Educated at the ancient English universities, Anglicans by upbringing, well-connected within metropolitan legal and intellectual circles, and having access to official preferment, they were well-placed to promote their arguments—obviously so in the case of Lushington. The closeness of their ideas with the mainstream of Liberal governmental thought is remarkable, and suggests one explanation for the immediately favourable response with which the minority report was received, and the receptiveness of Lowe to their critique of the criminal law in the early 1870s.

Permanent officials were the conduit through which new theoretical approaches initially flowed into policy-making: Thring was the first individual in government to recognize the implication of Longe's attack on the wage fund theory and of the Social Science Association's findings about the results of strikes; Lushington absorbed the historicist critiques of labour law to supply an intellectual foundation for the eventual settlement. Thring reached his conclusions in favour of legalization and decriminalization of non-violent collective action before E. S. Beesly's outspoken defence of unionism at Exeter Hall, in July 1867—the latter event being assigned importance elsewhere as 'the first turning point in the Labour Laws question'.[21] Thring's practical conclusions also anticipated Harrison's report, which was, in this respect, an extended statement of a position which was already forming within the Home Office. The approach suggested by Thring and carried forward by Lushington detached economic considerations from the resolution of the contested legal issues. Unlike the liberal-tories in the 1820s, who referred explicitly to the role of the criminal law in protecting capital and trade, and their own successors in the Home Office in

---

[20] Harrison, *Before the Socialists*, 277–306.
[21] Ibid. 282.

the 1890s, who were concerned to avert welfarist governmental intervention in the labour market,[22] Lushington and Thring had little or nothing to say about the state of the economy, the competitiveness of industries affected by unions, and trends in industrial relations. These matters, they assumed, could take care of themselves. Nor—beyond a general preference for openness over secrecy, and peaceful activity over violence—did they view legalization as a means of promoting certain models of unionism. J. M. Ludlow, the only official to attempt to direct the apparatus of legal recognition to that purpose, was firmly stifled.

Both political parties proved able to subscribe to the terms of the settlement—the Conservatives albeit more slowly and reluctantly than their Liberal counterparts. That it fell to a Conservative government to enact legislation drafted by its predecessor in office merely indicates how far 'liberal' attitudes were shared by both parties in the mid-Victorian period. It also reinforces the long-established conclusion that much of the domestic legislation of Disraeli's administration was simply the fulfilment of schemes already in the departmental pipeline.[23] Conservatives brought few distinctive perspectives to bear after the collapse of the protectionist patronage of labour in the early 1850s. One participant in that alignment was literally pensioned off when Lord John Manners used his patronage as commissioner of works in Derby's third administration to appoint Thomas Winters, the former secretary of the NAUT, to a life position as gatekeeper at Brompton cemetery.[24] During the mid-1860s some Conservatives, viewing their popular appeal as resting among the majority of working men who were not organized in unions, espoused the short-lived free labour movement. But by 1869 Conservatives came to adopt the view of the Liberal government that unions had to be formally recognized. They showed no determination to press the proposals for separation of trade and benefit funds, and full incorporation of unions, which some individuals within their party espoused. Perhaps the only significant Conservative contribution to the movement of opinion, A. K. Rollit's formulation of a business approach to Master and Servant law, concerned the aspect of the subject which affected all wage-earners, and not just those acting in combination.

Why, then, did the Liberal government fail, in the first instance, to resolve the question of criminal liabilities? As is clear from its attitude towards the freedom to combine, the government's difficulties did not stem from any unease about the exercise of collective power. A strong element of

[22] Stack, *Thomas Hodgskin*, 113, 117; Davidson, *Whitehall and the Labour Problem*, 180–6.
[23] Steele, *Palmerston and Liberalism*, 4; Smith, *Disraelian Conservatism*, 322
[24] *Glasgow Sentinel* (24 Apr. 1869).

contingency has been implied in the fact that crucial decisions were vested in a minister whose own perceptions were conditioned by personal involvement in the 'industrial feudalism' of the South Wales coalfield.[25] The paralysis of Bruce's department in the face of a popular agitation owed something also to the internal weaknesses which bedevilled its handling of the licensing question:[26] a reversal of policy became possible only when Gladstone ended his detachment from the subject, which had left Bruce's handling of it unscrutinized by the Cabinet for over two years. The ministerial view was critical in forming the party's position: a large majority of Liberal MPs supported Bruce's position on the labour laws; they were equally ready to support Lowe when he took policy in a new direction.

Bruce's attempt to settle the union question foundered ultimately on a matter of citizenship—whether working people, collectively or individually, should be subjected to exceptional and unequal laws—rather than a question of collective rights. He was unwilling to recognize the implication that labour law questions were now ones of democratic principle. Some anti-democratic Liberals, sensitive to the results of household suffrage, saw this clearly enough and urged a speedy resolution of the conflict. Fitzjames Stephen pressed for reform of the law of conspiracy because he feared that justifiable popular disaffection with its application would weaken the rule of the law. In 1867 Lowe had turned to the common law as a bulwark against a democratic electorate; by 1873 his anxiety was that class questions would intrude upon politics if the TUC's demands for equality before the law were not treated with proper seriousness. The emergence of a national employers' federation dedicated to defending the existing law had, from its organizers' point of view, the counterproductive result of making a removal of the TUC's grievance urgent; those who apprehended special interest groups vying for control of labour legislation now regarded it as all the more important to place the subject beyond politics. It was an index of Lowe's success that when the Victorian political system was disrupted, it was over a question of nationality rather than of class. 'Trade unionism, as an institution', the historians of the party re-alignment of 1885–6 conclude, 'could not have counted less if it had been a minor nonconformist church'.[27]

The same, of course, might have been said of the organized employers. That both the positions which they embraced—a restrictive form of trade

---

[25] As the South Wales industrialists were characterized in Creed and Williams, *Handicraftsmen*, 75.

[26] Harrison, *Drink and the Victorians*, 262–3.

[27] A. B. Cooke and J. Vincent, *The Governing Passion: Cabinet Government and Party Politics in Britain, 1885–86* (1974), 9; C. Matthew (ed.), *The Nineteenth Century* (2000), 104; Harris, *Private Lives*, 9.

union legalization and the perpetuation of penal laws in the field of industrial relations—were rejected by governments serves to reaffirm the well-attested ineffectiveness of those associations as pressure groups. The basis of the entrepreneurial programme elaborated by the spokesmen of the ironmasters, Creed and Williams, was exposed to ridicule within weeks of its publication. The General Builders' Association appeared to make the running during the early phase of the Erle commission, was swift to exploit the unions' financial insecurity after *Hornby v Close*, and obtained the actuarial evidence which exposed the potential insolvency of the amalgamated societies' benefit schemes. But the postscript is telling: by 1871 the association was on the verge of collapse, and its secretary and propagandist, the solicitor Alfred Mault, resigned in the face of mounting debts and allegations of mismanagement, if not actual peculation.[28] The organized employers had their day when the Lords' amendment to the CLAA was carried in 1871, but this was not as significant as they hoped. Lowe brusquely dismissed the promoters of the national employers' federation; Cross let them down more gently. Nor, it might be added, were the so-called 'new model' employers, such as Mundella, much more influential in the sphere of policy-making, however important their example may have been in forming public opinion.

It would be absurd to discount the input of the TUC and its predecessors so readily. Their constitutional agitation for civil and legal equality was undeniably successful, though there is a danger of exaggerating the extent to which they abandoned the old language of usage rights to advance their claims. The amalgamated trades had emphatically laid down the limits within which any legalization would have to take place, and to that extent the eventual form of the 1871 Act was dictated from below. During the phases of departmental legislative drafting, however, the unions were kept very much at arms' length. The exception to this pattern was in November 1873, when Lowe drew them in to establish, for his own purposes, whether his plans were likely to represent a viable solution. Apart from this, Liberal politicians involved the representatives of the unions only at moments of crisis: in July 1869 to shore up labour's attachment to Liberalism; and to secure the TUCPC's adhesion to Liberal amendments to the Conservative legislation during the summer of 1875.

Perhaps the TUC's most important contribution was to reinforce the hopes of politicians of both parties that, with the withdrawal of the criminal law from industrial relations, the subject of labour law was now politically

[28] GBA Minute Book of General Meetings, 129–30 (4 Jan. 1873); Minute Book of the Committee, 148–51 (16 June 1871)

closed. 'The work of emancipation is full and complete', Howell's report for the congress held at Glasgow in October 1875 declared.[29] In the immediate aftermath of the legislation, the development of collective bargaining gave contemporaries reasonable grounds for believing that, with the injustice and inequality of penal laws eradicated, industrial relations could be placed on a new moral basis, with each side equally respected as fellow-citizens. In 1894 the majority of the royal commission on labour claimed to discern a trend towards industrial peace brought about by 'natural forces' and saw no legislative solution to conflict.[30]

By the early twentieth century changing views of the state led others to reconsider options which had been discarded in 1871: incorporation, separation of trade and benefit funds, and compulsory arbitration.[31] Mark Judge, the former branch president of the amalgamated carpenters and joiners whose protests against the Trade Union Act had embarrassed the TUC and discomfited the Home Office, resumed his campaign for individual members to be given legal rights to union welfare benefits for which they had subscribed. In 1905, having established his own architect's practice, he helped to found the British Constitution Association, an anti-collectivist pressure group which pledged to resist 'political socialism', uphold personal liberty, and curb the powers of 'governing bodies'. He also took up the cause of another dissident branch officer, W. V. Osborne of the amalgamated railway servants, whose legal challenges to his union's compulsory political levy to support Labour parliamentary candidates resulted in the celebrated Osborne judgment (1909).[32] Lushington himself—by now retired from the Home Office and once again able publicly to voice his opinions—was willing to reopen questions which he had previously worked to settle. In 1903 he was officially invited to do so, as a member of the royal commission on trade disputes appointed by Balfour's Conservative administration following the Taff Vale judgment (1901).[33] Unlike his fellow commissioner Sidney Webb, Lushington did not regard Taff Vale as an opportunity to utilize the power of the state to achieve a more efficient system of industrial relations, and was not persuaded by arguments for compulsory arbitration (and concomitant curbs on strikes).

[29] Roberts, Trades Union Congress, 88.
[30] Toynbee, Industrial Revolution, 200–1; Toynbee drew heavily upon Henry Crompton's writings: A. Kadish, Apostle Arnold: The Life and Death of Arnold Toynbee, 1852–1883 (1986), 98–100; Royal Commission on Labour (PP 1894 xxxv) 5th Rep. 112.
[31] They were recommended by Lord Dunedin, Arthur Cohen, and Sidney Webb in their majority report of the Royal Commission on Trade Disputes (PP 1906 lvi), Rep. 7–12.
[32] M. H. Judge (ed.), Political Socialism: A Remonstrance (1908), 186; M. H. Judge and W. V. Osborne, Trade Unions and the Law (1911), 31–6.
[33] Clegg, Fox, and Thompson, History, 322–5.

Lushington's belief that the freedom to strike should be upheld against judicial encroachment remained unshaken. He regretted the decision of the House of Lords in *Quinn v Leathem* (1901) to extend the doctrine of civil conspiracy so as to make a strike against non-unionists actionable, exposing unions to claims for damages. Judges should not be permitted, upon the basis of their own discretion, and where 'there was no breach of criminal law or any known civil right', to prevent men collectively from refusing to work for any reason, good or bad. The right of workmen to refuse to be employed should have priority over the right of an employer to employ.[34] If limitations on that freedom should ever in future be thought necessary (for example, to prohibit a general strike directed against a government, of which he saw an alarming precedent in the proceedings of continental socialists) then those restrictions should originate from parliament and not from the courts.[35]

Lushington was disturbed by the violent methods and threats to public order associated with the 'new' unions of the 1890s. He hoped that the existing criminal law would be vigorously applied against what he termed their 'terrorism' and criminal intimidation.[36] Indeed, he came to regard picketing as a form of 'industrial conscription', which he now wanted to forbid altogether.[37] Yet he continued to affirm his faith in the morally elevating effect of trade unionism, as an embodiment of the collective sentiment of the class which it represented.[38] His views recalled the optimism with which he and his contemporaries in the 1860s had regarded the civic virtue that they discerned in the amalgamated societies. The claims of those unionists to seek only equality before the law, and to respect contracts, had strengthened the mid-century Liberal belief that a democratic electorate would uphold the rule of law.[39]

At the turn of the twentieth century Lushington proclaimed the principle of making union funds liable for injuries caused by their wrongful acts—provided that those acts would be regarded as wrongful if committed by other citizens—as 'just and salutary law'. Imposing financial responsibility upon unions for actions which no one disputed to be unlawful was

---

[34] G. Lushington, 'Trade Unions and the House of Lords', *National Review*, 33 (Dec. 1901), 559.
[35] Ibid. 560–3.
[36] G. Lushington, 'The Trade-Union Triumph: *Allen v Flood*', *National Review*, 30 (Jan. 1898), 713–14.
[37] Lushington's report in Royal Commission on Trade Disputes (*PP* 1906 lvi), Rep. 71–90; Clegg, Fox, and Thompson, *History*, 318, 324–5.
[38] Lushington, 'Trade Unions and the House of Lords', 560.
[39] Harvie, *Lights of Liberalism*, 167–8; D. Sugarman, 'The Legal Boundaries of Liberty: Dicey, Liberalism, and Legal Science', *Modern Law Review*, 46 (1983), 109–11.

merely a means of placing upon their members the duties of citizenship, to which many of them had been admitted after 1867. He regretted only that this result of the Taff Vale judgment was not law emanating from parliament. Hence his publicly expressed indignation at the passage of the Trade Disputes Act (1906), by which Campbell-Bannerman's Liberal administration, with a huge majority in the House of Commons, conferred a blanket immunity on unions from the effects of that judgment.[40] Drawing on the language with which the TUC had assailled the labour laws in the early 1870s, Lushington insisted that the demand of trade unionists to be allowed 'irresponsibility for wrongdoing is a claim that they should be stigmatized by Parliament imposing on them a degraded *status*'.[41] That would be to corrupt the objective which he and others had sought to achieve a generation earlier, when they attacked the persistence of 'class' legislation directed against labour and sought to establish the freedom to combine, in its broadest extent, as one of the foundations of the liberal state in Britain.

[40] H. C. G. Matthew, *The Liberal Imperialists* (1973), 247–9; J. Thompson, 'The Genesis of the 1906 Trades Disputes Act', *Twentieth Century British History*, 9 (1998), 198–200. Lushington accused his former political master at the Home Office, H. H. Asquith, who privately regretted the concession of such extensive immunity, of bowing to electoral pressure, *The Times* (4 Dec. 1906), 4.

[41] *The Times* (2 Apr. 1906), 7.

BIBLIOGRAPHY

Order of items:

1. Personal papers
2. Government departments
3. Trade unions and labour organizations
4. Employers' and other non-labour organizations
5. Parliament and parliamentary papers
6. Statutes
7. Law reports
8. Newspapers and periodicals
9. Contemporary writings
10. Later works
11. Theses

[Key to abbreviations for locations: (BL) British Library; (BLPES) British Library of Political and Economic Science; (Bodl.) Bodleian Library, Oxford; (GL) Goldsmiths' Library, University of London Library; (HC) Howell Collection, Bishopsgate Institute; (Liverpool RO) Liverpool Record Office; (LMA) London Metropolitan Archives; (HOLRO) House of Lords Record Office; (MCL) Manchester Central Library; (MRC) Modern Records Centre, University of Warwick; (PRO) National Archives: Public Record Office; (SCL) Sheffield City Library; (UCL) University College London; (WALS) Wolverhampton Archives and Local Studies]

All places of publication are London unless stated.

1. PERSONAL PAPERS

Anson MSS	(Staffordshire RO)
Beesly MSS	(UCL)
Bright MSS	(BL)
Brougham MSS	(UCL)
Bruce MSS	(Glamorgan RO)
Cabinet Letters at Windsor	(Bodl. MS Film 596, 597)
Carnarvon MSS	(PRO 30/6)
Carnarvon MSS	(BL)
Cross MSS	(BL)
Cross MSS	(Lancs RO)
Derby (14th Earl) MSS	(Liverpool RO)

Derby (15th Earl) MSS	(Liverpool RO)
Disraeli MSS	(Bodleian Library)
Erle MSS	(Bodleian Library)
Foster MSS	(MCL)
Gladstone MSS	(BL)
Granville MSS	(PRO 30/29)
Harcourt MSS	(Bodleian Library)
Gathorne Hardy MSS	(Suffolk RO)
Harrison MSS	(BLPES)
Howell MSS	(Bishopsgate Institute)
Knatchbull-Hugessen MSS	(Centre for Kentish Studies)
Ludlow MSS	(Cambridge University Library)
Melly MSS	(Liverpool RO)
Mundella MSS	(Sheffield University Library)
Northcote MSS	(BL)
Ripon MSS	(BL)
Sotheron Estcourt MSS	(Gloucester RO)
Walpole MSS	(private collection)
Wharncliffe MSS	(Sheffield Archives)

2. GOVERNMENT DEPARTMENTS

(i) Home Office (PRO)

HO 34	Departmental out-letters
HO 36	Out-letters to Treasury
HO 43	Domestic letter books
HO 44/56	Report by Senior and Tomlinson on combinations
HO 45	Registered papers
HO 46	Registers of in-letters
HO 136	Miscellaneous out-letters
HO 158	Circulars

(ii) Treasury (PRO)

T 13	Treasury out-letters
T1/7400A/17267	Parliamentary Counsel, 1869
T1/6988A/14555	Registry of Friendly Societies, 1870
T1/7236/17272	Registry of Friendly Societies, 1871
T1/7559A/19735	Memoranda as to the granting of Special Authorities under the Friendly Societies Act, 1875

(iii) Metropolitan Police (PRO)
MEPOL2/69 London Builders' Strike, 1859
MEPOL2/146,148; MEPOL3/131,132 Police Pay Grievance, 1872

(iv) Court of Chancery (PRO)
C16/528/S92 Springhead Spinning Company v Riley and Others

(v) Post Office Archives, London
POST 30/2/5 Telegraphists' strike, 1872

(vi) Office of the Parliamentary Counsel, London
Bills and Memoranda 1871 (Henry Jenkyns):
Bills and Memoranda 1874 (Henry Thring):
Bills and Memoranda 1875 (Henry Thring):

3. TRADE UNIONS AND LABOUR ORGANIZATIONS

Amalgamated Society of Carpenters and Joiners, Monthly reports, Annual reports (HC)
Amalgamated Society of Engineers, Monthly reports
Associated Carpenters and Joiners of Scotland, Annual reports, Reports of delegate meetings (MRC MSS 78/C&JS/4)
Birmingham Trades Council, MS Minutes (Birmingham City Library)
Bradford Trades Council, MS Minutes (Bradford City Library)
Conference of Amalgamated Trades, MS Minutes (Webb TU Coll. BLPES)
Friendly Society of Ironfounders, Annual reports, Half-yearly reports, Monthly reports (MRC MSS 41/FSIF/4)
General Union of Carpenters and Joiners, Annual reports, Monthly reports (MRC MSS 78/GUC&J/4)
Glass Bottle Makers of Yorkshire, MS EC Minutes, Quarterly reports (Leeds district TGWU)
Journeymen Cabinet Makers, Reports (MRC MSS 78/CU/4)
Labour Representation League, MS Minutes (BLPES)
Liverpool Trades Council, MS Correspondence (Liverpool RO)
London Society of Compositors, Annual reports, Quarterly reports (MRC MSS 28/CO/1)
London Trades Council, MS Minutes (BLPES, Film 1061)
Manchester Order of Bricklayers, Monthly reports (MRC MSS 78/MB/4)
Operative Bricklayers' Society, Trade circular (MRC MSS 78/OB/4)
Operative Stonemasons' Society, Fortnightly returns (MRC MSS 78/OS/4).

Power Loom Carpet Weavers, MS Minutes (Worcs RO)
Provincial Association of Operative Cotton Spinners, Annual reports (Oldham Library)
Reform League, MS Election Reports (HC)
Trades Union Congress Parliamentary Committee, MS Memoranda (HC)

4. EMPLOYERS' AND OTHER NON-LABOUR ORGANIZATIONS

Association of British Chambers of Commerce, Annual reports, MS EC Minutes (Guildhall Library)
Birmingham Chamber of Commerce, Half-yearly reports (Birmingham City Library)
Birmingham Chamber of Commerce, MS Council Minutes (Birmingham Chamber of Commerce and Industry)
Central Association of Master Builders, MS Minutes (LMA)
Gas Light and Coke Company, MS Minutes (LMA)
General Builders' Association, MS Minutes of General Meetings, and Sub-Committees (National Federation of Building Trades Employers)
Leeds and District Association of Factory Occupiers (Brotherton Library, Leeds, MS200/58)
Manchester Chamber of Commerce, MS Minutes (MCL)
Oldham Master Cotton Spinners Association, MS Minutes (Oldham District Textile Employers' Association)
Railway Companies' Association, MS Minutes (PRO RAIL 1098/2)
Royal Society of Arts, MS Correspondence regarding 1854 Conference on Strikes (LMA)
Sheffield Chamber of Commerce, MS Minutes (SCL)

5. PARLIAMENT AND PARLIAMENTARY PAPERS

Hansard, *Parliamentary Debates* (2nd, 3rd, and 4th series)
House of Commons, *Division Lists* (HOLRO)
Appendices to the Reports of the Select Committee of the Commons on Public Petitions (HOLRO)
House of Commons, *Votes and Proceedings*
House of Commons, *Notices of Motions*

Parliamentary Papers:-

PP 1824 (51) v. Select committee on artizans and machinery
PP 1825 (417, 437) iv. Select committee on combination laws
PP 1837–38 (488, 646) viii. Select committee on combinations of workmen

PP 1837–8 (673) xli. Penal code prepared by the Indian law commissioners

PP 1839 [169] xix. First report of the constabulary force commissioners

PP 1841 [296] x. Royal commission on hand-loom weavers

PP 1845 [618, 641] xv. Report of the commissioner on frame-work knitters

PP 1847–8 (648) xvi. Select committee on provident associations fraud prevention bill

PP 1850 (508) xix. Select committee on savings of the middle and working classes

PP 1854 (412) vii. Select committee on friendly societies bill

PP 1854–5 (421) xiv. Select committee on stoppage of wages (hosiery)

PP 1856 (343) xiii. Select committee on masters and operatives (equitable councils of conciliation)

PP 1857 (273) xxxix. Report of the registrar of friendly societies in England, 1857

PP 1860 (307) xxii. Select committee on masters and operatives

PP 1860 (525) xxxix, pt I. Report of the registrar of friendly societies in England, 1860

PP 1861 (72-I) xliv. East India (indigo commission)

PP 1865 (370) vii. Select committee on the Master and Servant Act

PP 1866 (499) xiii. Select committee on the Master and Servant Act

PP 1867 (75) xl. Number of societies which have deposited their rules with the registrar of friendly societies

PP 1867 [3873] xxxii. First report of the royal commission on trades unions; [3893] second report; [3910] third report; [3952] fourth report; [3952-I] Sheffield outrages inquiry

PP 1867 (354) lviii. Numbers of shareholders in the thirteen metropolitan gas companies, distinguishing the numbers of ladies, clergymen, and holders on trust account

PP 1867–8 [3980]. Manchester outrages inquiry; [3980-I] xxxix. Fifth report of the royal commission on trades unions; [3980-II] sixth report; [3980-III] seventh report; [3980-IV] eighth report; [3980-V] ninth report; [3980-VI] tenth report

PP 1867–8 (239) xlix. East India (contract law)

PP 1868–9 [4123] xxxi. Eleventh and final report of the royal commission on trades unions; [4123-I] Appendix

PP 1868–9 (399) lvi. Report of the registrar of friendly societies in England, 1868

PP 1871 [C.326] xxxvi. Commissioners on the truck system

PP 1872 (394) liv. Reports of the registrar of friendly societies in England, 1871

PP 1873 (313) x. Select committee on dearness and scarcity of coal

PP 1873 (348) xv. Select committee on imprisonment for debt

PP 1873 [C. 842] xxii. Royal commission on friendly societies, 3rd report

PP 1873 (315) liv. Chipping Norton magistrates

PP 1873 (313) x. Select committee on dearness and scarcity of coal

PP 1873 (385) liv. Return of convictions under 34 & 35 Vict. c. 32

PP 1873 (386) liv. Return of convictions under the Master and Servant Act, 1867

PP 1874 (359) liv. Return of convictions under 34 & 35 Vict. c. 32

PP 1874 (360) liv. Return of convictions under the Master and Servant Act, 1867

PP 1874 (132) lvii. Gaslight and Coke Company and Imperial Gaslight and Coke Company

PP 1874 [C.1094] xxiv. First report of the royal commission on the labour laws

PP 1875 [C.1157] xxx. Second and final report of the royal commission on the labour laws; [C.1157-I] appendix

PP 1875 (171) lxii. Master and Servant (law of foreign countries)

PP 1875 (237) lxi. Central Criminal Court (*R v. Hibbert*)

PP 1875 (273.) lxi. Central Criminal Court (Charge of the Recorder)

PP 1875 (280) viii. Select committee on Acts of Parliament

PP 1875 (408) lxxi. Reports of the registrar of friendly societies, 1874

PP 1876 (424, 424-I). Report of the chief registrar of friendly societies, 1875

PP 1877 (429, 429-I). Report of the chief registrar of friendly societies, 1876

PP 1894 [C.7421-I] xxxv. Fifth and final report of the royal commission on labour

PP 1906 [Cd.2825] lvi. Report of the royal commission on trade disputes and combinations

6. STATUTES

4 Geo. IV c. 34	Masters and Servants Act, 1823
5 Geo. IV c. 95	Combination Laws Repeal Act, 1824
6 Geo. IV c. 129	Combination Laws Repeal Act, 1825
18 & 19 Vict. c. 63	Friendly Societies Act, 1855
22 Vict. c. 34	Molestation of Workmen Act, 1859
30 & 31 Vict. c. 141	Master and Servant Act, 1867
31 & 32 Vict. c. 116	Larceny and Embezzlement Act, 1868
32 & 33 Vict. c. 61	Trades Unions Protection of Funds Act, 1869
34 & 35 Vict. c. 31	Trade Union Act, 1871
34 & 35 Vict. c. 32	Criminal Law Amendment Act, 1871
38 & 39 Vict. c. 86	Conspiracy and Protection of Property Act, 1875
38 & 39 Vict. c. 90	Employers and Workmen Act, 1875
39 & 40 Vict. c. 22	Trade Union Act Amendment Act, 1876

Theobald, W. (ed.), *The Legislative Acts of the Governor General of India from 1834 to the end of 1867* (3 vols., 1868).

7. LAW REPORTS

R v Mawbey (1796)	101 English Reports, 736
R v Bykerdike (1832)	174 English Reports 61
R v Harris (1842)	174 English Reports 678
R v O'Connor and Others (1842)	J. E. P. Wallis, *Reports of State Trials*, n.s. 4 (1892), 1202–3

R v Selsby (1847)	5 Cox Criminal Cases 495
R v Hewitt (1851)	5 Cox Criminal Cases 162
R v Duffield (1851)	5 Cox Criminal Cases 406
R v Rowlands (1851)	5 Cox Criminal Cases 438
Hilton v Eckersley (1855)	119 English Reports 781
In Re William Perham (1859)	157 English Reports 1088
Walsby v Anley (1861)	30 Law.Journal Magistrates Cases 121;
	121 English Reports 536
O'Neill and Galbraith v Longman (1863)	9 Cox Criminal Cases 360
O'Neill and Gailbraith v Kruger (1863)	122 English Reports 500
Shelbourne v Oliver (1866)	13 Law Times Reports New Series 630
Wood v Bowron (1866)	10 Cox Criminal Cases 344
Hodgson v Graveling (1867)	31 Justice of the Peace 115
Hornby v Close (1867)	10 Cox Criminal Cases 393
Cowan v Milbourn	2 Law Reports Exchequer 230
Skinner v Kitch (1867)	10 Cox Criminal Cases 493
R v Druitt (1867)	10 Cox Criminal Cases 592
R v Bailey (1867)	16 Law Times Reports New Series 859
R v Dodd (1868)	18 Law Times Reports New Series 89
The Springhead Spinning Company	
(Limited) v Riley (1868)	37 Law Journal Reports Chancery 889
R v Blackburn (1868)	11 Cox Criminal Cases 157
R v Shepherd (1869)	11 Cox Criminal Cases 325
Farrer v Close (1869)	4 Law Reports Queen's Bench 602
R v Stainer (1870)	11 Cox Criminal Cases 483
Purchon v Hartley (1871)	51 Law Times 294
R v Bunn (1872)	12 Cox Criminal Cases 316
Manners v Fairholme (1872)	Sessions Cases 3rd Ser. x. 520
Young v Allan (1873)	8 Law Journal 185
M'Kernan v Greenock Lodge of United	
Operative Stonemasons' Association of	
Scotland (1873)	Sessions Cases 3rd Ser. xi. 549
McKernan v. The United Operative	
Masons' Association of Scotland (1874)	Sessions Cases 4th Ser. i. 454
R v Hibbert (1875)	13 Cox Criminal Cases 82
R v Bauld (1876)	13 Cox Criminal Cases 282
Rigby v Connol (1880)	42 Law Times Reports New Series 139
Taff Vale Railway Company v	
Amalgamated Society of Railway Servants	[1901] Appeal Cases 426
Yorkshire Miners' Association v Howden	[1905] Appeal Cases 256
Amalgamated Society of Railway Servants	
v Osborne	[1910] Appeal Cases 87

8. NEWSPAPERS AND PERIODICALS

Bee-Hive
Bookbinders' Trade Circular
Builder
Builders' Trade Circular
Capital and Labour
Colliery Guardian
Commonwealth
Daily News
Daily Telegraph
Economist
Flint Glass Makers' Magazine
Glasgow Sentinel
Journal of Jurisprudence
Jurist
Justice of the Peace
Labourers' Union Chronicle
Law Journal
Law Magazine
Law Times
Lloyd's Weekly Newspaper
Morning Chronicle
Pall Mall Gazette
Potteries Examiner
Reformer (Edinburgh)
Reynolds's Newspaper
Saturday Review
The Scotsman
The Solicitors' Journal
The Spectator
The Times

For the provincial newspapers referred to in the text but not listed above, see:
British Library, *Catalogue of the Newspaper Library at Colindale* (8 vols., 1975);
For the labour press, see:
Harrison, R., Woolven, G. B., and Duncan, R., *The Warwick Guide to British Labour Periodicals, 1790–1970* (1977).

9. CONTEMPORARY WRITINGS

Akroyd, E., *On the Present Attitude of Political Parties* (1874)
Alison, A., 'Practical Working of Trades' Unions', *Blackwood's Edinburgh Magazine*, 43 (Mar. 1838)
—— 'Trades' Unions and Strikes', *Edinburgh Review*, 67 (Apr. 1838)
Amalgamated Society of Engineers, *Abstract Report of the Council's Proceedings, 1862–3* (BLPES)
Amalgamated Society of Engineers, *Full and Authentic Report of the Speeches delivered at the Great Demonstration of Trade Societies in Exeter Hall, London, on Thursday, 21st February 1867* (1867) (HC)
Amalgamated Society of Engineers, *Registration of the Society under the Trades' Union Act, 1871. Case Submitted to J.M. Ludlow Esq, and Opinion Thereon* (1874) (GL)
(Anon), 'Trades' Unions', *Companion to the Newspaper*, 12 (1833)
—— 'Combinations and Combination Laws', *Law Magazine*, 11 (Feb. 1834)
—— 'Report of the conference on Strikes and Lockouts held on 30 January 1854', *Journal of the Society of Arts*, 2 (1854)
—— *Trades-Unions, Strikes, and Lock-Outs* (Chambers's Social Science Tracts, ed. W. Chambers, 1861)
—— 'Labour and Capital', *Westminster Review*, n.s. 36 (July 1869)
—— 'The Demand of the Artisans', *Journal of Jurisprudence*, 18 (Mar. 1874)
Argyll, eighth duke of [George Douglas Campbell], *The Reign of Law* (1867)
Ashworth, H., *The Preston Strike, an Enquiry into its Causes and Consequences* (Manchester 1854)
Bagehot, W., *The Collected Works of Walter Bagehot*, ed. N. St John Stevas, vol. viii (1974)
[A Barrister], *Strikes and Lock Outs, or, The Law of Combination* (1867) (HC)
—— *Trades Unions Bill, 1869: Observations upon the Law Affecting Combinations and Trades Unions* (1869) (HC)
Beesly, E. S., 'Trades' Unions', *Westminster Review*, n.s. 20 (Oct. 1861)
—— 'The Trades' Union Commission', *Fortnightly Review*, n.s. 2 (July 1867)
—— 'Amalgamated Society of Carpenters and Joiners', *Fortnightly Review*, n.s. 1 (Mar. 1867)
—— *The Sheffield Outrages and the Meeting at Exeter Hall: Two Letters* (1867)
—— *Letters to the Working Classes* (1870)
—— 'Positivists and Workmen', *Fortnightly Review*, n.s. 18 (July 1875)
Brabrook, E. W., *The Law Relating to Industrial and Provident Societies and Remarks on Trades Unions* (1869)
Brabrook, E. W., *The Law Relating to Trades Unions* (1871)
Brassey, T., *Trades' Unions and the Cost of Labour* (1870)
Brentano, L., 'The Growth of a Trades Union', *North British Review*, n.s. 14 (Oct. 1870)

Brentano, L., *On the History and Development of Gilds and the Origin of Trade Unions* (1870)

British Association for the Advancement of Science, *Report of the Committee on Combinations of Capital and Labour* (1875).

Callender, W. R., *Trades Unions Defended: A Review of the Evidence Laid before the Royal Commission, 1867–8* (Manchester, 1870) (BLPES)

Cecil, R., 'The Programme of the Radicals', *Quarterly Review*, 135 (Oct. 1873), repr. in P. Smith (ed.), *Lord Salisbury on Politics* (1972)

Central Association of Master Builders, *Report of the Executive Committee* (1860) (GL)

Chalmers, T., *The Christian and Civic Economy of Large Towns* (3 vols., Glasgow, 1826)

Chamberlain, J., 'The Liberal Party and its Leaders', *Fortnightly Review*, n.s. 14 (Sept. 1873)

Charge of Conspiracy and Intimidation against Members of the Manchester and Salford Coarse Spinners' Association, tried at the Manchester Assizes, August 4th, 1874, by Baron Pollock (HC)

Chitty, J., *A Practical Treatise on the Criminal Law* (2nd edn., 4 vols., 1826)

Church Congress, *Authorised Report of the Church Congress held at Bath, 1873* (1873)

Creed, H. H., and Williams, W., *Handicraftsmen and Capitalists: Their Organization at Home and Abroad* (Birmingham, 1867)

Crompton, H. 'Arbitration and conciliation', *Fortnightly Review*, n.s. 5 (May 1869)

—— 'Class Legislation', *Fortnightly Review* n.s. 13 (Feb. 1873)

—— 'The Government and Class Legislation', *Fortnightly Review*, n.s. 14 (July 1873)

—— *The Criminal Law Amendment Act and other Laws affecting Labour* (1873) (HC)

—— 'The Workmen's Victory', *Fortnightly Review*, n.s. 18 (Sept. 1875)

—— *The Law of Conspiracy* (1875) (HC)

—— *The Labour Laws Commission* (1875) (HC)

—— *Industrial Conciliation* (1876)

Davis, H. F. A., 'Trades' Union Legislation', *Law Magazine*, 28 (Feb. 1870)

—— *The Law and Practice of Friendly Societies and Trade Unions* (1876)

Davis, J. E., *The Labour Laws* (1875)

Dicey, A.V., 'The Balance of Classes', in *Essays on Reform* (1867)

—— 'The Legal Boundaries of Liberty', *Fortnightly Review*, n.s. 3 (Jan. 1868)

—— 'The Ethics of Trades' Unions', *Saint Pauls Magazine*, 1 (Oct. 1867)

Dronfield, W., 'A Workingman's View of Trades' Societies' (read at the Social Science Congress at Sheffield, 5 Oct. 1865), repr. in *Seventh Annual Report of the Executive of the Association of Organized Trades of Sheffield and the Neighbourhood* (Sheffield 1866) (GL)

Duff, M. E. Grant, *Sir Henry Maine: A Brief Memoir of his Life* (1892)

Dunkley, H., *Strikes Viewed in Relation to the Interests of Capital and Labour* (1853)

Dunning, T. J., *Trades' Unions and Strikes: Their Philosophy and Intention* (1860) (HC)

Escott, T. H. S., *England: Its People, Polity, and Pursuits* (1885)

Essays on Reform (1867)

Fawcett, H., 'Strikes: Their Tendencies and Remedies', *Westminster Review*, n.s. 18 (July 1860)

—— *The Economic Position of the British Labourer* (1865)

Final Reports of the Royal Commission on the Working of Trades' Unions with a Copy of the Trade Union Bill (1869) (HC)

Forster, W. E., ' "Strikes" and "Lock-Outs" ', *Westminster Review*, n.s. 5 (Jan. 1854)

Fyfe, J. H., 'The Despotism of the Future', *Quarterly Review*, 136 (Jan. 1874)

Glasgow United Trades' Council, *Report, 1872–3* (HC)

Graham, P., *A Lecture on the Tendency of Trades Unionism and Some of the Relations between Capital and Labour* (1875)

Greaves, C. S., *A Treatise on Crimes and Misdemeanours by W.O. Russell* (4th edn., 1865)

Greg, W. R., 'The Relation between Employers and Employed', *Westminster Review*, n.s. 1 (Jan. 1852)

—— 'The Great Social Problem', *Edinburgh Review*, 100 (July 1854)

Guthrie, W., *The Law of Trade Unions in England and Scotland* (Edinburgh, 1873)

Hammersmith Defence Fund Report and Balance Sheet: Trial and Defence of George Turk (1872). (HC)

Harrison, F., 'The Good and Evil of Trade Unionism', *Fortnightly Review*, o.s. 3 (Nov. 1865)

—— 'The Trades-Union Bill', *Fortnightly Review*, n.s. 6 (July 1869)

—— *Imprisonment for Breach of Contract, or, the Master and Servant Act* (Tracts for Trade Unionists, 1, 1873) (BLPES)

—— *Workmen and the Law of Conspiracy* (Tracts for Trade Unionists, 2, 1873) (BLPES)

—— *The Criminal Law Amendment Act* (Tracts for Trade Unionists, 3, 1873) (HC)

—— *Order and Progress* (1875)

Howell, G., *The Conflicts of Capital and Labour* (1878; 1890)

—— *Trade Unionism New and Old* (1891)

—— *Labour Legislation, Labour Movements, and Labour Leaders* (1902)

Hughes, T., 'More about Masters and Workmen', *Macmillan's Magazine*, 4 (Oct. 1861)

—— 'Trades' Unions, Strikes and Co-operation', *Macmillan's Magazine*, 13 (Nov. 1865)

—— 'Problems of Civilization', *Macmillan's Magazine*, 28 (May 1873)

Hunter, W. A., *A Lecture on the Criminal Laws Affecting Labour* (Glasgow Tracts for Trade Unionists, 4, 1874) (HC)

—— *The Master and Servant Act, 1867, and the First Report of the Royal Commission, 1874: A Lecture Delivered before the Dialectical Society, London, on 20th Jan, 1875* (1875) (HC)

—— 'Mr Cross's Labour Bills', *Fortnightly Review*, n.s. 18 (Aug. 1875)

Innes, A. T., 'The Common Law Status of Trade Unions', *Journal of Jurisprudence*, 18 (1874)

—— 'Trade-Unionism: Its Limits and its Future', NAPSS, *Transactions, 1874*

—— 'The Paradox in the Law of Trade Unions', *Law Magazine*, n.s. 4 (Apr. 1875)

Iron Trades Employers' Association, *The Piece-Work Question and a Report as the Financial Position of the Amalgamated Society of Engineers* (Manchester, 1876) (GL)

Jenkin, F., 'Trade-Unions: How Far Legitimate', *North British Review*, n.s. 9 (Mar. 1868)

Jevons, W. S., 'Industrial partnerships', in *Lectures on Economic Science* (1870)

Kettle, R., *Strikes and Arbitrations* (1866)

—— *Masters and Men* (1871) (HC)

—— 'The Law of Conspiracy and its Modern Application', NAPSS, *Sessional Papers* (1873–4)

Kirk, R. S., *The Second Annual Congress of Trades Unions held on August 23rd, 24th, 25th, 26th, 27th, and 28th 1869, in the Odd Fellows' Hall, Upper Temple Street, Birmingham* (1869) (HC)

Le Marchant, H. D., *Trades' Unions and the Commission Thereon* (1867)

Lewis, G. C., 'Legislation for the Working Classes', *Edinburgh Review*, 83 (Jan. 1846)

The London Gas Stokers. A report by the committee of their trial for conspiracy, of their defence and of the proceedings for their liberation (1873) (BLPES)

Longe, F. D., *An Inquiry into the Law of 'strikes'* (1860) (HC)

—— *A Refutation of the Wage-Fund Theory of Modern Political Economy as Enunciated by Mr Mill, MP and Mr Fawcett, MP* (1866)

—— 'The Law of Trade Combinations in France', pts. I and II, *Fortnightly Review*, n.s. 2 (Aug., Sept. 1867)

Lowe, R., 'Reform Essays', *Quarterly Review*, 123 (July 1867)

—— 'Trades' Unions', *Quarterly Review*, 123 (Oct. 1867)

—— *Speeches and Letters on Reform* (2nd edn., 1867)

Ludlow, J. M., *The Master Engineers and their Workmen: Three Lectures on the Relations of Capital and Labour* (1852) (GL)

—— 'Trade societies and the Social Science Association' pts. I and II, *Macmillan's Magazine* 3 (Feb., Mar. 1861)

—— and Jones, L., *The Progress of the Working Class, 1832–1867* (1867)

—— 'Old Guilds and New Friendly and Trades Societies', *Fortnightly Review*, n.s. 6 (Oct. 1869)

—— 'Proposed Legislation in Reference to Companies and Friendly Societies', *Law Magazine*, n.s. 4 (Feb. 1875)

Lushington, G., 'Workmen and Trade Unions', in *Questions for a Reformed Parliament* (1867)

—— 'The Trade Union Triumph. Allen v. Flood', *National Review*, 30 (Jan. 1898)

—— 'Trade unions and the House of Lords', *National Review*, 33 (Dec. 1901)

McCulloch, J. R., 'Combination Laws—Restraints on Emigration', *Edinburgh Review*, 39 (Jan. 1824)

—— 'Combination', in *Encyclopaedia Britannica*, (8th edn., 1854), vol. vii

Macdonald, W., *The True Story of Trades' Unions Contrasted with the Caricatures and Fallacies of the Pretended Economists* (1867)

Manchester and Salford Trades Council, *Sixth Annual Report, 1872* (HC)

Manchester Free Labour Society, *First Annual Report of the Manchester Free Labour Society* (1870) (BL)

The Master Spinners and Manufacturers' Defence Fund: Report of the Committee Appointed for the Receipt and Apportionment of the Fund, to the Central Association of Master Spinners and Manufacturers (Manchester, 1854) (GL)

Maule, J. B., *Burn's Justice of the Peace and Parish Officer* (13th edn., 5 vols., 1869)

Martineau, H., 'Secret Organization of Trades', *Edinburgh Review*, 110 (Oct. 1859)

Mill, J. S., *Principles of Political Economy* (1848–71), repr., in *Collected Works of John Stuart Mill*, vols. ii–iii, ed. J. M. Robson (Toronto 1965)

—— 'Thornton on Labour and its Claims', pts. I and II, *Fortnightly Review*, n.s. 5 (May, June 1869), repr., in *Collected Works of John Stuart Mill*, vol. v, ed. J. M. Robson (Toronto 1967)

Morley, J., 'The Five Gas Stokers', *Fortnightly Review*, n.s. 13 (Jan. 1873)

—— *The Life of William Ewart Gladstone* (3 vols., 1903)

Morrison, C., *An Essay on the Relations between Labour and Capital* (1854)

Mundella, A. J., *Arbitration as a Means of Preventing Strikes* (1868)

National Association for the Promotion of Social Science, *Trades' Societies and Strikes* (1860)

—— *Transactions* (1858–75)

—— *Sessional Proceedings* (1866–71)

—— *Lectures on Economic Science, Delivered under the Auspices of the Committee on Labour and Capital* (1870)

National Association of United Trades, *Report of the Central Committee of United Trades on the Proceedings Connected with the Combination of Workmen Bill in the Parliamentary Session, 1853* (1853) (GL)

—— *Rules and Regulations* (1853) (HC)

—— *Arbitration of Disputes between Employers and Employed* (1854) (GL)

National Federation of Associated Employers of Labour, *Report of the Interview on 13 December 1873 between a Deputation from the National Federation of Associated Employers of Labour and the Right Hon Robert Lowe MP* (Manchester, 1874) (MCL)

—— *Report of the Executive Committee to be Presented at the First Annual Meeting of Members, 26 February 1875* (1875) (HC)

Neate, C., *Two Lectures on Trades Unions Delivered in the University of Oxford in the Year 1861* (1861)

Osborne, W. V., and Judge, M. H., *Trade Unions and the Law* (1911)

Paris, Le Comte de [Louis Philippe D'Orléans], *The Trades' Unions of England*, ed. T. Hughes, trans. N. J. Senior (1869)

Perry, E., *The Tinmen's 'Strike': A Letter to George Robinson, Esq., Late Mayor of Wolverhampton* (Wolverhampton, 1850) (WALS)

Potter, E., *Some Opinions on Trades' Unions and the Bill of 1869* (1869) (BLPES)

Price, B., 'Trade Unions', *Blackwood's Magazine*, 107 (June 1870)

Price, G., *Combinations and Strikes: Their Costs and Results* (1854)

Report of the Conference on the Law of Masters and Workmen under their Contract of Service held in London on 30th and 31st May, and 1st and 2nd June, 1864 (Glasgow, 1864) (BLPES)

Report of the St Martin's Hall United Kingdom Trades' Conference Committee on the Trades' Union Inquiry Commission until 7th August 1867 (1867) (TUC library)

Report of the Speeches of John A. Roebuck Esq, together with Mr Roebuck's Answers to the Questions on Trades' Unions (Sheffield, 1868) (SCL)

Report of the Trades Conference held at St Martin's Hall on March 5, 6, 7, and 8, 1867 (1867) (HC)

Report of the Various Proceedings taken by the London Trades' Council and the Conference of Amalgamated Trades, in Reference to the Royal Commission on Trades' Unions (1867) (HC)

Rickards, G. K., 'Trades' Unions', *Edinburgh Review*, 126 (Oct. 1867)

—— 'Thornton on Labour', *Edinburgh Review*, 130 (Oct. 1869)

Roberts, W. P., *The Trade Union Bill, 1871: A Letter* (1871) (HC)

Robinson, D., 'The Repeal of the Combination Laws', *Blackwood's Edinburgh Magazine*, 18 (July 1825)

—— 'The combinations', *Blackwood's Edinburgh Magazine*, 18 (Oct. 1825)

Rogers, J. E. T., 'Trades' Unions', *British Quarterly Review*, 46 (Oct. 1867)

—— 'Strikes', *British Quarterly Review*, 58 (Oct. 1873),

Rollit, A. K., *"The Master and Servant Act": A Letter to the Right Hon. R. A. Cross, MP* (Hull, 1875) [Hull Local Studies Library]

Russell, W. O., *A Treatise on Crimes and Misdemeanours*, ed. C. S. Greaves (3rd edn., 2 vols., 1843; 4th edn., 3 vols., 1865)

Ryland, A. (ed.), *The Crown Circuit Companion* (10th edn., 1836)

Senior, N. W., *Historical and Philosophical Essays* (2 vols., 1865)

Stafford Summer Assizes, Monday July 28, 1851, The Queen versus George Duffield, Thomas Woodnorth, and John Gaunt: Shorthand Notes of Mr Walsh (Wolverhampton, 1851) (WALS)

Stafford Summer Assizes, Tuesday, 29 July, 1851, The Queen versus William Peel, Frederick Green, Thomas Winters, Henry Rowlands, Thomas Pitt, Charles Pitt, George Duffield, Thomas Woodnorth, and John Gaunt (Wolverhampton, 1851) (WALS)

Statement of the Receipts and Expenditure for the Defence of the Five Cabinet-Makers tried at the Old Bailey for Picketing (1875) (HC)

Stephen, J. F., *A General View of the Criminal Law of England* (1863)

—— *Roscoe's Digest of the Law of Evidence in Criminal Cases* (7th edn., 1868)

—— 'Codification in India and England', *Fortnightly Review*, n.s. 12 (Dec. 1872)

—— *A History of the Criminal Law of England* (3 vols., 1883)

Stephen, L., 'The Good Old Cause', *Nineteenth Century*, 51 (Jan. 1902)

Stirling, J., *Unionism* (Glasgow, 1869)

Sturgeon, C., *Letters to the Trades' Unionists and the Working Classes* (1868)

Swift, H. G., *A History of the Postal Agitation* (1900)

Terrell, T. H., *Capital and Labour: A Plan for their Reconciliation, for a New Organisation of Labour, and for the Prevention in Future of Strikes and Locks Out* (1873) (BLPES)

Thornton, W. T., *On Labour: Its Wrongful Claims and Rightful Dues* (1869)

Thring, H., 'Simplification of the Law', *Quarterly Review*, 136 (Jan. 1874)

—— *Practical legislation, or, The Composition and Language of Acts of Parliament* (1877)

Thurlow, T. J. Hovell, *Trade Unions Abroad and Hints for Home Legislation* (1870)

Toynbee, A., *Lectures on the Industrial Revolution in England* (1884)

Trades' Societies and Lock-Outs: Report of the Conference of Trades' Delegates of the United Kingdom held in the Temperance Hall, Townhead Street, Sheffield, on July 17th 1866, and Four Following Days (1866) (HC)

Trades Union Congress Parliamentary Committee, *The Criminal Law Amendment Act: A Memorial to the Right Hon Henry Austin Bruce, MP* (1872) (HC)

Trades Union Congress Parliamentary Committee, *The Plot Discovered; or, Conspiracy amongst the Masters* (1873) (HC)

Trades Union Congress Parliamentary Committee, *Criminal Law Amendment Act, Master and Servants Act, and the Law of Conspiracy: correspondence with Mr Gladstone in Reference Thereto* (1873) (HC)

Trades Union Congress Parliamentary Committee, *The Trades' Union Act, Criminal Law Amendment Act, Master and Servants Act, and the Law of Conspiracy: A Special Report of the Deputation to the Home Secretary on Wednesday, November 5th, 1873* (1873) (HC)

Trades Union Congress Parliamentary Committee, *The Law of Contract of Masters and Servants, and the Law of Conspiracy: Report of the Debates in the House of Commons and House of Lords* (Tracts for Trade Unionists, 4, 1873) (HC)

Trades Union Congress Parliamentary Committee, *The Trades Union Congress Parliamentary Committee and the National Federation of Associated Employers of Labour* (1873) (HC)

Trades Union Congress Parliamentary Committee, *Important Case under the Master and Servants Act: Hague and Another v Cutler* (1874) (HC)

[Tufnell, E. C.], *Character, Object, and Effects of Trades' Unions, with some Remarks on the Law Concerning Them* (1834)

United Kingdom Alliance of Organized Trades, *Minutes of Conference, Preston, 24, 25, 26 September 1867* (1867) (HC)

United Kingdom First Annual Trades' Union Directory, 1861 (1861)

Waley, J., 'On strikes and combinations', *Journal of the Statistical Society of London*, 30 (Mar. 1867)

Watts, J., 'On strikes', *Report of the Thirty-First Meeting of the British Association for the Advancement of Science, Manchester, September 1861* (1862)

Wood W. H., *Trades Unions Defended* (Manchester, 1867) (MCL)

Wright, R. S., *The Law of Criminal Conspiracies and Agreements* (1873)

Authorship of articles, where applicable, as given in Houghton, W. E., *The Wellesley Index to Victorian Periodicals, 1824–1900* (5 vols., Toronto, 1966–89)

10. LATER WORKS

Alborn, T., *Conceiving Companies: Joint-Stock Politics in Victorian England* (1998)
Alderman, G., *The Railway Interest* (1973)
Allen, E., Clarke, J. F., McCord, N., and Rowe, D. J., *The North-East Engineers' Strikes of 1871: The Nine Hours' League* (Newcastle upon Tyne, 1971)
Allen, V. L., 'The Origins of Industrial Conciliation and Arbitration', *International Review of Social History*, 9 (1964)
—— *The Sociology of Industrial Relations: Studies in Method* (1971)
Anderson, A., 'The Political Symbolism of the Labour Laws', *Bulletin of the Society for the Study of Labour History*, 23 (1971)
Ariouat, J. F., 'Rethinking Partisanship in the Conduct of the Chartist Trials, 1839–1848', *Albion*, 29 (1998)
Armytage, W. H. G., *A. J. Mundella, 1825–1897: The Liberal Background to the Labour Movement* (1951)
Aspinall, A., *The Early English Trade Unions* (1949)
Atiyah, P. S., *The Rise and Fall of Freedom of Contract* (1979)
Bagwell, P., *The Railwaymen: The History of the National Union of Railwaymen* (1964)
Behagg, C., *Politics and Production in the Early Nineteenth Century* (1990)
Belchem, J., *Industrialization and the Working Class: The English Experience, 1750–1900* (1990)
Bellamy, J. M. and Saville, J. (eds), *Dictionary of Labour Biography* (8 vols., 1972–87)
Biagini, E. F., 'British Trade Unions and Popular Political Economy, 1860–1880', *Historical Journal*, 30 (1987)
—— *Liberty, Retrenchment and Reform: Popular Liberalism in the Age of Gladstone, 1860–1880* (1992)
—— and Reid, A. J. (eds), *Currents of Radicalism: Popular Radicalism, Organised Labour and Party Politics in Britain, 1850–1914* (1991)
Boyd, C. W. (ed.), *Mr Chamberlain's Speeches* (2 vols., 1914)
Brent, R., 'God's Providence: Liberal Political Economy as Natural Theology at Oxford, 1825–1862', in M. Bentley (ed.), *Public and Private Doctrine* (1993)
Breuilly, J., *Labour and Liberalism in Nineteenth-Century Europe: Essays in Comparative History* (1992)
Briggs, A., *Victorian People: A Reassessment of Persons and Themes, 1851–67* (1954; pbk. edn., 1975)
Brown, H. Phelps, *The Origins of Trade Union Power* (1983)
[Bruce, H. A.], *Letters of the Rt Hon Henry Austin Bruce GCB, Lord Aberdare of Duffryn* (2 vols., privately printed, Oxford, 1902)

Burgess, K., *The Origins of British Industrial Relations: The Nineteenth-Century Experience* (1975)

Burn, W. L., *The Age of Equipoise* (1968 edn.)

Challinor, R., *A Radical Lawyer in Victorian England: W. P. Roberts and the Struggle for Workers' Rights* (1990)

Chase, M., *Early Trade Unionism: Fraternity, Skill, and the Politics of Labour* (2000)

Checkland, S. G., *British Public Policy, 1776–1939* (1983)

Church, R. A. with Hall. A., and Kanefsky, J., *Victorian Pre-eminence* (History of the British Coal Industry, vol. iii, 1986)

Clegg, H. A., Fox, A., and Thompson, A. F., *A History of British Trade Unions since 1889* (1964)

Cocks, R., *The Foundations of the Modern Bar* (1983)

Cole, G. D. H., 'Some Notes on British Trade Unionism in the Third Quarter of the Nineteenth Century', *International Review of Social History*, 2 (1937), repr. in E. M. Carus-Wilson (ed.), *Essays in Economic History*, iii (1962)

——and Filson, A. W., *British Working-Class Movements: Select Documents, 1789–1875* (1967)

Coleridge, E. H., *Life and Correspondence of John Duke, Lord Coleridge* (2 vols., 1904)

Collini, S., *Public Moralists: Political Thought and Intellectual Life in Britain* (1991)

Collins, H., and Abramsky, C., *Karl Marx and the British Labour Movement* (1965)

Collins, H., Ewing, K. D., and McColgan, A., *Labour Law: Text and Materials* (2001)

Coltham, S., 'George Potter, the Junta and the *Bee-Hive*', *International Review of Social History*, 9 (1964), 10 (1965)

Connell, B., *Regina v Palmerston* (1962)

Cooke, A. B., and Vincent, J., *The Governing Passion: Cabinet Government and Party Politics in Britain, 1885–86* (1974)

Cordery, S., 'Mutualism, Friendly Societies, and the Genesis of Railway Trade Unions', *Labour History Review*, 67 (2002)

Cornish, W. R., and Clark, G. de N., *Law and Society in England, 1750–1950* (1989)

Cronin, J. E., 'Strikes and Power in Britain', *International Review of Social History*, 32 (1987)

Davidson, R., *Whitehall and the Labour Problem in Late-Victorian and Edwardian Britain* (1985)

Davies, P., and Freedland, M., *Labour Legislation and Public Policy: A Contemporary History* (1993)

Deakin, S., and Morris, G. S., *Labour Law* (3rd edn., 2001)

——'The Contract of Employment: A Study in Legal Evolution', *Historical Studies in Industrial Relations*, 11 (2001)

Dewey, C., 'Celtic Agrarian Legislation and the Celtic Revival: Historicist Implications of Gladstone's Irish and Scottish Land Acts 1870–1886', *Past and Present*, 64 (1974)

Diamond, A. (ed.), *The Victorian Achievement of Sir Henry Maine* (1991)

Dicey, A. V., *Lectures on the Relation between Law and Public Opinion in Nineteenth-Century Britain* (1905; 2nd edn. 1914)

Duff, M. E. Grant-, *Sir Henry Maine: A Brief Memoir of his Life with some of his Indian Speeches and Minutes* (1892)

Dunbabin, J. P. D., *Rural Discontent in Nineteenth-Century Britain* (1974)

Dutton, H. I., and King, J. E., *'Ten Percent and No Surrender': The Preston Strike, 1853–1854* (1981)

Eastwood, D., 'The Age of Uncertainty: Britain in the Early Nineteenth Century', *TRHS*, 6th ser. 8 (1998)

Evans, E. W., *The Miners of South Wales* (Cardiff, 1961)

Everard, S., *The History of the Gas Light and Coke Company, 1812–1949* (1949)

Ewing, K. D., 'The State and Industrial Relations: "Collective Laissez-Faire" Revisited', *Historical Studies in Industrial Relations*, 5 (spring 1998)

Fairfield, C., *Some Account of George William Wilshere, Lord Bramwell of Hever* (1898)

Feaver, G., *From Status to Contract: A Biography of Sir Henry Maine 1822–1888* (1969)

Finn, M. C., *After Chartism: Class and Nation in English Radical Politics, 1848–1874* (1993)

Fox, A., *History and Heritage: The Social Origins of the British Industrial Relations System* (1985)

Frank, C., ' "He might almost as well be without trial": Trade Unions and the 1823 Master and Servant Act—the Warrington Cases, 1846–47', *Historical Studies in Industrial Relations*, 14 (2002), 40

Fraser, W. H., *Trade Unions and Society: The Struggle for Acceptance, 1850–1880* (1974)

—— *A History of British Trade Unionism, 1700–1998* (1999)

Freeden, M., *The New Liberalism* (1978)

Freund, O. Kahn-, 'Labour Law', in M. Ginsberg (ed.), *Law and Opinion in England in the Twentieth Century* (1959)

—— *Labour and the Law* (2nd edn. 1977)

—— *Selected Writings* (1978)

Friedland, M. L., 'R. S. Wright's Model Criminal Code', *Oxford Journal of Legal Studies*, 1 (1981)

Garrard, J., *Democratization in Britain: Elites, Civil Society, and Reform since 1800* (2002)

Gash, N., *Mr Secretary Peel: The Life of Sir Robert Peel to 1830* (1961)

George, M. D., 'The Combination Laws Reconsidered', *Economic History*, 1 (1927)

Ghosh, P., 'Style and Substance in Disraelian Social Reform', in P. J. Waller (ed.), *Politics and Social Change in Modern Britain: Essays Presented to A. F. Thompson* (1987)

Gillespie, F. E., *Labor and Politics in England, 1850–1867* (Durham, North Carolina, 1927)

Goldman, L. (ed.), *The Blind Victorian: Henry Fawcett and British Liberalism* (1989)

Goldman, L., 'Civil Society in Nineteenth-Century Britain and Germany: J. M. Ludlow, Lujo Brentano and the Labour Question', in J. Harris (ed.), *Civil Society in British History: Ideas, Identities, Institutions* (2003)

—— *Science, Reform, and Politics in Victorian Britain: The Social Science Association, 1857–1886* (2002)

Gordon, B., *Economic Doctrine and Tory Liberalism, 1824–1830* (1970)

Gosden, P. H. J. H., *Self-Help: Voluntary Associations in the Nineteenth Century* (1973)

Grampp, W. D., 'The Economists and the Combination Laws', *Quarterly Journal of Economics*, 93 (1979)

Gray, P., 'The peculiarities of Irish Land Tenure, 1800–1914', in D. Winch and P. K. O'Brien (eds), *The Political Economy of British Historical Experience, 1688–1914'* (2002)

Gray, R. Q., *The Labour Aristocracy in Victorian Edinburgh* (1976)

Griffiths, C. 'Remembering Tolpuddle', *History Workshop Journal*, 44 (1997)

Hall, C., McClelland, K., and Rendall, J., *Defining the Victorian Nation: Class, Race, Gender, and the British Reform Act of 1867* (2000)

Hamer, D. A., *Liberal Politics in the Age of Gladstone and Rosebery* (1972)

Hanson, C. G., *Trade Unions: A Century of Privilege* (Institute of Economic Affairs Occasional Paper, 38, 1973)

—— 'Craft Unions, Welfare Benefits, and the Case for Trade Union Law Reform 1867–75', *Economic History Review*, 28 (1975)

—— 'Craft Unions, Welfare Benefits, and the Case for Trade Union Law Reform, 1867–75: A Reply', *Economic History Review*, 29 (1976)

Harling, P., *The Modern British State: An Historical Introduction* (2001)

Harris, J., ' Victorian Values and the Founders of the Welfare State', *Proceedings of the British Academy*, 78 (1992)

—— *Private Lives and Public Spirit: Britain, 1870–1914* (1993)

Harris, S. H., *Auberon Herbert: Crusader for Liberty* (1943)

Harrison, B. H., *Drink and the Victorians: The Temperance Question in England 1815–1872* (1971; new edn., 1994)

—— *Peaceable Kingdom: Stability and Change in Modern Britain* (1982)

Harrison, R., 'Practical, Capable Men', *New Reasoner*, 6 (autumn 1958)

—— *Before the Socialists: Studies in Labour and Politics, 1861–1881* (1965; repr. with new intro., 1994)

—— *The Independent Collier: The Coal Miner as Archetypal Proletarian Reconsidered* (Brighton, 1978)

—— *The Life and Times of Sidney and Beatrice Webb, 1858–1905: The Formative Years* (2000)

Harvie, C. T., *The Lights of Liberalism: University Liberals and the Challenge of Democracy 1860–86* (1976)

Hay, D., 'The State and the Market in 1800: Lord Kenyon and Mr Waddington', *Past and Present*, 162 (1999)

—— 'Master and Servant in England', in W. Steinmetz (ed.), *Private Law and Social Inequality in the Industrial Age* (2000)

Hilton, B., *Corn, Cash, Commerce: The Economic Policies of the Tory Governments, 1815–1830* (1977)

—— *The Age of Atonement: The Influence of Evangelicalism on Social and Economic Thought, 1785–1865* (1991 edn.)

—— 'Disraeli, English Culture, and the Decline of the Industrial Spirit', in L. Brockliss and D. Eastwood (eds), *A Union of Multiple Identities: The British Isles, c.1750–c.1850* (1997)

—— 'The Gallows and Mr Peel', in T. C. W. Blanning and D. Cannadine (eds), *History and Biography* (1996)

Hobhouse, L. T., *Liberalism and Other Writings*, ed. J. Meadowcroft (1994)

Hobsbawm, E. J., *Labouring Men* (1964)

Holdsworth, W., *A History of English Law*, vol. xv, ed. A. L. Goodhart and H. G. Hanbury (1965)

Hoppen, K. T., *The Mid-Victorian Generation, 1846–1886* (1998)

Howard, N. P., 'The Strikes and Lockouts in the Iron Industry and the Formation of the Ironworkers' Unions, 1862–1869', *International Review of Social History*, 18 (1973)

Howe, A., *The Cotton Masters, 1830–1860* (1984)

—— *Free Trade and Liberal England, 1846–1946* (1997)

Hutt, W. H., *The Theory of Collective Bargaining* (1930)

Inns of Court Conservative and Unionist Society, *A Giant's Strength: Some Thoughts on the Constitutional and Legal Position of Trade Unions in England* (1958)

Jaffe, J. A., *Striking a Bargain: Work and Industrial Relations in England, 1815–1865* (2000)

B. Ll. James (ed.), *G. T. Clark: Scholar Ironmaster in the Victorian Age* (Cardiff, 1998)

Jenkins, T. A. (ed.), 'The Parliamentary Diaries of Sir John Trelawny, 1868–73', in *Camden Miscellany*, 32 (1994)

Johnson, N. E. (ed.), *The Diary of Gathorne Hardy, later Lord Cranbrook, 1866–1892: Political Selections* (1981)

Johnson, P., 'Class Law in Victorian England', *Past and Present*, 141 (1993)

Jones, A., 'Workmen's Advocates: Ideology and Class in a Mid-Victorian Labour Newspaper System', in J. Shattock and M. Wolff (eds.), *The Victorian Periodical Press: Samplings and Soundings* (Leicester, 1982)

Jones, G. Stedman, 'Rethinking Chartism', in *Languages of Class* (1983)

—— 'Some Notes on Karl Marx and the English Labour Movement', *History Workshop Journal*, 18 (1984)

Jones, H. S., *Victorian Political Thought* (2000)

Jones, I. G., *Explorations and Explanations* (1981)

Joyce, P., *Work, Society and Politics: The Culture of the Factory in later Victorian England* (Brighton, 1980)

—— *Visions of the People: Industrial England and the Question of Class, 1848–1914* (1991)

Judge, M. H. (ed.), *Political Socialism: A Remonstrance* (1908)

——and Osborne, W. V., *Trade Unions and the Law* (1911)

Kadish, A., *Apostle Arnold: The Life and Death of Arnold Toynbee, 1852–1883* (1986)

Kauffman, C. J., 'Lord Elcho, Trade Unionism and Democracy', in K. D. Brown (ed.), *Essays in Anti-Labour History* (1974)

Kent, C., *Brains and Numbers: Elitism, Comtism, and Democracy in Mid-Victorian England* (1978)

Kent, H. S., *In on the Act: Memoirs of a Lawmaker* (1979)

Kiddier, W., *The Old Trade Unions: From Unprinted Records of the Brushmakers* (2nd edn., 1931)

Kirby, R. G. and Musson, A. E., *The Voice of the People: John Doherty, 1789–1859* (1975)

Kirk, N., *The Growth of Working-Class Reformism in Mid-Victorian England* (1985)

——*Change, Continuity, and Class: Labour in British Society, 1850–1920* (1998)

Klarman, M. J., 'The Judges versus the Unions: The Development of British Labor Law, 1867–1913', *Virginia Law Review*, 75 no. 8 (Nov. 1989)

Koot, G. M., *English Historical Economics, 1870–1926: The Rise of Economic History and Neomercantilism* (1987)

Lawrence, J., *Speaking for the People: Party, Language, and Popular Politics in England, 1867–1914* (1998)

Leventhal, F. M., *Respectable Radical: George Howell and Victorian Working Class Politics* (1971)

Levy, S. L, *Nassau W. Senior, 1790–1864* (1970)

Lloyd, D., *The Law Relating to Unincorporated Associations* (1938)

Lobban, M., 'Strikers and the Law, 1825–51', in P. Birks (ed.), *The Life of the Law* (1993)

Lowe, R., *Adjusting to Democracy: The Role of the Ministry of Labour in British Politics, 1916–1939* (1986)

McCarthy, W. E. J., *The Closed Shop in Britain* (1964)

McCord, N., 'Taff Vale Revisited', *History*, 78 (1993)

McCready, H. W., 'The British General Election of 1874: Frederic Harrison and the Liberal–Labour Dilemma', *Canadian Journal of Economic and Political Science*, 20 (1954)

——'British Labour's Lobby, 1867–75', *Canadian Journal of Economics and Political Science*, 22 (1956)

MacDougall, I. (ed.), *Minutes of Edinburgh Trades Council, 1859–73* (Edinburgh, 1968)

McGill, B., 'A Victorian Office: The Parliamentary Counsel to the Treasury, 1869–1902', *Historical Research*, 63 (1990)

McIlroy, J., 'Financial Malpractice in British Trade Unions, 1800–1930: the Background to, and Consequences of, *Hornby v Close*', *Historical Studies in Industrial Relations*, 6 (1998)

McKibbin, R. I., 'Why was there no Marxism in Great Britain?', *English Historical Review*, 99 (1984), repr. in *The Ideologies of Class* (1991)

McWilliam, R., *Popular Politics in Nineteenth-Century England* (1998)

Machin, F., *The Yorkshire Miners* (Barnsley, 1958)

Mack, E. C., and Armytage, W. H. G., *Thomas Hughes* (1952)

Martin, A. P., *Life and Letters of Robert Lowe, Viscount Sherbrooke* (2 vols., 1893)

Martin, R. M., *TUC: The Growth of a Pressure Group 1868–1976* (Oxford, 1980)

Mather, F. C., 'The Government and the Chartists', in A. Briggs (ed.), *Chartist Studies* (1959)

Matthew, H. C. G., *The Liberal Imperialists: The Ideas and Policies of a Post-Gladstonian Elite* (1973)

—— (ed.), *The Gladstone Diaries*, vols. v–viii (1978–82)

—— (ed.), *The Nineteenth Century: The British Isles, 1815–1901* (2000)

Moher, J., 'From Suppression to Containment: Roots of Trade Union Law to 1825', in J. Rule (ed.), *British Trade Unionism, 1750–1850: The Formative Years* (1988)

Monypenny, W. F., and Buckle, G. E., *The Life of Benjamin Disraeli, Earl of Beaconsfield* (6 vols., 1910–20)

Morgan, J., *Conflict and Order: The Police and Labour Disputes in England and Wales, 1900–1939* (1987)

Mortimer, J. E., *A History of the Boilermakers' Society, 1834–1906* (1973)

Murray, A. D. (ed.), *John Ludlow: The Autobiography of a Christian Socialist* (1981)

Musson, A. E., *The Typographical Association: Origins and History up to 1949* (1954).

—— *The Congress of 1868: The Origins and Establishment of the Trades Union Congress* (1968).

—— *Trade Union and Social History* (1974)

—— *British Trade Unions, 1800–1875* (1972)

Nead, L., *Victorian Babylon: People, Streets, and Images in Nineteenth-Century London* (2000)

Norman, E., *The Victorian Christian Socialists* (1987)

O'Brien, D. P., *J. R. McCulloch: A Study in Classical Economics* (1970)

Offer, A., *Property and Politics, 1870–1914* (1982)

Orth, J. V., *Combination and Conspiracy: A Legal History of Trade Unionism, 1721–1906* (1991)

Parker, C. S., *Sir Robert Peel from his Private Correspondence*, vol. i (1891)

Parris, H., *Constitutional Bureaucracy* (1969)

Parry, J. P., 'Religion and the Collapse of Gladstone's First Government, 1870–74', *Historical Journal*, 25 (1982), 71

—— *Democracy and Religion: Gladstone and the Liberal Party, 1867–1875* (1986)

—— *The Rise and Fall of Liberal Government in Victorian Britain* (1993)

—— 'Gladstone, Liberalism, and the Government of 1868–1874', in D. Bebbington and R. Swift (eds.), *Gladstone Centenary Essays* (2000)

—— 'The Impact of Napoleon III on British politics, 1851–1880', *TRHS*, 6th ser. 11 (2001)

Pellew, J., *The Home Office, 1848–1914: From Clerks to Bureaucrats* (1982)

Pelling, H., *A History of British Trade Unionism* (2nd edn., 1975)

—— *Popular Politics and Society in Late Victorian Britain* (2nd edn., 1979)

Pollard, S., 'The Ethics of the Sheffield Outrages', *Transactions of the Hunter Archaeological Society*, 7 (1957)

—— (ed.), *The Sheffield Outrages* (1971)

Porter, J. H., 'David Dale and Conciliation in the Northern Manufactured Iron Trade 1869–1914', *Northern History*, 5 (1970)

Price, R., *Masters, Unions, and Men: Work Control in Building and the Rise of Labour, 1830–1914* (Cambridge, 1980)

—— ' "What's in a Name?" Workplace History and "Rank and Filism" ', *International Review of Social History*, 34 (1989)

Prothero, I. J., *Artisans and Politics in Early Nineteenth-Century London: John Gast and his Times* (1979).

—— *Radical Artisans in England and France, 1830–1870* (1997)

Rathbone, E., *William Rathbone: A Memoir* (1905)

Reid, A. J., *Social Classes and Social Relations in Britain, 1850–1914* (1992)

Richards, P., 'The State and Early Industrial Capitalism: The Case of the Handloom Weavers', *Past and Present*, 83 (1979)

Rubin, G. R., 'Law, Poverty, and Imprisonment for Debt, 1869–1914', in G. R. Rubin and D. Sugarman (eds), *Law, Economy, and Society, 1750–1914* (1984)

—— 'The Historical Development of Collective Labour Law: The United Kingdom', in M. van der Linden and R. Price (eds), *The Rise and Development of Collective Labour Law* (Bern, 2000)

Rule, J., 'The Property of Skill in the Period of Manufacture', in P. Joyce (ed.), *Historical Meanings of Work* (1987; pbk. edn. 1989)

—— (ed.), *British Trade Unionism, 1750–1850: The Formative Years* (1988)

Roberts, B. C., *The Trades Union Congress, 1868–1921* (1958)

Sanders, L. C. (ed.), *Lord Melbourne's Papers* (1889)

Sanders, V. (ed.), *Harriet Martineau: Selected Letters* (1990)

Saville, J., *1848: The British State and the Chartist Movement* (1987)

Sayer, K., *Women of the Fields* (1995)

Searle, G. R., *Entrepreneurial Politics in Mid-Victorian Britain* (1993)

Shannon, R., *The Age of Disraeli, 1868–1881: The Rise of Tory Democracy* (1992)

Simon, D., 'Master and Servant', in J. Saville (ed.), *Democracy and the Labour Movement* (1954)

Smith, K. J. M., *James Fitzjames Stephen: Portrait of a Victorian Rationalist* (1988)

Smith, P., *Disraelian Conservatism and Social Reform* (1967)

—— (ed.), *Lord Salisbury on Politics* (1972)

Spain, J., 'Trade Unionists, Gladstonian Liberals, and the Labour Law Reforms of 1875', in E. F. Biagini and A. Reid (eds), *Currents of Radicalism* (1991)

Stack, D., *Nature and Artifice: The Life and Thought of Thomas Hodgskin (1787–1869)* (1998)

Steele, E. D., *Irish Land and British Politics: Tenant Right and Nationality, 1865–1870* (1974)

—— *Palmerston and Liberalism, 1855–1865* (1991)

Steinfeld, R. J., *Coercion, Contract, and Free Labor in the Nineteenth Century* (2001)
Steinmetz, W., 'Was there a De-juridification of Individual Employment Relations in Britain?', in W. Steinmetz (ed.), *Private Law and Social Inequality in the Industrial Age* (2000)
Stewart, W. A. C., and McCann, W. P., *The Educational Innovators, 1750–1880* (1967)
Stokes, E., *The English Utilitarians and India* (1959)
Sugarman, D., 'The Legal Boundaries of Liberty: Dicey, Liberalism, and Legal Science', *Modern Law Review*, 46 (1983)
Supple, B., 'Legislation and Virtue: An Essay on Working-Class Self-Help and the State in the Early Nineteenth Century', in N. McKendrick (ed.), *Historical Perspectives: Studies in English Thought and Society* (1974)
Sutherland, G. (ed.), *Studies in the Growth of Nineteenth-Century Government* (1972)
Taylor, M., *The Decline of British Radicalism, 1847–1860* (1995)
—— *Ernest Jones, Chartism, and the Romance of Politics, 1819–1869* (2003)
Thane, P., 'Craft Unions, Welfare Benefits, and the Case for Trade Union Law Reform, 1867–75: A Comment', *Economic History Review*, 29 (1976)
Thomas, W. E. S., 'Francis Place and working-class history', *Historical Journal*, 5 (1962)
—— *The Philosophic Radicals* (1979)
Thompson, A. F., 'Gladstone's Whips and the General Election of 1868', *English Historical Review*, 63 (1948)
Thompson, J., 'The Genesis of the 1906 Trades Disputes Act: Liberalism, Trade Unions, and the Law', *Twentieth Century British History*, 9 (1998)
—— ' "A Nearly Related People": German Views of the British Labour Market, 1870–1900', in D. Winch and P. K. O'Brien (eds.), *The Political Economy of British Historical Experience, 1688–1914* (2002)
Thurlow, T. J. Hovell-, *Trade Unions Abroad and Hints for Home Legislation* (1970)
Vernon, J., *Politics and the People: A Study in British Political Culture, c.1815–1867* (1993)
Vincent J., *The Formation of the British Liberal Party, 1857–68* (1972 edn.)
—— (ed.), *Disraeli, Derby and the Conservative Party: Journals and Memoirs of Edward Henry, Lord Stanley, 1849–1869* (1978)
—— (ed.), *A Selection from the Diaries of Edward Henry Stanley, Fifteenth Earl of Derby (1826–93) between September 1869 and March 1878* (1994)
Vint, J., *Capital and Wages: A Lakatosian History of the Wages Fund Doctrine* (1994)
Vogeler, S., *Frederic Harrison* (1984)
Waddams, S. M., *Law, Politics, and the Church of England: The Career of Stephen Lushington, 1782–1873* (1992)
Wallace, R., *'Organize! Organize! Organize!': A Study of Reform Agitations in Wales, 1840–1886* (Cardiff, 1991)
Walling, R. A. J. (ed.), *The Diaries of John Bright* (1930)
Watkins, C. C., 'Edward William Cox and the Rise of Class Journalism', *Victorian Periodicals Review*, 15 (1982)

Webb, R. K., *The British Working-Class Reader, 1790–1848* (1955)

—— 'A Whig Inspector', *Journal of Modern History*, 27 (1955)

Webb, S., and Webb, B., *The History of Trade Unionism* (1920 edn.)

—— *Industrial democracy* (1902 edn.)

Wedderburn, K. W., *Labour Law and Freedom: Further Essays in Labour Law* (1994)

—— Lewis, R., and Clark, J., *Labour Law and Industrial Relations: Building on Kahn-Freund* (1983)

—— *The Worker and the Law* (3rd edn., 1986)

Williamson, P., *Stanley Baldwin: Conservative Leadership and National Values* (1999)

Winter, J., *Robert Lowe* (Toronto, 1976)

Witherell, L. L., 'Direct Parliamentary Representation of Labour and the Controversy of 1872', *Parliamentary History*, 12 (1993)

Wrigley, C. J. (ed.), *A History of British Industrial Relations, 1875–1914* (Brighton, 1982)

Yeo, E., 'Some Practices and Problems of Chartist Democracy', in J. Epstein and D. Thompson (eds), *The Chartist Experience: Studies in Working-Class Radicalism and Culture, 1830–60* (1982)

Zeitlin, J., 'From Labour History to the History of Industrial Relations', *Economic History Review*, 40 (1987)

—— ' "Rank and Filism" and Labour History: A Rejoinder to Price and Cronin', *International Review of Social History*, 34 (1989)

Zetland, marquis of (ed.), *The Letters of Disraeli to Lady Bradford and Lady Chesterfield* (2 vols., 1929)

II. THESES

Buchanan, R. A., 'Trade Unions and Public Opinion, 1850–1875' (Cambridge Ph.D., 1957)

Dwyer, F. J., 'The Rise of Richard Assheton Cross and his Work at the Home Office, 1868–80' (Oxford B.Litt., 1954)

Stainton, D. C., 'Aspects of Trade Union Interest in Judicial Reform, 1867–1882' (Southampton M.Phil., 1969)

INDEX